CODEBREAKERS' VICTORY

CODEBREAKERS'

VICTORY

How the Allied Cryptographers
Won World War II

HERVIE HAUFLER

NEW AMERICAN LIBRARY

NEW AMERICAN LIBRARY
Published by New American Library, a division of
Penguin Group (USA) Inc., 375 Hudson Street, New York, New York 10014, U.S.A.
Penguin Books Ltd, 80 Strand, London WC2R 0RL, England
Penguin Books Australia Ltd, 250 Camberwell Road, Camberwell, Victoria 3124, Australia
Penguin Books Canada Ltd, 10 Alcorn Avenue, Toronto, Ontario, Canada M4V 3B2
Penguin Books (N.Z.) Ltd, Cnr Rosedale and Airborne Roads,
Albany, Auckland 1310, New Zealand

Penguin Books Ltd, Registered Offices: 80 Strand, London WC2R 0RL, England

First published by New American Library, a division of Penguin Group (USA) Inc.

First Printing, November 2003
10 9 8 7 6 5 4 3 2 1

REGISTERED TRADEMARK—MARCA REGISTRADA

LIBRARY OF CONGRESS CATALOGING-IN-PUBLICATION DATA:

Haufler, Hervie.
    Codebreakers' victory : how the Allied cryptographers won World War II / Hervie Haufler.
        p.   cm.
    ISBN 0-451-20979-6
    1. World War, 1939–1945—Cryptography.   2. Cryptography—United States—
History—20th century.   3. Cryptography—Great Britain—History—20th century.
I. Title.
    D810.C88H38   2003
    940.54'86—dc21
            2003008200

Set in Times New Roman
Designed by Eve L. Kirch

Printed in the United States of America

BOOKS ARE AVAILABLE AT QUANTITY DISCOUNTS WHEN USED TO PROMOTE PRODUCTS OR SERVICES.
FOR INFORMATION PLEASE WRITE TO PREMIUM MARKETING DIVISION, PENGUIN GROUP (USA) INC.,
375 HUDSON STREET, NEW YORK, NEW YORK 10014.

For my untiringly supportive family:
Patricia, Christopher and Marsha, Jonathan and Carolyn

Contents

Introduction

WITHIN the history of World War II lies a vital story that has become public knowledge only decades after the war's end: the role cryptanalysts played in securing the Allies' victory. The story remained cloaked for so long because, with victory won, the cryptanalytic geniuses and their thousands of support staffers pledged themselves to secrecy about their wartime activities. It was only when Allied military authorities agreed that relaxing their hold on disclosure would no longer harm their national interests that the full story of the codebreakers began to emerge.

As more and more details have come to light, growing awareness of the codebreakers' impact on the course of the war has forced revisions in its history and in the perceptions of many of its prominent figures. Yet these changes have seemed to come grudgingly. Histories written after the codebreaking revelations became available to the public frequently give the impression that the cryptanalysts' efforts were mere appendages to the larger war, inconvenient afterthoughts that had to be tacked on simply for accuracy's sake.

Furthermore, the effects of the codebreakers' successes have been given a standardized assessment: they shortened the war and saved thousands of lives. These are, to be sure, no small accomplishments. Survivors of the cryptologic war have, themselves, tended to accept that the sum total of their work was that they knocked a couple of years off the war's calendar and kept legions of men, women and children from becoming war victims.

This book's argument is that the tacked-on acknowledgment of cryptanalytic successes and the mantralike repetition of the results of those successes sell the codebreakers short. Their contributions to the Allies' triumph amount to more than that—a great deal more. An in-depth probe into those hundreds of thousands of decrypted enemy messages and a study of how Allied leaders used them in developing their battle plans leads to a different conclusion: that the tremendous advantage given to the Allies by the codebreakers was no less than the decisive factor tipping the scales in the war.

To state this book's premise another way, if a fully informed jury could sit in judgment to select the men who most influenced the war's outcome, it would pass over the celebrated heroes—the generals such as Dwight Eisenhower, Bernard Montgomery and Douglas MacArthur, and the admirals Chester Nimitz, Bull Halsey and their ilk. Instead, it would single out much less heralded men, including Poland's Marian Rejewski, Jerzy Różycki and Henryk Zygalski; Britain's Alan Turing, Gordon Welchman, Max Newman and Tom Flowers, and America's William Friedman, Frank Rowlett, Joseph Rochefort and Thomas Dyer. These were the individuals who led the way in deciphering enemy radio-transmitted messages that bestowed upon Allied commanders the great boon of "playing a card game with your opponent's cards visible to you."

Axis cryptologic teams had some codebreaking successes, and by these means inflicted grievous losses on the Allies. But their breakthroughs diminished as the war progressed, largely because the Allies' superior mastery in cryptanalysis revealed when their own forces' ciphers were being penetrated. As a result, Axis commanders were increasingly blinded in making their decisions while Allied leaders moved with ever greater certainty.

The stories of star-studded pistol-packing generals inherently make for more rollicking reading than those of analysts locked away in rear echelon cells solving the intricacies of military ciphers. But there is an added reason why the personalities and exploits of the codebreakers are known far less than those of the top brass. The generals and admirals could begin to trumpet their triumphs the day after the war ended—and often before. The cryptologists, on the other hand, were sworn to silence by those pledges they signed at the war's end.

Soon after V-J Day, congressional hearings into the debacle at Pearl Harbor forced some disclosures of the U.S. codebreaking efforts against Japan. But in England, even though more than ten thousand men and women were involved in various aspects of the codebreaking—including nearly five hundred Americans—no word of their achievements leaked out until thirty years after hostilities had ceased. Winston Churchill, a great admirer and advocate of Britain's cryptologic program, spoke of his codebreaking team in a visit to their center at Bletchley Park as "the geese that lay the golden eggs but never cackle."

Churchill himself respected the secrecy pledge. In all his many volumes of World War II history, he included no more mention of the codebreaking than an occasional oblique reference to "special intelligence" or "trustworthy sources." In this regard, his reporting is incomplete. One can imagine, if he had lived, what joy he would have taken in revising his scripts to give full recognition to his secret weapon.

This book can do what Churchill was duty-bound not to do. It can present the evidence that codebreaking in World War II was the single most important factor enabling the Allies to win the war.

The first step toward Allied victory came when Polish cryptanalysts, as early as 1932, began breaking the Germans' supposedly impregnable Enigma code machine and then, on the brink of war, turned their discoveries over to their French and British allies.

At that point, the story passes primarily to the British who, at Bletchley Park (BP), assembled the masterminds and their support staff to carry the Poles' technologies to new levels of proficiency. Bletchley cryptanalysts made inroads into German codes within a few months of the war's beginning. But these early successes came too soon to have effect against the overwhelming might the Germans displayed in their invasion of Norway and their blitzkriegs in France. Together with Britain's superiority in radar development, however, BP's decrypts, code-named Ultra, helped British air marshal Hugh Dowding prevent the Germans from sweeping the skies clear of the Royal Air Force—which Adolf Hitler saw as a prerequisite to the invasion of England. Decrypts of Italian codes were also key factors in two of the first British victories—over the Italian armies in North Africa and the Italian navy in the Battle of Matapan.

British codebreaking fully came into its own as a precursor to victory in the long, seesaw Battle of the Atlantic. Analysis of that struggle provides convincing evidence that Britain's gradual advance to dominance in cryptology was a key factor in preventing the German high command from using its U-boats, surface raiders and Luftwaffe aircraft to sever Britain's supply lifeline and starve the English into submission. With U.S. entry into the war, American signals intelligence (Sigint) teams joined in turning the tide so that German losses became so great they were forced to withdraw their U-boats from the North Atlantic and grant Allied convoys virtually free passage.

U.S. cryptanalysts' greatest contribution to Allied victory was their mastery of Japanese codes. The first American successes, code-named Magic, were against the code machines used by Imperial diplomats. Because Japanese militarists scorned including the diplomatic corps in their plans, however, U.S. decrypts provided no definite warning of the attack on Pearl Harbor. Afterward, U.S. Navy analysts quickly began breaking the codebook messages of the Imperial Navy. Their decrypts prevented another Pearl Harbor by revealing Japanese plans for a second surprise attack—this one on Midway atoll. Japanese admiral Isoroku Yamamoto hoped that his assault on Midway would draw what was left of the U.S. Pacific fleet to its doom. Hawaii-based codebreakers made sure there would be no follow-up Japanese surprise. They gave Admiral Nimitz the information he needed to place his fleet so that planes from his carriers, along with those from the island itself, could descend unexpectedly on the Japanese ships. When all four of the Japanese carriers were sunk, the battle was over and the Japanese retreated. Midway, described by Nimitz as "a victory of intelligence," changed the entire course of the Pacific war by ending the long march of triumphs by the Japanese and putting them immediately on the defensive.

Later in the war, Magic decrypts became invaluable assets when they unveiled the reports of Japanese emissaries and military attachés who used the diplomatic machines to inform Tokyo of such matters as German plans for withstanding the Allied invasion of France.

In Europe, on the eastern front, where the Germans were striving to subdue Mother Russia, a host of intelligence forces combined to set up three critical Soviet victories. First, the USSR spy in Tokyo informed his spymasters of the Japanese decision to strike to the southeast rather than make war against Russia, a disclosure that freed many Red Army Far East divisions to be rushed to the battle that stopped the Germans short of capturing Moscow. At Stalingrad, Marshal Zhukov relied on his network of informants in planning his attack on the weak spots in the German lines and conducting his enormous entrapment of German troops. Finally, preparing for the horrific clash of arms in the Battle of Kursk, Zhukov based his strategy on what secret intelligence was telling him and, as a consequence, broke the back of German military might.

Ultra decrypts lit the way for the Allied invasions of Sicily and Italy that drove Benito Mussolini out of power and, ultimately, Italy out of the war. When German armies took over the defenses of Italy, Ultra decrypts warned of counterattacks by the German war machine—the Wehrmacht—that could have pushed Allied beachheads at Salerno and Anzio back into the sea. Knowledge of German intentions gleaned from broken intercepts helped tie down and decimate German divisions that could otherwise have been fighting in Normandy or on the eastern front.

As D-Day approached, Ultra and Magic intelligence greatly aided the planners of the Normandy landings by supplying details of the Germans' West Wall defenses and orders of battle. Decrypts were also essential to the clever deceptions that fooled Hitler and his generals into massing formidable German forces in the wrong places, anticipating landings that never came. The invasion marked the high point in the exploits of the network of agents in Britain whom the Germans believed to be working for them but who, in actuality, were under British control and misinforming their German masters. These agents' false reports were skewed to make the Germans believe that the Normandy landings were only a feint preceding the main Allied thrust on the Pas de Calais. Many observers believe that but for these measures, the landings would not have been attempted in June 1944 or would have failed, with unimaginable consequences for the further course of the war.

In the Pacific theater, meanwhile, U.S. Admiral Nimitz and General MacArthur relied on their codebreakers to advise them in conducting the giant pincer movement that climbed up the islands and closed on the Japanese homeland. Decrypts of Imperial Navy messages pinpointed targets for Allied submarines, enabling them to devastate Japanese shipping and withhold from the military machine the Southeast Asian oil it needed in order to keep operating.

Similarly, in the China-Burma-India theater, the codebreakers were indispensable in dashing Japanese hopes to drive into India and link up with their Nazi partners for control of both Asia and Europe. Informed by his cryptanalytic teams, Lord Louis Mountbatten and his generals, with American and Chinese support, stopped the invaders at the borders of India and turned that "forgotten war" into a series of massive Japanese defeats.

The codebreakers also played a significant part in slowing Germany's technological progress. With decrypts revealing where menacing new developments were under way, Allied teams hampered nuclear advances, blasted sites where advanced work was being done on V-weapons and delayed the introduction of new jet aircraft and snorkel-equipped U-boats.

In the war's final phases, a flood of decrypts and captured intelligence documents sped the Japanese collapse. Allied leaders were kept informed of the standoff between Tokyo militarists and moderates over a surrender agreement. And Harry Truman gained insights into the unbending minds of enemy militants that gave him cogent reasons to drop the atomic bombs.

This, then, is a record of the war told from the perspective of, and in special appreciation of, the codebreakers. It is a record documenting that in battle after battle, and across all the war's theaters, they swung the balance.

In this war, as in no other, secret intelligence supplied the edge that produced Allied victory.

To make this claim is not to undervalue the importance of the soldiers, sailors and airmen who did the fighting and dying. They bore the brunt; their courage and sacrifice were the sine qua non on which all else depended. The argument here is that it is time that signals intelligence be recognized for giving the Allied fighting men the advantage that enabled them to conquer.

As Churchill wrote of "the secret war," "If we had not mastered its profound meaning and used its mysteries even when we saw them only in the glimpse, all the efforts, all the prowess of the fighting airmen, all the bravery and sacrifice of the people, would have been in vain."

The account here is meant for the general reader, with as little reliance as possible on the mind-bending intricacies of cryptologic processes and technologies. Rather, this telling emphasizes Sigint's decisive influence on all the war's major turning points while also highlighting the remarkable men and women and the engrossing incidents that make up the codebreaking story. Where it has seemed relevant, the report includes my own experience as one of the "Ultra Americans" involved in the British attack against the Enigma, and the experiences of colleagues I have come to know during my years of research. These additions, it is judged, throw a revealing individual light on those times that are so irrevocably slipping away.

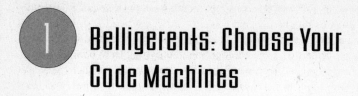

1 Belligerents: Choose Your Code Machines

Down through military and diplomatic history, where there has been an adversary there has been cryptology. It is a two-sided art. On one side are the methods used to prevent communications with colleagues and allies from being read by rivals. On the other are the technologies for penetrating shielded messages and extracting their meaning for information that can provide an advantage in acting against the opposition.

Historians of cryptology, such as David Kahn, can trace the beginnings of this art back to some of the earliest civilizations of recorded history, including the ancient Egyptians, Mesopotamians, Babylonians, Hebrews, Greeks, and Romans. The Greek Herodotus tells us, as a celebrated example, how a Spartan, Demaratus, scratched on a wooden tablet the letters warning the Greek nations that the Persians under Xerxes were about to invade and then covered the letters with wax in order to conceal them from guards along the way. So alerted, the Greeks beat off the Persians and ended the threat of conquest.

In those early days, the simplest encoding was enough to throw off would-be codebreakers. The most-used systems were *ciphers*, in which the original letters of a message—its plaintext—were transposed or replaced by other letters. One of Julius Caesar's ciphers, as an instance, consisted of substituting plaintext letters with those that were three places farther along in the Roman alphabetic sequence. Even that was too complicated for his great-nephew Augustus, the first emperor of Rome, who simply substituted the very next letter in the alphabet. Use of these single-alphabet—or monoalphabetic—ciphers could convert the plaintext order *attack* into the meaningless jumble *taktac* by the transposition of letters, or *buubdl* by applying Augustus's substitution method.

Over time, a second type of cryptographic system that came into widespread use was that of *codes*. For key words he wanted to communicate, the codemaker would create lists of unintelligible equivalents—letters, numbers or symbols—and assemble them in codebooks to be held both by senders and receivers. To signal *attack* the sender would look up the equivalent—1502, say—in his book. The receiver would, in turn, track down that number in his codebook, read its plaintext meaning and know what his commander was ordered to do.

Those primitive types of codes were easy prey for cryptanalysts who discovered the technique of frequency analysis. By counting the number of times a given letter appeared in a message, the analyst could take a good guess that the most frequently used code letter stood for the most common plaintext letter in a given language—*e*, in English for example—and thus gain a lever for opening up the remainder of the plaintext.

It was essential that codemakers come up with new ways to outwit the cryptanalysts. One way to foil frequency analysis was to treat the consonants of a code alphabet as usual, but to add several different variants for *e* and each of the other vowels. An even better system was invented by Leon Battista Alberti, a Florentine born in 1404. Alberti developed a cipher disk, with the plaintext alphabet on the outer ring and a cipher alphabet on the inner ring. By prearrangement between sender and receiver, the sender would set his cipher ring at, say, *G* under the plaintext *A* and encode several words. But then he would turn the cipher ring so that *Y* would fall under *A*. In effect he would bring a whole new cipher alphabet into play. With other shifts, he would employ additional alphabets. This was the start of the multi-alphabet, or polyalphabetic, substitution system that, in ever more advanced forms, remained a cryptographer's mainstay for centuries.

So it went, down through the ages. In medieval England, both Roger Bacon and Geoffrey Chaucer were ardent users of cryptography. During the Renaissance, the city-states of Italy raised the art to high levels of sophistication. Napoléon Bonaparte's neglect of more secure forms of codemaking led to his first great defeat. In a preview of a much later cryptanalytic triumph, the Russians read Napoléon's dispatches and combined these disclosures with the rigors of the Russian winter to turn back the invaders at the gates of Moscow.

New technologies necessitated new security safeguards for communications. Invention of the telegraph, for example, led Union commanders in the American Civil War to seek better ways to prevent their messages from being betrayed to Confederate generals. For Union generals McClellan and

Grant, cryptographers devised codebooks in which user-friendly ordinary words substituted for plaintext. *Colonel* became *Venus*, *Neptune* was *Richmond*, and *Adam* was *President Lincoln*.

Superior cryptography gave Union leaders an advantage over their Confederate opponents. The South relied on ciphers that included a version of the venerable Vigenère system that Kahn has described as "probably the most famous cipher system of all time." Its origination is attributed to Blaise de Vigenère, who lived in the sixteenth century. He used a square bounded on the left side by a vertical alphabet and across the top by a horizontal one. Within the square, each horizontal row is another alphabet, which begins with the letter of the left-hand column. To replace a plaintext letter with a cipher one, the cryptographer traced the column beneath the top horizontal letter down to its row on the vertical alphabet. In other words, this was a creative complication of Alberti's polyalphabetic ciphers. When combined with a key word or phrase and such complications as reversed alphabets, Vigenère confounded cryptanalysts for a long time. But as early as the 1840s, America's Charles Babbage demonstrated how to solve the Vigenère system, and Union analysts' unraveling of the Confederates' use of them contributed to the South's defeat.

Another cipher invented to assure secrecy in telegraphic messages was named Playfair, after a British baron, although it was devised not by him but by his friend Charles Wheatstone. This cipher also uses a square, with a key word rather than an alphabet across the top. Instead of yielding just letter transpositions, though, it delivers "digraphs," in which two letters of a message are enciphered together. Since there are 26 letters but 676 digraphs, the use of digraphs overcame the limitations of alphabets and sharply complicated life for the cryptanalyst.

Great War Debacles Demand Cryptologic Change

As the Great War of 1914–18 began, military communications faced a formidable new technological challenge, that of radio. Marconi's not-yet-twenty-year-old invention put telegraphy on the air. With streams of Morse code sprayed out from their command center, deskbound admirals could direct warships far out at sea, and generals were able to better control highly mobile gasoline-driven armies.

Along with this positive came a negative. Skulduggery was no longer necessary to secure an enemy's messages; interceptors as well as intended recipients could pluck them out of the ether by monitoring message-transmitting frequencies. Cryptanalysts were given masses of enemy communications to work with.

The situation called for groundbreaking new codes. They weren't forthcoming. Military communicators were still relying on pen-and-paper ciphers left over from the previous century, often no more than variations of Vigenère or Playfair systems.

Cryptanalysts of warring nations were presented with opportunities they moved quickly to exploit. The French were best prepared, with a group of codebreakers who had been working together since well before the war began. They also had in place both a line of intercept stations and the beginnings of sites for the direction-finding of enemy transmitters. In London, the British organized the now famous Room 40, where some of the nation's best minds concentrated on messages fetched in by a new line of coastal intercept centers. Germany launched into the conflict without a single cryptanalyst on the western front, but then strove mightily to catch up.

With all this emphasis on codebreaking, the Great War soon became a codemaker's nightmare. Cryptanalysts held the upper hand. Everyone was breaking everyone else's codes.

The Germans were the first to reap a major victory from their opponent's cryptographic failures. They did this against the Russians pressing in on them from the east. The French tried to help their more primitively equipped allies by supplying them with codebooks, but the czarist government and military were so corrupt that the code was quickly betrayed, for a payoff, to the Germans. Efforts by the Russian commanders to introduce a new code came to nought. In August 1914, as they approached the Battle of Tannenberg, the decisive struggle on the eastern front, the Russian leaders ran short of the wire and wire-laying equipment to communicate by telephone. Trying to coordinate their huge two-pronged pincer movement, they had no choice but to use radio—and to send their messages unenciphered. The Germans intercepted them and translated them. They revealed the Russians' entire plan of attack.

Intercepted messages in hand, the Germans knew how to counter the offensive. Aware that the Russians' northern wing, after an initial victory against the Germans, was pausing to reorganize, Generals Hindenburg and Ludendorff held that front with a thin screen of cavalry and concentrated their main forces to fall on the southern wing. They enveloped the Russian armies, killed some thirty thousand troops and captured one hundred thousand others, setting Russia on the long downward slide that ended in 1917 with the Bolshevik revolution and the Russian withdrawal from the war.

Early on, Britain's Room 40 began breaking German naval codes. The decrypts led to two relatively inconsequential British forays, but then were used with great effect on May 31, 1916, when decrypted messages warned that German navy commanders were massing their ships for a major offensive in the North Sea. The result was the climactic Battle of Jutland. "Without the cryptographic department," Winston Churchill wrote, "there would have been no Battle of Jutland." Although both navies were badly battered, the surviving German ships retreated into their home ports and did not again take on the Royal Navy throughout the rest of the war. With Room 40's aid, the British navy also ended the threat of German U-boats in their attempt to choke off Britain's Atlantic supply line.

Britain's breaking of another German message, the infamous Zimmermann telegram, brought the U.S. into the war. Wanting the U.S. to be a mediator for peace rather than a belligerent in the war, President Woodrow Wilson maintained American neutrality even after the Germans lifted their embargo on submarine attacks against neutral ships and sank the Cunard liner *Lusitania*, with the loss of 128 American lives. The U.S. public reacted with such fury that the Germans reconsidered and, for four months, suspended their U-boat campaign. But then Arthur Zimmermann, the German foreign minister, hatched what he considered an inspired scheme, one that would keep the U.S. so occupied with troubles close to home that American leaders would be unable to think about involvement in Europe. His idea was to induce Mexico to join with Germany in an alliance that would provide German financial backing for the Mexican army to cross its northern borders and reclaim its lost territories in Texas, New Mexico and Arizona. Moreover, he proposed that the Mexican president persuade the Japanese to attack the American West Coast. He sent encrypted instructions via a cablegram to the German ambassador in Washington, who was to forward them to the German ambassador in Mexico City and thence to the Mexican president.

The British, however, were tapping Atlantic cable communications. They intercepted the telegram and deciphered it. But they weren't sure what to do next. To reveal its contents to the Americans would give away the fact that they were breaking the German codes, which was an unacceptable disclosure. Yet they knew that Zimmermann's plan would infuriate the Americans and would likely draw them into the war. They came up with a bright solution. The German's Washington ambassador would have to strip off the instructions meant just for him before the relay to Mexico. Consequently, the version arriving in Mexico City would vary from the intercept as well as have a different transmission date. Germany's ambassador to

Mexico would deliver a deciphered version of the message to the Mexican president. The British scheme was to have one of their agents in Mexico City obtain a copy of this second message and then have *that* turned over to the Americans. It was all done so skillfully that the Germans blamed treachery in Mexico rather than suspecting the British.

Once the telegram was leaked to the press, headlines across the U.S. blared the incredible news. Any doubts about the message's authenticity were dispelled when Zimmermann admitted that he had sent it. With that, Wilson could no longer withstand the storm of rage the telegram stirred up; the U.S. declared war on Germany.

In March 1918, came the foremost cryptanalytic victory of the war. The German armies were closing in on Paris, preparing for the push that would seize the capital and drive France to make peace. German generals had been launching devastating surprise attacks because their cryptographers had devised a new cipher the French were unable to break. Known as the ADFGVX, it used only these letters of the alphabet because their Morse code equivalents were distinct from one another and less liable to be garbled in transmission. With German salients only thirty miles from Paris, close enough that the city was being bombarded by long-range Big Bertha artillery, French commanders were desperate to know where the next assault would fall. The task of breaking ADFGVX was left to France's most able cryptanalyst, young Lieutenant Georges Painvin. In an incredible feat of sleepless concentration, he broke the cipher and revealed when and where the Germans would strike. This time the French were ready for the German advance. The assault was beaten back and France was saved from defeat.

When the U.S. sent the American Expeditionary Force to France, Herbert O. Yardley, organizer of the first serious U.S. cryptographic program, went along to help with code work at the headquarters of the AEF commander, General John Pershing. Yardley was horrified to find the American forces relying on "schoolboy codes and ciphers" that, he was sure, the Germans were decoding as quickly as American operators. Nonetheless, the doughboys turned the course of the war toward triumph by their fresh vitality and overwhelming numbers, despite having their leaders' orders almost instantly known to the enemy.

The Great War was, indeed, a cryptographer's nightmare.

Well before the war's end, it was evident that a new order of military communications was required. The gasoline-powered mobility of modern armed forces needed radio to coordinate and direct their movements, which, in turn, called for faster and more secure methods of encryption and decryption than were possible with manual systems out of the past. It was time for machines to take on the tasks of cryptology.

Inventors Concentrate on Rotor Machines

Late in the war, the British put forth a code machine, the work of J. St. Vincent Pletts, that they recommended for immediate use by Allied commands. To convince their U.S. allies, they sent over a sample to be tested. The machine was delivered to American cryptanalyst William Friedman, along with five encoded messages the British were sure would prove undecipherable. Friedman broke them in three hours, ending this early try at machine encoding.

The need for mechanical systems was so evident, however, that almost simultaneously inventors in four different countries began work on machines, each of which relied on the same idea. This was the application of the electric-powered rotor, a revolvable code wheel.

Of the four inventors, the one whose development was to have the greatest consequence in World War II was the German, Arthur Scherbius. His work on a rotor device gained a boost when the Dutch inventor who had received the first patent on the machine, Hugo Alexander Koch, assigned the rights to Scherbius a year before he himself died. After going through several transformations, the Scherbius machine emerged as a device resembling an ungainly typewriter housed in a wooden box. It had a keyboard like a typewriter, but with only three rows of keys for the twenty-six letters, and none left over for numbers, punctuation or other extras. Atop the machine to the rear of the keyboard was a plate in which twenty-six round glass apertures were labeled with the letters of the alphabet and positioned above glow lamps. When the operator pressed down a key, rather than a skeletal arm rising to print an impression on paper, one of the glow lamps would illuminate a letter.

The trick was that the lighted letter—the cipher letter—was never the same as the depressed key—the plaintext letter. Pushing down a key fed a battery-powered electrical impulse into the machine's interior, and thereby hangs a tale of clever complexity.

The Scherbius machine depended primarily on three rotors on a single shaft to do the encoding and decoding. Each rotor was a small hockey-puck-like disk of insulating material. Around its rim were double rows of electrical contacts, twenty-six in number, representing letters of the alphabet. The contacts on one side of a rotor were wired in a random internal arrangement to those on the other side. As a result, the plaintext letters of the message delivered to one side emerged on the other side as different letters, transposed and scrambled. Thus, if the plaintext letter entered the right-hand rotor as A, it might exit it as Q. Then, entering the second rotor as Q, it emerged as W. And entering the third rotor as W, it came out the far side as X.

On the left-hand wall of the machine was a fourth scrambling element: a fixed half rotor with thirteen contacts only on one side. This was the reflector, which the Germans called "the turnaround wheel." It bounced the electrical impulse back once again through the three rotors, rescrambling the order in the passage through each one.

The electrical surge did something else as well: it caused that first rotor to rotate one space, one twenty-sixth of a revolution. Otherwise, each plaintext letter entering the right side of the disk would invariably activate the same ciphertext letter on the other side—easy prey for cryptanalysts. By edging forward a notch each time a key was pressed, the entry letter's current flowed through a different contact on the cipher side. As a result, when a plaintext letter—B, say—was hit a second time—BB—the repeated plaintext letter became a different cipher letter. That is, with the first B enciphered as, say, M, the second would be different—X, say. When the first rotor completed its twenty-six-letter cycle, it triggered the second rotor to move forward a notch and, after *its* twenty-six-letter rotation, to activate the third rotor. In this way, the machine was constantly changing the interconnections, additionally altering the plaintext inputs.

As if that amount of letter scrambling weren't enough to foil cryptanalysis, Scherbius and his colleagues added a further complexity: the order of the rotors on their shaft could be changed. What had been the right-hand rotor could be switched to the left-hand slot or the middle one, and so on.

Another important feature of Scherbius's machine was the reciprocity of its lettering. If plaintext A lighted the glow lamp for ciphertext X, then on the deciphering side of the cycle, X invariably equaled A. It was this reversibility that allowed the receiver to instantly decipher what the sender had transmitted.

Scherbius called his machine the Enigma. Ironically, considering its subsequent history, he is said to have derived the name from a musical composition, *Enigma Variations*, in which the British composer Edward Elgar used melodic codes in characterizing some of his friends.

In seeking customers for his Enigma, Scherbius pointed out a critical advantage: the machine itself could be captured, but unlike a purloined codebook, it would still be useless to the captor. The reason was that in order to decode a message on the Enigma, it was necessary to know the starting positions of the rotors. This essential information was called the key. With the multirotor Enigma, the number of the key variations ran into the billions. To determine even one key, he argued, would take cryptanalysts years of effort.

His first attempts, in the 1920s, to market the Enigma to business customers as well as military chiefs met with rebuffs. The German navy considered the machine but turned him down. So did the commercial prospects he approached. But then English writers on the war, including Winston Churchill, gave Scherbius a lift. In Churchill's book *The World Crisis*, he revealed how British successes against the German fleet in the Great War stemmed in part from the breaking of German naval codes. His disclosures prompted German navy officers of the twenties to have second thoughts. They bought the Enigma and decided it was their cryptographic answer. The navy began using Enigmas in 1925. The army followed suit in 1928 and the newly reborn air force in 1935.

To make their Enigmas even more secure against cryptanalysis, the Germans introduced two major changes. The first was an increase in the number of rotors. They had their Enigmas built with slots to store two extra rotors. Their machines continued to operate with just three rotors, but the operator's ability to vary the sequence among the five available code wheels enormously increased the difficulties facing the would-be analyst. Later the navy upped the ante by adding an extra rotor and altering their machines to operate with four instead of three.

The second change was the introduction of an entirely new scrambling element, the plugboard, which looked like a miniature telephone switchboard. It included cables to facilitate the pairings of plugs and sockets for twenty-six letters. The operator could change these pairings to send current through the machine by entirely different paths.

With these changes, the Germans could instruct their Enigma operators on the sequence of rotors to insert, the start-up position of each rotor and the order of plugboard pairings. Now, when a German operator pressed down a key of his Enigma, the electrical impulse ran a most tortuous course. First it went through the plugboard maze of wiring, then proceeded one way through the rotors. At the end it was bounced back by that fixed-wheel reflector and returned by a different route through the rotors. Only then did it light the glow lamp.

In peacetime, changes in the settings were first made at quarterly intervals, then once a month and, later, once a week. When the war came, changes were made once a day or, in some cases, every eight hours.

The Enigma required at least two operators, one to strike the plaintext keys, the other to read and copy down the lighted ciphertext letters. For the fastest operation, extra operators were used, the final one transmitting the gobbledygook letter groups over the air.

Progressively altering and improving the Enigma, the Germans made it their all-purpose code machine. It was selected by the security police organizations, railroads and other governmental departments, in addition to the military services.

Thousands of Enigmas were put into use. During the course of the war the number of different keys rose to nearly two hundred, and at some stages of the war the various German networks employed fifty different keys simultaneously.

The Germans had good reason to believe their Enigmas were secure against cryptanalysis. Dr. Ray Miller, a computer scientist at the U.S. National Security Agency, has calculated the exact number of key settings faced by Enigma codebreakers. The possible permutations for the plugboards alone, he has determined, run to more than 500 trillion. And that was just one of the machine's five variable components. All the variables together multiply out to 3×10^{114}. That number compares with only 10^{80} as the estimated number of atoms in the entire observable universe. "No wonder," he concluded, "the German cryptographers had confidence in their machine!"

Did the Germans ever suspect that their enemies were reading their Enigma-encoded messages? At times when the Allies seemed to benefit from what seemed like amazing coincidences and incredible streaks of good fortune, questions were raised. Investigations were conducted. Always, at least until the very end of the war, the answers came back uniformly: the Enigma-based communications systems were inviolate. It was inconceivable that human minds could cope with such astronomical numbers of variations. If the Allies fared better than could be explained by brilliance or luck, the cause had to be secret agents, not penetration of the Enigma.

Alternatives to the Enigma

The first rotor code machine was developed by an American, Edward H. Hebern. He was also the inventor with the most grandiose ideas for his device.

Hebern began with two electric typewriters connected by twenty-six wires in random fashion. Strike the key on the first and the other would type out its enciphered equivalent. But since the connections were fixed, decryption was too easy.

He moved on to a rotor machine, filing his patent on it in 1921. This complex device used five rotors. He brought his machine to Washington and demonstrated it to the U.S. Navy's Code and Signals Section. Naval officials were "thrilled when he showed us what it could do." They seemed ready to commit to navywide use.

This positive reaction was good enough for Hebern. Without having secured a signed order, he planned big. He sold a million dollars' worth of stock in his new company and built a substantial factory to produce his machines. The navy, however, was not accustomed to moving so swiftly. Not until 1923 did it convince a board to investigate the machine. In the end, it ordered only two machines for six hundred dollars each. Hebern's company filed for bankruptcy and he ended up in court, sued by his stockholders. Even though he later sold thirty-five machines to the navy, Hebern never succeeded in establishing a viable code machine business.

In Stockholm another inventor resolved to try his luck with a rotor-type code machine. This was Arvid Damm, who already had patents for weaving looms. Although his code machines were clumsy constructions that invariably broke down during critical tests, he incorporated a company to market them. His smartest move was to add to his staff a young man named Boris Hagelin, son of a wealthy investor in the firm.

One day in 1924, when Damm was in Paris, word came that the Swedish military was considering a mass purchase of Enigma machines. Hagelin resolved not to let that happen. He made quick changes to simplify the Damm model, making it more like an Enigma. The Swedish army placed a large order.

At this point Damm died, and Hagelin took over. Under his direction, the company developed a very compact code machine, no larger than an attaché case. The French army gave him what seemed an impossible challenge: to produce a pocket-size machine. Not only that, they wanted a machine that could print out the ciphertext and could thus be operated by one man. Hagelin met the test. His clever little device used the same elements to handle both the deciphering and the printing. The French ordered five thousand of them.

Hagelin came to the U.S. and got American cryptologic authorities interested. William Friedman made suggestions that he incorporated. In the end the U.S. Army adopted his machine as its field-use cryptographic system that offered at least midlevel security, and arranged with Hagelin to have the U.S. version mass-produced by a typewriter manufacturer. In World War II, GIs knew the not quite pocket-size but still very compact little wonder as the M-209.

As David Kahn has said, Hagelin "became the first—and the only—man to become a millionaire from cryptology."

Other Nations Make Their Choices

For the U.S., the M-209 was considered suitable for tactical use, but not for the higher-level transmissions the enemy must never succeed in deciphering. To secure a machine promising full security, the military turned to Friedman. He developed an American equivalent of the Enigma that also applied the rotor principle. It was larger and more cumbersome than the Enigma but more secure. Friedman, for instance, had determined that the Enigma's "fast" rotor, the one that inched forward after 26 clicks of the keyboard, was most vulnerable to cryptanalysis when used as the right-hand entry rotor, so he avoided that placement in his machine. He received help from Frank Rowlett, who, seeing that Friedman's keying process was erratic and unreliable, came up with an electromechanical keying unit that worked much better. They received U.S. patents on their inventions. Their machine became known as Sigaba in the army and M-134 in the navy. It was never broken during the war.

The British also studied the Enigma and saw ways to improve upon it. They added "Type X attachments," with the result that their machine became known as Typex. It, like the Sigaba, avoided reliance on glow lamps; it printed out its messages, enciphered one way, deciphered the other. Instead of the military Enigma's plugboard, it included two stationary entry rotors in addition to three stepping rotors. The Typex's rotor movements were much less regular than Enigma's. These modifications to the Enigma concepts gave Britain, too, a machine that handled top-level cryptography without ever being broken.

By a fortunate happenstance, the British and American machines were similar enough that adapters could be used in exchanging enciphered communications between them.

After their terrible cryptographic disasters of the Great War, the Russians developed better code systems in World War II. They depended primarily on codebooks and the secure but burdensome onetime pad system, which required both sender and receiver to use the duplicate top sheets of keyed paper pads, and then discard the sheets after a single use. The Russian military's codebook systems relied on four series of numerical codes, with five-digit codes for the top-level strategic messages scaling down to two-digit codes for frontline exchanges. They also made some field use of Hagelin's M-209 machines, which they received in lend-lease from the U.S. and copied.

Soviet espionage agents across Europe and in Japan had their own codes for communicating with Moscow. These were onetime numerical systems with the key numbers lifted from published statistics tables and given an additional scrambling. For the most part, these were systems that frustrated German cryptanalysts.

As for the Italians, Mussolini's navy bought Enigmas but did not add plugboards to them. This simplified choice would have provided the Allies a cryptanalytic bonanza, except that the Italians made very limited use of their Enigmas. Much more fruitful for the Allies was the Italian use of a Hagelin machine for enciphering information concerning the Mediterranean convoys sent to supply Rommel's armies in North Africa. Otherwise, the Italian military services relied mainly on codebook systems, some of which proved very difficult to break.

Japan's decisions about cryptography were influenced by a 1931 book, *The American Black Chamber*, written by U.S. cryptologist Herbert Yardley. In the twenties, Yardley's secret operation was breaking the codes of a number of nations, including Japan. The funding of the operation was supplied mostly by the U.S. State Department. When, in 1928, president-elect Herbert Hoover appointed Henry L. Stimson as his secretary of state, Yardley sought the approval of his new boss by sending him a batch of messages revealing the Japanese government's plans for gaining the best possible deal in a forthcoming international conference on the naval armaments levels the leading nations would be allowed to maintain. Yardley anticipated that the new secretary would welcome this inside information. Instead, Stimson took offense. "Gentlemen," he has been famously quoted as saying, "do not read each other's mail." Yardley's funding was withdrawn and the Black Chamber closed down. He got even—and temporarily rich—by writing his no-secrets-held-back best-seller.

Forewarned by Yardley's irresponsible disclosures, the Japanese set about developing more-secure code systems. They were faced by a language problem, for their written language relied heavily on some two thousand ideographic characters that evolved from Chinese. These characters, however, convey meaning but not sounds. To represent their language's sounds, the Japanese added phonetic symbols called kana. Only the kana characters lent themselves to radio codes. For radio transmissions, the Japanese developed their own Morse code, using Morse dots and dashes to represent forty-eight kana characters. As an alternative, they transmitted radio messages in Romaji, a Romanized spelling of the kana characters.

Japanese cryptologists inspected the available code machines and then developed their own design. The Imperial Navy began the work but then decided against machine encipherment, relying instead on codebooks whose number equivalents of essential words and phrases were further secured by a complex upper layer of scrambling. The Foreign Office took over the machine project for enciphering diplomatic messages.

Their first try was known to the Japanese as the *angoo-ki taipu A*, the "Type A cipher machine," or as the *91-shiki Oo-bun In-ji-ki*, "Alphabetical Typewriter 91." The 91 was derived from the year of the machine's development, since 1931 was 2591 in the Japanese calendar. Employing Romaji letters, the device had two electric typewriters, one for typing in the plaintext, the other for typing out the enciphered message for the radio operator to transmit. In addition to the two typewriters, it had an Enigma-like plugboard and an encipherment mechanism. The Japanese developed two versions of Type A, one for diplomats, the other for naval attachés.

Soon after, however, the Foreign Office introduced a new machine, one the Japanese called *angoo-ki taipu B*, the B machine. It made its first appearance on March 20, 1939, and gradually replaced the A machine. Type B was, as will be discussed later, a machine based on principles that radically departed from those of any other code device. For the cryptanalyst, it presented a challenge of an entirely different order from that posed by the Enigma.

So it was that in the aftermath of the Great War, and with another world conflict looming, each major nation gave hard thought to its cryptologic procedures and technologies. Most intelligence organizations changed from manual practices to the use of code machines. Others introduced codebook complexities that their intelligence leaders felt sure the enemy could not solve. Overall, the codemakers brought their art to the point where their systems seemed secure against the codebreakers—so secure, in fact, that Yardley, after viewing the demonstration of one such scrambler machine, lamented, "When all governments adopt such a system, cryptanalysis, as a profession, will die."

The story to be told next, however, relates how one lesser nation found bright young men who, well before World War II commenced, pierced the tight security screen and proved that even code machines could be mastered. The cryptanalysts of Poland, struggling to meet the threat of a renascent German military, began the slow, faltering change that brought codebreaking into the ascendant and set the war on its course toward Allied victory.

2 Breaking the Enigma: Poles Show the Way

On a Saturday in January 1929, a crate arrived at the customs office in Warsaw addressed to a German firm with offices in the city. The box bore a label specifying that its contents consisted of "radio equipment." The German firm's representative arrived and, claiming that the crate had been shipped from Berlin by mistake, demanded that it be returned to Germany *before* going through customs. Their suspicions aroused, the customs officials decided not to comply with the demand right away. They used the excuse that their people did not work on Saturday afternoons, but assured the representative that the box would be returned on Monday morning. By this stratagem the Polish Biuro Szyfrów, or "Cipher Bureau," alerted by the customs officials, had a whole weekend to investigate the suspicious "radio equipment."

Carefully disassembling the crate, Cipher Bureau experts found that it contained not radio equipment but a code machine. They took photos, made a diagram of its construction and measured its dimensions before repackaging it. Their information was tucked away in a file in the Intelligence Cipher Department.

This was the Poles' introduction to the Enigma.

The people of Poland had good reason to be sensitive to their neighbors' communications equipment. After being wiped off the map of Europe in the 1790s by a series of partitions that awarded its lands to Austria, Prussia and Russia, Poland had been re-created with the agreement of the Allies even before the cessation of hostilities in 1918. With their nation locked in a vise between Germany and the USSR, Polish leaders felt a desperate need to read the other countries' intentions by breaking their codes. The importance of codebreaking had been borne home to them in 1920 when decrypts of Russian military messages helped stave off an attempt by the new Soviet Union's armies to march through Poland and link up with pro-Communist German revolutionaries. In those early days, the Germans' pencil-and-paper codes were also yielding to Polish cryptanalysts.

During the 1920s the Poles did two things that proved critical to their later cryptanalytic triumphs. In 1921 they signed a political and military pact of mutual assistance with France, since the French wanted to hold their old German nemesis in check with the threat of a two-front war. In addition, the leaders of Poland's Cipher Bureau in 1929 enrolled some twenty young mathematics students in a course in cryptology at the University of Poznan.

The latter move was in response to a disturbing change: the Poles could no longer decipher the messages the Germans sent by radio. The head of the Cipher Bureau surmised that their potential enemy had switched from codebook to machine cryptography. Coping with code machines, they reasoned—long before the French or British came to the same conclusion—required advanced mathematical skills rather than the linguistic bent that had heretofore left cryptanalysis largely to philologists and classical scholars.

Faced with successively tougher trial cryptograms, most of the Poznan students dropped out. Three of the brightest—Marian Rejewski, Jerzy Różycki and Henryk Zygalski—continued their interest in cryptography and were eventually employed by the Cipher Bureau. The stage was set for the contents of that sequestered file of information about the German code machine to be reexamined and the attack on Enigma to begin.

The first step was to acquire one of the commercial Enigmas then on the market. For cover, the Cipher Bureau made the purchase through a cooperative Warsaw electrical firm whose business interests could logically justify the machine's use. Comparison of the machine with the file photos and diagrams proved that it was almost identical to that earlier model and suggested that Enigma was the German military's choice for mechanical encipherment. Experiments with the purchased machine, however, verified that the Germans had made changes that increased the Enigma's security. The Poles realized that they could make no headway against the Germans' military Enigma until they learned to build a working model of it.

At this point, in December 1931, the Cipher Bureau received some unexpected help from Poland's French allies.

The Captain and the Turncoat

France, as noted earlier, had been a leader in cryptology before and during World War I. In the postwar period, however, the military command relaxed this phase of its operation, reducing the number of army cryptanalysts to just eight. These analysts bothered themselves only with some of Germany's simpler pencil-and-paper codes. Army leaders had grown complacent because Germany's military preparations were severely restricted by the Treaty of Versailles. No matter how adept the Germans became in cryptography, the forces they were allowed could in no way compare with the superb armies of France.

Fortunately for the eventual course of the war, this thinking was reversed by Captain Gustave Bertrand, who had worked in cryptology since the close of the Great War. Bertrand believed strongly that the coming era of machine cryptography required new approaches, including a readiness to buy or steal opponents' cipher secrets. He formed a new army intelligence department specifically for this purpose.

In the summer of 1931 he received a letter from a young German employed in the cipher section of the German Foreign Office. Hans-Thilo Schmidt was nursing grievances because of his low pay and conspicuous lack of success in comparison with that of his older brother, a high-ranking officer who had arranged for Schmidt's job as a code worker. Schmidt also longed for the richer life that French intelligence payouts could provide. He was willing, for a price, to assume the code name of H.E.—in French the acronym sounds like *Asché*—and turn over to Bertrand the secrets of the very machine that his brother Rudolf had approved for German army use.

Bertrand's first meeting with Schmidt was arranged by a wily go-between named Rodolphe Lemoine, code-named Rex. At the meeting, Schmidt supplied documents that included the instruction manual for the use of the Enigma and the directions for setting its keys. Bertrand's enthusiasm for his find, however, was dampened by France's leading cryptanalyst of the time, who found the material of little value without an indication of the wiring of Enigma's rotors and the actual keys in use for a given period. Bertrand received the same lukewarm response from British intelligence. Not one to give up, he sent photocopies of the two booklets to Warsaw by diplomatic courier while he himself flew there to meet with the Poles.

There, his reception was much warmer. The Poles immediately recognized the value of the booklets Bertrand had received from Asché. As recalled by Rejewski, "Asché's documents were like manna from heaven, and all doors were immediately opened."

Of the three young Polish recruits joining the Cipher Bureau, Rejewski was the one in whom those in charge had the most confidence. Previously he had spent a year studying advanced mathematics at a German university to prepare himself for a career as an insurance actuary. After four years in which they themselves had made no headway in solving the Enigma, the bureau elders handed Rejewski the task. In addition to the manuals received from Schmidt, all he had to work with were some scraps of paper left over from earlier attacks against the Enigma, an outmoded machine and stacks of intercepts.

Studying these meager resources, Rejewski saw that two enormously complex tasks awaited him. One was to determine the internal wiring of the Germans' military Enigma so that replicas of it could be built. The second was to find a way to match what the German operators did in setting their keys for the day.

He went at the wiring problem first. An obvious beginning, Rejewski recognized, was to reduce the number of unknowns. He concentrated on the procedures the manual set forth for German code clerks to follow in operating their Enigmas. Clerks in all units were to arrange the three rotors on their shaft in the same sequence for a given time period—at that early date, for a quarter year. The clerks also followed daily directions for turning the rotors to their assigned letters as that day's "ground setting" common to all the operators. The instructions then told the clerk the order for coupling the plugboard cables. With all the machines set uniformly, it was left to the individual operator to choose, at random, three letters—the message key—indicating the starting positions for a specific transmission. After using that day's ground setting to encipher his message key twice, the operator was ready to change his rotors to the three letters of his choice and begin encoding the message. The procedure was complicated, but it had the virtue of giving each message its own key and then concealing that key in the enciphered first sequence of six letters—the "indicator."

Rejewski's attention focused on the penultimate step of the instructions: the requirement that the operator tap in the three letters of his message key *a second time*. As an example, he might type in *LTBLTB*, and the glow lamps would light up, say, *XMYRVO* as the indicator to be sent over the air. The Germans' apparent intention in doubling the encipherment of the message key was to guard against garbles in transmission because of radio interference or operator error. The repeat of the three letters gave the receiving operator a second chance to set *his* rotors correctly in order to convert the scrambled code groups back into German.

Those six letters at the head of each message, Rejewski saw, represented a major flaw in the German system. For in each grouping of letters, the plaintext behind the first letter was the same as for the fourth, the second as for the fifth, and the third as for the sixth.

These relationships held for the entire day's transmissions. Every time an operator began the indicator with L, enciphered into X, his fourth letter was also L, this time enciphered, say, into R. By stacking a series of indicators one beneath the other, Rejewski saw ways to begin sequences of interconnected letters. If, for example, the indicators were

XMYRVO

RTLGAS

he would know that the first and fourth letters X and R were the same in the plaintext but then, also, that in the next series beginning with an R, the plaintext letter underlying G was the same as R and X. He would link together *XRG* as the first links in a chain. If an additional indicator was *GOV-XPW*, the appearance of another X, now in the fourth position, would close the loop and complete the chain. Rejewski could assume that all the cipher letters in that chain were the same plaintext letter. Some chains extended for many cipher letters, some for only a few, but in the end, by stacking the first six letters of sixty to eighty intercepts, he would fashion chains covering the whole alphabet. He would repeat the process for the second and fifth linkages and the fourth and sixth. He called the three sets of chains the "characteristics" of that setting.

From the commercial Enigma, Rejewski would have learned that the three rotors worked on different cycles. The right-hand one turned a notch every time a typewriter key was pressed. It was the "fast" rotor. Only after it had gone through an entire twenty-six-letter cycle did it trigger a move in the middle rotor, which in turn had to edge forward twenty-six times before activating the third rotor. Rejewski's quick mind seized upon the fact that while the fast rotor was going through its cycle, the other two rotors and the reflector remained fixed as a single unknown factor that could be disregarded while he solved the wiring of the fast rotor.

He also applied mathematical theory to determine that his chains of letters, his characteristics, were entirely the product of the rotors. The plugboard could change the individual letters within a chain but could not alter the number of the chains or their lengths. At least for this part of the crypt-analysis, encipherment by the plugboard could be ruled out.

His characteristics told him the alphabetic substitutions performed for a given day in the six consecutive positions of the indicators. By applying numbers to his characteristics, he used them to set up six complex equations that, if he could solve them, would disclose the fast rotor's wiring sequence. When he tackled the equations, however, he was overwhelmed by too many unknowns. His Cipher Bureau superiors came to his aid. Hoping that Rejewski could solve the Enigma on his own and make the Polish program independent of external help, they had deliberately withheld much of the information they had received from Schmidt. Now they relented and, in early December 1932, gave him a copy of the daily keys for the past months of September and October.

The keys removed one of Rejewski's unknowns—the plugboard connections—and simplified his work on the rest of his equations. Yet they still resisted solution—until it occurred to him that the linkage between the typewriter keyboard and the rotor entry could be the problem. Studying the top row of letters on the typewriter keyboard—*QWERTZUIO*—he had thought the far-left typewriter keyboard *Q* connected with the first, or *A*, position on the input to the fast rotor, that the next letter, *W*, connected with *B*, the *E* with *C* and so on through the alphabet. This was, after all, the order of pairings in the commercial Enigma. But what if, in their military Enigmas, the Germans had decided on a different order of pairings?

If the connections were randomized, he knew, they would present an almost infinite number of variations, an all but insuperable stumbling block. But what if this was a point at which the Germans' fondness for orderliness, or a desire to make life less complicated for Enigma operators, had prevailed? What if instead of randomizing, the German planners had taken the simplistic course of arranging the connections in straight alphabetical order, keyboard letter *A* to the *A* contact on the entry rotor, *B* to *B* and so on through the alphabet?

It turned out that was exactly what they had done. When Rejewski adjusted his equations, he later recalled, "the very first trial yielded a positive result. From my pencil, as by magic, began to issue numbers designating the wiring of drum N"—his "drum" was that rightmost rotor.

The wiring of one rotor had been converted into a known quantity. What about the other two rotors and the reflector? By a stroke of good fortune, Schmidt's two monthly key tables spanned two different calendar quarters. This meant that in the second quarter another of the three rotors was shifted into the right-hand slot. Rejewski could apply to it the same formula he had used on the first rotor. After that, he wrote, "finding the wiring in the third drum, and especially in the reflecting drum, now presented no great difficulties."

Now, with Różycki and Zygalski assigned to help him, Rejewski was ready to turn over to the Bureau's collaborative electrical firm the details for building a working model of the Germans' military Enigma. He and his coworkers could also use Schmidt's information to begin learning how to decipher German messages.

In his reminiscences, Rejewski describes the scene that unfolded during the last days of 1932. While others were celebrating Christmas, the three young analysts, sleepy, unshaven, exhausted, but very content, placed on their superior's desk the first completely decrypted German army messages enciphered by the Enigma.

Mastering the Daily Key Settings

The Poles now faced a second, equally formidable challenge. They had learned how to reconstruct the Enigma machine, but they still lacked the know-how, without relying on the uncertain largesse from the German turncoat, to determine the daily settings. The messages they had decrypted at Christmastime were from the past, using outdated keys. The test now was to find out how to unravel the current keys and decrypt ongoing traffic.

They had to deal with four keying elements: the order of the three rotors on their shaft; the three letters—one for each rotor—which were that period's "ground setting" common to all operators; the three-letter key the individual operator chose for enciphering a specific message; and the connections of the plugboard cables.

They began their attack on the key settings with the discovery that also eased the way for later analysts: German code clerks misused their machines. Whether from boredom, laziness or overconfidence in the security of their Enigmas, they took shortcuts the Poles were able to exploit.

Faced with the necessity of choosing three-letter combinations as their message keys for every message they sent, as an example, clerks frequently chose not to make random selections but to use repeated letters such as *AAA* or *ZZZ*. The letter chains Rejewski derived from indicators tipped him off when the letters of the message key included a repeat. The discovery greatly reduced the number of trials the Poles had to run through in their search for the message key.

When German intelligence officers woke up to the shortcuts the code clerks were taking and issued orders prohibiting repeated letters in key settings, Rejewski was not discouraged. He saw that he could use his letter chains the other way around and rule out any combinations that included a repeat. By the process of elimination extended over a sufficient number of messages, he arrived at the point where only the correct settings were left.

These methods, however, identified only the three rotors' top letters that showed through the windows on the Enigma's lid. They did not reveal which rotor was where. Yet there were only six possible arrangements of the rotors. Rejewski and his colleagues invented an ingenious but laborious process by which they could identify the fast rotor. They used sheets of paper with six slots cut into them marked with the letters from one of Rejewski's chains. They then slid these grilles over tables of the cipher alphabets generated by each rotor, searching for pairings of the letters. Six pairings told them which was the right-hand rotor as well as its starting position. Repeating the process enabled the Poles also to identify the middle rotor, with the remaining rotor obviously going into the third slot.

Use of these techniques was tedious and time-consuming. Rejewski realized his letter chains offered a better way. They differed with each day's setting of the Enigma. Because of the reciprocal nature of the Enigma's wiring connections, the number of chains for each rotor was limited to thirteen (twenty-six letters divided by two). One day's setting might have thirteen chains for each rotor; the next day's could be thirteen, thirteen, twelve, one, and so on through all the various possibilities. He realized that these distinctive patterns were the fingerprints for identifying each day-key. If he and his colleagues could catalog all the variations in the chains and the number of links in each chain, they would have a ready reference with which to determine the ground setting for that day's transmissions. It was a daunting task since there were six variants for the order of rotors multiplied by 17,756 different letter placements on the three rotors ($26 \times 26 \times 26$) for a total of 105,456 entries that had to be tracked down and recorded. Still, that total was far less than the billions of permutations the Germans thought they had built into their machine.

Even with all this, the Poles still did not know where the alphabet rings had been set on the rotors. This step had to be taken in order to know where the notch on each rotor was located to trigger the turnover of its neighbor.

Rejewski and his colleagues observed that a great many messages began with *AN* (German for "To") followed by an *X* used as a word separator. They ran a message through all positions of the rotors in search of *ANX*. Finding a message with this beginning left "only" 26 × 26, or 676, ring positions to be tested for the other two rotors. That was a lot easier and faster than having to run through all 17,756 possible positions.

Measures such as these enabled the Poles to narrow their unknowns to one: the single-letter substitutions resulting from the plugboard connections. But this test was simpler because in those early days, the German code clerks were instructed to connect only six cables, producing just twelve letter substitutions. Rejewski saw that he could run a test decipherment on one of the Enigma replicas now arriving from the electrical supplier and find passages where the underlying plaintext could be discerned. An example in English could be *QEPOQXONXANMQEPAIQ*, which sharp eyes could translate into *REPORT ON TANK REPAIR*, with the plugboard substituting *Q* for *R*, *X* for *T* and *M* for *K*. Other passages revealed the remaining linkages and solved the plugboard in which the Germans placed so much faith.

By grinding through these burdensome procedures each day, the young Poles began reading the German messages and delivering to their superiors glimpses into the Reich military's plans. The process, however, used up most of the day. While that was a far cry from the endless millennia the Germans assured themselves it would take cryptanalysts to break into the Enigma, Rejewski and his mates recognized that their methods of decipherment were too slow to be of practical value. They had to improve the efficiency of the process and greatly increase its speed.

Machines to Defeat the Machine

Time was not the only problem they faced. Although the Germans were confident that their modified Enigmas were impervious to cryptanalysis, they also knew that prudent security precautions called for making changes in their systems periodically. The Poles could not rest on their laurels; they had to deal with a series of changes, each of which could make obsolete the process with which they had been succeeding.

The pressures on the young cryptanalysts were enormously increased by the ascendance of Adolf Hitler and his National Socialist Party. With their military strength on the rise, the Nazis raised an ever-mounting cry to regain their lost lands, particularly the corridor that gave Poland access to the seaport of Danzig, since it separated East Prussia from the rest of Germany.

Rejewski came up with a daring vision: to beat the machine, he and his team would create other machines that would help to find the Enigma keys far more swiftly than they could by their pencil-and-paper methods.

He turned first to that problem of developing a card index of all the 105,456 variations in the letter chains and their linkages. He conceived a device called the Cyclometer, which was designed to automate the process of identifying the characteristic cycles so that the results could be cataloged. It consisted of the interlinked elements of two Enigmas, with twenty-six glow lamps to cover the alphabet. Its function was to determine the length and number of chains in each set of characteristics for all six arrangements of the three rotors. The number of glow lamps that lit up indicated the length of a chain. When, after a year's work, the index was completed, the analysts had only to compare that day's notations on the number and lengths of the chains with the index to pin down the rotor order and settings. Developed in 1934 or '35, the Cyclometer together with the index sped the Poles' cryptanalysis efforts until November 1937.

All this work was then undone when the Germans changed the reversing reflector in the Enigma in a way that voided the Poles' catalog. Rejewski and his team started over, but it took them months to complete a new index and again succeed in decoding German communications.

In mid-September 1938 the Enigma output once more became an incomprehensible jumble. This time the Germans had made their first major change in procedures. Instead of all the operators setting their basic daily key uniformly, the code clerks were now told to choose a new basic setting for each message they transmitted. Their own three-letter choice would be sent unenciphered at the head of the message and was to be followed by a double encipherment of the message key. Since the Poles could no longer stack indicators to form letter chains, all that painstaking work in compiling cycle indexes went out the window.

The fact that the new procedure called for the German code clerks to continue enciphering their message keys twice was fortunate. The same relative positions of plaintext letters and cipher letters were there, providing the opportunity to link the first enciphered letter and the fourth, the second and the fifth, and the third and the sixth. Rejewski's response was to invent a new and more complex Cyclometer the Poles named after the ice cream confection they were eating at the moment Rejewski came up with the idea. The desserts, in Polish, were called "bomby," but subsequently the machines became known as "bombes." When the machines were built and began ticking away like a time bomb working its way toward an explosion, the name seemed appropriate.

Each bombe, consisting of six Enigma machines connected together, was capable of swiftly running through the entire cycle of possible permutations, looking for those relatively rare places where, in an indicator, the plaintext letter would have the identical cipher letter, as in *WGYWMC*. Out of the thousands of combinations, however, the bombe would locate the identical letters in all three 1-4, 2-5, and 3-6 positions. When it found this lineup, it would stop, giving the analysts the information they needed to reconstruct the daily keys.

Yet the determination of the settings did not disclose the order in which the three rotors had been inserted in their Enigma slots—an order which was now also changed daily. Rejewski proposed six bombes to try all six possible rotor sequences in one parallel process.

The machines were built. They worked well when the trios that included the identical letter were free of substitutions introduced by the plugboard. To produce results irrespective of the plugboard connections, Zygalski devised what became known as Zygalski Sheets, sheets of cardboard about two feet square. Each sheet was divided into a grid of small squares representing horizontal and vertical alphabets. For each of the six rotor orders, a set of 26 sheets was prepared, 156 in all. The complex procedure involved cutting holes in the grids where a repeat of plaintext letter and cipher letter from that day's indicators was possible. Zygalski and his coworkers used razor blades to cut out thousands of holes. By stacking the sheets over a light source and shifting them systematically, they found places where the light shone through, indicating a rotor order, and a few trial runs on a replica Enigma could determine whether or not this order was the right one. If it was not, gibberish appeared. If it was, the men read the German message. Together with the bombes, the Zygalski Sheets put the Poles back in the business of speedily deciphering the German traffic, which was now so voluminous that a new rank of Enigma-using technicians had to be added to the Cipher Bureau.

By the winter of 1937–38 the Poles were deciphering about seventy-five percent of the messages passed to them by their intercept stations. In all, during those five years after they first broke through in 1933, they read about one hundred thousand of Germany's military transmissions. They were able to inform Poland's government and military leaders about the German mobilization plans, the order of battle of the German forces and the output of their armaments industry.

Passing the Torch to the French and British

In December 1938, the Poles' entire operation again came to a screeching halt. Once more the Germans changed their system, and this time the change was, from the cryptanalysts' point of view, catastrophic.

The Germans put into service two additional rotors. As mentioned earlier, the Enigma had slots for only three code wheels at a time. To have the three chosen from the five available, however, multiplied the number of code wheel orders ten times, a huge additional cryptanalytic burden.

The Poles were confident they could solve the new system, but to do it they would need not 6 bombes but 60, and not 156 Zygalski Sheets but 1,560. These requirements simply outran the Cipher Bureau's resources. In addition, the Nazi drums of war were beating ever more loudly, and the Poles could see that time was running short.

Even though they could still read the messages of the Nazi Party's intelligence service, which continued to use the old keying system, the Poles came to a momentous decision. They would pass on to their allies, who now included the British, the knowledge they had acquired about the Enigma and the machines they had developed to break its output.

On July 24, 1939, the French delegates, including Bertrand and an aide, along with three top intelligence officials from Britain, arrived in Warsaw. They were taken to the building the Poles had created for their cryptanalysis crew outside the city. "At that meeting," as Rejewski depicted it, "we told everything that we knew and showed everything that we had." Ironically, the common language for their meeting was German.

The head of the Cipher Bureau, Lieutenant Colonel Gwido Langer, showed the visitors around the facility. Then he took them into a room in which several objects under covers rested on tables. Like an artist unveiling a new creation, Langer whisked off the covers. Under them were Polish clones of Enigmas. Everyone recognized what they were, yet they could not believe that the Poles had built the machines on their own. Bertrand called it "*un moment de stupeur*," "a moment of stupor."

Among the English party was Dillwyn "Dilly" Knox. Back in England, Knox had been wrestling fruitlessly with the Enigma, and he had a question for his Polish hosts: in what sequence had the Germans ordered their connections in the entry rotor? When told they were wired in alphabetical order, he blinked in disbelief. Something so obvious had never entered his mind. According to one report, later that evening when he was in a taxi with Bertrand returning to their hotel, he chanted happily, "*Nous avons le QWERTZU, nous marchons ensemble*": "We have the QWERTZU, we march together."

Langer led the way to another room. Here, lined up, were the six bombes. Langer switched on the machines and demonstrated how they worked. Rejewski answered questions. Zygalski explained his perforated sheets. Bertrand's moment of *stupeur* deepened.

Alastair Denniston, chief of the British delegation, wanted to telephone London right away to have technicians fly in to size up the specifications for the Enigmas and the bombes. That wouldn't be necessary, the Poles told him. They were ready to ship Enigmas by diplomatic pouch to Paris, where one could be forwarded to England, and to supply technical drawings of the bombes as well as samples of the Zygalski Sheets.

The conference ended, as Kahn has described it, "in an atmosphere of warmth, astonishment, gratitude, and anticipation."

The disclosure came none too soon. Just five weeks later, the German blitzkrieg overran the armies of Poland. The Cipher Bureau had to quickly destroy its files and smash its machinery. The cryptographic team also needed to escape, for in their heads was information the Gestapo might well extract by methods of torture.

Rejewski and his mates headed south and soon crossed the border into Romania. At the French consulate in Bucharest, the code name for Captain Bertrand brought a quick passage. Making their way through Yugoslavia and Italy, they joined up with Bertrand at his headquarters outside Paris. Soon, with British help that included providing new stacks of Zygalski Sheets, they were back to tackling the Enigma.

The Poles were not again to become the leaders in the attack on the Enigma, but before their flight they had shown what no one else, least of all the Germans, believed possible. The Enigma could be beaten and the secret contents of its messages divulged.

3 Britain Takes Over the Cryptologic War

BRITAIN'S cryptanalysts were busily making up for their years of half-hearted attempts to crack the machine. The Government Code and Cypher School (GC&CS)—a deliberately understated title—was moved out of crowded and bomb-vulnerable London. For its new home, the chief of the Secret Intelligence Service, eccentric millionaire Hugh Sinclair, had purchased the Bletchley Park estate in the town of Bletchley, a homely manufacturing and railway hub fifty miles to the northwest in Buckinghamshire. In August 1939, Alastair Denniston, picked by Sinclair to head up GC&CS, had investigated the accommodations at Bletchley Park. Even though the mansion was an architectural monstrosity, Denniston saw that the Park had other virtues. Chief among them was that it was located on a main rail line out of London and another line that connected Bletchley to both Oxford and Cambridge. Convinced, he made BP the GC&CS headquarters just before England was plunged into war against Germany.

British progress in cryptology owes much to Denniston. During the Great War, he was a bright young man in Britain's Room 40. He could have pursued a much more lucrative career elsewhere, but he stayed with the agency. With World War II approaching, he led the way in making changes that proved critical to BP's success. He realized, as the Poles had a decade earlier, that the new cryptology demanded different mind-sets, individuals with advanced mathematical skills, puzzle solvers, chess players, bridge addicts. He began tracking down such individuals, mainly in Cambridge and Oxford, and recruiting them. He launched a cryptography course to begin their training. Most important, he was a persuasive advocate for having most of Britain's cryptologic program centered in Bletchley. He knew that the kind of brains that excel in cryptanalysis are not common, and to have them joined in collaboration at one place was a distinct advantage. The Germans had bright analysts, but there were so many chiefs contending for Hitler's favor, with each zealously guarding his own turf, that the available brainpower was too fragmented ever to mount a coherent and consistent codebreaking program.

Denniston was not particular about his recruits' backgrounds. He combed the military; he used his old-boy contacts among the universities; he brought in civilians; he tapped the Wrens (Women's Royal Navy Service) and Waafs (Women's Auxiliary Air Force) for legions of young women. BP became a melting pot of cryptologic expertise. When the war began, three of Britain's master chess players were attending an international Chess Olympiad in Buenos Aires. They promptly caught the blacked-out, unconvoyed *Alcantara* for home and joined Denniston's team at Bletchley.

GC&CS denizens formed a society ruled by meritocracy. Military rank didn't count. No saluting or other military hocus-pocus was tolerated. Everybody went by first names or nicknames. The only way to gain respect was by doing a superlative piece of work.

Most brilliant, and most eccentric, of the lot was Alan Turing. He had a strange and wonderful combination of talents: he was a mathematical and theoretical genius, yet he could descend from his visionary cloud to become the most practical mechanic. To look back at those times is to marvel at how fortuitous it was that this man became the pivotal figure in the conquest of the Enigma.

Turing's powerful and independent mind made him, as a schoolboy, intolerant of conventional classroom teaching. Frequently he neglected regular studies because his real attention was given to probing advanced mathematical theorems on his own. Adding to his drive to excel was his memory of an ardent friendship with a fellow student, Christopher Morcom. When Morcom died of tuberculosis while still in school, Turing resolved to achieve what he believed his friend would have achieved if he had lived.

Morcom had won a scholarship to Cambridge. Turing followed suit by attending Cambridge and being elected to a fellowship at the university's King's College when he was twenty-two. He was also sure Morcom would have sought stimulus by searching out the university's outstanding academic scions. Turing was strongly influenced, first, by David Hilbert, who raised the question, did there exist a definitive method which could, in principle, be applied to any mathematical assertion and produce a correct decision as to whether it was provable? Hilbert believed there was no such thing as an unsolvable mathematical problem.

The second Cambridge lecturer who most influenced Turing's thinking was Maxwell H. A. "Max" Newman, who asked if there wasn't a mechanical process that could put mathematical theorems to the test.

From this point on, Turing—in the words of his biographer Andrew Hodges—"dreamed of machines." In the early summer of 1935, when he was just twenty-three years old, he saw his answer. He created a theoretical "universal machine"—afterward known as the Turing machine—that could, by using the binary system that later became the basis for digital computers, replicate logical human thought. The Turing machine could also write a verdict as to whether a specific assertion was or was not provable. This, together with his work on determining computable versus noncomputable numbers, proved Hilbert wrong: there could be unsolvable problems.

The world of advanced mathematics was then centered in Princeton, New Jersey. There men such as Albert Einstein, Alonzo Church and Kurt Gödel provided leadership in probing into mathematical unknowns. In 1936, Turing went to Princeton University and benefited from exchanging ideas with the older masters. While there he indulged both his theoretical and his mechanical bents in, as though by predestination, cryptology. He worked on a cryptographic system for which he needed an electrical multiplier. To build it he had to construct his own electrical relays.

Princeton Ph.D. in hand, and his multiplier in his luggage, Turing returned to Britain in July 1938 and soon afterward wound up at Bletchley Park. There, in the summer of 1939, spirits were animated by the knowledge that the Poles had broken the Enigma. Turing led BP's attack.

To him the German machine was a practical application of his theoretical machines. The Poles were right: to defeat the Enigma required counter-Enigmas. Yet the Poles were also wrong: their machines attacked the German machine through the message key indicators, and in his estimation, that was not the right way to go as indicators could be changed overnight, sending the codebreakers back to square one.

With astonishing speed Turing created an English bombe that took little from the Poles except the machine's name. Turing's bombe passed over the indicators; it sought to extract the key from the message itself.

Turing and Welchman Team Up

Brilliant as he was, to make his bombe effective, Turing had to have help from a colleague, Gordon Welchman. A lecturer in mathematics at

Cambridge, Welchman had a frustrating time when he first came to Bletchley Park. Denniston assigned him to join Dilly Knox's small group at work in the BP building known as the Cottage. But Knox seemed to take a dislike to him and banished him to another building. There Welchman was told to study some German army messages and draw whatever information and patterns he could through an external examination. Welchman soon went beyond those parameters. On his own he realized the vulnerability of the double enciphering of the message key and independently evolved an equivalent of the Zygalski Sheets. When he reported his work to Knox, Welchman was dismayed to find that he had simply been duplicating the efforts of another BP associate and Cambridge alumnus, John Jeffreys, who had produced Bletchley's version of the Polish sheets.

Welchman's fortunes changed when he teamed up with Turing. Turing's approach to cracking the Enigma was to work with "cribs," or what Welchman called the "probable words" in a message. Since military parlance was highly standardized and repetitious, one could presume that certain words or phrases would appear in the text. The Poles had made rudimentary use of the technique by searching for messages that began with *ANX*. Turing meant to use his bombes to carry the method much further by finding longer passages embedded in the message itself.

The British were aided, as the Poles had been, by German overconfidence in the security of their machine. The Germans could have made the use of cribs far more difficult if not impossible. All they needed to do was to add random bits of nonsense into their message beginnings and/or endings, or to insert *X*s into long words, or to translate officers' titles into coded references—any such steps would have prevented accurate cribs from being applied. But they remained punctilious about spelling out honorifics and titles, and they continued to use repetitive phrases without any masking.

Turing's bombe, possessing the power of at least twelve Polish bombes, was designed to run an automatic test to determine whether a specific crib was contained in the message. He, however, had a limited view of what could be obtained even when his bombe succeeded. Essentially, he meant to look for the same sorts of closed letter loops that had been at the center of the Poles' technology. Turing's loops, however, had the great advantage of being drawn from cribs within the message rather than from its indicator. His bombe used the loops to detect incorrect positions and, by rejecting them, to arrive at the correct settings.

When it was built, though, this first bombe did not work well. To seek out merely small strings of letters did not produce enough rejections. There were many "Stops" that were found to be false only by hand testing. It was a slow and uncertain process.

Then Turing showed his plans to Welchman. In a flash of inspiration, Welchman saw that they didn't have to settle for closed loops. "By interconnecting the scramblers in a completely new way," he wrote in his memoir, *The Hut Six Story*, "one could increase the effectiveness of the automatic test by a very large number."

His new method involved adding to Turing's bombe the circuitry of what Welchman called a "diagonal board"—a matrix of terminals in a square in which the twenty-six letters of the alphabet were arranged horizontally, with another twenty-six vertically. His scheme capitalized on the reciprocal nature of the Enigma's plugboard connections. That is, if A is connected with Z and becomes Z in the encipherment, then the reverse is also true: Z becomes A. His change ruled out false stops that the plugboards could make in Turing's bombe. The insertion of the diagonal board, as Welchman described it, "greatly reduced the number of runs that would be needed to insure success in breaking an Enigma key by means of a crib."

Turing, Welchman wrote, was incredulous at first, "but when he had studied my diagram he agreed that the idea would work, and became as excited about it as I was."

Turing's earlier design had guided the British Tabulating Machine Company in producing the first BP bombe. Now an improved design incorporating Welchman's diagonal board was put into production. The conversion benefited from Turing's mechanical bent. To do their required switching jobs, the bombes needed fast-working electrical relays. Turing drew from his electric multiplier to suggest designs for the bombes.

Patricia Bing, a teletypist who worked for Turing, later recalled how fellow workers at BP quickly adjusted to the unconventional ways of the man they began referring to as "the Prof." They understood that Turing thought little of his appearance or the impression he made. His clothes were a mess; his chewed-up fingernails most often had crescents of dirt beneath them; he could show up at BP entirely unaware that he was wearing two odd shoes. To control his allergies in pollen season he donned a gas mask when riding his bike. The bike had a bad habit of periodically throwing its chain; instead of taking the time to fix it he would count off the number of revolutions and stop just in time to make an adjustment. Bing remembered seeing Turing arrive on his bike and then "scuttle past us giggling girls, eyes downcast, as though in fear he might have to speak to one of us before he disappeared into his office." The papers he wrote and the designs he produced were made almost unintelligible by scratch-outs and inkblots. When invasion threatened, he melted down a collection of silver coins into ingots, buried them and then, when the crisis had passed and it was time to dig them up, could not remember where they were buried.

In the hunt to unlock the Enigma, though, the Germans never dreamed they would be up against a man of Turing's genius. In those few months between the outbreak of the war and early 1940, he had analyzed the machine, discerned the chinks in its supposedly impenetrable armor and, with Welchman's help, devised the countermeasures that would defeat it.

Months must pass, however, before the redesigned bombes, with all their thousands of soldered connections, would be available. How were the codebreakers to achieve at least partial success in the meantime?

British patience and meticulous attention to detail came to the rescue. GC&CS analysts had been studying the habits of German Enigma operators and had found two subtle mistakes that could be exploited.

The first became known as "Herivel's tip," after John Herivel, a young mathematician recruited by Welchman. Much like Rejewski, Herivel tried to put himself into the shoes of a German code clerk and imagine what the operator might do incorrectly because of laziness or work pressure. Herivel had an insight. At the beginning of each new encoding day, the German operator had a boring series of steps he had to go through. Following instructions, he must choose the correct set of three rotors out of the five available, slide the rotors in proper sequence onto the axle, turn their alphabet rings to the required positions and link up the proper arrangement of the plugboard cables. Then he was supposed to select three random letters for his message key. It was all a big bother. Suppose, Herivel asked himself, the lazy or hurried operator didn't take that final step? Suppose he sent his first message of the day using the same three letters as his rotor ring settings? Herivel suggested collecting the new day's first messages. If there was more than one shortcutting operator, there would be repeats—and the rotor settings could be surmised.

The second sloppy practice consisted of what BP labeled "cillis." The name may have been derived from the initials of one German clerk's girlfriend, which he used often instead of randomizing his three-letter selections. That was one type of cilli—the repeated use of familiar sequences, such as *HIT* and *LER*. Another form was supplied by German operators who, instead of plucking their three letters out of the air, simply lifted them from their keyboards. A sequence down from the *Q* key read *QAY*. One down from *W* read *WSX*. Although these practices were expressly forbidden in the Enigma operators' manuals, lazy or rushed code clerks did resort to them, and from these cillis BP's clever analysts could determine the wheel order for the day as well as the setting for these particular messages. "Unbelievable?" Welchman wrote. "Yet it actually happened, and it went on happening until the bombes came, many months later."

Using these and similar ingenious methods, the BP crew early in 1940 began deciphering the Luftwaffe messages known as Red because that was the color of the pencil Welchman used to demark it from other systems.

By then it had been decided that Welchman and Turing would divide the main Enigma decrypting responsibilities between them. Welchman had moved into Hut 6, one of the wooden structures hastily erected on the park's grounds, and took over its operation when the young John Jeffreys became terminally ill. Welchman's team concerned itself with breaking German air force and army traffic, then passed the decrypts on to Hut 3. There, another team translated them, judged their importance and urgency and determined where they should be disseminated. Turing was responsible for Hut 8, heading up work on the naval Enigma signals, with Hut 4 as his analysis center.

When the bombes arrived in August 1940, allowing cribs to be put to use, the Hut 6 team simply accelerated the breaking of the Red cipher. It was of particular value because it was used in army/air force coordination and disclosed information about both services.

German Enigma operators continued their inadvertent cooperation. Each month, for example, the operators had to create new sheets covering the next month's ring settings, rotor orders and plugboard connections. One German operator decided he could save himself much work by simply rearranging blocks of settings from previous months' key sheets. Having broken those of the previous months, BP could quickly break the new settings.

In North Africa's Qattara Depression, a bored German officer reported every day the same message, *"Nichts zu melden"*—"Nothing new to report"—giving Welchman and his team a ready-made crib for solving the new Enigma setup.

The Britons' attention to detail steadily paid dividends. In her self-published book, *England Needs You*, about her life at Britain's Beaumanor intercept station, Joan Nicholls has told of two Germans, either friends or relatives, who served as code clerks at different stations in a panzer division network. They would end each of their messages to each other with the smallest of flourishes. One would sign off with "—••—", or *X*; the other would answer with "— —", *M*. It was, Nicholls wrote, "such a small transgression on their part, but we were able to log these two and, of course, the whereabouts of their unit, from North Africa through Sicily, Italy, France and finally into Germany."

The bombes quickly proved their worth. The Wren operators of a bombe would receive a "menu" of settings phoned to them from BP and set the rotors accordingly. The bombe would whir through its rounds, testing a Luftwaffe message. When it came to a Stop, this indicated that all the links on a menu were confirmed. From a successful Stop, the GC&CS team could determine the order in which the three rotors had been placed as well as the three letters which were the settings for the alphabet rings on the rotors. One of the Wrens would check out the settings on her replica Enigma. If German text appeared, and a member of the overseeing watch approved, the exultant cry would ring out: "Red's up!" The operators would then await their next menu.

Mechanically, the bombes were a bit tetchy. The stiff wire brushes on each rotor that connected the two sets of contacts could, in use, widen and cause the machine to short out. Before each run the Wrens applied tweezers to reposition each wire correctly. RAF mechanics also appeared, either regularly or on emergency call, to repair the bombes. With these measures of correction, the machines operated around the clock, week after week, month after month. With the Tabulating Machine Company massproducing new units, several bombes could be set to work on the same menu, greatly reducing the time required for achieving a productive Stop.

It was well that Hut 6 was breaking Red because over in Hut 8 Turing was having a far harder time. He was facing a much more formidable opponent. While Welchman was dealing with Hermann Göring, who was as lax with his Enigma systems as he was with his personal fitness, Turing had to match wits with Admiral Karl Dönitz, the much more rigorous leader of the U-boat command. The German navy drilled its Enigma operators in following strict security procedures, kept introducing improvements into its systems and made regular changes in key methods. As an example of Turing's difficulties, the navy Enigma gave operators a choice of three out of eight rotors, while other German clerks selected three out of only five—a difference that put much greater barriers in the way of the cryptanalyst.

Before Turing eventually triumphed over the naval Enigma, a story told in a later chapter, he and his team experienced a harrowing time. Every day of continuing failure conjured up new visions of men trapped in their sinking vessels or escaping only to freeze to death in the North Atlantic's frigid waters; of desperately needed food, gasoline and other supplies plunging uselessly to the ocean floor; of Britain's ability to survive hanging in the balance.

Welchman made another significant contribution to the early development of Bletchley Park. He looked ahead and realized how inadequately Dilly Knox was preparing for the intelligence war that was to come. The small staff Knox had gathered would be inundated, Welchman foresaw, once the Enigma was conquered and masses of German intercepts began pouring in. Welchman developed an organization plan calling for a major expansion of the forces at BP. With his plan quickly approved, he became needed as much for his leadership and administrative skills as for his codebreaking abilities.

BP's Triumph over "Fish"

In the autumn of 1940, BP's analysts were faced with a cryptologic challenge decidedly different from that presented by the Enigma. This new traffic was based not on Morse code but on the international code—the Baudot-Murray code—developed for teleprinter machines. Instead of dots and dashes, Baudot-Murray employed electrical impulses triggered by holes and spaces in paper tapes. Unlike the Morse system, whose characters varied in length from one dot (letter *E*) to five dashes (numeral 0), each symbol in the Baudot code was represented by a group of five equal-length hole (*x*) or space (*o*) elements. Thus, in the nonsecret international system, *A* was *xxooo*, *B* was *xooxx*, and so forth. It was, in short, another forerunner of digital computers' binary system.

The Germans, it became clear, were adding a second machine to the standard Teletype machine to encipher its output. Messages transmitted by radio were most often sent automatically at high speed and were direction beamed so that interception was more difficult. In addition, each of the three German armed services was using a different cipher machine. Because the Germans called one of their systems Sägefisch, or "Sawfish," BP chose "Fish" as shorthand for this whole separate type of transmission.

How was BP to cope with the immense new problems presented by Fish? The question took on greater urgency as it became evident that after intermittent use at the beginning, the Germans were relying on Fish ever more heavily. BP also determined that the system was being used for higher-level communications, such as those between army commands, or from headquarters to commanders in the field. Further, the messages tended to be much longer, running to thousands of characters, compared to the few hundred typical of Enigma traffic. And there was the threat that the Teletype code machine might in time completely replace the Enigma. Harry Hinsley has written that Fish represented "intellectual, technological and organisational problems of a still higher order than those presented by the Enigma."

But BP had triumphed over Enigma. They were confident they could do the same with Fish.

Britain's top intelligence authorities came to a decision. To tackle three different types of Fish encoding machines would require too great a commitment of resources. Intelligence directed that the effort be concentrated on the cipher machine used by the army, subsequently known to be produced by the Lorenz firm. A greater flow of information about the Wehrmacht was, at that point, the prime need of Allied war planners. Carrying on the piscatorial analogy, BP called the Lorenz machine Tunny.

Hinsley was right: Tunny made a formidable opponent. In addition to two drive wheels, it used ten rotors, and none of them sat idle; they all worked together in linked sequences. The rotors were different from those of the Enigma. Instead of being wired internally, each enciphering rotor had around its rim a number of spring-powered pins that could be either retracted or extended to form either a hole or a space. To encode a message, the machine applied an additive system invented in 1918 by an American, Gilbert Vernam. The sender's machine automatically added to each plaintext letter a random letter, resulting in still a third letter which was sent over the air. The receiver's machine automatically canceled the additive, leaving the original character to be printed out.

BP's John Tiltman, a man who had entered Oxford at the age of thirteen, set his mind to unraveling Tunny messages by hand methods. He was making only slow progress until, once again, a German operator error opened the door. The operator had a long message of nearly four thousand characters to be sent from his high command post to another. The operator set up his Lorenz machine correctly and sent an indicator so the receiver could set up his machine. Yet trouble developed. After the sender had patiently typed out the long text and transmitted it, the receiver radioed back that he hadn't got it, so please send it again. The two of them took the absolutely forbidden tack of turning their machines back to the same initial settings of the rotors. The sender then committed a second mistake. Probably bored by having to repeat the message, he began to take shortcuts. The first word was *Spruchnummer*—"message number." He abbreviated it to *Spruchnr*. With similar cuts, the second message came out about five hundred characters shorter than the first. If the two messages had been identical, they would have been no help to Tiltman. But by crossruffing the streams of dissimilar ciphertexts against each other, he was able to recover both messages completely. What was more, he found the elements that had been added by the Lorenz.

Studying this information, another young Cambridge graduate, William T. Tutte, realized that certain patterns tended to repeat after forty-one bits. From this he deduced that the first rotor had forty-one pins. In four months of intense concentration, Tutte worked out the machine's complete internal structure. His discoveries resulted in the building of a simulated Tunny. Later, when the capture of a German unit permitted comparison, the BP team exulted, "We got it right."

Throughout 1942, work on the Lorenz intercepts had to be done by hand methods. The decrypts yielded some useful information, even though many of them were weeks old before the cryptanalysts could deliver them.

Max Newman, who had stirred the mathematical imagination of young Alan Turing at Cambridge, also entered the picture. Seeing that decryption of Fish traffic would remain of limited value until the process was mechanized, he proposed a device that would go beyond the strictly electro-mechanical functioning of Turing's bombes; it would make use of the emerging technology of electronics by including vacuum tubes, which worked much more swiftly than electrical switches.

Newman's machine resembled an eight-foot-high cupboard. The women working on it dubbed it "Heath Robinson," the name of the cartoonist who, in Britain, created the same sort of absurdly overcomplicated devices that Rube Goldberg did in America.

Comical or not, Heath Robinson could scan one thousand telegraphic symbols a second. It was designed to keep two paper teleprinter tapes in synchronization at thirty miles per hour. One tape carried the enciphered text of a message; the other contained the wheel patterns worked out by the codebreakers. The machine's comparison of the two tapes determined the settings of the five most active rotors and greatly speeded up the process of decryption.

It was a promising start, but Heath Robinson soon showed severe weaknesses. It caused the sprocket holes in the tapes to stretch, ruining the synchronization, or it completely broke the tapes. It sometimes became so hot that it began to smoke.

Turing, at that point in early 1943 a member of the Fish team, suggested that Newman call on the services of Tom Flowers, who had worked at Britain's Post Office Research Station, and who had developed postal equipment that used vacuum tubes. After the years of secrecy had ended, Flowers recalled about the Heath Robinson machine, "I was brought in to make it work, but I very soon came to the conclusion that it would never work. It was dependent on paper tape being driven at high speeds by means of spiked wheels, and the paper couldn't stand up to it."

He saw that combating the Lorenz required a fully electronic machine, one that would use as many as fifteen hundred vacuum tubes. The machine he envisioned would do a job much faster because it would not require the synchronization of two tapes. Its one tape would carry the enciphered message and would be read photoelectrically. To forestall the tape's tearing itself apart, it would run on smooth-surfaced wheels. Instead of running on a second tape, the wheel patterns would be generated electronically. He was confident his machine could process five thousand characters a second and could thus spin through all the possible combinations of keys for the Lorenz in about an hour.

The authorities at BP, having to husband their funds, thought Flowers's plans were too big and impractical. The vacuum tubes were unreliable; they burned out too quickly. Besides, since this was already the spring of 1943, the war would be over before he could possibly produce a machine.

Flowers and his Post Office colleagues were not to be dissuaded. They would build the machine without BP support. Flowers found that if vacuum tubes weren't turned on and off, if they were just allowed to run on and on, they were quite reliable. As for the completion date, he and his team, working on their own, produced Colossus I in ten months.

The results were dramatic. Colossus reduced the time required to decrypt Fish messages from weeks to hours. The timing was also dramatic. The machine came into use soon enough to provide invaluable information for Eisenhower's D-Day planning. Its decrypts helped prove that the Germans were swallowing the Allies' deception programs for the invasion. During the remainder of the war, it kept Allied leaders informed of the decisions of the German high command.

In volume, Fish decrypts numbered far less than the monthly averages of ninety thousand decrypts from Enigma traffic in the war's final phases. But the Fish messages were longer, some of them running to ten thousand characters, and they provided an ear to the most intimate planning of Hitler and his top generals, their discussions, orders and reports on the disposition and strengths of their commands.

As suppliers of intelligence, Enigma and Fish complemented each other. While Enigma decrypts most often revealed information of operational and tactical value, Fish supplied knowledge of strategic importance.

As the war progressed, the Germans relied more and more heavily on their Fish communications. These networks proliferated, rising from six links in July 1943 to twenty-six in early 1944. The Germans also kept changing and improving their systems. But Flowers and his men stayed with them, building ever more powerful Colossi. With BP approval, they had twelve machines working by the end of the war. Their Colossus II used twenty-five hundred vacuum tubes. George Vergine, an American who worked with the Colossi at BP, later recalled having one of the suppliers at the vacuum tube manufacturing plant ask him, "What the hell are you doing with these things—shooting them at the Jerries?"

Hinsley called the availability of Fish decrypts "the outstanding signals intelligence achievement in this last phase of the war."

Unknowingly, the engineers who produced Colossi were reaching another milestone. Their machines were forebears of the modern digital computer, a success that should have been attributed to British science but that had to be suppressed by the long postwar secrecy imposed on all things cryptographic. On orders from Churchill after the war, the Colossi were destroyed and Tom Flowers burned the blueprints.

At Bletchley Park in the 1990s, however, the Colossus was reborn. Tony Sale, a determined engineer of the postwar generation, secured the aid of Flowers and others who had worked on the original development to help him build a working model. This Colossus is now seen on summer weekends by thousands of visitors during tours of the Park.

4 BP Begins Exploiting Its "Gold Mine"

THE bright young people assembling at Bletchley Park very quickly realized that by building on the beginnings passed on to them by the Poles, they were on to a cryptologic opportunity surpassing anything known before. As Gordon Welchman said, "We were faced with an unprecedented situation quite unlike cryptanalysis of the old days when messages were broken one by one. If we could discover a 'daily key' which told German operators how to set up their Enigmas, we would be able to decode all messages using that key. . . . Even in the autumn of 1939, when no military operations were in progress, we were intercepting hundreds of messages each day." Welchman saw this mass of intelligence inflow as a "potential gold mine."

BP's first bonanza from the mother lode came in April 1940, when Hitler ended the edgy, idle "phony war" that had lasted for seven months. Hearing rumors that Britain was planning to occupy Norway, the German chancellor resolved to strike first. He would delay his planned drive into France and let the phony war continue until his troops had removed the threat of a flanking attack through Scandinavia. When the campaign began on April 9, Britain's intercept stations were suddenly flooded with the messages of a new Enigma code BP labeled as Yellow. Gratifyingly, the breaking of Yellow took Bletchley's cryptanalysts less than five days.

Very quickly the BP team learned how unprepared they were to handle the great influx. The sheer volume of the intercepts overwhelmed the cryptanalysts. Also, the messages they did decipher were filled with bewildering abbreviations, oblique references and arcane military jargon beyond the ken of the largely academic translators. The experience, moreover, pointed out the inadequacies of Bletchley's system for disseminating its information to the various commands. The people who could make the greatest use of the information simply weren't in the loop. In addition, security measures deemed necessary to prevent the Germans from knowing that their Enigma messages were being broken were now seen as serious deterrents to the effective use of decrypts. Up to that point, the scheme devised to protect security in case a BP summary fell into enemy hands was to attribute it to a spy code-named Boniface. It was a thin mask that, as the volume of traffic mounted, soon became an obvious fabrication. Further, British services had little faith in the espionage wing of British intelligence; as long as they thought they were reading the reports of a spy, they tended to reject or ignore even the most valid signals conveyed to them. BP minds began to realize they had to submit their internal systems to a drastic overhaul.

Young Harry Hinsley, the man who would long afterward take the lead in writing *British Intelligence in the Second World War*, was involved in one of the sadder aspects of the Norwegian disaster. Although BP was not yet breaking the German naval codes, Hinsley's study of the increased flow of naval wireless traffic, combined with direction-finding analyses that ascertained the buildup of signals was coming mainly from North Sea ports, convinced him in early April that a German attack in Norway was approaching. He phoned his warnings to the Royal Navy's headquarters, the Admiralty, in London. But his was merely a youthful voice, a voice, in the eyes of the Admiralty, of a civilian who knew little about naval operations. Moreover, the planes for British aerial reconnaissance were unable to range as far as the Baltic ports, so they could not verify his claims of a German naval buildup. Consequently, the Admiralty refused to heed his alarms or those of British agents on the continent, or even the advices of the diplomatic observers of "neutral" countries. If the navy had acted, Britain's warships could have ravaged the troop-filled transports and barges moving to the attack. Instead, the Germans achieved complete surprise, quickly overran Denmark and invaded Norway. On April 15 the British sent troops to aid the small, game Norwegian army. But it was all too improvised and far too late. The Germans crushed the Norwegian defenders and forced the British to evacuate.

Hinsley tried to prevent another grievous incident. The aircraft carrier HMS *Glorious* had steamed to Norway to bring home RAF planes and aircrews urgently needed to help defend Britain against the expected German air assault. The ship, headed back toward England and escorted by two destroyers, was oblivious to German warships in its path and failed to send out air patrols. From Yellow decrypts, Hinsley saw the danger and again tried to warn the Admiralty. And again he was ignored. The battleships *Gneisenau* and *Scharnhorst*, guided by German cryptanalysts decrypting the Admiralty's orders, moved in on the British trio and sank them all, with great loss of life.

In fact, the Germans had broken the British naval code in 1938 and were reading the Admiralty's dispatches throughout the Norwegian campaign. During the critical period when the German landings in Norway were most vulnerable, German decrypts disclosed the positions of most of Britain's capital ships in the North Sea. As one British commander ruefully commented, "It is most galling that the enemy should know just where our ships always are, whereas we generally learn where his major forces are when they sink one or more of our ships." At that early stage of the sea war, the Germans clearly held the intelligence advantage.

The British made Norway a bitter but fruitful learning experience. New personnel flowed into Bletchley Park in increasing numbers. Military experts were brought in to unscramble the Germans' military shorthand. A new legion of translators and interpreters were sought out. Fred Winterbotham solved the dissemination security problem by organizing SLUs—Special Liaison Units—which were assigned to the headquarters of each command and served as conduits by which summaries of BP decrypts were passed on to those who could make use of them. A new method was devised to indicate the relative importance attached to each report: one *Z* for lower-value material and up to five *Z*s for signals that clamored for immediate attention. Also, the Park's staffers began using special headings to designate Enigma information: *Hydra* identified naval traffic for a time, and later, because Churchill called BP his "Ultra Secret," reports based on Enigma decrypts were then labeled *Ultra*. As to where the information came from, messages simply cited *Source*. Boniface was laid to rest.

And miracle of miracles, the tradition-encrusted Royal Navy came around, changing its mind about the importance of BP's information. Hinsley, in a memoir, has reported that he was

> full of admiration for the alacrity with which the OIC (Operational Intelligence Center of the Admiralty) responded to the loss of the *Glorious*. It immediately invited me to spend a month in the Admiralty. It sent me on the first of several visits to the Home Fleet at Scapa, where I stayed on board the flagships and walked the deck with Admiral Tovey and his staff. And on my return it did all in its power to ensure through the regular exchange of visits, and with the

assistance of new scrambler telephones, that there should be complete collaboration between the OIC and the Naval Section at Bletchley.

When a question arose as to the source of a specific bit of news, it was sufficient now to answer only, "Hinsley."

One other result of the catastrophe in Norway was that Neville Chamberlain stepped down as prime minister, and was succeeded by Winston Churchill.

Ultra and the Battle of France

On May 10, 1940, when Hitler was confident that his Scandinavian flank was under control, he unleashed the fury of the German blitzkrieg on the British Expeditionary Force (BEF) and the armies of France.

Again the Germans possessed the advantage in intelligence. They were breaking the high-level French military code and consequently knew in detail the disposition of the French divisions. At this same critical moment, the German air force blinded BP by making a change in its Red system. German security controllers had evidently realized the vulnerability of having Enigma operators repeat the three-letter encoding of their machine settings—the flaw that had enabled the Poles to begin breaking the system—and had issued new regulations for the second encipherment to be dropped. Astonishingly, BP's codebreakers needed only twelve days to cope with this change. After May 22 they began deciphering as many as a thousand Red signals a day—"a flood of operational intelligence," as Hinsley put it.

It was intelligence that should have proved of high value to the British divisions in France because it contained clues to the intentions of both the German air force and army. By then, however, the situation on the continent had become a shambles. The French had used high percentages of their annual armaments budgets to build the Maginot Line—that concrete bastion designed to keep German invaders at bay—and had neglected to supply their military units with up-to-date arms. Even so they had completed only eighty-seven miles of the line, leaving open to attack the entire northern area from the English Channel to the Ardennes forest. The French didn't want to wall themselves against their Belgian, Dutch and Luxembourgian neighbors and persuaded themselves that the Ardennes forest was invulnerable to tank attack.

The Germans called their plan for the offensive "sickle stroke." They would frontally attack the Allies through the Holland-Belgium corridor and swing a mighty sickle of armored divisions through the Ardennes and then northward toward the Channel to cut the French and British armies in two.

The plan was brutally successful. The attack in the north drove the Allies into a grudging withdrawal, while the armored push through the Ardennes swiftly pierced the thin French lines and began the circuit west and north to encircle the northern armies. By the time the large flow of Ultra summaries was again reaching the BEF commander, Field Marshal John Gort, the situation was too chaotic for intelligence to have much effect.

The decrypts did, however, help in two important ways. In his book *The Ultra Secret*, Winterbotham related that Gort later told him of Ultra's value in convincing London to accept his decision to get out of France as quickly as possible. BP had decrypted an order from General Walther von Brauchitsch that commanded his two army groups "to continue the encircling movement with the utmost vigor." This came at a time when the French were pressuring Gort to launch a counterattack southward. To do so, he saw, would imperil the British Expeditionary Force in a cause that was already hopeless, and would rob Britain of the men who would be needed to stand off a German invasion attempt. Gort's decision to turn toward the sea was seconded by Churchill. Gort began pulling his troops back toward the coastal town of Dunkirk.

In view of Brauchitsch's order, the second decrypt was highly puzzling. Sent by Hitler himself, it called for the attack against the encircled Allies to be "discontinued for the present." Just when the BEF appeared to be backed up against the sea with little hope of escape, the pressure let up, and the panzer divisions stayed put. Gort gained the breather he needed to build a perimeter defense around Dunkirk and begin the massive evacuation of the BEF.

Hitler had his reasons for holding up the attack on the forces beleaguered at Dunkirk. Without an equivalent of Ultra to inform them, the Germans greatly underestimated the numbers of Allied troops trapped on the Channel coast and considered them a secondary target compared with completing their conquest of the French. The urgency of the attack was eased by Göring's assurance that if any evacuation was attempted, his planes would smash it. Further, German generals welcomed a pause that would let them regroup their armor and give the infantry time to catch up. Hitler himself, remembering his Great War experiences, viewed the coastal rivers and marshes as threats to German armor.

Above all, Hitler continued to hope that the British, recognizing their commonality with the superior German race and their united need to withstand the hated Bolsheviks, would agree to peace. This was a cause that might be aided by avoiding the massacre of those pitiful remnants of the BEF at Dunkirk.

The Germans delayed for two crucial days—a reprieve that spelled the difference for Great Britain and the war. During that time, the British launched Operation Dynamo—the gathering up of thousands of small craft, everything from fishing boats to private yachts—which crossed the Channel and rescued the Allied troops from the Dunkirk beaches. French and Belgian vessels joined the motley armada. By the time the last ship drew away on June 4, some 337,000 Allied soldiers, including more than 100,000 French troops, had been saved from capture.

And the codebreakers of Bletchley Park had strengthened their status. For the first time, intelligence derived from their decrypts had become a factor in the making of strategic decisions.

Battle of Britain: For Ultra a Stronger Role

As it had in the time of Napoléon, the twenty-plus-mile strip of water known as the English Channel once more came to the rescue of Britain. Although Operation Dynamo had brought the soldiers home, virtually all of their heavy equipment had been left on the continent. But with the sea as their moat, and with the Royal Navy and Air Force to make it impassable, the British prepared themselves to stave off the Germans' expected attempt to invade their island.

British leaders knew they had two other secret advantages to bolster their defense. One was the superiority of British radar, which enabled the RAF to avoid having to fly continuous patrols and instead to send up its fighters only when the time was right to intercept the German bombers. The other was signals intelligence, most particularly the decryptions of the Luftwaffe's Red code, which was providing a steady stream of information about the Germans' plans, their order of battle and the equipment they would hurl against Britain.

For the month after Dunkirk, the German air force launched only scattered raids against Britain's southern coast and shipping in the Channel. Hitler had never anticipated having to invade Britain. He refused to give up hope that the people would come to their senses and send Churchill to the conference table to negotiate for peace. Churchill fanned the embers of this delusion by seeming to encourage the appeasers and pro-Fascist elements among the British and in neutral countries. He also directed that plans be made to relocate the government in Canada to carry on resistance from there in case Britain was invaded and occupied. Historical revisionists have interpreted his actions at this critical juncture as proof that he was, in actuality, more ready to capitulate and negotiate than admiring biographers have admitted.

More likely, Churchill was merely being pragmatic, keeping open all the options, even the grimmest ones. He was also playing for time. Every day that Hitler could be put off allowed the British to step up their preparations to meet the onslaught. Under the energetic direction of the press mogul Lord Beaverbrook, as minister of Aircraft Production, British industry was currently turning out more warplanes than the Germans.

Hitler's attitude toward the invasion of Britain remained ambivalent. After waffling on the issue through June and into July, he sent to his commanders his Directive 16, which began, "Since England, in spite of her hopeless military situation, still shows no signs of readiness for rapprochement, I have decided to prepare a landing operation against her, and if necessary to carry it out." The "if necessary" still allowed room for the slow-witted British to come to terms.

Three days later, Hitler went before the Reichstag in Berlin and delivered a speech in which he offered his "peace plan" to the British. Speaking "as a victor," he could see "no reason why this war must go on. We should like to avert the sacrifices that claim millions."

In meetings with his generals and admirals to plan the invasion, Hitler appeared only half attentive. He gave the impression of thinking more about attacking the Soviet Union than about invading Britain. His antipathy toward the Bolsheviks had intensified when Stalin exploited Germany's preoccupation with the West by annexing Lithuania, Estonia and Latvia. General Brauchitsch told Liddell Hart after the war that the invasion of Britain "was not pushed forward. Hitler scarcely seemed to bother about it at all—contrary to his usual way—and the staffs went on with their planning without any inclination. It was all regarded as a 'war game.'"

The German army and navy spent weeks squabbling over how to organize the invasion. In the end, as Churchill wrote, "Both the older services passed the buck to Reichsmarshal Göring."

Göring was delighted to take on the responsibility. He assured Hitler that in a matter of a few weeks, the Luftwaffe would wipe the skies of the

RAF, clearing the way for the army and navy to land troops on England's southern shores.

BP learned of the operation, code-named Seelöwe, or "Sea Lion," when Göring passed on the gist of Hitler's directive to the generals commanding his air fleets. Winterbotham has claimed that it was the relay of this signal to 10 Downing Street that prompted Churchill to go before Parliament and make his ringing promise to "defend every village, every town and every city . . . we would rather see London in ruins and ashes than that it should be tamely and abjectly enslaved."

British intelligence employed a wide range of resources in order to discern German intentions. Young women who were fluent in German joined units that were listening in to conversations between GAF pilots and ground control centers as well as between pilots themselves—conversations that quite often gave away that day's intended target. The Cheadle intercept station took on the added responsibility of breaking lower-level nonmachine codes such as that used by the GAF Air Safety Service for airfield takeoff, approach and landing control. This station also kept track of the GAF's navigational aid beacons—the turning on of these beacons warned when a raid was about to start, and their sequence indicated the direction it was headed. Coast watchers phoned in their observations. All this was funneled into Bletchley Park, which added to the mix its own decryptions of the Red code.

These resources gave chilling evidence of how Hitler's directive was being carried out. Cheadle's low-level Sigint reported when GAF bomber and fighter squadrons were moved from their bases in Norway and Denmark to new airfields in Holland and France. Decrypts of Enigma messages warned of GAF units being rested and refitted for the attack on Britain, of airfields being extended to accommodate bombers, of dive-bomber squadrons being assembled, of long-range guns being positioned to fire across the Channel, and of the postponement of a ceremonial parade in Paris so that those troops could instead be shifted to the north coast. Photoreconnaissance showed barges being hurried to French ports.

Digesting these inflows, Bletchley sent its reports to the mansion outside London housing the RAF Command Headquarters. The hub of Britain's defensive air operations was a giant gridded map over which young women with croupier-like poles followed instructions to move symbols marking the course of aircraft squadrons, both German and British, keeping the onlooking officers abreast of the fast-changing aerial scene.

Hinsley has recounted one other significant contribution GC&CS made before the offensive began. Britain's Air Ministry had to estimate the number of German bombers available for the battle, and the bomb capacity they could be expected to deliver. The ministry had believed the RAF faced 2,500 bombers capable of dropping 4,800 tons of bombs per day. These alarming figures prompted the preparation of disaster evacuation and hospitalization measures. BP decrypts scaled down the estimates to a more realistic 1,250 bombers and 1,800 tons. The Air Ministry described the information as "heaven-sent" and felt able to "view the situation much more confidently than was possible a month ago."

The Battle of Britain began on July 10, 1940, when the GAF sent some seventy planes against British targets. The lines were drawn, pitting Göring firmly against Britain's Air Chief Marshal Hugh Dowding.

Dowding was a former Great War pilot who had risen to be a squadron commander and a brigadier. Frederick Pile, who commanded Britain's antiaircraft defenses during World War II, wrote of him that he was "a difficult man, a self-opinionated man, a most determined man, and a man who knew more than anybody about all aspects of aerial warfare."

Dowding clearly perceived that this would be a war of attrition, of whether the RAF could outlast the GAF. He wrote in his diary that time favored the British "if we can only hold on." To his advantages in radar and signals intelligence he added his own shrewd tactics for holding on. Instead of sending his Spitfires and Hurricanes aloft in masses to meet the German fleets head-on, which was what Göring wanted in order to shoot down more RAF planes, Dowding dispatched his squadrons piecemeal, ordering relatively small numbers of planes into the air at a time. His strategy gave his fliers the advantage of slipping in among the German formations and downing more planes than the RAF lost. Dowding's methods were hotly contested by other RAF commanders, but he alone among them was privy to BP decrypts, and these confirmed that his staggering of RAF planes and pilots was working. While reducing RAF casualties, it increasingly frustrated the Germans, especially Hitler.

At the outset of the battle, Göring's first goal was not only to shoot down RAF planes but also to destroy airfields, raze hangars, topple radar towers and smash aircraft-producing factories. In the days of July and August his generals sent wave after wave of German aircraft against these targets. Without a German Ultra to inform him, Göring never knew how close he came to succeeding. The RAF losses in planes and crews were so heavy, and their remaining pilots so exhausted from conducting as many as seven sorties a day, that by the end of the first week in September, Fighter Command feared it would hold out only three more weeks. Dowding confided to a colleague, "What we need now is a miracle."

The miracle came as, abruptly, the Germans changed their tactics. Their reason for the change came about because of a blunder. The crews of two German bombers on a night run became disoriented and dropped their bombs on London, going against Hitler's orders to avoid hitting English cities. Churchill retaliated by sending English bombers over Berlin. Hitler, in one of his rages that often led him to make bad decisions, ordered Göring to leave off his attacks against RAF facilities and focus future bombing runs on London.

As a consequence, just at the point when the Luftwaffe might well have gained dominance over the RAF, its planes changed course. The incessant pounding of London gave Dowding and his team the respite they desperately needed to recoup and reequip.

When repeated attacks on London failed to achieve the objective of breaking the morale of the British people, Göring again ordered new tactics. He sent his planes to concentrate on other cities, to devastate them one by one and so weaken the islanders' will.

Ultra's effectiveness in giving advance warning of Luftwaffe raids has been questioned. At this early stage of the war, Bletchley's mastery of Enigma was still too weak, and oftentimes too slow, for the decrypts to be of tactical value. Often, the raids were completed before the messages relating to them could be decrypted. Also, Göring relied largely on landlines to direct the attacks, leaving little to be intercepted.

But there was one development in which Ultra's aid was undeniable. This was the Germans' use of a radio beam system to guide Luftwaffe pilots, astonishingly untrained in navigation, to their targets and even to tell the crews when to drop their bombs. The German system was code-named Knickebein, or "crooked leg." On their runs over Britain, the German pilots steered between two streams of dot-and-dash signals; if the plane strayed too far to the left, dots grew louder, and if to the right, dash sounds increased. As they neared their targets, crossbeams told the crews the moment to unload their bombs, and in a later improvement actually triggered the releases. Bletchley decrypts tracked Knickebein's development all the way.

In his memoir *Most Secret War*, Churchill's young scientific adviser Dr. R. V. Jones told how he was alerted on June 12, 1940, to the existence of Knickebein and how he immediately began to plan countermeasures. His method was to develop signals more powerful than those of Knickebein and by this means to lure Luftwaffe bombers away from important industrial targets. Jones also used crossbeams that caused the crews to drop their bombs on open countryside. His measures succeeded. One German bomber crew dispatched to the west of Britain became so addled by Jones's trickery that they mistook the Bristol Channel for the English Channel and landed on British soil instead of France. Mindful of Jones's success in both thwarting Knickebein and developing two more sophisticated defense systems later, Churchill called Jones his "boy wonder—the man who broke the bloody beams."

One tragic error came on November 14, when the jamming transmitters were mistakenly turned to the wrong frequency, allowing Knickebein to guide a large assembly of bombers to their target, the city of Coventry. A Bletchley decrypt warned of three forthcoming attacks and gave the code name of *KORN* as the target for that night's intensive raid. Today, in Britain's Public Record Office at Kew, a visitor can gaze at BP's decrypt, with the code word thrusting itself on the eyes. But at that moment *KORN*'s meaning was not known. As a result, the German bombers got through virtually unchallenged to drop tons of high explosives and incendiaries on Coventry, burning out the city's center, killing 554 and wounding hundreds more.

A story that gained circulation was that the Coventry bombing thrust upon Churchill an agonizing decision: either he warned the citizens of the city to evacuate, which would have tipped off the Germans that their codes were being broken, or he allowed the raid to proceed. Though a touching story, it wasn't true. Warnings of the bombers' destination came too late to permit extraordinary defense or evacuation efforts. The most that could be done was to alert firefighters, rescue squads and antiaircraft batteries. Churchill faced many hard decisions, but this was not one of them.

A week after the Coventry raid, Bletchley Park endured its own Luftwaffe bombing. The crew of a lone aircraft who probably wanted only to jettison their remaining bombs on a nearby railway junction before turning for home missed their target. One of their bombs smashed into the outer building to which Gordon Welchman had originally been banished. Another landed in the garden of the vicarage next door. Two more landed inside BP, one of them close enough to Hut 4 to break some of its windows and move it several inches off its foundations. No one was injured, but to have the war come so close no doubt boosted the spirits of the men at BP. "They tended to think of themselves," recalled Pat Bing, one of Hut 8's young women, "as 'skivers'—the word for those who pick up money without doing any work for it—and in their case for being in the war but not actually fighting. So the bombing braced them up a bit."

The bombing may also have helped the men at BP counter the sneers of locals who observed healthy young blokes engaged in some dubious unspoken rear echelon activity. As a bit of doggerel circulated at the Park put it,

> I think that I shall never see
> a sight as curious as BP.
> . . . .
> Five long years our war was there
> subject to local scorn and stare.

Meanwhile, Ultra and other sources were reeling in a rich cache of intelligence regarding Operation Sea Lion. German top officers may have been lukewarm about plans for the invasion, but their underlings had no choice but to take the orders seriously and to throw themselves headlong into preparing for it. The Public Record Office file of Red translations includes the calls for embarkation rehearsals and practice landings, orders for transport and loading officers to remain at their ports until further notice, the training of crews for towed gliders, the plans for quick-turnaround airports to be used in shuttling troops and supplies across to England. The decrypts show how unprepared the Germans were to carry out an amphibious invasion. But that was what Hitler had ordered, and his service organizations substituted frenetic action for wiser consideration. Powered barges used on rivers and canals were hastily steered to Channel ports. Demands went out for engines to be mounted on the many other unpowered barges normally pulled in long strings by tugboats. It was a motley assortment, but the best the Germans could manage on such short notice.

On the night of September 7, after a day in which wave after wave of Luftwaffe planes had bombarded London, the code word *Cromwell* was sent to military units throughout Britain. It was the alert that the German invasion was about to begin. Church bells rang—a signal everyone recognized. Families crouched in candlelit shelters. The home defense forces were mobilized for "immediate action." Tomorrow the showdown would come.

But the German air force had not cleared the skies of the RAF. This was demonstrated on September 8 when, of two hundred bombers raiding London, eighty-eight were shot down. Adding strength to the RAF were Polish, Czech and Canadian pilots. The GAF raid was all that happened on that supposedly climactic day. The German invasion fleet never appeared.

The real climax of the Battle of Britain came on September 15. Göring, in desperation, hurled every plane he could muster against London, Southampton, Bristol, Cardiff, Liverpool and Manchester. Dowding, in response, departed from his piecemeal tactics and sent the RAF up in full force. When Churchill visited the RAF operations room and asked about reserves, he was given the answer: "There are none." The RAF lost twenty-seven fighters but destroyed fifty-five German aircraft.

Hitler was convinced: Göring had failed. On September 17, Hitler postponed the invasion of Britain, telling a subordinate that while the conquest of France had cost thirty thousand men, "During one night of crossing the Channel we could lose many times that—and success is not certain."

Word of his decision did not show up in Ultra decrypts. It had to be inferred from messages such as the one disclosing that equipment intended for installation on invasion barges "should be returned to store." Also, as October and November wore on, the rapid-fire rate of midsummer intercepts eased. Embarkation practices were postponed or canceled. Warships assembled for the invasion were sent on other missions. The threat evaporated.

Churchill did not wait long to be convinced. He ordered that 150 tanks being held to ward off German invaders should instead be dispatched to his hard-pressed divisions in North Africa.

The depleted Luftwaffe was reduced to making what were mainly nighttime attacks on London—the Blitz, as Londoners called it. Although the bomb runs killed many people and did great damage to the city, they came to be seen more as nuisance raids than elements of a consistent plan. Their effectiveness steadily declined. The Battle of Britain was over and, with the codebreakers' aid, handily won.

Albert Kesselring, who, in the first of his many command postings for Hitler, had led one of Göring's Luftwaffe fleets in the Battle of Britain, presented an interesting view of the effects of Britain's superior radar technology and signals intelligence on the Luftwaffe. Writing his memoirs in 1953, long before the role of Ultra had been revealed, Kesselring recalled that "losses soon increased to an intolerable extent owing to the quick reaction of the British defense—fighters and A.A. [Antiaircraft]—and quick concentration of fighters over the target and on the approaching route. With the alternative before us of letting the enemy's uncanny reading of our intentions bleed the Luftwaffe to death, we had no choice but to switch our targets, times and methods of attack."

"Uncanny reading of our intentions"—this could well be Ultra's epitaph, not just for the Luftwaffe but also for the whole German war effort.

During the depths of the Battle of Britain, Dr. Jones wrote in his memoir, "I used to look at my wall map every morning and wonder how we could possibly survive." By February 1941, he was finding "some hopeful signs," including an early victory in North Africa and "the strong voice of Franklin Roosevelt" in his support of Britain. Jones added, "Above all, there was the great advantage of being able to read much of the Enigma traffic. If only we could hold on, sooner or later this could turn the tide."

Ultra Guides a Victory in North Africa

Entering World War II, British intelligence was better prepared to sense what was happening in Benito Mussolini's Italy than in Hitler's Germany. GC&CS was reading the ciphers used by the Italian army, navy and air force in the Mediterranean, Libya and East Africa. Central Intelligence had also set up an interservice Middle East Intelligence Center in Cairo. The conclusion drawn from the decrypts, however, was that the state of Italy's armed forces left her unprepared for a long war and that Italian leaders would be anxious to preserve her neutrality.

These reasonable conjectures underestimated the ambitions of Mussolini. He felt overshadowed by Hitler's early successes and resolved to seek some conquests of his own. In April 1939, when Hitler took over Czechoslovakia, Mussolini sought to match him by seizing Albania—which gave in without a fight. In May 1940, with Hitler's defeat of France imminent, Il Duce declared war on Great Britain and France and even dispatched squadrons of Italian bombers and fighters to make token raids on England. He also tried to invade the southeast corner of France bordering on Italy, but his troops were repulsed by the French, with heavy losses. Undeterred, he planned for actions in North Africa, contenting himself with the thought that the victories he could achieve there fitted more appropriately into his dream of building a new Roman empire.

Mussolini's North African prospects looked highly favorable. The collapse of France freed the more than two hundred thousand troops in Italian-held Libya who were guarding the frontier against the French in Tunisia. They could join the Italian Tenth Army, which was in place to counter the British in Egypt. Conquest of Egypt would crown Mussolini's possessions in Eritrea, Italian Somaliland and Ethiopia, as well as Libya. To oppose the Italian might, the British had fewer than fifty thousand underequipped troops who were also supposed to defend British interests in nine other Middle Eastern countries. On June 28, Mussolini ordered the invasion of Egypt.

The situation was an acute worry for Winston Churchill, especially when he found out that those 150 tanks he had consigned to his Middle Eastern command, that "blood transfusion," as he put it, weren't going to be sped by convoy through the Mediterranean. He was "grieved and vexed" when instead the ships were routed the long, slow way around the Cape of Good Hope.

He needn't have worried. Control of the Italian armies to invade Egypt was placed in the hands of the cautious Marshal Rodolfo Graziani, a much bemedaled veteran of earlier conquests in Africa. A realist, the marshal saw how ill prepared his troops were, with archaic guns and antiquated tanks. He employed delaying tactics, arguing that the attack shouldn't begin until the Germans had invaded Britain. Consequently, all through the on-again, off-again plans for Operation Sea Lion, his vast forces simply camped out in the desert and waited. Fuming, Mussolini on September 7 gave him the choice either to attack or to resign his post. On September 13 Graziani finally did order his troops forward. In four days, to much trumpeting in Rome, he moved sixty miles into Egypt and took the outpost of Sidi Barrâni. But for the British it was only a planned withdrawal. When they settled at their base in Matruh, Graziani stopped his advance, still some eighty miles short of the British. All through October and November the Italian armies hunkered down in the desert while Graziani prepared a new base for his offensive. The British tanks and other equipment arrived in October.

Britain's commander in chief in the Middle East, General Archibald Wavell, had placed his Western Desert Force under the command of Richard O'Connor, a resourceful bantam of a general who much favored offense over defense. The day after Italy had declared war, O'Connor directed sorties that captured scores of Italians, including a general. Now he settled into planning his main attack. In this he was greatly aided by the British codebreakers. Their decrypts, relayed to him by the Cairo center, gave him copious and accurate information about the locations and strengths of the various Italian army concentrations. BP's breaking of Luftwaffe Enigma signals assured him that the Germans, as yet, were not planning a transfer to North Africa.

Aerial reconnaissance also came to O'Connor's aid. Photos showed the routes the Italians used to drive through the minefields protecting their main encampments. The paths left a wide gap that he, too, could use to slip between the Italian camps and then wheel his armor around to attack them from the rear.

O'Connor thought of every essential detail. In advance he had patrols store provisions in desert cisterns. Midway to the battle site he had his troops lie dormant for a day and night so they would be fresh for the attack. When, on the night of December 8, the Desert Force began its drive, hurricane lamps blinkered against the Italians' view showed troops and armor where to proceed.

The attack worked as O'Connor had hoped. At dawn the British completely surprised the Italians as they prepared breakfast. The Desert Force destroyed the Italians' armor and killed or captured them by the thousands.

Wavell had authorized O'Connor to launch only a five-day raid against the Italians. O'Connor's fighters were desperately needed elsewhere: to attack the Italian garrison in Eritrea that was threatening the Red Sea route to Egypt, to be ready to aid Greece, and perhaps to withstand German advances in Syria and Lebanon. Wavell did pull out the Fourth Indian Division, about half the Desert Force. All he could offer to replace them were poorly equipped Australians. He allowed O'Connor to continue his drive to the west.

After recapturing Sidi Barrâni and thus ending the Italian threat to Egypt, O'Connor's divisions routed the Italians and captured the strongpoints of Bardiyah, Tobruk and Benghazi. When BP decrypts told him the Italians were going to retreat along the coast road toward Tripoli, he made an end run in the desert and blocked the remainder of Mussolini's army. In a two-month campaign, O'Connor's men advanced five hundred miles, destroyed an army of 10 divisions, took 130,000 prisoners and seized some 400 tanks and more than 1,000 guns. Churchill gleefully read a battlefield report claiming the capture of "five acres of officers and two hundred acres of other ranks."

Following the Italian surrender, according to Hinsley's account, the head of British military intelligence in the Middle East observed that he "could not believe that any army commander in the field had [ever] been better served by his intelligence."

O'Connor set his sights on capturing his final prize, Tripoli, but it was not to be. While O'Connor was humiliating the Italian army, Adolf Hitler came to several major decisions. One was to send Erwin Rommel and German troops into North Africa to reinforce what was left of the Italians. The other was to mount a drive through the Balkans into Greece. His objective was to crush the British between these pincers and give Germany control over the eastern Mediterranean, its lands and its oil.

Wavell had to stop O'Connor's westward push and send much of his army to meet Churchill's commitments to the Greeks. O'Connor himself disappeared from the scene when, amid Rommel's first thrusts in North Africa, he was captured and forced to sit out the rest of the war as a prisoner.

Nevertheless, he had shown how Allied generals could, by taking heed of such secret aids as decrypted messages and photoreconnaissance, use intelligence to shape their planning and achieve victory.

Ultra Adds a Victory at Sea

Early in the war the Royal Navy suffered troubling losses, and later would experience other serious defeats. But a couple of Mediterranean triumphs buoyed English spirits. One was against the Italian fleet at anchor in the harbor of Taranto on November 11, 1940. The victory was set up not by signals intelligence but by photoreconnaissance. It will be described later in another context.

The second victory, once more over the Italians, resulted from a Bletchley Park breakthrough against the Italian navy's Enigma-encoded transmissions in March 1941. Dilly Knox, working with his young assistant, Mavis Lever, masterminded the breakthrough. They used a crib together with long strips of cardboard called rods—the cardboard replaced the actual wooden ferules originally employed. On the rods, the crib letters were lined up with letters of the ciphertext to determine the paths of electric current through the code wheels. It was a manual method of eliminating inconsistencies until only linkups between crib and cipher letters remained. By patient manipulation of their rods, Knox and Lever broke messages indicating that a strong force of Italian warships was about to leave port and attack British convoys traveling the sea between Alexandria and Greece. Decodes of air traffic disclosed plans to neutralize British air cover. The decrypts also pinpointed the time of this thrust.

Britain's naval chief in the Mediterranean, Admiral Sir Andrew Cunningham, made his plans on the basis of the intelligence. He knew he had to be cautious not to tip off the Italians that the Royal Navy was aware of their intentions. Cunningham's base in Alexandria was vulnerable to Axis spies, not to mention the Japanese consul general there, who was known to relay information to his Axis partners.

To put British shipping out of harm's way, Cunningham canceled a southbound convoy that was due to leave the Greek port of Piraeus. He arranged that a convoy bound for Piraeus from Alexandria should reverse course at nightfall. A British cruiser force already at sea was ordered to be south of Crete at dawn on March 28. After ordering his fleet to get up steam, he himself carried out a neat piece of deception against the Japanese consul general.

He knew that the Japanese official regularly played an afternoon round of golf at Alexandria's country club. On the afternoon of March 27, Cunningham made himself unmistakably visible with his clubs and an overnight bag. That night he slipped away to his flagship and led his battle squadron to sea. Sure enough, a BP decrypt confirmed that the Italians believed Cunningham's battleships and aircraft carrier had remained in Alexandria.

Instead, the British ships were in position waiting for the Italian fleet to sail into their trap. Mindful of the need for preserving the codebreakers' security, Cunningham sent an aerial patrol to spot the Italian ships—and to make sure they were *seen* spotting the Italian ships. Then he proceeded to dispatch the enemy. In the Battle of Matapan, three Italian cruisers and two destroyers were sunk, and the flagship *Vittoria Veneto* was heavily damaged. By contrast, the British lost only one torpedo plane. By so crippling the Italian navy, Cunningham eliminated the danger of attacks on British convoys between Egypt and Greece and gave Britain control of the eastern Mediterranean, proving crucial to the evacuations following defeats in Greece and Crete. What was left of the Italian fleet retreated to its base in Taranto and did not come out in force again until two years later, when the ships sailed to surrender to Admiral Cunningham at Malta.

By their early breaks of the Enigma and their solving of Italian ciphers, Britain's codebreakers had delivered to their commanders a golden flow of information that led to the successes at Matapan and in North Africa. But these gleams of hope were soon quenched. The Italian defeats made up Hitler's mind to come to the aid of his Axis partner and to secure his southern frontier. An entire corps of German planes was transferred from the Russian front to Italy and Sicily. Packs of U-boats with expertly trained crews shifted to the Mediterranean out of the North Atlantic. Erwin Rommel arrived in North Africa with disciplined, well-equipped troops to supplement and stiffen the backs of their Italian allies. It was a turn of events that was to prove in the period ahead a hard truth about secret intelligence: even the best of it cannot prevail unless there is sufficient force to exploit its revelations. In the sands of North Africa, that degree of force would be slow and long in coming.

5 Battle of the Atlantic: Cryptologic Seesaw

WHEN the Germans went to war in 1939, their navy was almost completely unready to take on the Royal Navy of Britain. German naval officers had considered an outbreak of hostilities with the English an unlikely prospect and had planned accordingly. Their aim was to give Germany a small, balanced fleet that could play a useful subsidiary role in a war against another continental power—France, say, or the USSR. The few state-of-the-art battleships they had designed were meant as much to be showpieces of German technology and expressions of German pride as to serve as meaningful war machines. As for submarines, which had been so lethal a force in the Great War, the German navy had failed to build even as many as permitted in postwar armaments agreements, and the ones they did commission were small vessels with limited range.

Almost completely unready. One important exception has already been noted: the Germans' cryptographic branch, B-Dienst, was reading a variety of the Royal Navy's codes. Britain's tradition-bound Admiralty had rejected Lord Louis Mountbatten's recommendation that it change over to code machines, as the RAF and army had done. Instead, it was clinging to the age-old practice of relying on codebooks whose listings of naval terms and their cipher equivalents had to be enciphered and deciphered by operators using manual methods. The naval officers believed that by employing superencipherment tables and changing them frequently, they could thwart cryptanalysis. It was a vain hope, especially when German divers recovered current codebooks from sunken British warships. By the summer of 1940, B-Dienst cryptanalysts were deciphering a high percentage of the traffic in the codes used by both the Royal Navy and the Merchant Navy. They were reading a total of some two thousand messages a month.

The German advantage came to the fore immediately after the war began. B-Dienst's decrypts more than made up for the U-boat fleet's limitations. The subs sent their first British ship to the bottom only days after war was declared, and between September 1939 and the end of the year they, together with other ships of the German navy, sank 150 merchant vessels, the passenger liner *Athenia*, the battleship *Royal Oak* and the aircraft carrier *Courageous*.

They had another advantage in the competence of the man commanding the *Unterseeboot*, or U-boat, command, Admiral Karl Dönitz. Dönitz was convinced that his U-boats could strangle Britain into submission, as they had almost done in the 1914–18 war. Germany's neglect of U-boat construction during the interwar years dismayed him; he needed at least three hundred boats—and preferably one thousand—to do the job. But he set to work skillfully with the fifty-six operational craft available to him at the war's outset, while thirteen boatyards began turning out newer and better designs of U-boats in a stepped-up building program.

To these positives should be added the German navy's development of the most advanced and secure code systems of all the Enigma users. As mentioned earlier, the navy's Enigma was equipped with three extra rotors—eight in all. Although only three were used at any one time until later in the war, to have eight available meant that they could be arranged in 336 different ways and not merely 60 as with the army and air force Enigmas. Further, the navy's method for indicating message settings was entirely different. Instead of having the Enigma encipher the keys—a practice that had betrayed other services' settings—the navy instructed code clerks to determine their settings using a two-letter "bigram" table that was, in effect, an extra code unto itself. The bigram substitutions made the system "operator-proof": no choosing girlfriends' initials or sequences copied from the keyboard. The navy's operators weren't likely to take those shortcuts anyway; they were much more disciplined in observing strict security measures than the code clerks handling Luftwaffe and army traffic.

Further, the German navy used its Enigmas for a bewildering variety of codes. The list of merely the principal codes compiled by British naval intelligence officer Patrick Beesly in his book *Very Special Intelligence* runs to thirteen, ranging from the Atlantic U-boats' Triton to the Bertok code used for communications between the naval attaché in Tokyo and the navy high command.

Dilly Knox and his team at Bletchley Park were inclined to give up on the navy Enigma. They had concluded that its system was impregnable.

Coupled with this spirit of cryptologic helplessness was the fact that the

British had woefully neglected the resources needed to conduct antisubmarine warfare. Control of the Admiralty had been taken over by Great War gunnery officers who believed that the scant funds available to the navy in the 1930s should be spent on battleships rather than convoy escort vessels or reconnaissance aircraft.

At the war's beginning, consequently, it appeared that Dönitz and his U-boat crews held the winning hand. They might well fulfill their promise to Hitler to turn Britain's protective moat into a garrote around the nation's neck.

This early air of pessimism did not apply to Alan Turing and his colleagues in Hut 8. He refused to be discouraged. As Stephen Budiansky has expressed it, "During those two months Turing had performed a feat that if anything surpassed Rejewski's. He had laid out the entire theoretical framework for tackling the Enigma in all its variations." Turing also recognized the importance of seizing any opportunity, or even *creating* opportunities, for the capture of naval Enigma materials. Nevertheless, except for small temporary successes, Dönitz's system defied Turing for the first twenty months of the war.

While his first bombe—the one without Welchman's diagonal board—was still being built, Turing went at the naval Enigma using manual methods. His approach, as ever, depended on applying cribs. What cribs could he hope to use to get at the naval Enigma messages?

One he borrowed from the Poles. They had found that often a message was a continuation of another and that this second message began with *FORT*, "forward from," followed by the time of origin of the preceding message. When it became known from a German POW interrogation that the naval Enigma procedure was to spell out numbers, the crib was extended. A message originating at 2330 could be enciphered as *WEEPY*. So the time that a message was sent could lead to identifying the plaintext letters. This method of cribbing was consequently called FORTY WEEPY. Using it, Turing and his small team managed to break messages from five days of Enigma traffic during the preceding November, before a more complex system of plugboard connections had gone into effect.

To break subsequent messages from those days, Turing invented what became known as the *EINS* catalog. He had observed that the word eins, German for "one," occurred in about ninety percent of all messages. By compiling a catalog of all possible encipherments of *EINS*, he was able to search out equivalents in the ciphertexts—another small opening into securing the plaintexts.

BP's "Prof" got his first boost from captured materials in February 1940. A German U-boat, *U-33*, tried boldly to lay mines in the Firth of Clyde, on the west coast of Scotland. The U-boat was discovered, depth-charged and driven to the surface. Mindful of the need to protect his Enigma, the skipper passed out the code wheels and insisted that when his crew members jumped into the sea they were to make sure that the wheels sank. The scheme didn't quite work. When the British rescued most of the crewmen, three code wheels were found in the pocket of a nearly drowned sailor. Two of the three were of the new code wheels added to the naval Enigma, and from them Turing learned the wiring of all but one of the new wheels.

Another helpful capture came in April 1940 when a British destroyer off the coast of Norway disabled a German trawler posing as a Dutch fishing vessel. Before surrendering, the German crew threw overboard two bags containing confidential documents and cipher materials. A British crewman dived into the icy water to rescue one of the bags, and other papers were found aboard the trawler. Included were the Enigma keys for the four previous days. With this gift Turing and his team were able, in May, to read some of Dönitz's April traffic and to advance their understanding of the naval Enigma. But they could still not decipher further messages.

Stimulated by the captures, however, Turing's inventive mind came up with another development that he could put to use when his first bombe arrived. This was a technique which, used on intercepts for which no cribs could be imagined, drastically reduced the number of bombe runs needed to determine the arrangement of the Enigma's rotors for a specific time period. It was an essential step, since to run through all 336 possible rotor orders would take as much as a week of full-time operation. His limiting method became known as Banburismus because the long sheets of paper used in it came from the town of Banbury. With Banburismus, Turing exploited a flaw in the naval Enigmas. The Germans thought they were adding to their system's security by having each rotor notch that caused its neighbor to turn located at a different letter of the alphabet. Thus, rotor one had its notch cut at the letter *R*; number two at *F*; number three at *W*; number four at *K*; and number five at *A*. The BP analysts created a meaningless but memorable mnemonic to keep the sequence in mind: "Royal Flags Wave Kings Above." Turing saw these disparate notch settings as a way to identify each rotor— if the Germans had cut their notches all at the same letter the Banburismus method wouldn't have worked. Later the Germans recognized the flaw. When they added three new rotors, all were notched identically.

The Banbury sheets were made of stiff white paper about ten inches from top to bottom but varying in width from two to five feet. On them were printed vertical rows of alphabets side by side. The narrower sheets accommodated shorter messages. The young women of Hut 8 took each intercept and punched holes in the alphabets for each of its letters. By sliding the sheets over each other above a dark table, analysts could spot the places where the same letters appeared in a pair of messages. By keeping score on the repeats, Turing and his colleagues could, by a series of logical—if formidable—deductions, apply the Royal Flags formula to determine the lettered notches at which the rotors in use that day were located. With luck, Banburismus could reduce the number of rotor orders to be tested by the bombes to as little as six runs. A detailed explanation of Banburismus is included as an appendix in Sebag-Montefiore's *Enigma* book.

Ascendance of the Wolf Packs

For all of Turing's brilliance, Hut 8's breaks in the naval Enigma remained, throughout 1940 and into 1941, too few and too slow to be of tactical use against Dönitz's U-boats. It was a time of havoc for British shipping. Merchant ship losses for 1940 totaled nearly four million tons, when only one million tons of new shipping was under construction in British shipyards. From B-Dienst, Dönitz knew the convoys' routes and sent his U-boats out in "wolf packs" to waylay them. To make matters worse for Britain, with the fall of France in mid-1940 both the Luftwaffe and the U-boats gained the great advantage of relocating in western France. The German air force added its own substantial totals to drowned tonnages of Allied shipping. For the U-boats, the new French ports markedly increased the times they could spend prowling the North Atlantic. They enjoyed what their crews thought of as a "happy time." The anguish in Hut 8 was deepened by press reports of victorious U-boat crews returning to their Bay of Biscay bases to the blare of brass bands and the popping of champagne corks, not to mention the presence of the führer himself, there to pass out Iron Crosses.

So desperate for new captures of naval Enigma keys did Turing and his team become that they supported a wild scheme put forward in December 1940 by Ian Fleming, a naval intelligence officer later to become the creator of James Bond. Fleming's idea was to seize one of the Enigma-equipped rescue boats the Germans manned in the Channel to pick up downed Luftwaffe fliers. To do this, Fleming advocated, and gained permission to implement, dressing an English flight crew in German uniforms and putting them aboard a captured German bomber. After the next raid on London, when the bombers headed home, the bogus bomber would sneak in among them. Over the Channel it would begin to emit fake smoke from its tail, send out an SOS and ditch. The crew would float in a rubber dinghy until deliverance appeared. "Once aboard rescue boat," his plan continued, "shoot German crew, dump overboard, bring boat back to English port." For the "word-perfect German speaker" among the English fliers, Fleming nominated himself.

The scheme almost came off. Fleming secured a plane from the Air Ministry, recruited "a tough crew" and settled in Dover to await his chance. The stumbling block was that neither reconnaissance flights nor radio monitoring turned up a suitable boat to be raided. The mission had to be aborted, much to the disappointment of all concerned.

BP did hatch an ingenious and successful stratagem for securing usable cribs. The codebreakers had discovered an interesting discrepancy in the Germans' use of naval codes when they dealt with mines sown by the British. German minesweepers were not equipped with Enigmas but relied instead on a manual code called the Dockyard Key, which BP had broken. When the British created new minefields, German warships had to be alerted, and they were equipped to handle Enigma traffic, not Dockyard transmissions. Oftentimes, when the RAF dropped mines, exactly the same message would be sent out in both ciphers. The new Bletchley scheme, appropriately called "gardening," was to have the Air Ministry sow a new minefield so that BP could reap the sudden sprouting of Dockyard and Enigma alarm messages. From the Dockyard decrypts, Hut 8 derived substantial cribs to be used in unlocking the naval Enigma. These cribs from two identical messages transmitted on different cryptographic systems were called "kisses."

In March 1941, Turing's team received another gift of captured materials. Once again off Norway, a trawler was disabled and driven ashore. This time the boarding crew seized the Enigma tables for the whole month of February. The resulting trove of decrypts was much larger. Moreover, Turing and his Hut 8 associates were learning enough about the naval Enigma to keep on reading the navy signals through the month of May. Then a new set of keys stymied them, and the flow of decrypts once more dried up.

None of this intelligence was of much use to the Admiralty. Messages that revealed important information were deciphered only long after it could have helped. However, the new batch of decrypts did yield one disclosure of supreme value. Young Harry Hinsley, studying the traffic, observed that some of the messages had been sent to small ships the Germans had stationed out in the North Atlantic to transmit weather reports back to headquarters. Although the weather trawlers were not enciphering their reports on Enigmas, they had to have the machines if they were to decode the Enigma messages transmitted to them. And since each ship was out there for stints of several months, they must have aboard a succession of naval Enigma tables.

Certainly, Hinsley told the Admiralty, if one of the weather ships was attacked, the crew would quickly jettison their Enigma and the current key tables. But wasn't it probable that future keys would be stored in a safe? And wasn't it also likely that in the stress of being attacked, the crew would forget about those hidden-away tables and they could be recovered by a boarding party?

The Royal Navy cooperated. A carefully planned foray on May 7, 1941, carried out by a flotilla of seven cruisers and destroyers, captured the trawler *München* east of Iceland. Sure enough, the weather boat crew, before surrendering, placed their Enigma and secret tables in a bag and threw it overboard. But also, as Hinsley had predicted, in the captain's quarters British sailors found the Enigma settings for the month of June.

Two days later, Bletchley analysts were handed an unexpected gift. A North Atlantic convoy escort group under Commander Joe Baker-Cresswell forced the German submarine *U-110* to the surface. The U-boat skipper, certain that the sub was sinking, ordered his crew to abandon ship. But she didn't sink. Baker-Cresswell saw his opportunity. Remembering from his naval training how in World War I the capture of a German warship had enabled the British to seize codebooks and break the German navy's codes, he launched a similar mission aboard the *U-110*. He had the sub's survivors picked up and stowed out of sight belowdecks before his own crewmen boarded the U-boat and removed two boatloads of useful papers as well as the sub's Enigma.

The documents retrieved from the *München* and the *U-110* gave Hut 8 a heartening, if temporary, breakthrough. Before, analysts had taken days to obtain Enigma decrypts. Now, with the June keys in hand, they lowered their decryption time to an average of six hours. The information they passed on to the sub trackers was current enough to locate U-boat wolf packs and deflect convoys to safer routes.

However, this heady time soon ended. The bigram tables they had so painstakingly compiled were replaced in mid-June, after BP had been reading Enigma traffic for only two weeks. Turing figured he needed a month of decrypts to work out the new tables. Could Hinsley persuade the navy to capture another weather ship?

He could. The navy would cooperate in tracking down the *Lauenberg*, which Hinsley selected as the most promising target. She had left her Norwegian base at the end of May to take over the North Atlantic patrol from a sister ship. Hinsley figured that she would be out there for at least a six-week tour of duty and would consequently be carrying the Enigma keys for both June and July.

This time when the Royal Navy task force steamed off to find the weather ship, GC&CS staffer Allon Bacon went along. The operation came off smoothly. Informed about the little trawler's location by BP decrypts, the British flotilla found her behind an iceberg. The British fired shells that came close but deliberately avoided hitting the trawler, forced her crew to take to lifeboats, took the Germans aboard and sequestered them so that they could not see what the boarding party was doing. The Germans had ditched their Enigma and tried, only partially successfully, to burn the confidential papers in the ship's stove. The boarders presented Bacon with thirteen mail sacks of documents. Sorting through them, he found just what he hoped for: the Enigma settings till the end of July.

Once again, Hut 8 needed only a few hours in which to decipher the German navy's Enigma traffic. Of much larger significance, the learning curve had been completed. Turing's team could now proceed on its own, without need for further captures.

An additional benefit came from the *U-110* materials. Besides the regular German naval Enigma, Dönitz used an "Offizier," or "Officer," code for higher-level communications. It was doubly enciphered, first in the special code and then again in the regular Enigma cipher. The *U-110* papers included the special Offizier settings for the month of June 1941 and so allowed Offizier messages to be broken for that month. But when the settings were replaced, BP was again shut out—that is, until Rolf Noskwith, a German Jew who had emigrated to England with his parents in 1932, studied the earlier decrypts and hit upon a crib that he used to crack open the code. Offizier was broken for the remainder of the war.

For the last half of 1941, and until February '42, the cryptologic battle of the Atlantic swung sharply in favor of the British. While B-Dienst was still breaking the Admiralty's codes, Bletchley Park had an ally whose contributions more than made up the difference. This inadvertent aide was Admiral Dönitz himself. Early in the war the German admiral had decided, as he wrote later, that "I myself could quite easily direct the whole tactical operation against a convoy from my headquarters ashore." The result was a flood of communications back and forth as he instructed the U-boats where he wanted them to be and what he wanted them to do, while also expecting that they transmit regular situation reports back to him. The masses of advice BP was teleprinting to the Submarine Tracking Room far exceeded in value whatever B-Dienst was disclosing.

The statistics of shipping losses reflected the change in cryptographic fortunes. From April to June 1941, another 150 Allied ships were sunk. The July-to-September period showed a decrease to ninety, and from October to December the score declined to seventy. Factors other than the codebreaking helped account for the decline. The support by convoy escort vessels was strengthened, especially by the deployment of fifty World War I destroyers that the U.S. had taken out of mothballs and turned over to the British in a nominal exchange for ninety-nine-year leases on British bases in the Americas. Longer-range planes gave the convoys air cover for larger stretches of their journeys. Technological developments such as shipborne radar improved the convoys' chances. But the codebreakers had the most impact on the change. Their decrypts enabled the convoys to be rerouted, often in midcourse, to swing clear of the wolf packs. By pinpointing the U-boats' locations, BP decrypts caused more of them to be sunk. From a seemingly hopeless struggle, the Battle of the Atlantic, for this sunny period, swung in favor of the Allies.

BP Decrypts Help Sink Surface Raiders

While the U-boats posed the most serious threat to Allied shipping, they were by no means alone. The marvel warships the Germans had begun building in the 1930s stood ready to be released as hunters and raiders. The Sigint forces at Bletchley Park paid special attention to them because they were new and fast and, therefore, especially dangerous.

The first major engagement with the raiders came too soon for BP to have much effect. In December 1939 the pocket battleship *Admiral Graf Spee* was set loose in the South Atlantic, sinking three British merchant ships in five days. She was tracked down by three Royal Navy cruisers, whose guns scored some fifty hits, forcing the raider to take refuge in the harbor of Montevideo, Uruguay. Seeing no possibility of escape, the ship's captain ordered her to be scuttled. He then shot himself.

In the aftermath, though, British intelligence did score a notable success. Accompanying the *Graf Spee* was a supply ship, the *Altmark*. Before scuttling the battleship, the German captain ordered that some three hundred captured British merchant seamen be put aboard the *Altmark*, which was to be dispatched to Europe. British and French agents tracked her to Norway, where a Royal Navy destroyer intercepted her and liberated her prisoners before sinking her.

Admiral Erich Raeder, the German navy's commander in chief, next planned for his surface raiders to attack Atlantic shipping. He would unleash his newest battleship, the *Bismarck*, accompanied by the heavy cruiser *Prinz Eugen*. They would be joined by the battle cruisers *Scharnhorst* and *Gneisenau*. His plans were partially frustrated when *Scharnhorst* needed to stay behind for engine repairs and *Gneisenau* was severely damaged when a gallant Coastal Command torpedo plane pilot got off his missiles before being shot down. These setbacks did not deter Raeder from sending out the *Bismarck* and *Prinz Eugen*.

Since naval Enigma messages were then being broken only days and weeks after being intercepted, they were usually too late to be of use. However, an April message read in May did disclose that the *Bismarck* was to be loosed as a raider. Aerial recon found that she had first moved to the Norwegian port at Bergen and, subsequently, that she had left Bergen.

A British naval squadron located the *Bismarck* and engaged her, but she shot her way out, sinking the battleship *Hood* and damaging the *Prince of Wales*. She herself suffered a bomb blast that caused her to leak oil. In foul weather, the Royal Navy lost contact. When the German warships separated, British attention focused on the *Bismarck*. Where would she be headed? After escaping past the north of Britain toward Iceland, would she double back to Norway? Or keep on going in the Atlantic? The British could only guess.

Harry Hinsley weighed in with his opinion. He lacked decrypts for an answer, but he could see from direction-finding reports that messages being sent to the *Bismarck*, previously originating in Wilhelmshaven, were now being sent from Paris—a sure sign, to him, that the ship was bound for a French haven.

Admiralty authorities shook him off. His information was too tenuous to be relied on. August minds at the top were convinced that a more northerly route was most likely.

BP provided the clincher. Normally Gordon Welchman's breaking of the Luftwaffe's Red code would not have supplied any useful naval information, but this time it so happened that a Luftwaffe general in Athens had a close relative on the *Bismarck*, and he inquired as to the ship's destination. The word came back and was promptly decoded in Hut 6: the *Bismarck* was bound in a southeasterly direction for the French port of Brest.

She never made it. Even though one British flotilla misinterpreted the signals that intelligence transmitted to it and headed off in the wrong direction, the battleship *Ark Royal*, hurrying up from Gibraltar, found her. One of its aircraft torpedoed her, jamming her rudder so she could only travel in circles. Her captain ordered her to be scuttled.

As with the *Graf Spee*, supply ships had been dispatched to the Atlantic, both to serve the needs of the *Bismarck* and to aid the U-boats. By early June, Hut 8 had begun reading naval Enigma messages almost currently, and decrypts revealed the positions of eight supply ships. To avoid arousing the Germans' suspicions that the codes were being broken, it was decided that only six of the eight ships would be destroyed. As luck would have it, though, other Royal Navy ships, without advice from BP, happened upon the remaining two and sank them as well. Concern about Ultra was soon eased. The Germans continued to blame the sinkings on superior British direction finding or French agents or some other cause rather than accept that the Enigma could be compromised.

The *Scharnhorst* and the *Tirpitz*, the last two of Germany's battle cruisers, were hiding out in Norwegian harbors, ready to sail out and ravage convoys headed for the USSR. At Christmastime in 1943 the Germans decided to unleash *Scharnhorst* for an attack on convoy JW55B. Dönitz, succeeding Raeder as commander in chief, was sensitive to the plight of German soldiers now being battered on the Russian front and wished desperately to stanch the flow of supplies to the Soviets. He believed he could commit the precious battleship because he had lulled Britain into more relaxed convoy protection by allowing recent sailings to pass through unmolested. Bletchley decrypts, however, warned of his plans. Although key German messages relating to the *Scharnhorst* were in the Offizier code, whose doubled encipherment slowed decryption, and were of little tactical value, BP did inform the escort fleet when the *Scharnhorst* put to sea. Further, the decrypts guided the British warships in placing themselves to intercept the German battleship when she did try to attack the convoy. In the early hours of December 26, a star shell fired from a British cruiser lit up the *Scharnhorst* instants before a salvo from the fleet's battleship, HMS *Duke of York*, slammed into her. Left burning, she was finished off by torpedoes from swarming destroyers. Of her crew of more than two thousand, only thirty-six men were rescued from the Arctic waters.

The final chapter of warfare against Germany's surface raiders was not written until November 1944. This was the struggle against the *Tirpitz*. Fear of this capital ship had caused the British to attempt repeatedly to put her out of commission. In March 1941 a commando raid against Saint-Nazaire succeeded in seriously damaging the only dry dock on the Atlantic coast capable of handling repairs of the massive battleship. In October

1942 the Admiralty sent across the North Sea a Norwegian naval officer in a fishing boat that had two manned torpedoes slung beneath it. The idea was to enter the fjord where the *Tirpitz* was berthed and aim the torpedoes at the ship. The scheme went awry when the boat encountered a squall and lost both the torpedoes. In September 1943 a fleet of six midget submarines was towed into position to glide in close to the *Tirpitz* and her escort vessels and detonate explosives beneath their keels. Three of the tiny subs made it through and, as Enigma decrypts later confirmed, made hits on the *Tirpitz*, so badly damaging her that the Germans did not expect to have her ready for action until mid-March of 1944.

When, repaired, the ship again became a danger, she was attacked and once more damaged, this time by carrier aircraft. A second carrier-planned sortie in July, meant to finish her off, met with increased antiaircraft fire and made no hits. But on September 15, 1944, RAF bombers operating from north Russia again put her out of action.

With Ultra decrypts carefully monitoring every stage of the big ship's latest repairs, the finale came when *Tirpitz* was once more reported ready for raiding. On the twelfth of November, thirty-two British bombers, each carrying a single twelve-thousand-pound bomb, took off from Scotland. At least two of the bombs hit the *Tirpitz* and capsized her. German sailors, hopelessly trapped within the inverted hull, were heard singing the German national anthem, "Deutschland Uber Alles," to their last breaths. "What a tragedy," one observer commented, "that men like that had to serve the Nazi cause."

Removal of this last threat of the surface raiders enabled the Admiralty to dispatch warships to the Pacific for the war against Japan.

Bletchley Copes with Shark

In February 1942, when everything had been going so well, Hut 8's intelligence feast abruptly ended. Up until then, both the surface ships and the U-boats had used a common cipher, called Dolphin by GC&CS. Now the U-boat command gained its own cipher, which the British dubbed Shark. It was not only a new code; it involved a change in the design of the U-boats' Enigma machines. This was a thinned reflector that allowed a fourth rotor to be added in its slot. Applied to the machines Dönitz used in his communications with his Atlantic and Mediterranean U-boats, Shark plunged Bletchley into a ten-month blackout. During those long months,

Hut 8 penetrated the new cipher on only three days—and each of these times only because of a German error in sending a message in both the Dolphin and Shark ciphers. Banburismus no longer worked. Turing's *EINS* catalogs were of no avail. The Submarine Tracking Room reported, "Little can be said with any confidence in estimating the present and future movement of the U-boats."

What made those ten months doubly frustrating was that by breaking codes other than Shark, BP knew a great deal about the U-boats: the commissioning of new craft and their trial runs in the Baltic, their expected performance, their armament, the experience levels of their commanders, their transfers to the west of France, even the times of their departures for active duty and their arrivals back in port. What was lacking was the most important information, in Hinsley's words, what happened "between the time they left harbour and the time they returned from patrol."

To make this long blackout period still more disastrous, B-Dienst was again gaining the upper hand in the contest of which antagonist was breaking the other's codes. The British Admiralty had switched to a new nonmachine code, but B-Dienst was readily reconstructing it. Dönitz knew the schedules of the North Atlantic convoys and the courses they would take.

The Sigint seesaw had peremptorily swung back to the German side—at a time when Reich production was delivering increasing numbers of U-boats into Dönitz's hands. In addition, he was receiving large "milk cow" supply submarines, each of which could deliver seven hundred tons of spare fuel and torpedoes, saving the U-boats the forty-six-hundred-mile round-trip back to their bases.

The consequences were muted for a while by the fierce winter of 1941–42, for its violent seas decreased the U-boats' effectiveness. When the weather moderated, however, Dönitz and his commanders made up for lost time. They steadily increased their sinkings, while their losses of U-boats declined. The first half of 1942 resulted, again in Hinsley's words, in the U-boats' "greatest sustained period of success in the whole course of the war."

In view of the sudden inability of the convoys to steer clear of wolf packs coinciding with a change in code, the U-boat command might well have been tipped off that their earlier codes had been broken, if not for one momentous change in the war's course: the entry of the United States into the conflict. Four days after Pearl Harbor, Hitler had honored his Tripartite pledge to the Japanese by declaring war on the U.S. All that American shipping he had placed off-limits to the U-boats in order not to provoke the U.S. now became fair game.

As a result, instead of continuing to send his boats against the Atlantic convoys and finding them suspiciously vulnerable, Dönitz directed his boats against the coasts of the U.S. and Canada. He did not have as many to dispatch as he would have liked. Many had to be diverted to the Mediterranean to help protect the supply lines to Rommel in North Africa. In addition, Hitler, still fearing a flank attack through Scandinavia, had ordered other U-boats to patrols in Norwegian waters. For attacks on U.S. shipping, the German admiral had only a handful of boats, but they were the large, long-range Type IX craft now being supplied by German boatyards.

American unpreparedness enabled him to make the most of what he had. The U.S. could assemble few vessels suitable for escort duty, and the ones available were not assigned to convoy protection. The navy's head, Admiral Ernest King, did not approve of convoys; he preferred to go after the U-boats in open-sea hunts. These forays, however, proved fruitless. The U-boats simply hid out on the bottom until King's patrols had passed before rising to continue their slaughter of the busy traffic along the eastern coast. U.S. coastal cities, resisting the inconvenience and possible trade loss that would ensue from blackouts, kept their lights undimmed, providing the German prowlers neatly silhouetted targets. In just two weeks the U-boats sank twenty-five ships totaling more than two hundred thousand tons, a high percentage of them tankers, and continued the sinkings at roughly one a day. Crowds of watchers along the coasts witnessed the deadly pyrotechnics of exploding ships. Another "happy time" for the U-boats had begun.

If Dönitz's approach to sea warfare had a fault, it was in his belief that what mattered most was the tonnage sunk by his subs. Despite knowing that choking off British supplies in the North Atlantic was the real key to German victory, he was unable to resist the opportunities to pile up tonnage records elsewhere. His impressive statistics, it must be remembered, made for status-saving, job-preserving reports to Hitler. Yet while his U-boats were scoring easy points in U.S. waters, massive convoys were passing through to Britain almost unmolested.

Not until the summer of 1942 did the situation begin to change. By then Admiral King had given up the hunt missions and agreed to convoys. Coastal cities were blacked out. Plus, the navy established what it called its "bucket brigade." Tankers and merchant ships traveled up the coast in protected convoys by day and holed up in sheltered ports at night. The British helped by sending over escort corvettes and a squadron of RAF Coastal Command planes. Guided by visiting Britons, the U.S. Navy had begun setting up a Submarine Tracking Room similar to that of the Royal Navy. The happy time came to an end.

Dönitz rerouted his wolf packs to the North Atlantic. With few U-boat losses and strong inflows of new boats, his fleet had grown four times as large as when Shark had been introduced. Also he had found a chink in the Allies' defensive armor. This was the "Air Gap," a distance of three hundred miles between the extremity of air cover from Newfoundland and Iceland and that extending from the British Isles. In this gap he formed his boats into "picket lines." Aided by B-Dienst's decrypts, the pickets could detect approaching convoys and alert other subs to swarm in for the kill. Before Shark, when BP was breaking the naval Enigma, only one in ten convoys was sighted by the wolf packs. Now with BP blind, they found one of every three.

The carnage in the North Atlantic marked the second powerful German surge toward victory. In the first of the new round of convoy battles, eleven out of thirty-three ships went down. In the two months of September and October 1942, forty-three ships were sunk. By November the losses soared to 743,321 tons, the highest figure for any month in the entire war. During 1942 more than eight thousand merchant sailors were killed. Two of the ships sunk were carrying U.S. servicemen to England, adding to the lives lost.

The same grim story held true for convoys trying to deliver armaments and supplies to the Soviet Union. Grimmest of all was the fate of convoy PQ17, which set out from Iceland on June 27, 1942. The convoy was attacked in the Barents Sea by U-boats and aircraft. At that time the *Tirpitz* was still available as a raider. The convoy was given the misguided order to scatter. It didn't matter that the *Tirpitz* never got into the action. The U-boats and planes picked off the dispersed merchant ships one by one. Of the thirty-seven ships in the convoy, only thirteen reached Russian ports. As a result of the disaster, all convoys to Russia were suspended during the spring and summer of 1943.

The mounting destruction by the U-boats cast a pall of despair over news of the war that was otherwise turning in the Allies' favor. The British Eighth Army had defeated Rommel at El Alamein. The Allied landings in northwest Africa had surprised the Germans. The Germans' decision to occupy the whole of France had prompted the Vichy government to scuttle the French fleet at Toulon. But without Ultra's help, the situation in the North Atlantic was threatening to undo all the other triumphs.

Breaking Shark, Turing saw, required four-wheel bombes. Tabulating Machine Company engineers worked on their development, introducing some limited use of electronic tubes to speed their operation and race through the increased number of permutations introduced by the fourth rotor. Until these bombes could be delivered, Hut 8 could only wait. Luckily, an even harsher winter than the one preceding it slowed the U-boats in January and February 1943.

In March, however, they stormed back in force. During just the first twenty days, ninety-seven ships were sunk, with over half a million tons of supplies sent to the bottom. The official Admiralty verdict was that "the Germans never came so near to disrupting communications between the New World and the Old" as in those twenty days.

Behind the scenes, though, important changes were occurring. For one, the sheer productive might of the U.S. was tipping the scales. The Ships for Victory program was turning out standardized Liberty ships at a rate of three per day, enabling the Allies to produce more vessels than the Germans were sinking. The American merchant craft were faster, ensuring that convoys could move more swiftly. Escort patrol ships, aircraft carriers, destroyers and larger warships were being delivered by American shipyards. Recon aircraft with ever greater ranges were issuing from American factories in unprecedented numbers. Long-range American B-24 bombers were joining with British bombers to extend air cover over the convoys and close the Air Gap.

In addition, convoys were benefiting from British and American technology. Radiotelephones were installed to improve communications between ships and to coordinate their maneuvers. Escort vessels were equipped with their own direction-finding equipment to help them home in on lurking U-boats. Some larger freighters were fitted with airplane catapults, from which game pilots took off knowing they would, after their search-and-destroy missions, have to reach a land base or ditch near an Allied vessel in the hope of being picked up. Airborne radar and powerful new searchlights enabled Allied planes to detect and swoop in on U-boats traveling on the surface at night.

On December 13, 1942, the decisive change came. Shark was finally broken. This resulted from one last, all-important capture of German code materials and from the clever use Bletchley made of them.

The capture occurred in the Mediterranean, off the coast of Egypt. A British flying boat's crew sighted U-boat *U-559* and alerted four destroyers to pursue it. Later that night, a depth charge forced the sub to the surface, virtually under the guns of the HMS *Petard*. The *U-559*'s commander ordered his crew to abandon ship. Before escaping, the U-boat's engineer opened the sea cocks to scuttle the sub. But she remained afloat, her conning tower just visible above the waves. Four of the *Petard*'s crewmen either swam to the sub or jumped onto it from the deck of their ship—survivors' accounts vary. Three of the crew, Lieutenant Tony Fasson along with Colin Grazier and Ken Lacroix, clambered into the sub's interior while the fourth, young canteen assistant Tommy Brown, ran up and down the conning tower ladder in order to hand over to a whaleboat what the others could deliver to him. They grabbed the four-rotor Enigma from the radio room and an armful of charts and papers that Brown managed to transfer to the whaleboat alongside. At that moment the U-boat went under. Lacroix just managed to escape up the conning tower; Fasson and Grazier never made it.

Their sacrifice gave the Hut 8 team what it needed to crack Shark. In adding the fourth rotor, the Germans had taken into account that at times, in order to communicate with three-rotor machines, that rotor would have to be put in a neutral position—as, for example, when the U-boat had to communicate with a shore weather station. Among the papers the brave men of the *Petard* had delivered were the current editions of the three-rotor codebook for the Short Weather Cipher and the four-rotor U-boat key. The result was that when Shark was used for weather signals, the three-rotor bombes could be used to decipher the messages, and the remaining part of the day's key could be reconstructed by testing no more than twenty-six letters of the nonrotating fourth rotor. In the first hour after this breakthrough, a message revealed the positions of fifteen U-boats.

Those in Hut 8 felt both deep relief and huge elation. Pat Bing, then a teenaged typist, later recalled the excitement of finally being able to tap out German text on long strips of sticky tape, fasten the tapes to paper and send them by the compressed-air tubes the young women called "Spit and Suck" to Hut 4 for the interpreters and disseminators to work on. The deciphered Shark messages were, she said, "a great gift from the brainy boys' department."

Historian Patrick Beesly has recorded the impact of the conquest of Shark. The flood of decrypts and translated signals that poured into the Admiralty's Operational Intelligence Center, he noted, "made it possible, for the first time, for . . . the Submarine Tracking Room to build up a comprehensive and accurate picture of the whole operational U-boat fleet."

At this point the cryptologic war reached a stalemate. BP was reading Dönitz's copious exchanges with his U-boats, but B-Dienst was reading the Admiralty's output. As Hinsley put it, "Between February and June 1943 the battle of the Atlantic hinged to no small extent on the changing fortunes of a continuing trial of cryptographic and cryptanalytic resourcefulness between the B-Dienst and the Allies."

There was one significant difference. From their decrypts, Bletchley's cryptanalysts gained unmistakable proof that the Germans were breaking the Royal Navy's main code, and so set in motion the changes necessary to provide a more secure system.

It took the Admiralty until June to make the changeover. In the interim, U-boat warfare rose to its savage climax. As an example, during four days in mid-March, Dönitz's wolf packs hurled themselves against two intermingled convoys, HX229 and SC122, whose course had been plotted by B-Dienst, and sank thirty-two of their ships plus a destroyer, with a loss of only one U-boat. It was the greatest U-boat success of the war. Again the Admiralty was reduced to despair, even to considering that "we should not be able to continue convoy as an effective system of defence."

April produced a standoff. Shark decrypts enabled the Admiralty to reroute threatened convoys, but B-Dienst decrypts informed Dönitz how to counter the instructions and reposition his boats to the best advantage. So exhausted were his crews and their equipment by the March onslaught, however, that he could not maintain their previous level of sinkings. April's toll dropped to 277,000 tons.

Then came what those in U-boat command regarded as "Black May." Two calamities struck the U-boats. One was a sharp rise in their own losses: thirty-one boats were sunk during the month, and the total for the first six months of 1943 rose past one hundred. The second was a wavering in morale. Less experienced commanders exhibited a drop-off in zeal and a rise in caution compared with their predecessors. Dönitz was driven to increasingly shrill denunciations of his crews for their failures to press home their attacks.

The turn of the tide was dramatized by the passage of convoy SC130 in mid-May. Though attacked by a pack of U-boats, not a ship was sunk. By contrast, six U-boats were lost and others damaged.

The price was more than the German admiral, who had lost his own son in one of the downed boats, was willing to pay. On May 24 he sent out orders for his U-boats to withdraw from the North Atlantic and shift to less hazardous patrols southeast of the Azores.

Dönitz refused to concede, however. He later wrote, "Wolfpack operations against convoys in the North Atlantic . . . could only be resumed if we succeeded in radically increasing the fighting power of the U-boats." He was determined that in the autumn of 1944 he would launch a new campaign, using U-boats equipped with new developments from German science. The improvements included superior radar, better antiaircraft protection and more efficient acoustic torpedoes.

It was an abortive effort. By then the odds were stacked overwhelmingly against Dönitz. Long-range aircraft made the air cover for convoys complete, especially after Portugal permitted the Allies to occupy the Azores. Escort carriers were plentiful. New technological developments included "hedgehogs" that enabled destroyers to throw depth charges ahead of their course as well as behind. To counter the acoustic torpedoes, the Allies perfected the "Foxer," a device towed astern of the escort vessels; it attracted the torpedoes and caused them to explode harmlessly.

Above all, the cryptographic advantage had swung completely to the Allies. As Beesly expressed it, Dönitz "was now groping in the dark while our picture was so clear that convoys could be converted, Support Groups transferred, air cover increased or reduced in accordance with the daily or even hourly demands of a situation."

Few Allied ships were sunk, and too many U-boats were destroyed. On November 16 Dönitz ordered another withdrawal.

In the meantime, control of Shark had passed to American cryptanalysts. With a flood of super-high-speed bombes being produced by the National Cash Register Company in Dayton, Ohio, the Yanks were better equipped to deal in a timely fashion with the vast numbers of permutations that had to be run through to reach Shark Enigmas' settings. During the second half of 1943, National Cash delivered seventy-five bombes, more than the British produced during the rest of the war. American analysts informed the Tracking Rooms in London and Washington.

Dönitz still would not give in. He pressed U-boat designers to apply new techniques in a series of Super U-boats. Informed by Shark decrypts, British and American commanders watched these new developments with grave misgivings. The new boats' streamlined hulls and quiet new electric motors allowed them to slip along underwater at speeds matching those of most Allied escort vessels. Most worrisome of all, they were equipped with snorkel devices that took in oxygen and recharged batteries as the boats traveled at hard-to-spot periscope depths, enabling the subs to stay submerged for up to ten days.

Dönitz planned his Super U-boat convoy battles for early 1945, but his ambitious plans were thwarted as Allied bombardments of U-boat assembly plants and bases caused delays. Then the finished boats revealed flaws that had to be corrected. Before he could deploy his new subs, the war ended.

The Battle of the Atlantic was the longest sustained conflict of the war, one that cost both sides heavily. The Allies lost 2,603 merchant ships and 175 naval vessels. The lives lost exceeded 40,000, including 26,000 civilians. German U-boat losses numbered 784, killing 28,000 crewmen—two-thirds of the total force. The casualty rate was the highest suffered by any service during the war.

By June 1943, Churchill wrote, "The shipping losses fell to the lowest figure since the United States had entered the war. The convoys came through intact, and the Atlantic supply line was safe."

For Some Codebreakers, Unhappy Endings

Triumphant as they were during the war, both Alan Turing and Gordon Welchman suffered ill-fated deaths in the years that followed. Turing's fondness for Christopher Morcom turned out to be more than an adolescent aberration. He slowly surrendered to his true nature—at a time when British law still regarded homosexuality as a crime. Arrested after a petty encounter with the police, he was unable, because of his secrecy pledge, to assert his heroic wartime stature in his defense and was subjected to a humiliating trial and a judgment that his "cure" include the injection of female hormones that made this sturdy man who had run marathons become obese and grow breasts. Not long after, at the age of forty-two, he committed suicide.

Welchman, after the war, emigrated to the U.S., became an American citizen and served as a consultant on intelligence security during the Cold War. He became concerned that Allied codebreakers were making the same mistakes that had betrayed the Enigma. When Winterbotham's *The Ultra Secret* broke the walls of secrecy, Welchman felt released from security restrictions and had his book *The Hut Six Story* published by an American firm. But whereas Winterbotham had said little about the actual codebreaking methods used at Bletchley Park, Welchman, as a warning to current cryptographers, spelled out the "comedy of errors committed by the Germans" and how these errors had been exploited by Allied cryptanalysts.

Because of these disclosures, the book met with a storm of protests by both British and American authorities. The British banned publication in Britain and issued criminal charges against Welchman. The Americans withdrew his security clearance, making it impossible for him to continue his employment. Because of the harassment, Welchman wrote, "my health was seriously affected." British historian Nigel West has claimed that the persecution drove Welchman to a "premature death."

For both Turing and Welchman, however, these postwar troubles cannot dim the glory of their wartime achievements. The techniques they developed became the machinery of a huge intelligence factory at Bletchley Park, which ran so smoothly that in the war's latter stages they had only to oversee its almost routine production of war-winning decrypts by the hundreds of thousands.

6 When Superior Intelligence Was Not Enough

AFTER Adolf Hitler became chancellor of Germany, he was reported to have regretted revealing so much of his planning for the future in the book he dictated to Rudolf Hess while in prison in 1923–24 and later at an inn in Berchtesgaden. He called his book "Four and a Half Years of Struggle Against Lies, Stupidity and Cowardice," but his publishers sensibly shortened the title to *Mein Kampf*, or "My Struggle." The book spelled out his rejection of equality and democracy; inequality between individuals and races he saw as part of an unchangeable natural order. Topmost in this order was the "Aryan race," of which the German *Volk* was a supreme expression. Morality and truth were to be judged by their accordance with the interest and preservation of the *Volk*. As leader of the *Volk* the führer was endowed with absolute authority. Under the führer, the Aryans, as the superior race, must reign supreme over the *Untermenschen*, the lower orders that included the Jews and the Slavic peoples; these were to be eliminated or enslaved.

Hitler's racist beliefs underlay his plans for Germany's rise. As the master race, the Aryans were justified in acquiring *Lebensraum*, or "living space," land to be used in cultivating food and providing space for the expanding Aryan population. That land was to be taken by force from the *Untermenschen* in Poland and particularly from the hated Bolsheviks of Soviet Russia. "To guarantee to the German nation the soil and territory to which it is entitled," Hitler dictated to Hess, "we are bound to think first of Russia and her border states."

The opening step in this plan was to conquer France, following through to what he saw as the victory that was denied Germany in the Great War by political treachery and Jewish betrayal. The vengeful defeat of France would also secure the western border so that the Germans could then proceed to take over the lands to the east.

Once he was master of Germany, Hitler followed *Mein Kampf* as his blueprint for the future. He consolidated his power and made himself the führer. He directed Heinrich Himmler to begin excising the inferior peoples from among the Germans. He added living space by his occupation of Austria and his conquest of Czechoslovakia. He hoped to bluff France and England into accepting his invasion of Poland. When that part of his plan failed and precipitated war, he humbled the French and reduced England to a negligible barrier in the way of his larger goal: the submission of the USSR, the extermination or enslavement of its people and the absorption of its vast territories. He ordered his military chiefs to prepare for a campaign against Russia in the late spring of 1941.

Hitler was confident his surprise would be complete. He had ample evidence that Joseph Stalin was abiding by the German-Soviet nonaggression pact of 1939. Stalin was, for one significant instance, honoring his pledge to provide materials needed by the Reich's war machine. Trains bearing grain, petroleum and metals regularly rolled across the borders to supply the Wehrmacht.

With the fall of France, Europe became a highly productive rumor mill, grinding out estimates of what Hitler would do next. As early as August 1940 the respected British agent Paul Thümmel, code-named A-54, began sending reports directly from within the German military that Hitler was planning an attack on the Soviets. The intelligence branch responsible for the Russian area, Thümmel said, had been expanding since June, the counterintelligence had also been urgently increased and the whole intelligence organization was reinforced with specialists on Ukraine, the Crimea and the Caucasus. Other agents reported the eastward deployment of German divisions into Poland and, after a transit agreement agreed to by the Finns, to the eastern borders of Finland. In December a newly organized network of Polish agents sent word of a German push to increase west-east road and rail construction.

None of it was persuasive to British intelligence. Their myopic view was that Hitler could not possibly consider attacking Russia while the second-front war with Britain continued. The buildup of German forces in the east was simply to guard against a drive by the USSR or to blackmail Stalin into further concessions. Until Great Britain was defeated, Germany would not fight Russia "except in dire emergency." Churchill himself believed that the Germans and Russians had more to gain by "overrunning and dividing the British Empire in the East" than by going to war with one another.

Then Bletchley Park decrypts began to change his mind. On March 26, 1941, an Enigma message pinpointed the shift of three armored divisions and two important headquarters locations from the Balkans to Kraków in Poland. On March 30 a BP summary concluded that the evidence it was receiving confirmed a large-scale operation against Russia. Churchill became convinced. He wrote later that the information from his "most trusted source" had "illuminated the whole Eastern scene in a lightning flash." The sudden movement to Kraków of so much armor needed in the Balkan sphere could only mean Hitler's intention to invade Russia in May.

Some were astonished that Churchill, to whom Communism was anathema, should try so hard to awaken the Russian dictator to his peril. His answer: "If Hitler invaded Hell, I would make at least a favorable reference to the Devil in the House of Commons."

All through April and May Bletchley's GC&CS continued to amass evidence of German preparations on the Russian borders. On May 27, as an example, the Luftwaffe's Red code revealed that a German air corps was asking for maps of Latvia, Lithuania, Poland and northeast Russia. Perhaps most persuasive at this point were decrypts of the German Railways Cipher. In an endless stream they shuttled massive shipments of troops and armor supplies to the eastern frontier.

Obstinately, Britain's intelligence leaders held to the view that the Nazis were using these shows of force to achieve better terms in their negotiations with the Soviets. "With her usual thoroughness," one report declared, "Germany is making all preparations for an attack so as to make the threat convincing."

On May 31, GC&CS issued a special paper based on its Enigma decrypts. The report stated, "It becomes harder than ever to doubt that the object of these large movements of the German army and air force is Russia." The paper admitted that Hitler, no doubt, would prefer to blackmail Stalin into a bloodless surrender. "But the quiet move, for instance, of a prisoner-of-war cage to Tarnow looks more like business than bluff." To those still arguing the improbability that Hitler would be so rash as to take on a long struggle on two fronts, the paper answered that it "may well be that the Germans do not expect the struggle with Russia to be long," that Hitler was anticipating "a lightning victory."

The paper was right on target. In making his decision Hitler had been encouraged by the Soviets' earlier bumbling effort to subdue Finland. Announcing his plans to his generals back in July 1940, he had informed them that he expected no more than a five-month blitzkrieg against Russia. He had labeled the invasion Operation Barbarossa, deriving his code name from the medieval emperor who, as legend had it, lay sleeping in a mountain retreat ready to come to Germany's aid in her hour of need.

Seeking to avoid what had befallen Napoléon—"the 1812 factor"—Hitler wanted to make an early start and end the campaign before the Russian winter set in. In his Directive 21, issued on December 18, 1940, he specified that preparations for the attack must be concluded by May 15, 1941.

Churchill's messages to Stalin were only a small part of the flood of warnings pouring in on Moscow. As will be related in more detail subsequently, it was one of those times when superior intelligence did not suffice. Stalin refused to listen. In fact, he had the Soviet press fulminate against British "provocations," deploring them as efforts to drive a wedge between the USSR and Germany.

Whether he wanted help or not, the Russian dictator was about to receive it from an unexpected source.

Delaying Barbarossa's Start-up

As soon as Winston Churchill had accepted his codebreakers' assessment that the Germans planned to invade Russia, he began to think how fortuitous it would be if the date of that invasion could be pushed back, if the time between its launching and the arrival of the Russian winter could be shortened.

One of his principal aids in this endeavor was William Stephenson, Canadian-born industrialist and millionaire. Stephenson's story has become most widely known through a best-selling biography, *A Man Called Intrepid*, written by his near namesake William Stevenson. Unfortunately, the account is seriously flawed. Historian Nigel West has written of the book that it is "almost entirely fictional in content." Even the code name Intrepid, according to West, is false. It was the name given not to Stephenson as an individual but to the New York City operation he headed.

This much seems to be true. Stephenson was chosen to be the chief of British Security Coordination, the cover name for the New York outpost of Britain's Secret Intelligence Service. As head of the BSC he established, in his native Canada, a center for clandestine activities such as training spies and fabricating materials for large-scale deceptions of the enemy. He helped negotiate the deal by which fifty mothballed U.S. destroyers went into service for the British. Behind the scenes, he did much to carry out Churchill's scheme to delay Hitler's Russian adventure as long as possible.

The opportunity for delay was presented by fomenting trouble in the Balkans. Hitler believed that this southeastern doorway into Europe must be neutralized before he went ahead with Barbarossa. His planning was complicated by his Axis partner Benito Mussolini, who in October 1940 launched a campaign against Greece while also trying to drive the British out of North Africa. Both ventures foundered. The plucky Greeks had fought the Italians to a standstill at the same time that the campaign to take Egypt had met with embarrassing defeats. An additional problem for Hitler was that the British had occupied the island of Crete and established RAF bases in southern Greece.

He directed his generals to begin planning an early spring campaign against Greece. Otherwise, he sought to gain his objectives in the Balkans by diplomacy backed by threats. Stephenson saw his chance. Fear was supposed to compel the Balkan leaders to give in quickly and sign the Tripartite Pact, which would give the Germans military bases in, and unopposed passage through, their territories. Suppose that somehow those leaders' backbones could be stiffened and their negotiations with the Nazis dragged out for days, perhaps for weeks?

Stephenson found willing collaborators in President Roosevelt and Colonel William J. "Wild Bill" Donovan, FDR's envoy-at-large who was eventually to head up the Office of Strategic Services, the precursor to the CIA. When Churchill requested of FDR that Donovan travel to the Balkans on Britain's behalf, Roosevelt readily agreed. Donovan's departure was carefully leaked to the press, leading to headlines such as AMERICA'S SECRET ENVOY FLIES ON MYSTERY MISSION. Stephenson was his unseen companion.

By the time Donovan arrived in the Balkans, Hungary and Romania had already given in to Germany's demands, and Bulgaria was on the verge. He flew to Sofia, Bulgaria, for talks with King Boris. Donovan's message there, and to other Balkan leaders, was that any nation that tamely submitted to the Germans would be regarded less sympathetically when the U.S. came "to settle accounts" than any nation resisting the Nazis. The king couldn't be dissuaded, but he did hesitate. Churchill indicated he would have been content with a delay of twenty-four hours; Donovan put off Bulgaria's surrender by eight days.

The crux of any Balkan campaign was Yugoslavia. It offered more suitable terrain and the best railway system for German intervention in Greece. The British had tried to persuade Prince Paul, regent for young King Peter II, to have Yugoslavia join them in defense of Greece, but Paul refused. He had already been summoned to Berchtesgaden for a browbeating session with Hitler and felt driven to give in to the Germans' demands, even though the agreement was anathema to him: he was an Anglophile graduate of Oxford and had a Greek princess as his wife. Donovan flew to Belgrade and persuaded Paul, too, to drag out his negotiations with the Germans. Secretly Donovan also sent messages to Yugoslav opposition leaders: "If Prince Paul kneels to the Nazis, revolt."

That was what happened. After extending negotiations as long as he thought possible, Paul caved in to the Nazis. Immediately Serb general Dušan Simovic led a palace coup, forced Paul to abdicate and installed Peter II as monarch.

Back in the U.S., Donovan delivered a deliberately provocative report to the nation on the courageous Balkans' defiance of the Nazis.

The plotters hoped that Hitler would fly into a tantrum, as he had before, and do something foolish. Now, as Churchill expressed it, "He had a burst of that convulsive anger which momentarily blotted out thought and sometimes impelled him on his most dire adventures." Hitler called his generals together and told them that since the Yugoslavs had become an uncertain factor in the coming action against Greece and in his plans for Barbarossa, the German army must be diverted to punish them.

His orders were carried out with unmerciful harshness. For three days German bombers attacked Belgrade, flying in virtually unopposed to drop their missiles from rooftop height. Much of the city was destroyed, with heavy losses in civilian lives. The German army crossed the borders and in eleven days crushed the Yugoslav forces.

Yet the Germans also suffered damage—not in terms of military casualties, which were few, but in world opinion. People outside the Axis had been thrilled by the Yugoslav revolt and then horrified by the savagery of the Nazi response.

The sacrifice of the Yugoslavs had another effect, which world opinion at the time could not appreciate. The German command had hoped to begin their campaign in Greece on March 1. The trouble stirred up for them in the Balkans was a factor in delaying their attack to April 6.

Churchill felt obliged to support Greece, his one Balkan ally, in her resistance against the Nazi juggernaut, even though BP decrypts clearly showed that troops sent there would face a grim prospect. In fact, British intelligence warned the chiefs of staff, "We must be prepared to face the loss of all forces sent to Greece." Nevertheless, Churchill directed General Archibald Wavell in North Africa to detach three of his crack divisions and dispatch them to Greece—a transfer that began March 4.

The fight in Greece went pretty much as the pessimists had predicted. The Greek army and the British detachment were outnumbered and, within three weeks, overwhelmed. There was one significant high note. Bletchley Park had been reading the Germans' messages and for the first time arranged to send the substance of its decrypts directly to the commanders in the field. They made good use of the intelligence, managing a series of skillful withdrawals and, in the end, a substantial evacuation of the divisions that had been sent there.

The ships of Admiral Cunningham brought off a smaller Dunkirk, rescuing more than fifty thousand British and Greek soldiers while having to leave only eleven thousand behind. With the Luftwaffe in control of the air, the cost to the Royal Navy was high: twenty-six ships were lost in the operation.

Once again superior intelligence could not right the balance against too-powerful opposition. As Hinsley noted, however, "The high-grade Sigint sent out from the United Kingdom helped to reduce the scale of the calamity."

Crete, the Germans' Pyrrhic Victory

Even with the Balkans subdued, Hitler could not rest easy in his plans for Barbarossa as long as the British threatened from the island of Crete. Besides, he had a group of fighters who were chafing for action. These were the paratrooper corps under the command of Hermann Göring. Still smarting over his defeat in the Battle of Britain, Göring himself was eager for a chance to recoup the Luftwaffe's reputation.

His airborne brigades were made up of the cream of German youth, the most ardent of the young Nazis, and although they had made small-scale drops in Norway and the Netherlands, they were itching to win a major victory for the führer. They saw Crete as their opportunity.

The attack was intended to be a complete surprise to the island's Allied troops, mainly New Zealanders and Australians evacuated from Greece. Suddenly out of the skies on a May morning, following an air and sea softening-up bombardment, thousands of elite parachutists would come floating down and would be followed by a flight of eighty towed gliders hauling additional soldiers and heavy equipment. Still more firepower would come from sea convoys ferrying in troops and armor.

But of course the codebreakers knew all about the attack. "At no moment in the war," Churchill wrote, "was our intelligence so truly and precisely informed." He was pledged not to reveal the source of that intelligence, but we now know that Ultra cryptanalysts began disclosing the German intentions against Crete the day after Hitler issued his directive. Although Bletchley was still struggling with German army and navy codes, those of the Luftwaffe were an open book. Masses of information were accumulated as the Germans prepared their operation. On May 20, when the attack was to begin, Britain's commander, New Zealand general Bernard Freyberg, knew when, where and in what strength the Nazi parachutists and gliders would be attacking.

He also knew, however, that his troops would have to defend the island without air support. Crete's paltry force of thirty-six RAF aircraft had been evacuated to Egypt the day before the attack began.

The Germans' first objective was to capture at least one of the three airstrips on Crete. That would enable them to pour in heavy armor, artillery and supplies. Knowing what he did, Freyberg should have concentrated his forces at those three sites, and he did assign considerable strength to ward off the airborne landings. But he was also wary of the sea convoys and gave what critics later felt was undue priority to the seaborne operation. This disposition of the British troops was especially unfortunate, since the Royal Navy attacked the support convoys and prevented either of them from reaching the island. The only Germans to land on Crete from the sea were forty-nine soldiers in life rafts.

Even so, the carnage among the parachutists and glider forces was tremendous. The equipment for paratroopers was still at a formative stage. For example, they had little control over their chutes; they just drifted down like "beautiful kicking dolls," as a British officer described them, and were shot en masse while still in the air. Many of those who managed to come down alive were injured in landing on the rocky terrain, which also smashed a high percentage of the gliders. The New Zealand gunners quickly mopped up survivors.

The defenders came close to staving off the attack. At the critical moment, however, the British commander in charge of preventing the seizure of the airstrip at Maleme inexplicably withdrew his troops to the hills instead of keeping them in place at the landing site. Once the Germans were in control of the landing field the battle was effectively over. Although the German general in charge of the operation had used up even his reserves of paratroops, he was able to crash-land a mountain rifle regiment and to reinforce them with a flood of equipment. To the consternation and dismay of the codebreakers at Bletchley, the Germans succeeded in taking Crete and forcing another evacuation of defeated British troops.

It was a victory the Germans were not to repeat. Faced with accountings of the massacre of his paratroopers, Hitler ruled airborne assault out of his military repertoire. "Crete," he told his parachute general, "proves that the days of paratroops are over." The depleted parachute corps was never rebuilt.

Hitler had secured his southeastern flank and eliminated the threat of Crete. The costs were great. They were to continue: German divisions were bogged down in the Balkans by the need to battle the guerrilla forces that sprang up following the defeats of the regular armies. In Yugoslavia particularly, Germans found themselves locked in vicious fighting against the underground forces led by Draza Mihailovic, and later the Communist partisans under Tito.

Hitler had originally hoped to launch Barbarossa on May 15. It has been pointed out that this was an unrealistic scheduling. A late spring thaw turned the Russian frontier into a quagmire that would have rendered the passage of panzers impossible until well into June. But the Allied schemers could not have anticipated the weather as an ally. In any case, Barbarossa did not start until June 22. Despite all his efforts to avoid a Russian winter, Hitler had gained only two days on the date when Napoléon embarked upon his Russian adventure.

Churchill had no doubt as to the success of the delaying tactics. He believed they slowed the invasion by five weeks. In his war memoir he wrote, "It is reasonable to believe that Moscow was saved thereby."

7 The Spies Who Never Were

DID the benefits of secret intelligence flow only one way? Certainly the Germans did not think so. One of the important rebuttals that the Abwehr secret service would have offered was the network of spies they had established in Britain. These spies sent back such valuable information that the Germans awarded several of them the Iron Cross in recognition of their contributions.

At the war's outset, one of the agents the Abwehr would have cited was an electrical engineer code-named Snow. His firm did work for the British Admiralty, and Snow was also assigned to seek German customers. During his trips to Germany he let it be known that he was a Welsh nationalist bitterly opposed to the British. Recognizing that he could be a resource for useful information about the Royal Navy, the Germans had, in 1936, recruited him as an agent.

When war broke out, he quickly made himself the hub of an organization with a dozen or more Anglophobic agents throughout Britain. He trained them in the radio codes of the Abwehr, and his network became highly regarded by his spymaster for the information it transmitted about ship movements and deliveries of materials from the U.S. When, in 1940, Snow collapsed from the strain of his double life, his spy work was taken over by one of the subordinates he had so carefully trained.

A second agent, code-named Tate, was a sturdy young German fluent in English and trained in espionage. He parachuted into Britain equipped with special radio equipment that he used to receive orders from his controllers and to transmit back answers to their questions. Active to the war's end, he sent hundreds of messages about what he observed and was able to learn in

Britain. He was one of those granted the Iron Cross, First and Second Class.

Zigzag was the code name given to a criminal imprisoned by the British on the Channel Island of Jersey. When the Germans occupied the island, he offered his service in a spirit of vengeance against his former captors. The Germans trained him as a demolition expert and dropped him by parachute on the mainland. His primary mission was to sabotage the De Havilland factory where Mosquito light bombers were being produced. He was promised fifteen thousand pounds if he did the job. On January 29, 1943, he was able to report his success. An explosion had done extensive damage to the plant, as British newspapers indignantly reported and aerial reconnaissance could verify.

Tricycle was the code name of a youth from a wealthy Yugoslav family. Through his family's business he had high-level contacts in many countries—for example, he had once squired the Duke of York around during the duke's visit to Belgrade. Before the war he had gone to Germany's University of Freiburg to study law. When the war began, one of his German friends who worked for the Abwehr asked Tricycle to become a Nazi agent in Britain. The friend explained that while the Abwehr had many spies there, they wanted someone who could move in the upper strata of English society and help determine who would best cooperate in the coming invasion of Britain. To provide cover for his presence in England, he could carry on his business interests. The Germans knew he was a high liver and an inveterate womanizer, but they were willing to pay him well for his services. He gained his code name from the three-person spy agency he established—an agency the Germans relied on heavily for insights into the thinking of Britain's elite. When U.S. entry into the war began to seem inevitable, the Germans sent him to New York to begin structuring an American spy network.

The star of their show was the agent code-named Garbo—a Spaniard who presented himself at the German embassy in Madrid as one who so strongly hated Communism that he was willing to become a spy for German Fascism. Before sending him to Lisbon for his flight on to London, his German spymasters equipped him for his mission; he took with him a questionnaire covering information they most wanted to receive, along with secret ink, money and an address to which he could mail his findings. The Germans were delighted by his long, colorful, insightful reports from Britain, especially after he lined up a network of agents reporting to him from advantageous spots all over the island. The Abwehr also respected the care he expressed for his helpers, as when his agent in Liverpool sickened and died. In response to the obituary notice Garbo posted to them, his spy-masters wished him to extend their deepest sympathies to the agent's widow. He, too, was awarded the Iron Cross.

With these highly effective spies in place, along with a scattering of lesser agents, the Germans were content that their needs for special intelligence from Britain were being fully met. They soon saw no further necessity of dropping in new agents from the air or landing them from U-boats.

For the Allies, the most delicious irony of the war was that all of this complex infrastructure of German espionage was a chimera. Every one of some 120 agents and subagents the Nazis thought they had in their pockets was, in fact, a double agent, working under British control.

Snow, whose real name was Arthur Owens, made a practice during his prewar journeys back and forth to Germany of supplying snippets of information to the Nazis while also collecting facts that could prove useful to British authorities. As soon as war broke out, he immediately offered his services to Britain's Secret Intelligence Service. SIS chiefs were doubtful about him at first and actually locked him in a prison cell. But Snow proved his loyalty and became an enormous asset. His organization of a dozen agents was entirely imaginary. His reports to the Abwehr via radio included accurate tidbits mixed in with subtle misinformation. The reason for his end as a German agent was not that job pressures had caused him to collapse but that he had become an alcoholic and was no longer trustworthy. The British phased him out and had one of his "subordinates" take charge.

Tate really was a German who parachuted into Britain. Quickly captured, he was presented with the choice of being hanged or agreeing to be "turned" to work for the British. He chose life and underwent what was described as "an almost religious conversion to the Allied cause." Tate became one of the most trusted members of the British team, showing great resourcefulness in seeming to meet the demands of his Hamburg spymaster while larding his largely innocuous responses with carefully skewed data.

As for Zigzag and his destruction of the De Havilland factory, that was all neatly arranged by the British. Camouflage experts created a fake extension to the plant that could be blown up without hindering production at the real facility. The press, ignorant of what had actually happened, ran lurid accounts of the sabotage, which Zigzag could triumphantly report in order to collect his fifteen thousand pounds.

Tricycle's real name was Dusko Popov. During his studies in Germany he formed some close friendships but also, secretly, developed a fierce hatred of Nazism. Consequently, when Johann "Johnny" Jebsen, one of his friends, came to Belgrade to recruit him as a spy for German intelligence, Popov sought the advice of the British consul. He was told to go ahead and pretend to work for them. Settling in London, Popov lived well—largely at the Nazis' expense. He rented luxurious accommodations and enjoyed numerous romances. His reports of weekends spent at the country estates of the rich and powerful made good reading for his German overlords while misleading them as to the true situation in Britain. To the end the Germans considered him one of their ablest agents and regarded the reports that he and his support net sent from London as among the most valuable intelligence they received. In England, Popov worked with Ian Fleming and is thought to be one of the models Fleming used in creating James Bond.

In his way, Garbo—whose real name was Juan Pujol—was as creative as Fleming. Son of a father who instilled in him the desire to fight tyranny, he set out to do as much destruction to the Nazi cause as he could manage. Instead of going from Madrid to Britain, as his spymaster thought he'd done, he holed up in Lisbon and for nine months prepared a series of letters that he purported to write in England and convey by courier to be mailed to the Germans from Portugal. He had never been to Britain, and all he had to work with now was a tourist guide to England, an out-of-date railway timetable, a large map of the islands and whatever he could glean from bookstalls. He also had his imagination. His letters pictured him reporting from London while his first subagents fed him useful information from the West Country, Glasgow and Liverpool. It was all fiction, but the Germans were royally duped.

Twice Garbo approached the British to serve as an agent for them and twice he was rebuffed. He finally gained their approval in an unexpected way. Bletchley Park's codebreakers had found that the Germans were marshaling their forces to intercept a large convoy that was supposed to have left Liverpool bound for Malta. It was puzzling—there was no such convoy. The British took a different view toward Garbo when they discovered that the expedition, on which the Germans expended a huge waste of effort, was his invention. He was smuggled into Britain in April 1942 and given his code name in recognition of his chameleonlike ability to assume varied roles.

In London, Garbo blossomed. He expanded his network to six agents, all of them imaginary. From his facile pen flowed reports from all six, each revealing an individual style. The stream of information—always with a top spin of *mis*information—he sent to his masters was so bounteous that when gathered together after the war his reports totaled some fifty volumes.

The Liverpool agent, who had reported that nonexistent Malta convoy, came to be seen as a problem. With German aircraft closing the Thames as a convoy destination, Liverpool became the main convoy harbor. An agent there would be expected to see more than the Germans needed to know. Garbo's solution was simply to kill him off. The accounts he transmitted of the agent's declining health and subsequent death, together with the newspaper obituary he sent along, were all fakery. The Germans paid their respects to a widow who existed only in Garbo's imagination.

The most impressive indicator of the trust the Germans placed in Garbo is that they informed him of the code used by the Abwehr intelligence service in their station-to-station communications. When the code was changed, they sent him the new one—saving a great deal of work for Bletchley Park!

Garbo-Pujol's story had a glorious ending. After V-E Day, he honored his pledge to secrecy and slipped away to Venezuela. "I wanted to be forgotten," he said, "to pass unnoticed and to be untraceable." And so he remained for thirty-six years. But then, when the stories of the double agents became public knowledge, writer Nigel West tracked him down. Pujol returned to England to a hero's welcome, received a personal thanks from the Duke of Edinburgh at Buckingham Palace, and told his story in collaboration with West in their popular book *Operation Garbo*.

The XX Committee: Master Tricksters

Behind all this artful hocus-pocus is an equally inventive story. When the war began, the German secret service was bereft of spies in Britain. This was the result of deliberate policy. Ever hopeful of persuading those Aryan-blooded Brits to join, or at least acquiesce in, the German battle against the Bolsheviks, Hitler had forbidden placing any agents in Britain. He wanted to avoid having the unmasking of spies roil the relationship. Only when it became evident that Britain would remain an implacable foe did Hitler allow the creation of a spy network.

The Germans were clumsy in this task. While their agents were generally fluent in English, they were poorly trained in the vagaries of English social norms and quickly gave themselves away. One tried to use his forged ration book to pay for a meal at a restaurant. Another, when billed two-and-six, thought that meant two pounds and six shillings, not two shillings and sixpence. The agents' fake identity documents contained easy-to-spot errors that had been placed there on the sneaky advice of Snow. Germans landing with radios began immediately to send messages from one location as though not knowing that direction finding allowed the British to triangulate on them and track them down. And the Germans trusted agents such as Snow so unreservedly that they gave him the names of other spies, who were summarily captured.

In its first major attempt to place spies in Britain, from September to November 1940, the Abwehr landed twenty-one agents. All but one were captured or gave themselves up. The exception committed suicide.

When the British realized what a prime asset they had in their hands, questions arose as to how to make the most of it. How could they manage the finicky game of supplying information that would satisfy the Abwehr without doing real harm to Britain? In January 1941, representatives of the various services and the Foreign Office came together to establish the Double Cross Committee, also called the Twenty Committee because the Roman letters for twenty depict a double cross. Holding weekly meetings until May 1945, the Double Cross Committee took over responsibility for control of the double agents.

Chosen to head the committee was J. C. Masterman. Before taking on this wartime duty he had made his living as a writer of popular mystery novels. Now he turned his skills to the task of supervising the scripts to be transmitted to the Germans.

The committee started cautiously. Acceptance of the incredible fact that there were no undetected spies in Britain, and therefore no one to alert the Abwehr that its network was comprised of all double agents, was slow to sink in. Also, before becoming too bold with misinformation, the credibility of the double agents had to be established in order to make their spymasters confident they were being well served.

A case officer was assigned to each double agent. Usually this was an older man who could serve as a father figure to the uprooted, scared and often unstable youth under his control. The Twenty Committee saw to it that the agent's course was as authentic as possible. If an agent was requested by his spymaster to report on a specific defense factory, Masterman wrote later, "We arranged, if it was possible, that he should visit the place himself before he replied." The agent "must experience all that he had professed to have done." The committee also saw to it that each agent was provided with an identity card, ration books, clothing coupons, a place to live, a housekeeper and cook, day and night guards, possibly a car and driver, and a radio operator to monitor and transmit his messages.

Care was taken to back up agents' claims. In addition to the war plant explosion to justify Zigzag's reports, a mock generating station was blown up, and at a time when the Nazis were convinced that the U-boats were starving the British, a simulated food storage area was destroyed. Newspaper accounts of the shocking incidents of sabotage made good reading for the Abwehr and earned fresh plaudits for their hard-working agents.

Treading the narrow catwalk of responding to the German spymasters' queries and orders without surrendering information of real value, the committee members made it an ironclad practice never to release new material until it had been cleared by the appropriate authority. At times cautious reviewers crossed out whole sections of proposed scenarios. When the Americans came aboard, the same courtesy was extended to them. General Eisenhower and Admiral Stark were asked to name an army and a navy officer to approve what Double Cross would report about the American forces.

Always in the minds of Masterman and his team was the idea that, as he explained, "at some time in the distant future a great day would come when our agents would be used for a grand and final deception of the enemy." Awaiting that day, they satisfied themselves with less bold deceits.

When invasion of Britain was threatened, the agents accentuated the island's readiness to fend off attackers. The shore defenses were made to seem perceptibly stronger than they were. Warnings went to the Abwehr that antiaircraft resources were being effectively organized to destroy Luftwaffe planes. The numbers of Spitfires available to the RAF were boosted, and the production of new aircraft was exaggerated. German generals were not to be allowed to think the British people would give in tamely; the mood was reported to be defiant, the morale high.

During the Blitz, the Air Ministry gave the committee a special charge: persuade the Luftwaffe to ease off on bombing the cities and concentrate more on the RAF airfields. In order to win the war of attrition, the ministry wanted the German planes to fly where the antiaircraft defenses were strongest—RAF's airfields—and lessen their attacks against the less well protected urban centers. The committee responded by preparing papers purporting to report on a hand-wringing meeting of the Air Raid Review Committee. The papers expressed alarm about poor defenses at the airfields and the inadequacy of the training of their antiaircraft gunners. These were weaknesses that must be corrected: altogether too many planes were being destroyed on the ground. Naturally these distressing papers fell into the hands of Germany's agents.

Did the deception work? An Ultra decrypt told of the German air force's belief that "the British ground organization concentrated in the south of England is the Achilles' heel of the RAF. A planned attack on the ground organization will hit the British air force at its most tender spot."

Similarly, the Twenty Committee was given a role to play in the deception carried out in November 1942 to mislead the Germans about the Allied landings in northwest Africa. The Nazis were aware that something big was coming; they didn't know where. To keep them off guard, the double agents played to Hitler's fears of an attack through Norway and also raised the specter of a landing in northern France. As far as a landing in Africa was concerned, Ultra decrypts showed that the Germans felt sure the Allies lacked the shipping to manage a landing inside the Mediterranean; they believed any landing the Allies might try would be made down the West African coast at Dakar. The deception worked: there was little opposition when the Allies went ashore at Oran and Algiers, inside the Mediterranean, as well as at Casablanca, on the Atlantic coast.

Double Cross was a fragile venture. Everyone feared that each day the cover would be blown and the Germans would wake up to the fact that they were being gulled. Several times that moment came perilously close. Probably the closest call came with the agent code-named Summer. He was another of those German lads who had parachuted into Britain, been captured and chosen to cooperate. But his betrayal weighed on him. One day he half strangled his guard and raced off on the guard's motorbike, heading for the coast. Along the way he came across a canoe he could steal. He lashed it to the bike, apparently thinking he could use it to cross the Channel or the North Sea. Unfortunately for Summer, the bike broke down, and he was recaptured and, to make sure he would make no further attempt, executed. The reliable Snow reported to Summer's spymaster that his agent had come under suspicion by the police and had gone into hiding. So Double Cross survived another day, and in fact kept on fooling the Germans until the war's end.

The question remains: why did the Germans fail to realize that their agents were submitting more misinformation than material of true benefit? Masterman's answer was that much of this vulnerability derived from the Abwehr's flawed system. Each spymaster's prestige, job security and income depended on his having discovered an agent and launched him on his career. If an agent's reliability was questioned, his chief defender invariably turned out to be his own case officer, who would go to any lengths to protect him against doubt and criticism. After all, any case officer who admitted misgivings about his agent could face the prospect of a Gestapo prison or reassignment to the Russian front.

Soon after the war ended, Masterman prepared a report on the Twenty Committee, but for twenty-five years he could not get approval to have it published. His slim volume, *The Double-Cross System*, appeared in 1972.

That was too soon for him to reveal the role of the codebreakers in helping Double Cross succeed. He referred instead to "secret sources" that "permitted us to observe that the reports of our agents were transmitted to Berlin; that they were believed." Hinsley's later history spelled out BP's participation and detailed how Bletchley's codebreakers mastered each advance in the sophistication of the Abwehr's codes, including its conversion to Enigma.

Conquest of the Abwehr Enigma, as Sebag-Montefiore has related in *Enigma*, was another triumph for Dilly Knox and his "girls," the pretty young women he liked to have around him—all quite platonically, it would seem. Using the manual techniques Knox called "rodding," Mavis Lever and Margaret Rock broke the Abwehr cipher on December 8, 1941.

The rewards of the codebreaking went well beyond verifying that the double agents' skewed information was being accepted as truth. The spymasters' questions supplied rich clues as to the direction of the Germans' thoughts and intentions. They also pointed up gaps in the enemy's knowledge that could be exploited. In tandem, the Twenty Committee and Bletchley Park made "turned" spies and Nazi-hating volunteer agents into strong contributors to Allied victory. In Hinsley's words, they turned what the Germans thought to be a major asset into "a substantial liability."

Tricycle's Ignored Pearl Harbor Warning

Another series of incidents involving one of Britain's double agents, the Yugoslav volunteer Dusko Popov, deserves mention here. The first was that previously mentioned raid on Italian warships at Taranto. On a November night in 1940, Britain's fast new aircraft carrier *Illustrious*, guarded by a screen of four cruisers and four destroyers, slipped stealthily through the Mediterranean southeast of the boot of Italy. Just after eight-thirty, her crew began launching the carrier's twenty-one venerable open-cockpit Fairy Swordfish torpedo bombers. Their target lay 170 miles away: the good portion of Italy's war fleet that lay at anchor in Taranto's harbor.

The sneak attack completely surprised the Italians. Swooping in at mast height, the Swordfish sent their missiles crashing into ship after ship. At the cost of just two planes, the British sank or badly damaged three battleships, two cruisers and two destroyers, putting nearly half the Italian navy out of action for a long period. Most important, the raid frightened the Italians into moving their capital ships out of Taranto and into the safer harbor at Naples. The significance was that they were now too far away to be effective against British convoys in the Mediterranean.

In May 1941, the Italians were again surprised—this time by a visit of Japanese naval officers wishing to review their Tripartite partner's naval facilities. Rear Admiral Kobe Abe and his aides wanted to know every possible detail of the British Taranto raid and form in their minds a complete picture of how it was carried out.

Shortly afterward, Popov made one of his regular trips to Lisbon, ostensibly for business but actually to check in with his German spymasters. There he also met with Johnny Jebsen, who, although highly placed in the Abwehr secret service, was revealing himself to be as anti-Nazi as Popov. In fact, Jebsen did become a double agent, code-named Artist, working for the Twenty Committee.

In Lisbon, Jebsen reported on his own puzzling recent mission. He had been a German representative in the group escorting the Japanese at Taranto. It was clear to him, as he informed Popov, that Japan's military leaders were gathering information to guide their own surprise attack by carrier aircraft. But against whom? And where?

The answers, Popov was convinced, came when the top German intelligence officer in Lisbon met with him, instructed him to go to the U.S., asked that he set about establishing a new German spy ring in the country and gave him a questionnaire to which the Germans wanted answers. It was also urgent that Popov travel to Hawaii as soon as he could manage. When he read the questionnaire he could understand why. Of the hundred or so points of interest included, fully a third pertained to Hawaii, with a whole series of questions relating specifically to Pearl Harbor.

Popov was in no doubt, nor were his British colleagues when he returned to London, regarding the significance of these two events. The Japanese were planning a Taranto-style attack on the Pearl Harbor anchorage of U.S. Navy ships. The Germans were doing what they could to supply their Asian partners with useful information.

What to do with this vital intelligence? The British at the time were gingerly seeking to improve relations with the one U.S. agency then assigned to conduct counterespionage activities, the Federal Bureau of Investigation. Masterman and his associates judged that the FBI's credit-seeking director, J. Edgar Hoover, would jump at the chance to be the one to alert the U.S. military to Japan's planned raid. They also believed that Hoover would welcome the opportunity to work with Popov in developing an American equivalent of the Twenty Committee. It seemed right to Popov's British controllers that he himself should meet with Hoover and his FBI staff members, since, as Popov wrote, "the Americans might want to question me at length to extract the last bit of juice."

Ewen Montagu, a member of the committee, has reported in his *Beyond Top Secret Ultra* that the head of British intelligence, Stewart Menzies, called J. Edgar to acquaint him with Popov and prepare the way for his mission. Montagu himself was sent to the U.S. to assist Popov in establishing the American double-agent network.

Yet, because of the fierce clash of personalities, because the turf-protecting FBI was incapable of achieving the broad cooperation of agencies necessitated by a Twenty Committee, the entire venture came to nought.

On August 12, 1941, Popov took a Pan Am flying boat from Lisbon to New York. There he met with the FBI's agent in charge, Percy "Sam" Foxworth. Popov showed Foxworth the two German secrets he thought would be of greatest interest to the Americans. One was the questionnaire. The other was a sample of the microdot system the Nazis were developing as the means to condense a large amount of secret data into a dot that would appear like nothing more than a speck of dirt on the surface of an innocuous-looking letter.

To the question of when Popov could see the director, Foxworth hedged. The meeting couldn't take place for another two weeks. No explanation for the delay was given, but Anthony Summers, a biographer who has charged that Hoover was "a closet homosexual" and "a practicing transvestite," has determined that at the time Hoover was away on vacation with his near-constant companion, Clyde Tolson.

Popov decided he couldn't sit idle for a whole fortnight, and since one of the objectives asked of him on the questionnaire was that he investigate U.S. military bases, "especially in Florida," Popov decided he would drive to Florida in the flashy convertible he'd purchased. He couldn't take along Simone Simon, the French movie star he'd squired in the past. Instead, he would drive south with a new friend, an English model working in New York.

On his second day in Miami, he wrote in his memoir, he was lolling on the beach with his girlfriend when he was approached by a formidable figure in a business suit and tie who asked him to come along to the beach bar. There a second man, "looking like his half-brother," told Popov, "You are registered in this hotel as man and wife with a girl you're not married to."

House detectives, Popov thought, and suggested that he go get his wallet so things could be "cleared up."

The men were not house detectives. They were FBI agents and informed Popov he had broken the Mann Act, which made it a federal offense to transport a woman across state lines for immoral purposes. They did not add that it was one of the least-enforced measures in U.S. law. What they did tell him was that either he send the woman home immediately or he would be taken in, to face a minimum of a year and a day in prison.

Braving the model's annoyance that he had—disguising the real reason for his actions—given in to house detectives, Popov put her on a plane back to New York that same day and drove north alone.

These were the preliminaries to Popov's meeting with Hoover. Popov's memoir placed the meeting in Foxworth's office, with Hoover sitting at Foxworth's desk. The scene was set for a violent clash of personalities: the slim, suave, macho Yugoslav facing the pudgy, fussy but all-powerful American.

"Sit down, Popov," Hoover ordered, with what Popov remembered as "an expression of disgust on his face."

"I'm running the cleanest police organization in the country," Popov quoted Hoover as saying. "You come here from nowhere and within six weeks install yourself in a New York penthouse, chase film stars, break a serious law, and try to corrupt my officers. I'm telling you right now I won't stand for it." He pounded on the desk with his fist "as though to nail his words into my brain."

Popov defended himself. "I'm not a spy who turned playboy. I'm a man who always lived well who happened to become a spy." The Germans, he told Hoover, expected him to live well and would become suspicious if he didn't.

According to his memoir, he also told Hoover, "I did not come to the United States to break the law or to corrupt your organization. I came here to help the war effort." Popov explained about the questionnaire, the Pearl Harbor warning and the microdot system. He finished by dwelling on the plan to organize a double-agent network under FBI control. In describing what would be needed to make the system work, he said, "You cannot expect a crop if you don't put in the seed. You cannot deceive the enemy if you don't . . ."

He stopped. Hoover, giving in to braying laughter, had turned to Foxworth, saying, "That man is trying to teach me my job."

Popov saw that any further discussion was futile. He had communicated the critical information he had come to report. He stood up and walked out.

"Good riddance," Hoover yelled after him.

Popov refused to believe that his mission had been wasted. Several FBI officials, including Foxworth himself, saw the value of what had been handed them. The questionnaire alone should convince any thoughtful leader of its import. Besides, Popov thought, he could count on his British superiors to make the information known to high U.S. government officials.

He went off to Rio de Janeiro to meet with a German spymaster there and deliver a batch of double-cross material of his own devising. On December 7 he was on a passenger liner returning to the U.S. when news about the raid on Pearl Harbor began to trickle in. He anticipated hearing of a great U.S. victory. When instead he learned of the debacle, he couldn't believe his ears. "How, I asked myself, how? We knew they were coming. We knew how they were going to come. Exactly like at Taranto . . . I couldn't credit what I was hearing."

Like others involved in secret operations during the war, Popov was constrained by Britain's Official Secrets Act from telling his story until thirty years later. When his memoir, *Spy/Counterspy*, was published in 1974, it touched off a firestorm of controversy that has still not receded.

Apologists for Hoover and the FBI, for example, deny that Hoover and Popov ever met. The FBI says it has no record of any such meeting. They also claim that whatever was of value in Popov's questionnaire was passed on to the responsible military authorities and even to President Roosevelt. But subsequent research has found that while a paraphrased one-page version of the questionnaire was included in a sheaf of reports circulated by the FBI, it did not include the material on Hawaii.

So why didn't the British, knowing of Popov's troubles with the FBI, pick up the ball? The answer given by Masterman: "Obviously it was for the Americans to make their appreciation and to draw their deductions from the questionnaire, rather than for us to do so. Nevertheless, with fuller knowledge of the case and of the man, we ought to have stressed its importance more than we did."

Ironically, Hoover was much more taken with Popov's news about the microdot system than with the Pearl Harbor warning. In 1946 Hoover published in *Reader's Digest* an article telling how FBI agents had intercepted a Balkan playboy "son of a millionaire" in New York and in going through his possessions had discovered on the front of an envelope this "dot that reflected the light." Under a microscope that magnified the dot's contents two hundred times, he wrote, "we could see that it was an image on a film of a fully-sized typewriter letter, a spy letter with a blood-chilling text."

Hoover was careful not to add that the actual content of the first dot the FBI saw was a copy of the German questionnaire.

Where is the truth in all this? Certainly Popov, writing decades after the events, slipped up on some details and may well have embellished the account. But reading the questionnaire today in the context of what Popov and the British were trying to convey does raise the question of how those references to Hawaii and to Pearl Harbor could have failed, somewhere along the line of recipients, to set off alarm bells.

The FBI did, Montagu has written, use Tricycle's name in sending messages to his spymaster. But they were "low-grade, trumpery stuff that almost any half-witted agent could have got." Further, "It is almost impossible to believe—they never let Tricycle know what they had sent or what the Germans had asked." At the Twenty Committee's request, Popov was allowed to return to Britain and in "the greatest instance of cold-blooded courage that I have ever been in contact with" he met with his spymaster in Lisbon, explained away his American failures and again became a key member of the committee.

Postwar events also show that Popov's British masters did not share Hoover's disdain of him. Hinsley rates him as one of the three "most valuable" double agents in Britain's cause. In recognition of the daring and dangerous but vitally important work he carried out, the British promoted him to the honorary rank of colonel, granted him British citizenship and awarded him both the Distinguished Service Medal and the Order of the British Empire.

Jebsen, however, was arrested by the Gestapo, for reasons that are not clear. This was a development of great concern to the Twenty Committee because of what he could reveal. But he was killed, presumably trying to escape, and honorably carried his secrets with him.

Amid all the controversies swirling around Popov, this is for certain: he went to his grave believing that J. Edgar Hoover was "the person responsible for the disaster at Pearl Harbor."

8   The U.S. Tackles Japan's Codes

WHEN Secretary of State Stimson sniffed at the idea of reading other gentlemen's mail and closed down Herbert Yardley's Black Chamber, American cryptology seemed to have come to an end. It had not. Quietly, other agencies, from the FBI and the Federal Communications Commission to the army and navy, carried on the task, independently of each other and often involving rancorous internecine turf wars.

Inheriting Yardley's files, the U.S. Army Signal Corps in 1930 created the Signal Intelligence Service (SIS). To head it up, the corps hired William Friedman, whom many consider the greatest cryptologic genius of all time.

Friedman came to code work by a serendipitous route. Born in Russia in 1891, he was brought to the U.S. as an infant. His family settled in Pittsburgh, and as a high school youth, he became caught up in a Jewish "back to the land" movement which led him, when he was a graduate student at Cornell University, to plan a career in plant genetics. In 1915 an eccentric millionaire cotton merchant named George Fabyan went to Cornell in search of a geneticist to work at his Riverbank Laboratory, near Chicago, on improving crop strains. Friedman, recommended by one of his professors, became head of Riverbank's Department of Genetics and involved himself in such Fabyan projects as planting oats by the light of the moon to see whether the phases made any difference in their growth.

Fabyan, who had the wealth to support his flights of fancy, also became intrigued by a woman whose research had convinced her that Francis Bacon had written the works attributed to William Shakespeare and, what was more, had included coded messages to that effect in the early folios of the plays and poems. She claimed the secret messages also revealed that he was the illegitimate son of Queen Elizabeth I and the rightful heir to the British throne. To fill out his team conducting this research, Fabyan hired Elizebeth Smith, a Hillsdale College graduate, whose mother had insisted on the unusual spelling of her name to prevent its being shortened to *Eliza*.

The theory of the Bacon codes was based on variations in the typefaces in the folios. Handy with a camera, Friedman helped the project by making photo enlargements of the type fonts. He was drawn to the cryptographic work. "Something in me," he commented later, "found an outlet."

Since Europe was then at war and American military involvement was becoming increasingly likely, Elizebeth and William foresaw the need for the U.S. to become more proficient in secret communications. Ever the opportunist, Fabyan enthusiastically supported this new phase of their research. For a time Riverbank was the only organization in the country skilled in deciphering coded messages. Their mutual professional and personal interests led Elizebeth and William to marriage in 1917.

When, later that year, the army created its Cipher Bureau, Fabyan arranged for the Friedmans to conduct classes in cryptography for army officers. A famous photo from that era shows Elizebeth and William surrounded by their eighty bright young students in khaki. The students' faces are turned either directly toward the camera or away from it to register a bilateral coded message: Bacon's aphorism "Knowledge is power."

As texts for his classes, Friedman began writing a series of booklets on cryptography—one of them with Elizebeth as collaborator. Impressed, the army brass offered him a first lieutenant's commission. He spent the last five months of World War I on General Pershing's staff in France, concentrating on breaking German codes. The experience gave him ideas that subsequently he was to use with great effect. On his return to Riverbank he published a new booklet, *The Index of Coincidence and Its Application to Cryptography*. David Kahn has written that it "must be regarded as the most important single publication in cryptology. It took the science into a new world."

Cryptanalysis had, previously, been rather an occult process in which the would-be breaker pored over a ciphertext waiting for some intuitive insight to lead to a solution. Friedman's "new world" consisted of methodically applying a statistical and mathematical science to codebreaking. His new booklet added a useful technique. He had observed that if the horizontal lines of a message are arranged so that the letters are placed in vertical rows precisely below each other, now and then the same letter will appear, the one directly beneath the other. This coincidence, he had determined, will vary in frequency with each language. In English it occurs in 6.67 columns of every 100. This was a step forward in cryptanalysis that gave Friedman a tool in analyzing the new machine-encoded ciphers when they began to appear.

During the 1920s both Friedmans were engaged in code work for the government. William made national headlines when he cracked the codes of the conspirators in the Teapot Dome scandal and helped send several of them to prison. He also became chief codebreaker for the War Department, where he developed the reputation of being like Midas, except that everything he touched turned not into gold but into plaintext. Elizabeth, in addition to starting a family, helped the Department of Justice and later the Treasury Department in efforts to enforce Prohibition. She broke the increasingly sophisticated codes of the rum-running syndicate and testified against them in well-publicized court cases.

When, in the autumn of 1929, William became chief of the newly created Signal Intelligence Service, he was empowered to begin building a cryptographic staff. He requested mathematicians, and chance gave him Frank Rowlett, a high school mathematics teacher from Virginia, and two graduate mathematicians from the City College of New York, Solomon Kullback and Abraham Sinkov. Also foreseeing the need for a translator fluent in Japanese, Friedman was swayed by a congressman to hire his nephew, John Hurt.

There were only five of them, but what a team they turned out to be! Friedman adroitly challenged his staff, first by having them study his cryptography writings, then by giving them relatively easy ciphers before moving on to more difficult examples. He threw at them a Great War German cipher that he, with a French cryptanalyst, had had considerable trouble in cracking. The team surprised him by the speed with which they broke it. He turned them loose on the Hebern mechanical enciphering device, which had taken him six weeks of intense concentration to solve; they broke it in less than a month. They were ready, Friedman decided, to take on "real work": breaking the Japanese nonmachine "pencil and paper" codes then current. To Hurt's delight the cryptographers were soon giving him plaintext to translate and interpret. Sinkov recalled of Friedman, "His teaching was such that we developed on our own."

The second heavy responsibility placed on the Friedman five has already been mentioned: the work of developing secure cryptographic systems for the U.S. that resulted in the Sigaba M-134. Because of security restrictions, Friedman couldn't reveal even to his own lawyers the nature of the patents he was seeking. He had to write his own briefs.

Conquest of the Red Machine

As the 1930s unfolded, Friedman and his SIS team faced the challenge of breaking into the code machines the Japanese Foreign Office had introduced. First to be tackled was the Type A machine, the Alphabetical Typewriter 91.

Rowlett, in his memoir, *The Story of Magic*, gave a progressive account of how the Friedman team analyzed the Japanese machine and slowly solved it. They began by observing a quirk in the system. In their new machine ciphers the Japanese used the Roman alphabet to spell out phonetic equivalents of Japanese words, and in this new machine cipher, six letters occurred with high frequency, while the other twenty appeared less frequently. Friedman and his young analysts determined that the six consisted of the five vowels plus the letter *V*. The SIS was able to exploit this discovery by looking for patterns. One such pattern was that in the Japanese phonetics the *Y* was always followed by one of the other vowels and often by a doubling of them—*YUU* or *YOO*—and it was often preceded by *R* or *K*—*RYUU, RYOO, KYUU, KYOO*. Another pattern was the combination of the letters that, when deciphered, produced *oyobi*, the Japanese word for the English "and." In their analysis the Friedman crew noticed that their descriptions of these identifiable combinations held for only forty-two positions; then the machine introduced a stepping pattern, moving the whole process forward to a new equivalent of the letters. From those beginnings they were able gradually to open up the entire encoding system and produce plaintext from the messages.

Type A, they decided, was a rotor machine, a Japanese variation on the principles of the Enigma. Its encipherment mechanism included two rotors, each of which had twenty-six electrical contacts wired around the circumference of one of its sides. There was also a gear wheel with forty-seven pins projecting from it. A unique feature was that the gear wheel pins were removable. If a pin was in place, it moved the rotors forward with one stroke of the typewriter keys. If it was removed, the machine jumped over that contact, giving the machine an irregular movement meant to foil cryptanalysts.

The machine simply didn't have enough complexity to withstand the SIS team's attack. They were able gradually to open up the entire encoding system and produce plaintext from Type A's messages.

While solving its riddles, the cryptanalysts referred to it often as "the Japanese code machine." They realized that this term was so descriptive that its use might result in an inadvertent security break. They gathered together to settle on a cover name, and eventually the discussion got around to considering colors. "All of us were in agreement," Rowlett wrote, "that the first color of the spectrum was an excellent choice as a cover name for the first cipher machine that we had solved which was actually used for enciphering official messages of a foreign power. And from this moment on, the Japanese diplomatic cipher machine was always referred to as the 'Red Machine.' "

In short order the five team members began to flood the president, the secretary of state and the chiefs of the army and navy with John Hurt's translations of Japanese diplomatic exchanges. Friedman, incidentally, had overcome the usual interservice animosities and developed a friendly, mutually beneficial collaboration with Commander Laurance F. Safford, his counterpart in charge of the navy cryptologists.

Appreciation of the team's exploits took the practical form of increased funding for IBM processing machines, a move to more spacious quarters and an increased staff, including the hiring of bright young women such as Genevieve Grotjan.

The Breaking of Purple

In late 1938 and early 1939, Friedman and his expanded team began deciphering Red messages announcing the distribution of Red's replacement, *angoo-ki taipu B*, or "cipher machine Type B." They hoped that the new machine would be only a modification of Red, but a new series of messages sent in by U.S. intercept stations beginning on March 20, 1939, dashed that hope. They proved unbreakable by the methods applied to Red cryptanalysis.

As the Americans were to learn, slowly and painfully, Japanese cryptographers had built on their experience with Red and had perfected a machine whose principles were completely different from those in the German Enigma or other code machines and presented complexities greater than those of the Enigma.

Again Friedman met with his team to choose a new cover name. Sticking to the light spectrum, they chose the color Purple.

Ronald Clark, in his biography of Friedman, *The Man Who Broke Purple*, told of the felicitous decision made early in 1939 by General Joseph O.

Mauborgne, chief of the Signal Corps. Disturbed by the slow progress being made in solving the Purple machine, Mauborgne saw that Friedman was too burdened by administrative details and work on the Sigaba to be effective in the attack. In February 1939, consequently, he ordered Friedman to drop all other duties and concentrate on Purple cryptanalysis. "Friedman," wrote Clark, "now began the most acute eighteen months of intellectual effort he was ever to undertake."

Rowlett's memoir suggested that Friedman had much less to do with the cracking of Purple than did Rowlett and other members of the SIS. However it was, progress did come at a brisker pace. Japanese errors helped. Reliance on ceremonial diplomatic forms of address such as "I have the honor to inform your excellency" handed the analysts cribs of probable plaintext to test against the ciphertext. Purple messages sent to embassies equipped only with the Red machine were obligingly repeated in that code, offering another angle from which to unravel the cipher. And on occasion a sender would admit having erred in one of his settings and re-send the message correctly, supplying the analysts with an insight into the proper setting.

Exacting analysis also showed that Purple offered the same structural opening as Red. Its system included a subsequence of six often-used letters enciphered separately from the other twenty. Unlike in the Red, though, these six could include any letter rather than just the vowels plus V. Rowlett drew up plans for a machine that would be an equivalent of the mechanism the Japanese used for enciphering and deciphering the sixes. Friedman, impressed with the plan, recommended that SIS employ Captain Leo Rosen, who had joined the Reserve Officer Training Corps at MIT while studying to become an electrical engineer.

The hiring of Rosen turned out to be another fortunate choice. Very quickly after being briefed on the nature of the Purple machine and of Rowlett's plan for cracking the sixes, he saw what was needed. This was nothing more than the use of standard telephone switchboard stepping switches. The switches were acquired, the "Six Buster" machine was built, and it did its job perfectly.

One of Safford's cooperating navy analysts, young Harry L. Clark, has been credited with raising the question of whether the Japanese, in their new machine, might be using an entirely different enciphering mechanism than those of other code machines. Could it be that the machine was based on the same stepping switches Rosen had applied in the Six Buster? Rowlett, Rosen and the others thought so, but before that question could be answered they had to gain a great deal more knowledge about the groups of twenty letters. Being able to tell where the sixes' letters occurred in a message helped by pinning down likely cribs. What was needed was a much broader base of plaintext equivalents of the twenties. The team made up large worksheets on which they recorded from each day's intercepts the most probable pairings of plaintext and ciphertext equivalents.

The process took most of a painstaking year. Then Genevieve "Gene" Grotjan, who had been doing the monotonous task of compiling indicator worksheets, made the breakthrough. Rowlett has described being in his office conferring with colleagues Bob Ferner and Albert Small when Grotjan broke in, visibly excited. She wanted to show them something in her worksheets. Leading them to her desk, she indicated where she had drawn circles around selected plaintext and ciphertext equivalents. Further, she had circled the same relationships on other worksheets. What she had found were *consistent relationships*, proofs that the coded letters were invariably linked with the plaintexts. As Rowlett characterized her discovery, it was "the first case of positive evidence that we were on the proper course to a full recovery of the Purple machine."

After she had pointed to the last example, Rowlett recalled, "she stepped back from her desk, with her eyes beaming through her rimless glasses, obviously thrilled by her discovery." The others immediately realized the importance of what she had found. "It was a beautiful example," Rowlett wrote, "of what we had hoped our search would uncover."

He described what followed: "Small promptly started dancing around her desk, raising his arms like a victorious prizefighter, and yelled 'Whoopee.' Ferner, who was usually very quiet and not very much inclined to show enthusiasm, clapped his hands, shouting 'Hurrah! Hurrah!' I could not resist jumping up and down and waving my arms above my head and exclaiming 'That's it! That's it! Gene has found what we've been looking for!'"

They made so much noise that Friedman came out of his office and asked, "What's this all about?"

Rowlett led Friedman to Grotjan's desk and tried to let her tell the story of her discovery. But she was so overwhelmed, and by now weeping in her excitement, that he had to take over.

Friedman carefully examined each of the areas and grasped their implications. He saw that with this break his team could go forward with actually building a replica of the Purple machine. "Suddenly he looked tired and placed his hands on the edge of the desk and leaned forward, resting his weight on them," Rowlett recalled. "I pulled a chair forward and offered it to him. Seated, he addressed everyone in the room: 'The recovery of this machine will go down as a milestone in cryptanalytic history. Without a doubt we are now experiencing one of the greatest moments of the Signal Intelligence Service.' "

The team forged ahead toward producing a clone of the Purple machine. Further work along the lines of Grotjan's discovery confirmed what Rosen and his colleagues had suspected: the devices that caused Purple to advance at regular intervals from one encipherment stage to another were stepping switches, both for the sixes' subsequence and for the twenties'. "Rosen," Rowlett wrote, "promptly started to prepare the layout of a complete cipher machine to duplicate the cryptographic functions of the Purple machine."

Postwar comparisons with the real Purple machine verified that Rosen's replica reproduced the original's complex wiring, its use of stepping switches, its intricate plugboard. If ever there was a feat of visionary engineering, this was it: to imagine the inner workings of an intricate secret machine and produce a copy that was so close an approximation of the original that of the several hundred connections in the clone, only two were wired differently from the Japanese machine. As various commentators have noted, the achievement surpassed those of the Poles and the British, who had commercially available models to serve as guides.

On September 25, 1940, just two days after Germany, Italy and Japan had signed the Tripartite Pact pledging all three to mutual support, Rowlett sat at the keyboard of the new machine in Washington's Munitions Building and started typing the ciphertext of a message. "The machine performed beautifully," he wrote in his memoir, "producing a letter-perfect plaintext."

Once again the SIS had opened a secret window through which the U.S. could spy on Japan's diplomats. As we shall see, however, the eventual consequences of the conquest of Purple were to go far beyond listening in to diplomatic chitchat.

Documentary sources make it clear that William Friedman was not the man who broke Purple. He himself said, "Naturally this was a collaborative, cooperative effort on the part of all the people concerned. No one person is responsible for the solution, nor is there any single person to whom the major share of the credit should go."

Nevertheless, the strain of those eighteen months took their toll on him. In December 1940 he collapsed and was rushed to the neuropsychiatric ward of the army's Walter Reed Hospital. He remained there until March

1941 and returned to full-time duty only on April 1. By then additional Purple replicas had been built and distributed to Allied nerve centers. The flow of information meant that both Britain and the U.S. could navigate the twists and turns of Japanese diplomacy.

General Mauborgne thought of Friedman's team as "the magicians" and gave the whole U.S. codebreaking operation the cover name of *Magic*. Later in the war the English code name *Ultra* began also to be applied to the U.S. program. In these pages, to avoid confusion, *Ultra* has been applied to decrypts of the Enigma and *Magic* to the success over Purple.

Tracking the Imperial Navy

During the 1930s the U.S. Navy employed the largest cryptologic branch among the U.S. military services. This made sense in view of the navy's responsibility to provide the first line of defense against the mounting threat of Japanese naval power. Navy leaders needed to organize the strongest effort possible to decode the signals of the Imperial Navy. But these were times when isolationist America wanted to avoid a repeat of the Great War and also when the American economy was in the grip of the Great Depression. The consequent lack of funding starved U.S. military services almost to impotency.

With its share of the inadequate defense budget the navy nevertheless built and operated a circle of radio intercept stations around the Pacific Rim and conducted a three-phase cryptologic program. One was direction finding—the use of triangulation to locate specific Japanese transmitters. The second was traffic analysis—determining from merely the sending of messages and the call signs of the senders the movements of the Japanese fleet. The third was cryptanalysis—the attempt to penetrate the content of the messages themselves. The headquarters of the cryptanalytic program was based in Washington, with outposts at Pearl Harbor and at Cavite on the island of Luzon in the Philippines.

The navy took another foresighted step. It assigned bright young officers to three-year stints in Japan, expecting them to use this duty to become familiar with the Japanese people and to develop fluency in the Japanese language.

For all the navy's prescience, however, it placed serious obstacles in the way of any career officer interested in cryptology. One was the low esteem, even contempt, in which intelligence work was generally held; time spent at it was viewed as a detour, not a step forward. Another was the encrusted rule that an officer could put in only a certain time of desk work before going on sea duty. All through the 1930s, the main source of continuity in navy cryptanalysis work was supplied by a civilian, "Miss Aggie"—Agnes Meyer Driscoll, who stayed put in Washington, did whatever codebreaking she could and trained the young officers as they came and went.

So it took a strong element of determination and grit for the navy officer to persist in pursuing code work. Fortunately for the U.S., men such as Edwin Layton, Thomas Dyer and Wesley "Ham" Wright possessed that determination and grit. So did Joseph John Rochefort.

Rochefort began his navy duties as an enlisted man and rose, by sheer ability, to head the navy's cryptographic section from 1925 to 1927. Ordinarily the navy was sending only bachelors on the three-year Japanese-learning assignment. It made an exception in Rochefort's case: in 1929, despite his being a married man with a child, he went to Japan for three years as a language student. After another half year in naval intelligence he spent the next eight years on sea duty.

In June 1941, Rochefort returned to cryptology. He was given command of the radio intelligence unit in Hawaii, to which he applied the cover name of the Combat Intelligence Unit. Within the service it became more familiarly known as Station "Hypo"—the standard name for *H* in the International Signal Code. While Rochefort's command included one hundred officers and enlisted men, the great majority were assigned to direction finding and traffic analysis. Only a small number were left over to concentrate on cryptanalysis.

A contest of wills was already forming between the cryptologic staff of the Washington naval headquarters and the staffs of the two outposts, the one known as Cast, from the *C* of Cavite, and Rochefort's Hypo on Oahu. The Washington operation, known as Op-20-G, wanted to maintain overall control. Its chiefs decided which Japanese codes the other two stations would be assigned to work on and which ones it would hold to itself.

Japan's navy relied not on cipher machines but on codes in the old sense: the use of codebooks in which a vocabulary of thousands of information elements such as *harbor* or *battleship* were given letter or numerical equivalents—98765, say, or 12345. The Japanese went beyond merely using the codebooks. When a message was encoded in its four- or five-number equivalents, it was subjected to a superencipherment, a further scrambling of the code numbers. The cryptanalyst faced the formidable task of stripping away this first barrier before getting at the code groups themselves.

The Japanese used a diversity of codes with varying degrees of cryptographic security. The two toughest were the "flag officers' system" and the main naval standby, which the U.S. Navy cryptologists identified as JN-25 because it was the twenty-fifth of the naval codes they had worked on. Lesser codes dealt with administrative matters, personnel changes, weather forecasts and the like.

In an unfortunate turn, as subsequent events proved, Rochefort's Hypo unit was assigned work on the flag officers' system, while only OP-20-G and Cast were responsible for trying to solve the JN-25 code. Washington also monopolized work on a lesser code, J-19, even though this was the code used by the Japanese consul in Honolulu. In another strange twist, the Cast operation in the Philippines had a Purple machine, and three were sent to the British, but the one for Hawaii was not scheduled to arrive until late December 1941.

Rear Admiral Edwin T. Layton, head of intelligence for the Hawaiian commander Admiral Husband E. Kimmel, told in his revealing memoir, *And I Was There*, how Kimmel was, in July 1941, cut out of the loop of those receiving Magic information, ostensibly for security reasons, and how his own pleas to receive Magic decrypts were rebuffed.

These quixotic assignments of responsibilities helped precipitate the coming disaster.

Rochefort and his command's efforts were wasted on the flag officers' code. Neither they nor any other Allied group ever succeeded in breaking it—partly because it was used so sparingly they never had a sufficient number of intercepts to work with. One of the most troubling what-ifs of the war was subsequently raised by Layton, Rochefort's superior: what if Rochefort, whom Layton considered the navy's most gifted performer in both linguistic and cryptanalytic terms, had been concentrating on JN-25, with which neither OP-20-G nor Cast was making serious headway? Layton's answer was that if the mass of JN-25 intercepts that awaited decoding in Washington had been given to Rochefort to penetrate, the catastrophe at Pearl Harbor could have been averted. The same was true of the J-19 code. When it was eventually tackled, after the fact, its messages were found to include highly specific exchanges between Tokyo and the Oahu consulate about U.S. warships docked at Pearl Harbor.

Even though Rochefort's team had to derive most of their intelligence from direction finding and traffic analysis, they went at their work in a manner that differed sharply from the general practices then in force on Oahu. Even in 1941, with war an increasing menace, slack peacetime ways were the rule. In many units the men were on duty only one day out of four; a commander who tried to impose a change to one day out of three met with almost an insurrection, especially on the part of the servicemen's wives. Rochefort, by contrast, aware of the Imperial Navy's ever more belligerent actions, drove himself and his men hard. As W. J. Holmes has written in *Double-Edged Secrets*, his record of those times, "Had I not witnessed it, I never would have believed that any group of men was capable of such sustained mental effort under such constant pressure for such a length of time."

With estimates based on the limited means of Sigint available to Hypo, Layton and Rochefort did their best to keep Admiral Kimmel informed about the Japanese military's plans. They could tell him with confidence that the Imperial Navy had organized a powerful force in Taiwan and Indochina. And where might this force strike? The intelligence officers' best guess was that it was poised to conquer Southeast Asia and the Netherlands East Indies.

Their estimate made sense. The English, Dutch and Americans had imposed an oil embargo on Japan. The Imperial war machine faced declining energy reserves. Japan's most likely response, the officers told Kimmel, was to seize the oil fields of the East Indies.

Layton and Rochefort were also intensely aware that the Japanese were moving southward, island jumping in their progress toward Australia. They had moved into the Marshall Islands southwest of Hawaii. The intelligence officers saw the Marshalls as the most likely base for an attack on Oahu. On their say-so, Kimmel used his inadequate air fleet to patrol more to the south and west than to the north.

The guesses by Washington ranged all over the Pacific map. The navy's chief war planner dogmatically asserted the attack would fall on the Soviet Union's easternmost provinces. Others speculated the coast of California, the Panama Canal or the Aleutian Islands, off Alaska. In a memorandum submitted to President Roosevelt ten days before the attack, Admiral Stark warned that it might fall on sites as remote as Thailand, Malaya or the Burma Road, but made no mention of Pearl Harbor. The strongest response by Washington's top brass, however, was the decision to strengthen the air fleet under the command of General Douglas MacArthur in the Philippines. A large flight of B-17 bombers was sent from the West Coast to the Philippines, with stopovers on Midway and Wake Islands. As an indication of how little anyone in power expected an attack on Pearl Harbor, Kimmel was ordered to load half his fighter planes onto the two aircraft carriers available to him—the third was in the U.S. for an equipment refit—and deliver them to Midway and Wake. There the fighters would await the B-17s and escort them on their way to the Philippines. A smaller squadron of bombers was also to fly to Oahu.

For Layton and Rochefort, the most worrisome aspect of their reporting to Kimmel was that they could not determine with any certainty the whereabouts of Japan's aircraft carrier force. They could not know it, but they were being tricked. Fake radio traffic made the men both at Cast and Hypo believe that the carriers were in home waters. In fact, the carriers had been ordered to observe radio silence, so there was no direction finding or traffic analysis call signs to give their location away. Instead of idling close to home, the carriers, in the midst of their huge escorting fleet, were sneaking down toward Hawaii.

The Debacle at Pearl Harbor

The question still rankles those who lived through the experience: how, with Purple solved and three different signals intelligence units concentrating on Japanese naval codes, did the U.S. fail to anticipate Commander Isoroku Yamamoto's Hawaiian surprise that put out of action a large part of the U.S. Pacific Fleet and cost 2,403 American lives?

William Friedman himself gave the most succinct answer: "There were no messages which can be said to have disclosed exactly *where* and *when* the attack would be made"—at least not among the messages that were decrypted.

In retrospect, of course, investigators probing into the disaster found reams of evidence that *should* have awakened U.S. commands to the possibility of the assault. But the definitive proof that was necessary to pierce through lax peacetime attitudes and clouds of uncertainty never came.

Books and long Internet articles have been written supposedly "documenting" that American inaction was the deliberate result of a Franklin Roosevelt "conspiracy" to plunge the U.S. into war on the side of his friend Winston Churchill. These writers have characterized FDR as a "Communist" and a "traitor" who knew the Japanese plans but purposely avoided taking action because he wanted them to come to fruition.

Historian John Keegan has said these charges "defy logic." They fail to mention that to have achieved so malign a purpose, Roosevelt would have had to persuade the army chief of staff George Marshall and navy chief

Harold Stark to go along with him. Professor Gordon W. Prange, who spent thirty-seven years researching *At Dawn We Slept*, dismissed the conspiracy charges as "an absurdity." Ronald Lewin labeled them "moonshine." In her respected work *Pearl Harbor: Warning and Decision*, Roberta Wohlstetter wrote that hostile critics of FDR "confuse his frank recognition of the *desirability* of an incident with *knowledge* of the Pearl Harbor attack." In his 2001 book, *Roosevelt's Secret War*, Joseph E. Persico reported on his research showing that on the night before Pearl Harbor, FDR actually drafted an appeal to Emperor Hirohito "to join him in a statesman-to-statesman effort to stave off disaster"—hardly the act of a leader hoping to see that disaster happen.

The sacrifice of ships and sailors at Pearl Harbor is most honestly seen as the necessary price paid for shaking off the complacency that beset the public and military alike. The Japanese timed their attack to fall on a Sunday morning because they knew full well that the American navy wanted, like everyone else, to enjoy its weekend. More ships would lie in port then than at any other time of the week, and the guard systems would be least manned.

Even so, the codebreakers came agonizingly close to ringing the alarm bells. All during 1941 the Purple decrypts kept U.S. leaders informed on the instructions Tokyo's Foreign Office was sending its embassy in Washington. To read these messages is to glimpse a group of Japanese diplomats caught between the harsh demands of the military and the unwillingness of the Americans to accede to the terms the embassy was empowered to offer. Purple told of Japan's foreign minister desperately seeking some concession from the U.S., knowing the alternative was that "a lamentable situation will occur." This sense of urgency was heightened after October 16, when the moderate government of Prince Konoe fell and was replaced by the jingoistic Tojo cabinet. On November 26 the U.S. State Department presented its conditions for resolving the negotiations. Knowing these would be unacceptable to Tojo, Tokyo's diplomats pleaded with their embassy staff to secure some crumb of a compromise; otherwise "the fate of the Empire hangs by the thread of a few days" and "things are automatically going to happen." Finally, on December 6, Tokyo warned the Washington staffers to expect a long reply to the American proposal. It came in fourteen parts, the last of which was intercepted at three a.m. on December 7. Merely rehashing the Tojo cabinet's intransigence, it ends with the ominous words that "it was impossible to reach an agreement through further negotiations." A four thirty a.m. intercept instructed the ambassador to "submit to the United States government (if possible the Secretary of State) our reply to the United States at 1:00 p.m. on the seventh, your time." And at five a.m. the final message came through, ordering the embassy to destroy its code materials.

The Americans in Washington who saw these decrypts understood their meaning. Roosevelt himself said, "This means war." But from that point on, an incredible series of mistakes blocked effective response to the warnings.

FDR, failing to notice that the one p.m. deadline was just past dawn at Pearl Harbor, followed the general line of thinking that the attack would come on Southeast Asia. So, while he could have called Hawaii on his scrambler phone, he did not, because Pearl Harbor seemed an unlikely target for the Japanese.

Admiral Harold Stark, chief of Naval Operations, could have called Kimmel, but not realizing that the Hawaiian commander was no longer receiving Purple decrypts, he presumed Kimmel was as fully informed about the crisis as he was.

General Marshall could have used his scrambler phone to call General Walter Short, his commander in Hawaii. Not trusting the phone's security, however, he asked that his warning message be sent by radio. It happened that radio interference that morning was bad; Marshall's message went by commercial telegraph to San Francisco and from there was relayed seven hours later. A messenger on a motorcycle delivered it to General Short only after the Japanese planes had completed their first run.

In Hawaii, as well, the alarm was nullified by slipups and errors of judgment. Two privates manning a radar station on Oahu detected the oncoming Japanese planes and phoned in their report. But the lieutenant on duty knew that the flight of B-17s from the mainland was due to arrive that morning, presumed that these were causing the blips on the privates' screen and told them to forget it. The navy had both air and ship patrols operating. Both reported seeing unescorted submarines and launched attacks against what were later revealed to be Japanese midget subs trying to augment the mayhem at Pearl Harbor. The officer in the Naval Operations office, hearing these reports, knew immediately that "we were in it." Before he could rouse an official response, though, the Zeros were already incoming.

One possible warning in which the cryptanalysts of OP-20-G in Washington placed great store came to be known as the "winds execute" message. The Japanese had signaled to their outposts that in the case of an emergency, such as cutting off diplomatic relations, they would add to regular radio weather forecasts a "hidden phrase code" calling for the destruction of code machines and materials. The code for the termination of relations with the U.S. was "east wind rain," that for the USSR "north wind cloudy," and that for Britain "west wind clear." Ralph T. Briggs, then a twenty-seven-year-old U.S. Navy communications intelligence technician in Washington, has sworn that he did receive the fateful words "*higashi no kase ame*"—"east wind rain"—embedded in a Tokyo weather broadcast on the morning of December 4. Briggs recalled recognizing the message's importance and reported that with his "heart pounding and adrenaline flowing," he informed his superiors and received the congratulations "Well done" from Captain Laurance Safford, founder of the navy's Communications Intelligence operation. Together, Briggs and Safford thought they had produced the bit of vital information that would alert the navy to the coming attack.

From that point on, however, the story of Briggs's intercept becomes clouded in mists of confusion and, it would appear, deliberate cover-up. Higher officials in the chain of command failed to act on the message and later denied receiving it. Briggs's report on the message disappeared from the files.

In planning the Pearl Harbor raid, Admiral Yamamoto saw it as the way out of a personal dilemma. A blunt bullet of a man who had been a language student at Harvard and had served as a naval attaché in Washington, he understood America and the Americans better than his colleagues and had argued in prewar councils that to provoke war with the U.S. was folly. "The United States would never stop fighting," he was quoted as saying, "and ultimately we would not be able to escape defeat." Yet he also came to realize that the momentum toward war could not be stopped. He persuaded himself that by destroying the U.S. fleet in Hawaiian waters, he could strengthen the isolationist spirit in the U.S. and weaken the will to fight, generating a desire for a negotiated peace. As Admiral Samuel Eliot Morison wrote in his multivolume *History of United States Naval Operations in World War II*, Yamamoto "knew that he must annihilate the United States Fleet in 1942 or lose the war."

The attack on Pearl Harbor, carried out by a task force under the command of Vice Admiral Chuichi Nagumo, achieved nearly everything Yamamoto had hoped for. His planes sank or seriously damaged eighteen U.S. naval vessels, including eight battleships at anchor. Because General Walter Short, the army commander, had interpreted the warnings from Washington as orders to guard against sabotage from within the islands rather than attacks from without, he had grouped his aircraft in tight circles to make them easier to guard, allowing Yamamoto's raiders to destroy them en masse. And the Japanese admiral could take satisfaction in knowing his planes had put out of action broad ranks of servicemen who died or were seriously wounded.

Yamamoto had secured *nearly* everything he sought. He remained discontent, however, for two reasons. He had been led to believe the leaders in Tokyo would declare war before his planes struck. That was the plan, but it was thwarted by a series of blunders and delays. The admiral felt his honor had been sullied, and he knew the effect on Americans would be the opposite of desiring to negotiate a peace settlement. His second disappointment was that the U.S carriers were absent—they were on their plane-delivering mission to Midway and Wake.

The Japanese celebrated Pearl Harbor as a great victory. As for the U.S., the wound to the American psyche seemingly could be healed only by the cashiering of Kimmel and Short, the injustice of which is richly documented in Layton's memoir, and by the interminable investigative commissions and embittered congressional hearings that filled thirty-nine volumes of discordant testimony.

Yet in the long sweep of history it was a huge miscalculation by the Japanese. Admiral Morison's history summed up the attack as a "strategic imbecility." To have an enemy plot a vicious sneak attack even as its diplomats were carrying out a pretense of polite negotiations united the American people as nothing else could have. Pearl Harbor cleaned the decks of questionable commanders and brought in bright, energetic new leaders. It accelerated the American productive machine in turning out the masses of matériel that in the end would overwhelm the enemy's resources. It dashed the Japanese hope that they could achieve in the 1940s what they had accomplished in the 1905 settlement with the Russians: an advantageous peace without any attempt at invading enemy territory. As for its real effect on American naval power, the Japanese, as a U.S. admiral told Gordon Prange, "only destroyed a lot of old hardware." In fact, the raid failed to accomplish even that. The shallow waters of the anchorage permitted the salvage and repair of most of the crippled vessels; only two battleships—*Arizona* and *Oklahoma*—were beyond recovery. And the obvious surprise of the attack confirmed the Japanese in the belief that their codes were inviolable.

An odd corollary to the Pearl Harbor raid came in the Philippines, where Douglas MacArthur was the commander in charge. The Japanese planned their raid on the American bases on Luzon to follow as soon after Pearl Harbor as they could manage. But there was a two-hour time zone difference. In addition, fog delayed the departure of the mission. Consequently, MacArthur and his aides had nine hours to prepare for the Japanese assault. Yet they were strangely dormant, not even dispersing the aircraft lined up on their airfields. Dwight Eisenhower subsequently told an interviewer that MacArthur, his former commander, had some notion that the Japanese would not attack the Philippines. But attack they did, and their surprise was complete. "We still could not believe," a Japanese flier later recalled, "that the Americans did not have fighters in the air waiting for us." The U.S. lost more than one hundred planes—a good portion of the Philippines force—and suffered more than two hundred casualties. Admiral Layton has tartly pointed out that for this dereliction, in contrast to the treatment of Kimmel and Short, MacArthur was not even censured.

Though a smashing victory, Pearl Harbor's effects were so temporary that Yamamoto felt compelled to begin quickly the planning of another surprise strike—one whose outcome would be entirely opposite to his success at Pearl. Japanese Admiral Tadaichi Hara perhaps summed it up best in his postwar analysis: "We won a great tactical victory at Pearl Harbor and thereby lost the war."

They lost it in good part because of the harsh light the Pearl Harbor raid cast on the inadequacies of the U.S. intelligence system. The lack of a Purple machine in Hawaii has already been noted. Also highlighted were the system's ridiculously slow methods of gathering information. Sigint results from Oahu and Cavite were often dispatched to Washington in weekly bundles aboard a Pan American clipper; if the flight was canceled, they went by surface ships. The list of high-level recipients was also seen as far too restrictive: commanders with the strongest of all needs to know were not included. In Washington the methods for disseminating the information were cumbersome in the extreme. Copies of that vital fourteenth part of the final Japanese series to its embassy, for example, were locked into dispatch boxes and hand-carried by two officer-couriers making the rounds of the White House, the State Department and the offices of the military chiefs.

Japan's Pearl Harbor raid had two powerful effects on Station Hypo and Joe Rochefort. First, it left him with a profound sense of guilt that he had been unable to warn his admiral of the coming attack. Despite the fact that he had not been assigned the code from which he, with his deep knowledge of the Japanese mind and the Japanese language, might well have extracted the information, he felt that he had let his boss down. As he said in his oral reminiscence recorded in 1969, "An intelligence officer has one task, one job, one mission. That is to tell his commander, his superior, today, what the Japanese are going to do tomorrow. . . . We did not inform Admiral Kimmel prior to December 7th that the Japanese were going to make the attack. . . . Therefore we failed." His wounded conscience drove him and his closest associates to work twenty-hour days to make sure nothing like it happened again.

The second result was that just days after the raid, Washington had second thoughts about Hypo. Rochefort and his team were ordered to drop their work on the flag officers' code and join in the attack on JN-25b, the latest version of the Imperial Navy code. That change would make all the difference.

Purple and the Obliging Baron

When the cryptanalysts of Friedman's Signal Intelligence Service distributed their replicas of the Purple machine, they could not have imagined that Purple's decrypts of diplomatic traffic would ever throw more than an indirect light on military affairs, especially in Europe. Yet, by an odd twist, Purple decrypts became a vital contribution to military intelligence in the European theater.

The reason for this unexpected cryptanalytic plum was Hiroshi Oshima, the Japanese ambassador to Germany. Both a baron and a general, he was also ardently pro-German. William L. Shirer wrote of him that he was "more Nazi than the Nazis." His strong advocacy of German interests won him the approval of top Nazi officials, including Foreign Minister Joachim von Ribbentrop and Hitler himself. Speaking fluent German, Oshima had hours-long interviews in which Hitler disclosed his innermost thoughts and plans. The Germans took him and his military attachés on tours of German production facilities, defense installations and frontline attack formations. An excellent reporter, Oshima prepared multipage summaries of his observations, which his subordinates encoded on his Purple machine. And of course Allied analysts in Washington and Bletchley read his transmissions almost as quickly as they were decoded in Tokyo.

Moreover, the Japanese reports from Berlin were not the only rich sources of inside information for the U.S. and Britain. The Japanese ambassador in Moscow kept Washington and London advised on their less-than-forthcoming Soviet ally. The ambassador in Rome used his Magic machine to report what he could learn of Mussolini and the Italians. Japanese ambassadors and military attachés in the neutral countries of Switzerland, Sweden, Portugal and Latin America were eager to transmit their findings.

General Marshall said of Oshima's reports that they were "the main basis of information regarding Hitler's intentions in Europe."

As early as January 1941, for example, the baron began informing Tokyo of Hitler's plans to attack the Soviet Union. He tried to persuade Japanese leaders that when this happened they, too, should declare war on the Soviets. Later, he persuaded Hitler to pledge that, in Oshima's words, "if a clash occurs by any chance between Japan and the United States, Germany will at once open war against the United States."

He, Ribbentrop and Hitler liked to get together and dream of the time when Japan would gain mastery over Burma, India and the Indian Ocean while Germany pushed through Ukraine and the Middle East for a linkup in Asia that would presage "a new world order." Oshima's persistence in urging this dream on Tokyo eventually drew a sharp rebuke from a new foreign minister, who let him know that any such idea was completely unrealistic.

Oshima was bold enough to offer criticism to the short-tempered führer. When the Germans did invade Russia and sent in the SS troops to liquidate masses of Russian citizens, he told Hitler what a serious mistake this was. It had turned the conflict into "a war of the peoples" when it could have become a struggle to free the Russian masses from Bolshevism. How much better, he said, if Germany had followed Japan's example in seizing Manchukuo, where they had granted the people a degree of independence that included the formation of a puppet government. How much wiser to have allowed a share of autonomy to Ukraine instead of savagely eradicating masses of its people. His advice fell on deaf ears.

For the U.S. a tragic omission in Oshima's reports was any word about Pearl Harbor. If the Japanese military had let him in on their plans, he would no doubt have wired back that he had relayed this information to Hitler. But since the generals were cagey about what they told the diplomats, there was nothing explicit for Allied eavesdroppers to overhear.

As the war progressed, the Allies learned more about the fighting on the eastern front from Oshima than from the Russians themselves. In March 1943, for instance, the Soviet gave a large Japanese contingent permission to travel across Russia, east to west and then down through neutral territory and on to Berlin. Everyone in the troupe was a spy, eager to gather information as the tour progressed. From Berlin, using Oshima's Purple machine, they reported back to Tokyo—and to Anglo-American analysts—their copious findings on Soviet rail transport, lend-lease aid, and the rebuilding and relocation of factories, oil storage facilities, food resources and the like. They also confided their observations of the solidarity of the people in support of the war. The tone of their reports reflected their awe at the enormous reserves of Soviet manpower and matériel as well as their feeling that the tide had turned against Germany.

Oshima fought against such pessimism. When he realized how the shortages of rubber and other materials were hampering the German war machine, he led the way in establishing the Mutual Economic Aid Pact for Winning the War. Central to this pact were what were called the Yanagi operations, blockade runners carrying vital Far East materials to Germany in exchange for German machinery and sophisticated armaments. Oshima envisioned a steady traffic back and forth that would ease the most urgent needs of both Axis partners. But since the Allies were decrypting his messages as well as those of the Japanese navy, Allied subs knew exactly where to go to intercept and sink the Yanagi ships. The Germans were soon reduced to converting old U-boats in order to transport minimal supplies through the blockade and then abandoned the operation altogether.

Throughout the war, Oshima kept the Allies informed of shifts in the attitudes of Axis leaders. Early on, the partners were wary toward each other about the possibility of one or another splitting off to sue for peace. On December 14, 1941, the baron reported the signing of a war alliance supplement to the Tripartite Pact: it pledged that none of the three Axis powers would negotiate a separate peace with the U.S. or Britain. As for Oshima's pleas that Tokyo declare war on the USSR, in July 1942 Oshima was told unequivocally that there would be no Japanese attack on the Soviets—information that President Roosevelt immediately relayed to Stalin. In the dark days when German armies were plunging deeper into Russia, Churchill and Roosevelt feared that it was the Soviets who would yield to a separate peace. Oshima's messages confirmed that Stalin was holding staunchly against any such temptation. When the tables were turned and the Russians were overpowering the Germans, the baron reported that now it was Hitler who stood adamant against a peace initiative.

It is one of the war's great ironies that the reports of Japan's German ambassador and his consular colleagues were of far greater value to the Allies than they were to their masters in Tokyo.

It seems almost unfair that after all he'd done for them, the Allies after the war tried Oshima as a war criminal and sentenced him to life imprisonment. However, Hitler's Japanese confidant was paroled in December 1955 and granted clemency in April 1958.

Baron Oshima's story adds an incredible extra dimension to the importance of U.S. cryptology during World War II. From the low point of Pearl Harbor, American cryptanalysis swiftly climbed to a dominance that made the plans of Japanese leaders an open book to Allied commanders, while Japan's widespread use of its Purple machine helped extend that dominance to the European conflict. The combined effect was to make the contribution of U.S. intelligence to Allied victory second to none.

9 North Africa: A Pendulum Swung by Codebreakers

DURING the war in North Africa, Allied and Axis forces continually pursued each other back and forth over harsh desert sands, losing vast numbers of men in the process. Many factors could be cited for the swings of fortune, but close study shows that none had more impact than signals intelligence. When the Axis was breaking Allied codes, they were the winners. When the Allies sealed their informational leaks and gained cryptologic superiority, they in turn were triumphant.

Rommel's early victories certainly owed much to the unconventional generalship and unexpected moves in the midst of combat that earned him renown as "the Desert Fox." What was not known at the time was that he also gained a powerful advantage through two secret sources. One was a field cryptographic team that expertly listened in on enemy radio exchanges to inform Rommel of British tactical plans. The other was the American military attaché in Cairo, who was kept informed of British strategic decisions and, all unknowingly, passed them on to Rommel.

Captain Alfred Seeböhm led the mobile unit that stayed close to the front lines and tuned in to British wireless traffic. His intercept operators sopped up every bit of undecoded chat and every message transmitted in a field code the Germans were readily breaking. Seeböhm added to his intelligence haul by using call signs to identify British units, and direction finding to ascertain troop concentrations and movements.

One example illustrates the use Rommel made of this information. On the morning of June 16, 1942, when Rommel was driving to isolate Tobruk, Seeböhm's team overheard a radiotelephone conversation between the Twenty-ninth Indian Brigade and the Seventh Armored Division. It disclosed that the garrison at the strongpoint of El Adem intended to launch an attack that night. Rommel responded by ordering his Ninetieth Light Division to strike first. The British, surprised, had to surrender. The larger import was that with the capture of El Adem, Rommel was able to surround and isolate Tobruk, which had been a thorn in his side for months. He soon forced the Tobruk garrison to capitulate, handing over enormous stores badly needed by the Afrika Korps. The surrender also delivered to the world press another disheartening story of British failure.

The U.S. Cairo-based military attaché was Colonel Bonner Frank Fellers. He became Rommel's unwitting dupe because of the code he used. America's Black code, so called because of the color of its binding, had been surreptitiously copied by the Italian secret service and made available to the Germans. As America's chief military observer in Egypt, Fellers was like Japan's Baron Oshima, an energetic gadabout and a tireless reporter. The British were obliging to him because they hoped he would aid them in securing much-needed lend-lease equipment for the desert forces. He himself felt driven to help prepare the American military for desert warfare. He toured the battlefields, talked with commanders, studied their tactics, was often made privy to their plans and then spilled all that he had collected in long, meticulous dispatches that he dutifully enciphered in the Black code and radioed off to Washington—and to Rommel.

Reading Fellers's reports makes one's skin crawl in horror. Through him Rommel turned unexpectant British garrisons into sitting ducks ready to be pounced on by the Desert Fox. Of course, Fellers's giveaways were only a turnabout of what Allied decrypts were routinely doing to unexpectant Axis garrisons. But somehow the sheer nakedness of his disclosures and the awfulness of their consequences are especially penetrating.

For example, he told of forthcoming commando raids by the British, which the Germans met and destroyed. He described defects the Allies had discovered in Axis armor and aircraft, and thereby facilitated corrections that made the equipment more killingly effective. He supplied a complete rundown on where the British armored and motorized units were located at the front, how many tanks were in working order and how many had been damaged. He tipped Rommel off to the withdrawal of 270 airplanes and a quantity of antiaircraft artillery to reinforce British strength in the Far East. He reported the locations of the air squadrons and how many of their planes were operational.

Fellers's revelations played a key role in another of the North African war's reversals. After his earlier successes against Wavell, Rommel had been hurled back by the British under General Claude Auchinleck at the end of 1941. But by receiving what Gordon Welchman called "just about the most perfect intelligence any general could wish for," Rommel knew exactly when and where to strike in his counteroffensive of January 1942. He made the British retreat three hundred miles, and destroyed or captured thousands of men in the course of the campaign.

Rommel might well have gone on to Cairo except for one obstacle: his tanks ran out of gas. The failure underlined the importance of the island of Malta, lying midway between Sicily and the Axis bases in North Africa. The supply shortages that hindered Rommel were a direct result of the depredations on Axis convoys carried out by Malta-based planes, ships and submarines. All-out bombing by German and Italian aircraft could not subdue the island, nor could the German commander in Italy persuade Hitler to commit the land forces to conquer it. Fellers handed the Axis an opportunity, if not to put Malta completely out of business, then at least to greatly hamper its raids on shipping.

The island, too, had its supply problems, and in June 1942 the British planned to have convoys converge simultaneously on Malta, one from the east, the other from the west, as the means of preventing the Axis from directing all its might against either one. To further neutralize Axis attempts to attack the convoys, the British planned to bomb the Italian warships, destroy Axis planes on the ground and air-drop commandos in Italy to sabotage other airfields. All of this Fellers learned about in advance and dutifully reported.

The result was a massacre. The Germans and Italians shot the descending parachutists, stood off the attacks on the airfields and sent ships, submarines and planes against the convoys. Britain's losses included a cruiser, three destroyers and two merchant ships. The convoy from Alexandria was forced to turn back. Of seventeen ships, only two got through to Malta, crippling for a time the island's effectiveness in sinking Rommel's supply ships.

At this low point the cryptologic pendulum again swung to the Allies. British cryptanalysts stopped the exploitation of Fellers by the simple expedient of breaking the Black code, reading his dispatches and putting two and two together. Convinced that the British suspicions were true, the American command recalled Fellers. He resumed his earlier service with MacArthur and became a brigadier general on Mac's staff. The new attaché to Cairo was equipped with a Sigaba code machine. Rommel lost his best informant and his strategic advantage.

Around the same time he was also deprived of his tactical weapon.

Amid the desert ebb and flow the British launched an armored thrust that overran the staff headquarters of the Afrika Korps. Seeböhm was killed, his men mostly wiped out or captured and many of the unit's records seized. An added asset from the strike was the surrender of a very coopera- tive German officer, Seeböhm's second-in-command. This lieutenant's ad- missions concerning the poor radio practices of British operators guided the tightening of their cryptographic disciplines. Plus, the Germans' new field unit proved very much inferior to Seeböhm and his team.

From then on, Allied cryptology in North Africa never again lost its leading edge. Rommel was shown to be much less prescient in his decision making. Or as Welchman expressed it, "Much of the foxiness of the 'Desert Fox' was due to German radio intelligence."

First El Alamein: Long-Delayed Turning Point

Despite being outclassed, for a time, by the Seeböhm-Fellers decrypts, British cryptologists were steadily strengthening the flow of intelligence they were supplying to North African commanders. Early on, GC&CS de- crypts kept General Wavell well informed about Rommel's posting to North Africa and about the forces under his command. Yet these authorita- tive disclosures could not offset command blunders.

Wavell thought the newly arrived Rommel would behave as he himself would have in the German general's situation. That is, he would delay any serious action until he was firmly in place and all of his equipment had ar- rived. Wavell was confirmed in these expectations by dispatches from Rommel's superiors in Berlin specifying that in view of the limited sup- plies of men and matériel they could send him, he should assume only a defensive position in North Africa.

That was not Rommel's way of thinking. He believed in boldness, speed, surprise. Knowing from Fellers's decrypts that Wavell's forces had been depleted by the need to send troops to Greece, Rommel decided that, ready or not, he should strike. He quickly organized what he had in men and machines, built fake tanks mounted on Volkswagens to create the im- pression he had more armor than he did, and went on the offensive. There were no messages to warn of his attack. Caught off guard, the British reeled back, giving up to the newly energized German-Italian assault troops most of the territories O'Connor had won. As Rommel wrote tri- umphantly to his wife, "I took the risk against all orders and instructions because the opportunity seemed favorable."

If Rommel, in that early stage of his North African adventures, could have captured Tobruk as an entry port for convoys from Italy, he might well have driven on into Egypt. When the Tobruk garrison held out, the overextension of his supply lines, especially for gasoline, forced him to bring his campaign to a halt.

While Wavell has been judged by analysts to have been an able commander, his attempts to recoup his losses against Rommel were doomed by rigidities in his and his subordinate generals' attitudes toward combat. One such shortcoming was their refusal to accept the tank-killing power of the Germans' 88-millimeter gun. Although this heavy weapon had been developed for antiaircraft use, the Germans had learned in the Spanish civil war that when its barrel was lowered and leveled against tanks, it could blast through the enemy's best armor. British commanders kept sending unescorted tanks against it and seeing them brew up into blazing hulks. The British had an antiaircraft gun whose penetrating power was greater than the 88's, but using it against anything other than aircraft was something one just didn't do.

Accompanying this failure was the generals' reluctance to break down the walls of interservice rivalries. Rommel excelled in combined operations, in which infantry supported tanks, artillery and antiaircraft units worked together and Luftwaffe planes were closely coordinated with ground forces. These tactics the British commanders were slow to adopt. Their units moved into battle splendidly independent of one another—and the Germans picked them to pieces.

So it was with Wavell's next big offensive, code-named Battleaxe. His multiple responsibilities as commander in chief of the entire Middle East kept him tethered in Cairo while his subordinate generals carried out his Battleaxe plans. They were no match for Rommel. Wavell came forward at the last minute to take control, but it was too late. His carefully amassed infantry battalions and armor had been shattered. The best he could do was keep the defeat from turning into a rout that would deliver Egypt into Rommel's hands.

In historians' eyes, Winston Churchill shared the onus for catastrophes in North Africa. Avid for victories that could strengthen world opinion about Britain's power to fight, and armed with BP decrypts that informed him of reinforcements headed for the Afrika Korps, he coerced his commanders into attacking before they were ready. Then, when the offensive stumbled, he peremptorily sacked his commander in chief and replaced him with another.

Having failed, in Churchill's estimation, to "save our situation in Egypt from the wreck" of Greece and Crete, Wavell was transferred to a less demanding post in India. Claude Auchinleck took over in Cairo. Although the Auk, too, was considered a sound leader, he had one crucial failing. He was a poor judge in choosing his frontline generals, and he was slow to remove them even when their deficiencies were glaring.

He withstood Churchill's impatience and reorganized what now became known as the Eighth Army. Freed from the threat of invasion as Hitler focused on his Russian offensive, Britain was pouring men, guns, armor and planes into North Africa in numbers that exceeded those going to the Afrika Korps. Auchinleck's field general, Alan Cunningham, should have had the edge when he attacked Rommel. But he made the same mistakes of sending his unescorted tanks against entrenched 88s and allowing infantry, armor, artillery and aircraft units to act too autonomously. The result was another disaster. The strain of command reduced Cunningham to a nervous wreck; he had to be relieved and sent to recuperate at a Cairo hospital. Auchinleck, like Wavell, hurried to the front, took over, held off another Rommel surge into Egypt and forced him to retreat—a narrow standoff victory for the Eighth Army.

The Auk did little better in his next choice of command, Neil Ritchie. In January 1942, when Rommel counterattacked and confronted Ritchie with the myriad decisions of combat, the new general went "all haywire," as one of his subordinates put it. Auchinleck flew in to stabilize the situation and stave off the Germans, but he left Ritchie in place.

The war settled into stalemate as each side prepared for new initiatives. It was the kind of seemingly stagnant situation Churchill couldn't abide. Relying strictly on the numbers of men and armor delivered to Auchinleck, he determined that the Eighth Army had a comfortable superiority that justified an early offensive. What the prime minister overlooked was the operational capability of those numbers. Although the British were receiving a steady inflow of American-made Grant tanks that were more than a match for most of Rommel's armor, the machines had to be prepared for desert warfare, and the crews trained in their use. Similarly, the new infusions of troops and armor from distant corners of the Commonwealth had to be organized and trained. The Auk was diligently handling these preparations when he received Churchill's ultimatum: either attack by June or resign.

Ultra decrypts, however, told Auchinleck that the issue was to be taken out of his hands. Rommel had decided to attack late in May. Auchinleck advised Ritchie of two points where Rommel was most likely to strike and insisted that Ritchie position his two divisions of armor at those points. Ritchie ignored the advice. When Rommel drove forward, the British armor was dispersed, ready to be destroyed one unit at a time. When Ritchie tried to counterattack with what was left of his tanks, he sent them, unescorted, to be smashed by the 88s.

This time Rommel even took Tobruk—at the embarrassing moment when Churchill was meeting with Franklin Roosevelt and trying to convince FDR that Britain was not a lost cause.

Rushing forward once again, Auchinleck withdrew his battered army to Matruh. When the Afrika Korps also took that strongpoint, Rommel wrote to his wife, "We're already 60 miles to the east. Less than 100 miles to Alexandria." All that stood in his way were the remnants of the Eighth, which Auchinleck was reorganizing at El Alamein. Rommel stopped for twenty-four hours to prepare his next attack.

Auchinleck, however, did the better preparing. He studied the Ultra decrypts and learned where Rommel would strike. Dispensing with interservice noncooperation, he faced the Desert Fox with his own version of a combined force. When Rommel, having to operate with little benefit from signals intelligence, grouped his tanks for a frontal strike, he was met by Auchinleck's massed artillery. Knowing that his adversary was starving for reinforcements of German troops and having to depend on Italian divisions, the Auk chose the Italian sector for his counterattack. His coordinated infantry and armor fell on the Italians and routed them.

Correlli Barnett, historian and author of *The Desert Generals*, has claimed that July 2, 1942, was the pivotal moment of the war in North Africa. On that day Auchinleck stopped Rommel, and on the days following he forced the German to change from an offensive into a defensive frame of mind. In the First Battle of El Alamein, Auchinleck turned back the last great Nazi thrust to conquer Egypt.

For Churchill, however, the Auk's effort was too little too late. He sacked Auchinleck and brought in Harold Alexander to be his Middle East chief of staff. Bernard Montgomery became the new commander of the Eighth Army.

Monty: Sigint Helps Make a Hero

Assigned to take over in North Africa in mid-August 1942, Alexander and Montgomery benefited from impeccable timing. Allied strength in the theater was on a mighty upsurge while Rommel's was in swift decline.

By then, U.S. war production had shifted into high gear. The supply of Grant tanks to Egypt was being supplemented by the arrival of thirty-six-ton but swift-moving Shermans whose 75-millimeter guns were, unlike the fixed weapons of the Grants, mounted on power-driven turrets. Britain was pouring reinforcements into the Eighth Army. By the time Montgomery was ready to go on the offensive, he had almost a two-to-one superiority over Rommel in men, tanks, antitank guns and artillery. In the air, the Royal Air Force was dominant over the Luftwaffe. Nor did Montgomery have any lack of gasoline to power his vast machine.

Monty profited from another tremendous advantage: Bletchley Park was breaking the ciphers Rommel most depended on. Four days after Montgomery took command, the complete details of Rommel's order of battle were handed to him. In his *Memoirs*, published well before the Ultra secrets were made public, Monty made much of his "intuition" for directing the winning moves in combat, intimating that his genius alone had crushed Rommel in North Africa. His chief intelligence officer's reply was, "Montgomery won his first battle by believing the intelligence with which he was furnished."

Montgomery's critics also point out that he exaggerated the poor state of affairs in the desert before he took over. His picture of the Eighth Army under Auchinleck was one of incompetence and ruin. He told Churchill, and repeated in his autobiography, the untruth that the Auk was ready to give up El Alamein and retreat to the delta if Rommel launched another attack in strength.

The more accurate description is that Auchinleck bequeathed to him a veteran staff settling down after their first defeat of Rommel to develop plans for a new attack. Their ideas formed the basis for Montgomery's self-touted "Master Plan."

Monty's many detractors, though, can't deny that he was a leader who inspired confidence and respect in his men. Dressed casually in a pullover sweater and the medallion-decorated beret that became his trademark, he went into the front lines to have tea with his troops, give them pep talks and exude a sense of sureness that the Goddess of Victory, not to mention the God in heaven, were on his side. His intelligence officer Edgar Williams's reaction after hearing Monty's first address to his headquarters staff was, "Thank God this chap has got a grip." Staffer William Mather told Monty's biographer Nigel Hamilton in an interview, "Monty absolutely deserves all the credit he could get for the way he changed us. I mean, we were different people. We suddenly had a spring in our step."

British codebreakers were doing him another service. Daily they were breaking some two thousand Hagelin-encoded Italian messages, many of them relating to shipments to Rommel. Decrypts of German air force and Fish signals were rising toward ninety thousand a month. All of these inside glimpses, put together, were providing so complete a picture of Axis shipping plans that Britain's Mediterranean forces were able to pick and choose which transports would go through—those with supplies for British POWs, for example—and which ones, especially the tankers carrying gasoline to Rommel, would be sunk. As Monty was preparing his El Alamein offensive, the Royal Navy and Air Force were sinking more than forty-five percent of the shipping meant to supply the Afrika Korps.

The British were careful, in carrying out this ravaging of the Axis marine, to preserve the security of Ultra. When decrypts specified the course of an Axis transport, an RAF reconnaissance plane would take off from Malta and seem, as merely part of a routine patrol, to happen upon the vessel. Meanwhile, a Malta-based submarine or bomber would already be on its way to intercept the ship. As Hinsley recalled the results in a 1996 reminiscence, "The Germans and the Italians assumed that we had 400 submarines whereas we had 25. And they assumed that we had a huge reconnaissance airforce on Malta, whereas we had three aeroplanes!"

A man with the sharp intelligence of Albert Kesselring, Hitler's commander in chief in Italy, was suspicious of the "extraordinary losses incurred during sea transport." He "suspected that the times of our convoy sailings were betrayed." But instead of questioning broken codes, he blamed the sinkings on "the efficiency and wide ramifications of the enemy system of sabotage."

The results for Rommel were catastrophic. He faced the Eighth Army short of ammunition, with rations for his troops at a low level, and so deprived of gasoline that he was robbed of freedom of movement. As he commented in *The Rommel Papers*, which his wife and son put together after his death, "The battle is fought and decided by the Quartermasters before the shooting begins." He leaves no doubt that with adequate supplies, including a sufficient tonnage of gasoline, he could still have defeated an enemy that was "operating with astonishing hesitancy and caution." As it was, El Alamein became, as he entitled one of his chapters, the "Battle Without Hope."

Added to his troubles was his vulnerability to the sort of deception he had earlier used against the British. Wanting Rommel to believe Eighth Army forces were being built up in the south, Montgomery ordered the creation of dummy battalions, with fake tanks, bogus artillery and troop simu-

lations that went so far as to have balloon soldiers sitting on inflatable la-
trines. A masterstroke was a mock water pipeline made up of discarded
gasoline cans. It was left unfinished to fool the Germans into believing the
attack would not come until the line was completed.

Rommel, a sick man, lulled by Monty's trickery, had actually returned
to Germany for treatment when the Eighth Army struck. His second-in-
command, fat General Georg Stumme, trying to cope with the complexities
of combat, died of a heart attack. Healthy or not, Rommel flew back to resume command.

Montgomery's critics can't deny that he divined the most likely point
of Rommel's attack: the Alam al-Halfa ridge. He prepared to meet and destroy Rommel's armor there. Four days after he'd made this decision, Ultra
decrypts confirmed that a thrust against the ridge was exactly what Rommel intended. Monty's acute military analysis, backed by the codebreakers,
gave him the victory in the defensive phase of El Alamein.

When the Eighth Army went on the offensive, however, Montgomery's
Master Plan turned out to have serious flaws. Needing to break through in-
depth minefields, Monty planned to have sappers clear a narrow channel
through which his infantry and armored divisions would pour during the
first hours of the offensive. The plan went awry when the minefields
proved to be a tougher, more time-consuming problem than he'd anticipated. His infantry and armor had to wait until a defile was cleared. Then
the mass of troops and tanks trying to crowd through it created confusion,
causing further delays and heavy losses. He had, in effect, to throw away
his Master Plan and improvise his further moves, but he did this with calm
authority and, in the end, carried the day.

Rommel, his armor all but immobilized by lack of fuel, had no choice
but to concentrate on evacuating his armies to avoid annihilation.

Here that "astonishing hesitancy and caution" he had observed of
Montgomery came to Rommel's rescue. To the amazement and dismay of
the onlookers at Bletchley Park, Montgomery made no move for three days
after Rommel had started his retreat. He seemed so dazzled by his victory
that he could not bring himself to order the end runs that could have
trapped the exhausted, near-helpless Afrika Korps, and send them into
prisoner-of-war camps. In his memoir Monty blamed heavy rains for his
failure to overtake Rommel, even though the rains did not begin until after
those first three days of idleness. However it was, the Afrika Korps kept
ahead of belated British sorties and reached Tripoli. They were headed
there at the time of Anglo-American landings in French North Africa and

were available to continue the war in North Africa for four more months of brutal fighting.

The Afrika Korps: Ultra Tightens the Noose

In 1942, after the U.S. had joined the war, Anglo-American planners held long discussions on how to conduct joint future campaigns. The Americans argued for a cross-Channel invasion in 1943. Knowing how much preparation was needed before that attempt could be made, the British advocated that the first substantial combined operation should instead be a series of North African landings. Agreement was reached and a timetable set for the autumn of 1942, with a little-known American general, Dwight D. Eisenhower, in charge.

It was just as well that the British won the argument. The North African landings showed up countless fumbles, mix-ups and snafus that needed to be corrected before taking on the Germans in northern France.

The North African expedition was, in fact, a tissue of bungles. The primary objective was to seize the Tunisian ports of Bizerte and Tunis, to prevent the Axis from using these ports that provided the nearest and best harbors for transports from Sicily and Italy and the best exits for an evacuation. To achieve the objective, the British felt sure, the landing should be made as far east as possible, hard on the Algeria-Tunisia border. The Americans were cautious about venturing so far. All sorts of fears entered in—among them the threat that Hitler might press France and Spain into allowing German passage through to capture Gibraltar, whose fall could maroon troops east of the Rock. To forestall any such eventuality, the Americans urged at least one landing in Morocco, west of Gibraltar. With that safeguard, a Mediterranean landing could also be contemplated.

A compromise was reached. Operation Torch would be made up of three landings: at Casablanca in Morocco, and at Oran and Algiers in Algeria. After securing these sites, it was thought, Allied troops could speed across land to capture the Tunisian ports.

The trouble was that even the easternmost landing, in Algiers, was still 450 miles from Tunis. They were tough miles, much of the way through rugged mountain terrain. As canny Scots general Kenneth Anderson noted, the race for Tunis was lost before it began.

The November 8, 1942, landings came just four days after Rommel's defeat at El Alamein. In themselves they represented a magnificent achievement. An armada of some five hundred American and British ships had set out from ports as far apart as Portland, Maine, and Lock Ewe, Scotland, and had converged on North Africa without ever being touched by German U-boats. GC&CS decrypts showed that Axis leaders knew something big was afoot, but the messages also disclosed uncertainty about the destination. Italy, Sardinia, Sicily, Malta, the Aegean? The Axis commanders' most favored answer, as Ultra made clear, was that this was a convoy bound for the relief of Malta. The Allies used that information to carry off a bit of deception. The Mediterranean ships made a feint as though heading for Malta, then wheeled about and sailed for Algiers. The Axis commanders were fooled, and the landings were a surprise.

Aside from the Allies' own foul-ups, the landings went off more smoothly than anticipated. Only at Algiers did the French troops, supposedly loyal to the Vichy regime, show troublesome resistance. The Axis Mediterranean submarines managed only two attacks and damaged one ship. The German and Italian air forces were caught unprepared and did little to harass the landings. Neither France nor Spain acceded to a German march on Gibraltar.

One big problem remained: Tunis and Bizerte were objectives too far. Algerian roads were in poor condition. Railroad equipment was ancient and the tracks were of mixed gauges. The intended harelike dash was slowed to a tortoise crawl.

In addition, the planners seriously misjudged the Axis response. With Rommel beaten and the Russian offensive demanding close attention, the Allies doubted that Hitler would try another major gamble in North Africa. Even if he did, they believed, the preparations would take weeks. They were wrong on both counts. Hitler saw the danger in allowing the enemy to gain possession of the ports providing the best jumping-off point for an invasion of Sicily and Italy. The troops, armor and planes that Rommel had pleaded for and been denied now flowed in great numbers and with stunning speed into Tunisia. The capable, aggressive General Jürgen von Arnim was called back from the Russian front to share command with Rommel.

The Allies' push to reach the ports foundered. In addition to the surprising resistance by the Germans, winter rains turned roads into quagmires. Eisenhower called off the offensive, and both sides settled down to a winter spent gathering their strength. The race for Tunis had, indeed, been lost.

By the time the Allies resumed their drive into Tunisia, their intelligence advantage had become even more overwhelming. With mastery of

Luftwaffe traffic a routine matter, BP cryptanalysts were also penetrating Wehrmacht Enigma ciphers. They had broken a new Enigma key that provided a fresh font of knowledge about Axis shipping. Italy's air force book code and Hagelin-encoded navy cipher were being quickly read. And Magic decrypts of Baron Oshima's reports continued to be helpful.

Axis commanders, by contrast, were reduced to guesses and hunches. An example of what this disadvantage could mean in battle came when Rommel—with his Afrika Korps troops safely dug in at the Mareth Line of old French fortifications in Tripoli—hurried west to join Arnim in organizing attacks against the Allies trying to hold the passes in the Atlas Mountains. Rommel's panzers succeeded in overpowering the untried American troops in the Kasserine Pass and fanned out into the plain beyond. He could have placed the whole North African operation in jeopardy if he had kept his drive going. But he had to guess at what lay ahead, and his guess was that the Allies were readying a counterattack that could trap him. Although his guess was wrong, he had no means of dispelling the uncharacteristic sense of caution that overcame him. When an American artillery division was hastily brought forward and began lobbing mortar shells onto Rommel's armor, he called off the offensive and withdrew through the pass. What was perhaps the greatest Axis opportunity in the campaign withdrew with him.

The battle for Tunisia was a series of gory thrusts and counterthrusts that continued through March and April and into May 1943. The codebreakers influenced the outcome in two critical ways. One was by keeping the Allied commanders informed about virtually every major action their Axis counterparts planned to take. The other was by directing the stranglehold on Axis supply lines.

Ultra's effects on strategic operations are exemplified by a March 3 decrypt that Hinsley described as of "decisive importance." It alerted Montgomery that Rommel, back with his old Afrika Korps troops, was organizing a surprise breakout from the Mareth Line against the Eighth Army on March 6. In a hard-driven day-and-night frenzy of activity, Monty used the three days to quadruple the forces in place at the point Rommel meant to strike. An in-depth massing of 470 antitank guns and 400 tanks was camouflaged to blast the Germans as they came forward. Rommel wrote later, "It became obvious that the British were prepared for us." After his attack had failed, the Desert Fox went home to Germany. This time he did not return.

Once more the Germans suspected that Enigma had been compromised.

The British high command rebuked Montgomery for not making a greater effort to disguise the source of his intelligence. But again the suspicions were quelled, and use of the Enigma never wavered.

U.S. general Omar Bradley told, in his *A General's Life*, how the code-breakers helped the American soldiery regain a measure of respect from their British allies after the near rout of the GIs at Kasserine Pass. Arnim planned, on March 23, a counterattack against the U.S. II Corps at El Guettar. "Our front-line codebreakers," Bradley wrote, "picked up and decoded the order, giving us a full day's notice. . . . A second decoded message provided us further valuable details on the attack." So warned, the Americans "mauled the Germans and Italians . . . it was the first solid, indisputable defeat we inflicted on the German Army in the war. Kasserine Pass had now been avenged."

As for the Axis supply situation, Ultra decrypts made the clampdown by the Allies all but total. Arnim's armored divisions, like those of Rommel before him, were immobilized by lack of fuel. Many of his soldiers were soon existing on two slices of bread per man per day.

Without transports and control of the sea, Axis commanders could not manage a Dunkirk. When resistance ended and Arnim surrendered on May 13, Hitler and Mussolini had no choice but to abandon 275,000 German and Italian soldiers and all their equipment.

From Tunis, Alexander sent a message to Churchill: "Sir, it is my duty to report that the Tunisian campaign is over. All enemy resistance has ceased. We are masters of the North African shore."

So ended an error-filled campaign that had resulted in more than one hundred thousand men—Germans, Italians, Britons, Americans, French— being killed, wounded or missing in action. As Rommel colorfully phrased it, "Rivers of blood were poured out over miserable strips of land which, in normal times, not even the poorest Arab would have bothered his head about."

But the campaign opened the underbelly of Europe to Allied attack, and it welded the Allied forces into a strong, unified and confident team. From the perspective of the codebreakers, the greatest significance was that the campaign proved to Allied generals the value of trusting their intelligence sources.

10 Turnaround in the Pacific War

FOR the six months following Pearl Harbor, the Japanese war machine was invincible. The U.S. islands of Guam and Wake fell within days after the Pearl Harbor raid. In the Philippines the Japanese sliced up the American and Filipino armies, forcing the Americans to retreat into the hopeless corners of Bataan and Corregidor and, in May 1942, to surrender. On the China coast, the American garrisons at Shanghai and Tianjin were seized. British-led forces were pushed out of Burma and Malaya. The Dutch East Indies yielded up their riches not only in oil but also in rubber, rice, timber and metals. The strategic stronghold at Rabaul in New Britain fell. The Japanese extended their Greater East Asia Coprosperity Sphere to include the whole arc of the central, south and southwest Pacific and were threatening the supply lines between the U.S. and Australia.

During those first months of 1942, the leadership that would direct the U.S. war effort in the Pacific had established itself. In Hawaii, Admiral Chester W. Nimitz had become the new commander of the Pacific Fleet. General MacArthur had been ordered to leave his besieged troops on Corregidor and escape to Australia in a torpedo boat. Moreover, the two commanders' cryptologic support teams were firmly in place. On Oahu, Edwin Layton, the fleet's chief intelligence officer, and Joe Rochefort were relieved to find that Nimitz refused to consider any shortcomings in their Pearl Harbor performance and wanted them to continue serving him. MacArthur had seen to it that his Cast cryptographers were spirited away to Australia on submarines before he himself left the Philippines, vowing, "I shall return."

In terms of cryptology, the explosive geographic expansion by the Japanese had one consequence that was to bring a decisive reversal in the course of the war. Japanese intelligence leaders knew that the security of their systems depended on regular replacement of the codebooks that were the basis of their nonmachine codes. They had planned to change their workaday naval code, JN-25, on April 1, 1942, but the distribution of their codebooks was made impossible by the twenty-million-square-mile spread of Japanese commands and the growing profusion of recipients. The date for the changeover was pushed back to May 1, then to the beginning of June. The delays gave Allied cryptanalysts those extra months to master JN-25.

In the windowless basement of the Fourteenth Naval District's Administration Building, known as "the dungeon," Joe Rochefort was on hand virtually nonstop. He paced around with a red smoking jacket over his uniform, both to keep him warm in the dank quarters and to provide the deep pockets he needed for his pipe, tobacco pouch and copies of messages of special interest. His work uniform was completed with house slippers because the concrete floors hurt his feet. In addition to overseeing the direction-finding, intercept, and traffic analysis operations along with cryptanalysis, Rochefort had to manage the influx and training of new recruits now flooding into his cellar headquarters.

Of these newcomers the most bizarre was a contingent of musicians left jobless by the severe damage to their ship, the USS *California*, in the Japanese attack. To the amazement of Rochefort and Dyer, the band provided capable and even some exceptional additions to the team.

The new, closer cooperation between the Allied cryptographic units in the Pacific and in Washington quickly began to produce results. Gone were the cumbrous communications methods of the pre–Pearl Harbor days. Now the cryptanalytic units flashed new discoveries to each other via radio-teletypewriter links. Soon the analysts were solving some forty percent of JN-25's code groups, but since those were the most often used words and phrases, the meaning of a high percentage of entire messages could be determined, or at least guessed at.

In April the U.S. military, knowing how badly the American people needed a morale boost, planned what became known as "Doolittle's raid" on mainland Japan. Colonel James Doolittle would load sixteen B-25 bombers on the flight deck of the aircraft carrier USS *Hornet*, slip within five hundred miles of Japan, lead the bombers so they could drop bombs and incendiaries on Tokyo and other cities, and fly on to those parts of China still held by Chiang Kai-shek. To carry out this bold act, the *Hornet* was joined by Admiral William F. "Bull" Halsey on the aircraft carrier *Enterprise* and by several escort vessels. Fortunately, Halsey's crew included an experienced intelligence officer and intercept operators. When the task force was still well short of its five-hundred-mile goal, the intelligence team picked up Japanese radio traffic revealing that Halsey's ships had been sighted. Japanese leaders took almost two hours to overcome their shock and disbelief, but then their radio channels crackled with transmissions as they sought to organize a huge sea hunt. Halsey decided to launch the bombers sooner than planned but not so late that his precious carriers and other ships would be endangered. While the attacks themselves were mere pinpricks, the raid gave the U.S. the semblance of a reprisal for Pearl Harbor, a publicity bonanza and a lift to American spirits. FDR stirred imaginations by claiming the bombers were launched from Shangri-La, the mythical kingdom in James Hilton's novel *Lost Horizon*.

The Doolittle raid had a much more important consequence than that of its bombs. In those early days of 1942 the Japanese high command, flush with victory, was debating its next offensive strategies. One group wanted to parlay the capture of Rabaul into the seizure of Port Moresby, on the south coast of the huge island of New Guinea, which hangs over Australia in the north like a giant incubus. Port Moresby was only a short hop across the Coral Sea to the Australian mainland. The group also advocated conquests in the Solomon Islands and beyond to sever Australia's links with the U.S.

Admiral Yamamoto pressed for an alternative plan. He wanted to extend the Coprosperity Sphere in the other direction: to establish a new perimeter that included the Aleutian Islands in the north and Midway Island on the eastern sea frontier. He argued that his strategy would lead to eliminating U.S. power in the Pacific in two ways. The capture of Midway would provide a base for the conquest of Hawaii. And the need for the U.S. to defend the island would draw the battered Pacific Fleet into deep water where he could complete the decisive battle he had started at Pearl Harbor.

The Decisive Battle was an important concept to Japanese sea lords, as John Prados emphasized in his book *Combined Fleet Decoded*. "The Japanese fleet," he wrote, "was built to engage in the Decisive Battle, trained to conduct it, and officers and men were imbued with the idea of the Decisive Battle almost as a tradition, an ideology, a cult." The pervasive idea traced back to the Japanese victory over Russia in the 1904 battle at Tsushima. Russia had put together a fleet in European waters and then sent it halfway around the world to engage the Japanese. Because of the long journey and a variety of tribulations along the way, the Russians had arrived in the Far East thoroughly dispirited, and they were soundly defeated. Just so, Yamamoto believed, could Japan humble the U.S. Navy. In traversing the vast distances of the Pacific, the American fleet could be harried, weakened and confused by submarine torpedo attacks, destroyer flotillas and aircraft strikes. Then the concentrated power of the Imperial Navy could fall on it and deliver the deathblow.

The loss of Midway, the seizures in the Aleutians and the annihilation of the U.S. fleet, Yamamoto stressed, would dishearten the American people. The admiral again held out the prospect of a negotiated peace on terms dictated by Japan.

Doolittle's raid swept away any resistance to Yamamoto's plan. As he himself commented, "Even though there wasn't much damage, it's a disgrace that the skies over the Imperial Palace should have been defiled without a single enemy plane shot down." It must not happen again. Midway was near enough to serve as a launching site for similar attacks in the future, and the Dutch Harbor base in the western Aleutians was also too close for comfort. The army, which had heretofore refused to participate in the admiral's scheme, now insisted on becoming a part of it.

Japan's military leadership, basking in the knowledge that their losses had been far less than anticipated, decided it was unnecessary to choose between the alternatives. They could do both: carry out the drive against Port Moresby while also proceeding with the Midway-Aleutians campaign.

Winning the Battle of the Coral Sea

Rebuffing the Japanese commanders' first attempt to take Port Moresby was primarily the task of the U.S. Navy. Rochefort's team informed Admiral Nimitz of the great flotilla of Japanese warships that were escorting transports carrying a whole division of invasion troops, heading down from Rabaul. The Japanese objectives were to capture Tulagi, one of the Solomon Islands, and build an airfield there while also entering the Coral Sea to seize Port Moresby.

In his memoir, Layton emphasized that Nimitz's entire Coral Sea operation was guided by Rochefort's "sixth sense" in assembling seemingly unrelated information in partially decrypted enemy messages and turning the puzzle into an accurate picture of enemy intentions.

Believing his codebreakers, Nimitz evacuated the small Australian detachment at Tulagi before the Japanese invaders arrived. He also relied on advice from decodes to station his ships to the best advantage in the Coral Sea.

Vice Admiral Shigeyoshi Inouye, commanding the Japanese fleet, was expecting that his passage would prove a surprise to the Allies. His shock was great, therefore, when U.S. carrier-based planes began to attack and sink his ships.

The Battle of the Coral Sea, fought from May 4 to May 8, 1942, was a mix of poor judgment, faulty leadership, missed opportunities and lucky hits on both sides. Admiral Morison thought it might better be called "the Battle of Naval Errors," but he also wrote, "It was an indispensable preliminary to the great victory of Midway."

For the U.S., a prime opportunity was lost when one of Nimitz's commanders, Vice Admiral Jack Fletcher, became antagonistic toward the mobile intelligence unit aboard his flagship and turned a deaf ear to them. What had miffed him was that when he had asked the unit's leader to describe his work to a wardroom of officers, the leader's consciousness of his security restraints had caused him to refuse. Consequently, when the unit pinpointed the location of nearby Japanese carriers and revealed that they were in the vulnerable stage of refueling aircraft, Fletcher, still piqued, declined to act on the information.

In the end, the U.S. traded the sinking of a Japanese light carrier and heavy damage to another carrier for the loss of the *Lexington* and the crippling of the *Yorktown*. American fliers also downed a large number of enemy planes. Technically, in terms of ships sunk, it was a Japanese victory. But without carriers to provide air cover for the Port Moresby invaders, Yamamoto on May 18 called his ships and his occupation force back to Rabaul. Round one clearly went to the Allies.

Of larger significance, the Japanese for the first time in the war had suffered a setback. That realization gave the Allies' esprit a powerful boost.

Midway: "A Victory of Intelligence"

While Rochefort and his team were busy tracking the enemy's advance toward Australia from decrypted fragments, he also began detecting Yamamoto's Midway-Aleutians operation. Of special help was a decrypt of April 29 referring to the dispatch of maps of the Aleutian Islands. Another signal dealing with the "forthcoming campaign" used the words *koryaku butai*—"invasion force"—aimed at a destination encoded as *AF*. Rochefort and Layton informed Nimitz that something big was heading toward Hawaii.

In hindsight, it can be seen that Yamamoto's plans were flawed in the extreme. In setting the three objectives of taking the atoll, establishing control in the Aleutians and luring what was left of the U.S. Pacific Fleet out into the open sea, he was violating the principle of massing his strength. He thought of the Aleutian campaign as a useful feint, a clever deception, as well as a needed blunting of that northern scimitar hanging over the Japanese mainland. Instead it resulted in a ruinous division of his ships and carriers.

Cockiness made him sloppy. He allowed two other carriers to be left behind in home waters—one to be repaired after the Coral Sea battles, the other merely to receive a new complement of planes and pilots—when a determined effort could have added both to his fleet. In addition, when his huge force sailed toward Midway, he placed his four carriers forward in a close grouping that proved terribly convenient for U.S. attack planes. And instead of covering these all-important carriers with his battleships, he had the war vessels, including his flagship, *Yamato*, lag far behind, a floating headquarters remote from the action.

Most damaging of all was his attempt to use the same deceptive tactics at Midway that had worked for him at Pearl Harbor. Again he used fake radio traffic to create the illusion that his ships were in training operations near Japan. This time, thanks to the delay in introducing the new JN-25 code, Rochefort and his team were not to be fooled.

The intelligence supplied in the Coral Sea battles had confirmed for Nimitz that he could trust his codebreakers. When they began submitting evidence of a massive new Japanese thrust aimed at Midway, he sided with them against the view held by Washington analysts, as well as Washington chief Admiral Ernest J. King, that Rochefort was being duped. The Washington unit believed any move toward Midway was only a feint masking Yamamoto's real objective: the aircraft factories of Southern California. The U.S. Navy even dispatched a fleet, Admiral Morison has reminded us, to search for a Japanese carrier falsely reported to be descending on San Francisco.

Further, the Washington intelligence staff advised King that Halsey and his carriers should be kept in the Coral Sea, since the Yamamoto offensive might be directed there rather than toward Midway.

Rochefort was not subtle in disparaging these interpretations. Regarding an attack on the U.S. West Coast, he knew the Japanese lacked sufficient transports, tankers and food refrigeration ships to take on so remote an objective. Also, he judged it "ridiculous" and "stupid" to think they would strike so far east while the U.S. Navy ships at Pearl remained on their flank.

As for leaving carriers in the Coral Sea, MacArthur's codebreaking teams in Melbourne came to Rochefort's support. Their decrypts verified that the Japanese had abandoned amphibious operations against Port Moresby and were planning an overland offensive instead. Halsey's carriers could head for Pearl Harbor and Midway.

In his recorded oral reminiscences, Rochefort stated, "Possibly the best thing that ever happened to the Navy during the war was Nimitz's acceptance of Station Hypo's estimate of what the Japanese were going to do, not only at Coral Sea but at Midway and subsequent."

Even with Nimitz's approval, though, one big question remained. Where was "*AF*"? Rochefort had worked with the Imperial Navy's geographical bi-letter designations enough to know that *AH* was Hawaii and *AK* was Pearl Harbor. He was sure that references to *AF* in the intercepts stood for Midway, but none of the decodes made the identification certain. How could he make sure?

Lieutenant Commander Jasper Holmes knew that the Midway command depended on a plant that distilled seawater to supply the garrison's water needs. What if Midway sent out, both in plaintext and in a low-level code the Japanese were sure to read, that the desalinization plant had broken down and the island's supply of water was running desperately short? If *AF* was Midway, surely some mention of this crisis would show up in subsequent traffic.

The scheme was carried out, with the extra fillip of an answering plaintext transmission from Hawaii that a freshwater barge would be sent at once.

The deception worked. As Holmes reported, "The Japanese took the bait like hungry barracudas." *AF*'s water troubles turned up in a decrypt, establishing beyond doubt that Midway was the target. Historian David M. Kennedy has called this resourceful stroke by Rochefort's team "the single most valuable intelligence contribution of the entire Pacific war." Its upstaging of the bigwigs in Washington, however, exacerbated their ill feelings toward Rochefort.

The ruse convinced Nimitz, who had already reinforced the defenses at Midway. He began preparing his David role against the Yamamoto Goliath, pitting twenty-seven surface warships against the enemy's eighty-eight. On May 25, Nimitz held a staff meeting that Rochefort had been ordered to attend. A punctual man, the admiral was annoyed when his chief cryptanalyst showed up a half hour late. But when Nimitz saw what Rochefort had brought with him, all was quickly forgiven. Rochefort and his colleagues had spent the night decoding a long intercept. It revealed nothing less than the complete Japanese order of battle for the Midway attack. Plus, the intercept confirmed that the attack was scheduled not for mid-June, as Washington was claiming, but for June 3 or 4.

On May 28, the Japanese did switch to a new version of their JN-25 code, blacking out the Allied codebreakers for a time. But the changeover came too late. The Americans knew all they needed in order to take on the Japanese fleet.

Unlike the overconfident Yamamoto, Nimitz hastened to amass every element of naval strength he could muster. Although not an aviator himself, he understood the importance of naval air power. On the afternoon of May 27, the battered carrier *Yorktown* limped from the Coral Sea into Pearl Harbor. If it could be patched up in time, it would add a third carrier to Nimitz's fleet. Given the extent of its damage, the repairs could easily have consumed a couple of months, perhaps even a trip to the West Coast. Instead, crews swarmed over the vessel and on the morning of May 29 had it ready to put to sea, at least marginally battle worthy.

Nimitz received what seemed a serious setback to his plans when Bull Halsey arrived at Pearl with a skin disease that sent him to the hospital instead of aboard a flagship. Postmortems of the battle, though, suggest that in reality this was a felicitous change. The impulsive Halsey might not have fared as well in the complex operation as his cool, clear-thinking replacement.

This was Rear Admiral Raymond A. Spruance, who in his service under Halsey had shown himself to be an aggressive fighting man and a shrewd strategist. He would command one of Nimitz's task forces, with Jack Fletcher in charge of the other. Knowing from the Hypo codebreakers that the Aleutian operation was only a diversion, Nimitz sent northward a motley assortment of ships under Rear Admiral Robert A. Theobald.

On June 1, Yamamoto planned to place two picket lines of submarines between Pearl Harbor and Midway. The subs would be stationed there primarily to alert him if the U.S. fleet emerged in response to his surprise attack on the atoll. The operation was badly coordinated, and the subs were late in getting into position, but even if they had been on time they would not have detected the American ships; they had already passed the barrier.

For the previous month the defenses of the Midway atoll had been reinforced by inflows of antiboat and antiaircraft guns, two additional companies of GIs, five tanks, ten torpedo boats, stores of aircraft gasoline and a variety of planes that included B-17 Flying Fortresses. Midway was as ready as Nimitz could make it.

He proceeded to set his sea trap. His two task forces met at "Point Lucky," 325 miles northeast of Midway, a position that was expected to place them on Yamamoto's left flank. The three carriers would lie in wait, undetected, while long-range search planes from Midway sought out the Japanese fleet. Then every type of air power the U.S. could marshal, both from Midway and the carriers, would fall on the Japanese ships.

In Washington, suspicions still lingered that Nimitz and Rochefort were being gulled by a Japanese force that was only a decoy. Consequently, they were greatly relieved when on June 3 a flying boat from Midway spotted the invasion fleet almost exactly where Rochefort had predicted it would be. The Spruance and Fletcher task forces, along with the defenders at Midway, knew for certain what they must do.

At this point Yamamoto's plan began to show its flaws. His battleships, with their powerful eighteen-inch guns, could have pulverized Midway's defenses, but they were three hundred miles away. The softening up was left to Pearl Harbor's hero, Admiral Chuichi Nagumo, commanding the invasion fleet that included the mission's four carriers. At dawn on June 4, Nagumo sent off nine squadrons of bombers escorted by four squadrons of Zero fighters. Their arrival at Midway was expected to be a surprise. Instead, the planes were met by heavy antiaircraft fire and a fierce swarm of game but outmoded and outclassed fighters.

Nagumo's Zeros shot down most of the U.S. planes. Overall, however, the initial resistance put up by Midway's defenders seemed to the Japanese leader of the raid too strong to permit a landing of troops. He radioed back to his commander that a second attack wave was needed.

That was not what Nagumo wanted to hear. His ordnance men were already arming aircraft with torpedoes and armor-piercing bombs, preparing to dispatch any Allied warships that might show up, especially the U.S. carriers that Yamamoto hoped to lure toward Midway. A second attack on the island meant canceling that order and equipping his planes with fragmentation bombs for a land bombardment. The necessity for the change, however, seemed to be confirmed by the arrival of a fleet of torpedo bombers from Midway. Even though antiaircraft fire and the Zero fighters massacred the obsolete U.S. planes, their attack verified that the defenders of Midway were far from neutralized. Nagumo sent off a second wave against the island.

While those planes were in the air, he received dumbfounding news: one of his reconnaissance planes had discovered American warships in the area. At first the spotter saw only cruisers and destroyers. Then he reported a carrier. He also warned that more torpedo planes were winging

Nagumo's way. How should he counter this incredible new development? After dithering for a precious quarter of an hour, Nagumo ordered that the returning planes be armed with the original torpedoes and bombs to be used against surface ships.

At that moment of maximum confusion and vulnerability, when the Japanese carrier decks were cluttered with torpedoes, bombs, gasoline hoses and aircraft, came what Gordon Prange in his monumental *Miracle at Midway* called the Americans' "uncoordinated coordinated" attack.

Spruance and Fletcher had planned for flights of torpedo planes, dive-bombers and fighters to converge simultaneously over the Japanese fleet, while Flying Fortresses from Midway dropped their bombs from great heights. But Nagumo had changed course, and the American planes had trouble finding his ships. The fighters, running out of fuel, turned back, many of them having to ditch. The torpedo planes, first to discover the Japanese, courageously swept in at low levels. The complete flight was shot to pieces by the Zeros, with only one of the thirty crewmen surviving. They were lost without scoring a hit. The Flying Forts were equally ineffective, managing nothing better than near misses.

The sacrifice of the torpedo planes, though, was not in vain. While the Zeros were occupied with them down near sea level, thirty-seven American dive-bombers from *Enterprise* arrived far overhead. They had traced their way to Nagumo's fleet only because their commander, Clarence Wade McClusky, had cannily let himself be guided by a Japanese destroyer returning after a try at sinking a pesky U.S. submarine. When McClusky and his mates went into their screaming dives, the huge rising suns painted on the flight decks as aids to Japanese fliers gave the Americans perfect targets. McClusky's crew wrecked the *Akagi* and the *Kaga*. A second flight of dive-bombers, from *Yorktown*, arrived almost simultaneously and concentrated on *Soryu*.

In less than five minutes the opportunity that had been slipping away from the Americans was turned into a flaming victory. Three of the four carriers were reduced to blazing hulks and later sank. As historian Keegan put it, "Between 10:25 and 10:30, the whole course of the war in the Pacific had been reversed." George Marshall called it "the closest squeak and the greatest victory."

The battle was not quite over. The *Yorktown*, only partially restored from her Coral Sea mauling, was further crippled by a flight of Japanese dive-bombers from the remaining carrier and was finished off by a submarine, which also sank a destroyer. Bombers from *Enterprise* exacted quick revenge. Her planes caught up with the retreating occupation force and sank the fourth carrier. Also, one cruiser was sunk and a second badly damaged.

Yamamoto still had a vast superiority in sea power, but with the only other two carriers of his fleet protecting the Aleutian landings, he knew he was defeated. He called off the Midway operation and sneaked back to home waters.

The one part of Yamamoto's overly complex plan that succeeded was his diversionary raid against the Aleutians. Ironically, his small victory there came about because Theobald, the American commander, refused to believe what his cryptographic team told him. Their decrypts warned that while the Japanese would bomb the American base at Dutch Harbor, they would land troops to seize Attu and Kiska. Theobald would not be swayed from believing the invasion would be against Dutch Harbor, and he positioned his ships accordingly. When Yamamoto's attackers did exactly what the decoders had forecast, Theobald's task force was in the wrong place by a thousand miles. It failed to prevent the Attu and Kiska landings.

Otherwise, the great surge of Japanese expansion was over. After Midway, despite a few abortive efforts to mount new drives, the war machine of the Rising Sun was put on the defensive.

"Midway was essentially a victory of intelligence," Nimitz later wrote. George Marshall added that as a result of cryptanalysis, "we were able to concentrate our limited forces to meet their naval advance on Midway when otherwise we almost certainly would have been some 3,000 miles out of place."

At a postbattle staff conference at Pearl Harbor, Admiral Nimitz singled out Joe Rochefort: "This office deserves a major share of the credit for the victory at Midway."

One result of the battle nearly caused disaster for the codebreakers. Along with accounts in the American press exulting over the Midway victory was a sidebar story that caused U.S. cryptographic teams consternation and dismay. The story's headline was NAVY HAD WORD OF JAP PLAN TO STRIKE AT SEA. Appearing in three large dailies owned by Roosevelt-hating Colonel Robert McCormick, the story related that navy commanders knew in advance about Japanese plans, the strength of their forces and the fact that a move against "another base" was only a feint. The gaffe could have cost the Americans their entire intelligence advantage over the Japanese. Investigations found that a reporter aboard American ships in the Pacific had been allowed to see U.S. intelligence summaries and had, with remarkable insensitivity, filed his account, to which equally obtuse censors had given

approval. Whether because of this break or as the result of their natural precautions about cryptographic security, the Japanese did make changes in
their codes that Allied codebreakers had difficulty in overcoming.

Countering New Drives on Port Moresby

Douglas MacArthur adopted a complex attitude toward codebreakers.
His powerful ego and adherence to old army values caused him to project
the image that reliance on such undercover chicanery was beneath him. In
making his decisions he needed no other source of advice than his own superior brain. His sycophantic staff, revering him as "The General," followed by practicing a studied "negligent indifference" toward signals
intelligence. Yet he was too shrewd a commander, and they were too intent
on seeing him win, not to make use of the advantages the codebreakers
provided.

After their escape from Corregidor in late March 1942, MacArthur set
up his cryptographic team, together with an Australian unit and a British
contingent from Singapore, as the nondescriptly named Central Bureau in
Brisbane. His real attitude toward signals intelligence, as Edward J. Drea
has pointed out in his book *MacArthur's Ultra*, was indicated by the fact
that one of his first appeals to the War Department was for cryptanalytic
support. In his study *MacArthur as Military Commander*, Gavin Long
commented about The General, "The prescience with which he may at
times seem to have been endowed was generally the outcome of the cracking of Japanese codes."

Intelligence informed him that the Imperial forces had decided on two
new campaigns against Port Moresby. An overland drive would be made
across the Papuan southeastern sector of New Guinea. In addition, decodes revealed that the Japanese would try to take the port in a new
seaborne invasion.

The overland campaign was launched first. On July 22 the Japanese
began unloading at Buna, on the northern coast of New Guinea, the army
division that had been turned back in the Coral Sea battles. The troops
faced a formidable obstacle: the Owen Stanley Range, thirteen thousand
feet high and almost constantly immersed in rain clouds. The sole passage
was by the Kokoda Trail, hewed through the jungle and up and over the
mountains, so narrow that in places only men walking in single file could
traverse it. The hot, humid climate and incessant pounding rain turned the

trail into a seventy-eight-mile-long horror of ankle-deep muck and slippery roots, the scene of what Morison called "the nastiest fighting in the world."

The troops sent in by the Japanese were crack infantry, trained in jungle warfare, their supplies carried on the backs of New Guinea natives. Driving the Australian defenders steadily before them, they came within sight of Port Moresby. There the determined Aussies, aided by rushed-in American GIs, dug in and stopped the advance. The battle dragged on for days, then weeks, while Allied planes smashed Japanese attempts to replenish their troops. In the end, the starving, disease-ridden remnants of the Japanese force retreated back to Buna.

Yamamoto's new sea campaign against Port Moresby concentrated first on taking the anchorage at Milne Bay, on the southeastern tip of New Guinea. The Australians had a small garrison there and had constructed an airfield. Yamamoto wanted the airfield to provide air cover for his landings at Port Moresby.

Allied decodes informed MacArthur of this new threat. He quickly reinforced the troops at Milne Bay and had his new air commander, Major General George C. Kenney, organize his meager forces into as strong a defense as he could manage. The aggressive Kenney directed preemptive air strikes against Japanese airdromes at Rabaul and Buna, greatly reducing the number of planes they could send to protect the landing at Milne Bay.

Lacking the equivalent of the Allies' codebreaking, the Japanese expected only a minimal defense of the port. On August 24, 1942, they sent in a landing force composed of overage recalled reservists. When this group was shot to pieces and radioed for help, a special Naval Landing Force went in. They fared no better. After another week of bitter fighting, the Japanese gave up. The Melbourne cryptanalysts deciphered the Imperial Navy's order for the evacuation of Milne Bay.

Yamamoto's grand design of using Port Moresby as a base against Australia was frustrated. In contrast, MacArthur brought a new spirit to the Australian people. On his arrival he had found a nation cowering in fear of conquest. Some among Australian military leaders had been convinced they must be ready to surrender the continent's less populated areas in the hope of holding the more populous parts. MacArthur rejected their pessimism, signaling his aggressive attitude by announcing that he meant to make his base of operations not in the relative safety of Melbourne or Brisbane but at Port Moresby. "We'll defend Australia in New Guinea," he proclaimed.

In view of MacArthur's successes at Milne Bay and Port Moresby, which supplemented the victory in the Coral Sea, the Aussies took heart that The General might well deliver on his promise.

11 USSR: Intelligence Guides the Major Victories

HISTORIES of World War II generally leave the impression that military intelligence had little to do with the Soviet Union's defeat of Nazi Germany. The reasons given are instead the inexhaustible resources of Soviet manpower, the grit of the Russian people, the vastness of Soviet territory and the miseries of the Russian winter. Yet disclosures released to the public only in recent years have shown that in the Soviet Union, as elsewhere on the Allied side, secret knowledge of German intentions, plans and orders of battle informed the Soviet responses and, at crucial moments, made the difference. While much of this information came from agents and spies, codebreakers also played their part.

The Soviets themselves became increasingly adept at conducting what they called *razvedka*, the gathering of intelligence from such varied sources as scouting parties, aerial reconnaissance, prisoner interrogation, reports from agents and partisans, electronic direction finding and the like.

In addition, their military intelligence benefited from two powerful political and ideological forces. One was hatred of Hitler and Nazism. The other was love of Marx and Communism. Together, these strong undercurrents kept a flood of diverse secret information flowing into Moscow to supplement their own *razvedka* operations.

The foremost source of intelligence reports delivered to the Moscow Central Bureau, which directed agents and volunteer informants, was a trio of transmitting groups in Switzerland that the Germans called *Die Rote Drei*, "the Red Three." While fierce debate still rages as to where the Red Three obtained their information, there is no argument that they supplied Moscow's bureau with staggering amounts of advantageous information drawn from within the highest circles of German society. The Red Three were prolific, their reports were most often accurate and their revelations pierced to the heart of the Nazis' military decisions.

Who were the individuals who made up this transmitting triumvirate? Heading up the first Switzerland-based group was a Hungarian, Sandor Rado, anagrammatically code-named Dora. A fervent Communist married to a fervent Communist, he was a paid Soviet agent. In Geneva he set up pro-USSR news agencies and then a successful mapmaking business that provided good cover for his covert operations. One of the uses he made of his cartographic skills was to prepare for his Russian masters a map showing the locations of all the munitions and armaments factories in Germany and Italy.

Rado combined forces with Otto Punter, a Swiss Communist who had organized a network of informants in Italy and Germany. His code name was Pakbo, an acronym of the principal places where he met with his confederates.

For a while Rado and Punter delivered their findings via courier, but in 1939, when the war came and Switzerland closed its borders, another devoted Communist, Ruth Kuczynski, a German woman code-named Sonia, arrived in Geneva. She had orders from Moscow to change Rado's modus operandi from couriers to radio. She subsequently recruited the owners of a radio repair shop to supply transmitters and learn Morse code.

Their teacher was an Englishman, Alexander Foote, a member of Sonia's group of agents. The second leg of the Red Three was formed when Foote was equipped with a newly built transmitter and moved to Lausanne to begin sending from there.

Unknown to Rado, another small network of Communist informants was also based in Geneva. Its head was a Polish Jew, Rachel Dübendorfer, code-named Sissy. She worked as a secretary in the International Labor Office of the League of Nations. In May 1941 Rado was ordered to meet with her and absorb this third leg of the clandestine groups serving the Soviets.

Into this web ventured the individual who became the most important informant of all. This was Rudolf Roessler, a German ruled not by Communist sympathies but by a strong Catholic faith and a consuming hatred of Hitler and the Nazis. The information he delivered to Moscow was of such importance that the Russians showered him with praise, medals and money.

What were the sources of the information transmitted by the Red Three? Rado and Punter depended on networks of agents and informants, as did Sonia. Sissy used her job in the International Labor Office to winnow out economic insights that were useful to the Soviets.

As for Roessler, he died in 1958 without ever revealing where his information came from or how he received it. His secrecy has left the door open for guesses, theories, myths and, in some cases, complete fabrication.

This much seems inarguable: during his life in Berlin, Roessler belonged to and was highly active in the Herren Klub, an exclusive circle of prominent Germans. The group included German officers who formed a conspiracy to dispose of Hitler and oust the Nazis, a cabal that became known as *Die Schwarze Kapelle*, "the Black Orchestra," picking up on the German secret service's shorthand for the clandestine organizations that kept the airwaves humming with the tunes of their illegal transmissions.

Roessler's antipathy toward the Nazis derived partly from having the successful and profitable theater business he had developed taken over by one of Hitler's henchmen. Roessler emigrated from Berlin to Lucerne, Switzerland, and established himself there as a publisher, primarily of anti-Fascist literature and of books banned by the Nazis. He began supplying the Soviets with bits of information that seemed to come from sources high up in German society, especially in the military. At first he followed a roundabout route, delivering his reports to an agent in Swiss intelligence who passed them on to the Soviets. Needing a proofreader for his business, Roessler hired Christian Schneider, not knowing that he was one of Sissy's band of informants. When Roessler and Schneider found they were two of a kind, they developed a new procedure. Roessler secured the information while Schneider acted as the go-between, carrying it to Sissy for wireless transmission to Moscow. It was agreed that Schneider would never reveal to his confederates in Switzerland that his material came from Roessler. All that Sissy, Rado and the others knew was that Schneider, who had been a minor informant, suddenly began delivering reports of great value and amazing timeliness. Even when Roessler's Moscow directors tried to order him to name his sources, he never responded. The Roessler-Schneider duo was given the code name *Lucy* because of their Lucerne location.

As to the identity of Roessler's sources, claims have been advanced for as varied a cast as top Nazi generals and even Hitler's close confidant, Martin Bormann. The CIA produced a paper advancing its theory. What matters is that Roessler's information was of decisive importance. Alexander Foote has written of it: "In fact, in the end Moscow very largely fought the war on 'Lucy's' messages—as indeed any high command would who had access to genuine information emanating in a steady flow from the high command of their enemies."

A Host of Other Informants

Lucy, Dora and others of the Red Three were far from the only sources dispatching secret information to the Soviets. One highly idealistic but only marginally effective source centered on two other members of the Herren Klub, Arvid Harnack and Harro Schulze-Boysen.

Harnack was a senior civil servant in the Reich Ministry of Economics. As told in Shareen Brysac's recent book *Resisting Hitler*, in his youth he studied at the University of Wisconsin, where he met Mildred Fish. When they married, she came to live with him in Germany and served as one of his anti-Nazi conspirators. While Harnack was pro-Marxist in his sympathies, he chose his dangerous course as much to alert Britain and the U.S. to the evils of Nazism as to help the Soviets.

Schulze-Boysen was a Luftwaffe lieutenant in the Reich Ministry of Aviation. A rebellious youth, he joined a revolutionary society and became editor of its newssheet, *Gegner* (*Opponent*). When the Nazis came to power, he made the journal more and more an anti-Nazi organ. He was seized by the secret police, thrown into an early concentration camp and tortured. His mother, from a high-placed family, got him released. He sought revenge by going underground and gathering around him a group of fellow dissidents. His job at the Aviation Ministry enabled him to obtain military information of value to the Soviets. He and his wife, Libertas, joined the Harnacks as conspirators in *Die Rote Kapelle*, "the Red Orchestra."

Until Germany went to war against the Soviets, the Harnack-Schulze-Boysen group turned their information over to Soviet runner-agents in Berlin. When the war began, they had to shift to the use of radio. Here they ran into troubles. The first transmitter the Russians delivered to them was defective; the second their inexperienced operator wrecked by connecting it to direct rather than alternating current. After early successes as informants, Harnack and Schulze-Boysen were largely reduced to aiding the cause by spreading anti-Nazi propaganda within Germany and trying to stir German factory workers to revolt.

A more effective section of the Red Orchestra was the network of informants led by Leopold Trepper, the code name for Leiba Domb, a Polish Jew who became a dedicated Communist. Trepper had served the Soviets in Palestine and France before being appointed resident director of the Russian secret service in Western Europe. Settling in Brussels, he took over a small nucleus of agents, developed his cover as a businessman marketing a line of raincoats and, as the *Grand Chef*, or "Big Chief," began building an espionage web. Moscow sent agents skilled in radio and code work to back him up. After the Germans overran Belgium in 1940, Trepper made Paris the center of his network. The successful raincoat business gave him the wealth to develop many useful friendships, including those with German officers. He kept a broad flow of information directed toward Moscow.

Still another Soviet informant was based in Tokyo. He was Richard Sorge, ostensibly working there as a German journalist but secretly a pro-Soviet agent heading up a spy ring that drew invaluable information from unsuspecting high officials in the Japanese government and the German embassy.

Add the British to the Soviet sources. As previously shown, Bletchley Park began deciphering messages of special import to the Soviets well before they became Britain's allies, and Winston Churchill overcame his personal distaste of Communism to convey the information to Stalin, always in a disguised form to protect Ultra's security. Bradley Smith, in his book *Sharing Secrets with Stalin*, has reported the on-again, off-again efforts by the British military mission in Moscow, and later by the American mission, to develop a useful exchange of intelligence with the Russians. The efforts were hampered throughout the war by mutual suspicion and distrust. The U.S. military in particular showed a penchant for assigning officers to Moscow who had a knee-jerk reaction against anything Communist. Even with these hindrances, a good deal of information of value did flow back and forth.

Another British group determined to aid the Soviets was the so-called Cambridge ring, or the "Cambridge Comintern," secret Soviet sympathizers impelled by their beliefs in Marxism. The ring's members burrowed into the heart of British intelligence and high government posts to winnow out information of use to the Soviets. It has been charged that men such as Kim Philby went so far as to reveal the names of British agents in the USSR, leading to their torture and execution.

Anthony Blunt was the kingpin, having recruited Philby, Guy Burgess and Donald MacLean. Others included John Cairncross, Leo Long and James Klugman. Although known to have been enamored of Communism in their student days, they evaded detection until well after the war. Partly this was because they took pains to disguise and seemingly to reject their true beliefs. Philby, as an example, worked as a journalist covering the Spanish civil war on the Fascist side and actually received a decoration from the victorious dictator, Francisco Franco.

At first the Cambridge ring had to overcome the same Russian mistrust encountered by Churchill and the British missions. In *The Crown Jewels*, Nigel West and Oleg Tsarev have documented from Russian archives that Moscow suspected that the entire Cambridge group were double agents under British control, assigned to pass disinformation to the Soviets. But in time the sheer volume and value of the documents the ring delivered to their contacts in London swept away doubts.

Philby progressed to the top ranks of Britain's Secret Intelligence Service, a position that empowered him to receive many Bletchley Park decrypts and to read the SIS sourcebooks, which included the names of British spies in Russia. Blunt wormed his way into the counterespionage branch, a rich source of information about the personnel and working methods of British intelligence, and revealed Bletchley Park's successes in breaking the Enigma. He also gave the Russians advance notice of the time and place of the Allies' D-Day landings in France. MacLean mined the Foreign Office for another load of vital data for the Soviets. Burgess was a charmer who developed a wide range of influential friends from whom he extracted information to be passed on to his control. Cairncross actually worked for a time at Bletchley Park, and on weekend trips to London in the automobile his control had supplied him, he conveyed thick sheaves of notes on traffic of interest to Moscow as well as actual copies of decrypts filched from disposal boxes. He also turned over BP training manuals on deciphering, and details of Turing bombes. Similarly, Leo Long did duty at BP, and while his scruples constrained him from delivering actual decrypted material, he did submit, as he admitted long after, "intelligence assessments based on it."

For the Secret Informants, Initial Defeats

What came of the varied efforts to warn Moscow that the invasion was coming, that Hitler had entered into the 1939 nonaggression pact only to lull the Russians while he subdued the West? At first the informants encountered nothing but bitter frustration.

Stalin's rejection of Churchill's warnings was only one in a series of rebuffs. The Cambridge Comintern fared no better. Nor did Sorge, reporting from Tokyo. Through links with the Lucy ring, the German conspirators in Berlin signaled the precise date and the exact hour the offensive would begin. The information supplied by Alexander Foote was so compendious that it took him four days to transmit the whole of it. As far as the effect their warnings had on Stalin, though, the informants might as well have stayed in bed.

Why did the Russian dictator act as he did? Since he left no known record of his thinking, his motives can only be guessed at.

One explanation is that he thought of himself as a man of his word. He had sanctioned the signing of the pact with Germany and he meant to stick by it, even going so far in his pledge to supply the Wehrmacht's material needs as to buy copper from the U.S. and transship it to Germany.

Also, he discounted the reports of German buildups on Russia's borders as merely Hitler's maneuvers to mask his real intent, which was to invade Britain.

The most charitable explanation is that Stalin was simply buying time. He knew the pact would not hold and Hitler would attack, but believed the evil day could be postponed by a demonstrable policy of nonprovocation. He was aware that the Red Army was woefully unprepared, and each day that passed helped it get ready. He may also have hoped to delay the German offensive until winter set in. He ordered his generals to do absolutely nothing that could be construed by the Germans as a justification for invasion.

Whatever his reasoning, the consequences were disastrous. His army leadership had been thinned in the 1930s by his ruthless culling of officers he suspected of opposing him, an extended bout of paranoia in which more than half his senior commanders were executed. This bloodletting, as noted by the leading U.S. historian of the Soviet military, David M. Glantz, had "stifled military thought and analysis." If now he, the boss, said that war was not imminent, his cowed officers disregarded all other signs and agreed: the Germans were not coming.

The result was that when the German armies crossed the Russian borders at four fifteen a.m. on June 22, 1941, they found the Red Army unready for war. Aware of the great reaches into which the Russians could retreat, the German generals planned pincer movements that would envelop huge numbers of Red Army soldiery. Aided by the chaos among Soviet defenders and the reluctance of Stalin to permit withdrawals, the German armies sliced through and around the confused troops. At Minsk they captured three hundred thousand prisoners and large amounts of equipment. The encirclements were repeated at Kiev, at Smolensk. The Germans' northern army closed in on Leningrad and began the thousand-day siege that caused two million Russian deaths because of starvation and the effects of malnutrition. Pushing toward Soviet oil fields, the southern army penetrated into the Caucasus Mountains and overran much of the Crimea. In the first two months of the war almost one million Russian soldiers were taken prisoner and seven hundred thousand more were killed. The Germans controlled the western five hundred miles of the country and half of Ukraine's breadbasket. It began to look as though what Hitler had told his generals as they prepared the campaign would come true: "You have only to kick open the door and the whole rotten edifice will come crashing down."

While everything seemed to be going Hitler's way, however, serious problems were developing for the Germans. Russian soldiers were proving to be tougher fighters, putting up a more stubborn resistance, than the Germans had anticipated. Their do-or-die spirit was caused by more than love of country. The word had spread among Russian troops that if they surrendered, they would only end up being shot—if not by German soldiers, then by the SS Blackshirts who followed them. Hitler had told his generals that since they were fighting inferior Slavs, the war "cannot be conducted in a knightly fashion"; it must be waged with "unprecedented, unmerciful and unrelenting harshness." Since the Soviet Union was not a participant in the Hague Convention that set down humane behavioral rules for troops in combat, he said, German soldiers would not be prosecuted for flouting those rules. As ghastly tales of massacres filtered down to the Russian soldiers, they fought with a desperation that caused the German victories to be achieved at high costs.

Also hampering the German advances were the primitive roads and paucity of rail lines. Repeated delays in the armies' progress, General Gerd von Rundstedt told Liddell Hart after the war, "were caused by bad roads, and mud. The 'black earth' of the Ukraine could be turned into mud by ten minutes' rain—stopping all movement until it dried. That was a heavy handicap, in a race with time. It was increased by the lack of railways in Russia—for bringing up supplies to our advancing troops." The poor roads also prevented the Germans' encirclement maneuvers from being as successful as they had planned. Although they captured legions of prisoners, many thousands escaped before the rings could be closed.

As his own commander in chief, Hitler made a decision that his generals opposed but could not alter. That came when the Army of the Center, in late August as the days were growing shorter and the Russian winter loomed, wearily slogged through to the approaches to Moscow, so close that forward troops could see the sun reflecting off the towers of the Kremlin. Hitler, however, postponed the advance. His reasoning was that it was more important to step up the stubbornly resisted drive into Ukraine, to take over those prime farm and factory areas, than to capture a city important only for its symbolic meaning. No less than sixteen divisions were redeployed to the south. When his generals protested, Hitler informed them that they knew nothing about economics. Let Germany seize Russia's principal agricultural and industrial centers, he said, and then Moscow would fall into German hands with scarcely a struggle.

Reinforced, the southern offensive went well. The whole of Ukraine was opened up. The Donets Basin, supplying sixty percent of the Soviet Union's coal, was overwhelmed. The advances pushed toward the mountains of the Caucasus and the rich oil fields beyond. Hitler was jubilant. His planning had led to triumph.

Now his armies could turn back to the taking of Moscow. On October 2 they launched Operation Typhoon, which Hitler described as beginning "the last, great, decisive battle of the war."

It has been said it took four years and twenty million Soviet lives to correct Stalin's mistake. The turn toward remediation was about to come.

Winning at Moscow, Stalingrad and Kursk

When, despite warnings, the Russian armies had been surprised and shattered during the opening phases of the war, Moscow's intelligence cadres could do little to stem the devastating series of Nazi conquests. Yet the information they supplied soon began to have consequences. As the Germans prepared to resume their assault on Moscow, Bletchley Park succeeded in breaking a new eastern-front Enigma cipher, whose messages revealed in detail the German order of battle. Reading these decrypts, Churchill asked Stewart Menzies, his chief of intelligence, "Are you warning the Russians of these developing concentrations?" When Menzies affirmed this was being done, Churchill nevertheless added, "Show me the last five messages you have sent."

A more vital contribution to the defense of Moscow came from Sorge. A big question hanging over the Soviets was whether Japan, as the third main partner in the Axis, would enter the war against Russia. The likelihood seemed good, given the long history of rancor between the two. To guard against this eventuality, the Soviets had to keep many divisions in the Far East. Now Sorge presented convincing evidence that an attack on Russia did not fit into the plans of the Japanese; their intentions were directed southward toward the English, Dutch and Americans.

From Switzerland, the Red Three confirmed Sorge's information. Sandor Rado quoted the Japanese ambassador in Bern as saying, "There can be no possible question of a Japanese attack against the Soviet Union until

Germany wins a decisive victory on the Eastern Front"—i.e., until Moscow falls.

By then, Stalin and his generals had enough confidence in their informants to rush eighteen divisions, half of the Eastern command, by rail to Moscow, with additional divisions drawn from Siberia and Outer Mongolia. Richard Overy, in his excellent history *Russia's War*, described how, suddenly in the days just before Stalin and his commander in chief, Marshal Georgi Zhukov, were planning their December 5 counteroffensive, the streets of Moscow were filled with "tough, fresh-faced 'Siberian boys,' " to whom bitter cold seemed a natural element. The arrival of divisions from the East added a powerful cutting edge to the new divisions Zhukov was skillfully organizing and training. Overy commented, "It was not the tough winter conditions that halted the German army but the remarkable revival of Soviet military manpower after the terrible maulings of the summer and autumn."

To have masses of fresh Russian troops coming at them in subzero weather surprised and shocked the Germans. Their own initiative was stalled. Instead of occupying the buildings of Moscow, the German soldiers were forced to endure the ravages of the Russian winter in open country. Many of them wore only summer uniforms. To equip the troops for winter war had been considered a defeatist attitude—the Russian edifice was supposed to have collapsed well before winter set in. The German army would be debilitated by more than 133,000 cases of frostbite.

Not only was the German advance stopped. The Russian counteroffensive harried the Germans into a retreat that almost ended in a rout. Stalin could tell the people of Moscow that the German attempt to encircle the capital had failed. The only sour note in this initial success came when Stalin grew too ambitious. Over Zhukov's objections, he ordered a broad offensive that would also relieve the siege of Leningrad. As did an ill-prepared attempt to retake the city of Kharkov, the attack failed. Russian losses ran into the hundreds of thousands.

In the spring of 1942 came the second important contribution by pro-Soviet informants. Roessler received and conveyed to Moscow the whole ten pages of Hitler's Directive 41. The directive showed the Soviets the plans for Hitler's summer offensive. His armies would have two goals. One was to capture the Volga port city of Stalingrad—a victory that would have the symbolic value of seizing Stalin's namesake. At the same time the city's capture would protect the left flank of the divisions driving south to achieve the other goal: the final conquest of the Caucasus, which would assure the Germans control of the region's oil fields.

Again Stalin rejected the informants' warnings. Certain that the Germans would resume their assault on Moscow, he refused to allow the capital's reserve forces to be sent to the relief of Stalingrad. And again his secret sources were proved right. The Germans ignored Moscow, closed in on Stalingrad and drove a deep salient into the Russian lines in the south.

In August 1942, when the situation became desperate, Stalin once more called on Zhukov to bail him out. After touring the battle site and studying intelligence about the forces arrayed against him, the marshal worked with his staff to devise a daring plan: they would enclose the German encirclers in a still wider encirclement.

To give the planners time to organize the counteroffensive, they needed the defenders inside Stalingrad to hold out for forty-five days. The Russians were up to the harrowing task. Under their commanders Vasily Chuikov and Andrei Yeremenko, they burrowed into the city's ashes and rubble and allowed the Germans' Sixth Army and Fourth Panzer Army only yard-by-yard, house-by-house advances, with tremendous casualties on both sides. Yeremenko set an example for his men by continuing to command even after being wounded seven times. At night, Russian boats and, after the river froze over, sleds crossed the mile-wide Volga to ferry in supplies and carry out the wounded. To help fend off the Germans, Russian artillery and rocket launchers fired from across the Volga. At a critical moment Stalin relented and allowed the Thirteenth Guards Division to be rushed to the city, just in time to stop a last German push that had cut a narrow corridor through to the river and split the defenders into two pockets of holdouts.

In his planning, Zhukov enjoyed a distinct intelligence advantage. He knew both the makeup and the placement of the armies facing him. The German commanders, by contrast, were blind. As a result, Zhukov was able to assemble a far larger concentration of attack forces than the Germans thought possible.

He was also aware of a major weakness in the German line. Hitler's armies, worn down by an attrition rate that totaled more than a million casualties by March 1942, could no longer rely entirely on German manpower to carry out the ambitious campaigns asked of them. Hitler resolved to fill the voids by ordering into combat the armies of satellite nations and his Axis partner. As General Paul von Kleist later recalled of the forces deployed along the Volga, "When I pointed out the risks of leaving such a long flank exposed, he said he was going to draw on Romania, Hungary, and Italy for troops to cover it. I warned him, and so did others, that it was rash to rely on such troops, but he would not listen." When Hitler's chief of staff suggested abandoning the now useless city and shortening the German line, he shouted, "I won't leave the Volga!"

Zhukov saw that the non-German armies were less experienced and not well armed. "Above all," he wrote in his memoir, "their soldiers, and many of their officers, had no desire to die for interests alien to them in far-away Russia."

The Stalingrad defenders gave him his forty-five days to arrange his divisions for his huge pincer movement. Zhukov knew where to hit. On November 19 his armies swept forward against the Romanian army assigned to hold the left flank. It collapsed in hours. From the south Zhukov's armor struck the Romanian army on the other flank and crushed it. Within four days the pincers had met, closing some 330,000 Germans inside the destroyed city.

The Sixth Army's General Friedrich von Paulus, a fastidious man abandoned in an abattoir, asked permission to try to break through the Russian enclosure. Hitler ordered him to stand fast and, to strengthen his resolve, promoted him to field marshal. Paulus was also assured that he would be supplied from the air and that a powerful German thrust would punch through the Russians to his rescue.

In London on December 8, Menzies was again reviewing Bletchley Park decrypts with Churchill. The messages dealt with German plans to regain the initiative around Stalingrad. "Is any of this being sent to Joe?" Churchill asked. Menzies replied that every bit of useful information Bletchley could pull out of the air was being relayed to Stalin.

The odds were too great against the Germans. Their offensive to supply von Paulus an escape route faltered. Airborne supplies dwindled as the Russians shot down the transports. The troops inside Stalingrad endured for seventy-two deadly days. When on February 2, 1943, Paulus surrendered, only ninety-one thousand of his troops remained alive to be locked into Siberian prison camps. Fewer than five thousand were to survive the war.

All during this tense time the stream of secret information flowing into Moscow's Central Bureau was at flood stage. The German conspirators were transmitting to Roessler the decisions of the German high command, often with an elapsed time of ten hours or less. The Red Three were so overwhelmed by the scope of traffic to be transmitted that Rado had to find and train additional helpers to handle it. The faithful members of the Red Orchestra, trying to answer the countless questions the Moscow bureau directed to them, jeopardized themselves by transmitting for five hours or more nightly, giving German counterespionage teams ideal opportunities to home in on them with direction-finding equipment. From Britain, in addition to inputs from Churchill and British intelligence, the Cambridge volunteer agents delivered piles of documents, including Cairncross's and Long's summaries from Bletchley Park, to their spymaster in London. These were reduced to reels of microfilm and dispatched by diplomatic couriers to Moscow. The Russians showed their appreciation by returning their usual largesse of laudatory letters, money and medals.

Although badly bloodied by the defeat at Stalingrad, the Germans on the eastern front were by no means finished. The Red Army found this out when once again Stalin overreached, hoping that one last blow would produce a German collapse. Instead, a brilliant counterstroke, directed by Army Group South's Field Marshal Heinrich von Vietinghoff, met the Soviet forces and hurled them back.

One climactic battle remained to decide who would be the masters of western Russia. The attacks and counterattacks during the winter of 1942–43 had left, around the city of Kursk, a prominent Russian-held salient thrusting into the German lines. In March 1943, Hitler decided the salient must be eliminated. First word of the operation code-named Citadel came from an April 13 Luftwaffe decrypt. Hitler initially set the date for the offensive in mid-April but then delayed its start in order to bring into action more of his new Tiger "miracle" tanks now rolling off the assembly lines. Finally he ordered Citadel to began on July 4 and sent a personal message to the soldiers around the salient: "This day you are to take part in an offensive of such importance that the whole future of the war may depend on its outcome." The führer was right, but not in the way he had hoped.

David Glantz, in his book *The Role of Intelligence in Soviet Military Strategy in World War II*, has detailed how adroitly the Soviets used *razvedka* to identify targets. From their many sources, they knew, in advance of the battles, the locations of German artillery and mortar batteries, separate guns and mortars, pillboxes, observation posts and machine gun nests. Now they were set to apply this superior reconnaissance in the battles at Kursk.

Hitler had hoped to keep Citadel a secret, but the informants were zeroing in on the operation even as it was being hatched. From Bletchley Park's Fish analysts came the warning that the Germans' planned pincer movement would begin with an attack from the north and another from Kharkiv in the south, together with a frontal assault on Kursk itself. These official signals from BP were, of course, sanitized for security reasons. Much more believable to Moscow were the materials supplied by Cairncross. Not only were the messages in their original German; they also came via the Soviets' KGB intelligence service. "The Russians were convinced," Cairncross later wrote, "that in its German version the Ultra I supplied was genuine, giving the full details of German units and locations, thus enabling the Russians to pinpoint their targets and to take the enemy by surprise."

On July 1, when Hitler drew his generals together at his East Prussian headquarters to impress on them the importance of the operation, at least one of the conspirators had to be among those present. Details of the conference were in Stalin's hands the next day.

Stalin argued that the best response was a preemptive strike. Zhukov counseled otherwise. "It would be better," he told Stalin, "for us to wear down the enemy on our defenses, knock out his tanks, bring in fresh reserves, and finish off his main grouping with a general offensive." He won Stalin's approval of his plan. The Soviet defenders laid a miles-deep series of traps for the German attackers. Some three hundred thousand civilians in the Kursk area, many of them women, joined the troops in constructing defensive positions. In the forward zone the lines of antitank ditches and World War I–type trenches extended for three miles. Seven miles to the rear lay another defensive zone similar to the first. Twenty miles still farther back, other tank traps and trenches were dug. The front area was heavily mined, antitank strongpoints were set up and masses of the Russians' best tanks, artillery pieces and tank-destroying guns were assembled. Advised by Cairncross, the Red Air Force had already swooped down on seventeen German airfields and destroyed more than five hundred aircraft caught on the ground.

In the early hours of July 5, as the Germans waited to launch their attack, they were suddenly subjected to an intense artillery bombardment. They went forward knowing the surprise was blown. The Red Army was waiting for them.

This, the greatest tank battle of the war, with armor in the thousands hurling themselves against each other, went on for a week. The Germans were stopped after making only minor advances, and on July 12 the Russians loosed their counterattack. The gigantic battle went on for seven more days. When, finally, on the nineteenth, Hitler called off the offensive, seventy thousand Germans lay dead and the steppes were littered with the smoking remains of Nazi armor. As V. E. Tarrant expresses it in his book *The Red Orchestra*, "Before Kursk a German victory was still a possibility; after Kursk defeat was inevitable."

After the war, German field marshal Paul von Kleist bemoaned to Liddell Hart that somehow "the Russians got word of our preparations." His rueful remark came well before the senders of that word were revealed.

Conspirators' End: Paying the Price

Churchill, his Bletchley Park colleagues and the military missions to Moscow could, after the war, recall the intelligence given to the Soviets with a large degree of satisfaction. So could the Cambridge ring, whose members kept on betraying their country well into the Cold War, until they were at last unmasked. Philby and others defected to the Soviet Union and lived to ripe old ages.

Most of those manning the information posts on the continent were not so fortunate. The Germans learned that encoded messages were flowing to the Russians from within their own realm. Incensed, Hitler ordered the Abwehr secret service and the Gestapo secret police to join forces in tracking down and destroying these traitors.

The Red Orchestra played a dangerous cat-and-mouse game with the counterintelligence agents. Early in the war the orchestra's units frustrated the agents' direction-finding equipment by changing their transmission sites and by broadcasting only in short bursts. As the war continued, however, and as the intelligence directors in Moscow realized the value of what they were receiving and became ever more demanding in their questions, the informants could no longer be so cautious. Their longer stints on the air enabled the Abwehr to narrow in on their areas, their streets and eventually their dwelling places. Sudden raids conducted by police with sound-deadening socks drawn over their jackboots caught many of the informants at their transmitters, with stacks of messages beside them still waiting to be sent.

The Abwehr achieved its first success in December 1941. Its agents raided an apartment in Brussels and seized several Red Orchestra operatives, only just missing the capture of the *Grand Chef*, Trepper.

Arrest by the Germans presented the Red Orchestra members with the same dilemma posed by the British to German spies: die as heroes or live as turncoats. Three of those arrested in Brussels remained tight-lipped even during the sessions of torture the Gestapo termed "intensified interrogation," and died proudly. The fourth, the mistress of one of the men, told the agents all she knew. For this she escaped torture, but in the end she, too, was condemned to death.

Liquidation of the Brussels unit proved to be a short-lived triumph. By mid-June 1942, a new unit began transmitting from the Belgian capital. Again, the Nazis' direction-finding task was eased by the senders' long hours on the air nearly every night of the week. The agents tracked down devoted Communist Johann Wenzel and so broke him through torture that he agreed to transmit misinformation dictated by his captors. Wenzel was brave enough to include in his messages a tip-off that they were false. Eventually he escaped from prison and remained in hiding for the rest of the war.

One of Wenzel's unenciphered messages seized when he was captured gave the Germans a stunning insight. It set forth in precise detail the plans for the Germans' summer offensive and clearly showed that the information came from somewhere in the top ranks of the Reich military. The Abwehr and the Gestapo redoubled their efforts to wipe out the Red Orchestra.

They soon trapped the units in Holland and Paris. In Paris they captured Trepper himself, who chose nonheroism, immediately declared he would cooperate and proved it by betraying one of his chief assistants. His cooperation led to the capture, torture and deaths of numerous others. Trepper's own fate was determined by the Germans' desire to use him in a *Funkspiel*, a turnabout series of transmissions meant to mislead Moscow. His captors treated him well and guarded him so loosely that he escaped and, with further sacrifices of those who tried to provide him with hideouts, remained free until Paris was liberated. He then flew to Moscow. He received no hero's welcome, however. Instead, his *Funkspiel* time was remembered and he spent nearly ten years in Soviet prisons.

In Berlin, the Abwehr was aided by an unforgivable blunder on the part of the Moscow Central Bureau. Managing to break some old intercepts, the German counterespionage team found one sent from the bureau that gave away the addresses of three agents in Berlin, Arvid Harnack's among them. The decrypts also incriminated Schulze-Boysen. Although he and the other three remained heroic to the end, the Abwehr found a weak link: Schulze-Boysen's wife, Libertas. Her information enabled the German agents to round up 117 members of the Berlin conspiracy.

In all, the Gestapo arrested 217 Red Orchestra members. Of these, 143 were executed or murdered during "intensified interrogation," while the rest died in concentration camps. Gaining nothing from her collaboration, Libertas herself was guillotined, as was Arvid Harnack's American wife, Mildred—the only American woman executed on direct orders from Hitler.

In Japan, Sorge was arrested by the Japanese two days after sending the message convincing Stalin he could release Far East divisions for the defense of Moscow. After being held in prison for two years, he was hanged by the Japanese on November 7, 1944. Others of his spy ring were rounded up and died on the gallows or in prison. His tombstone in a Tokyo cemetery bears the epitaph, in Russian, HERO OF THE SOVIET UNION.

The Germans were unable to get directly at the Red Three in Switzerland, but they had other ways. By making the threat of invasion seem imminent, they panicked the Swiss authorities into an agreement to shut down the illegal transmitters.

While the principals of the Red Three could look back with pride at their wartime exploits, postwar life was far from easy for Rado, Foote and Roessler. Rado and Foote took the same plane that bore Trepper to Moscow. Rado found himself under suspicion because he had, when his network was being broken up by the Swiss, suggested using British agents as conduits for Lucy's messages. The Russians also thought he had lived too well on the funds supplied him. He was tried and sentenced to ten years in Soviet prisons, after which he became until his death a minor Communist functionary in his native Hungary.

Disturbed by the treatment given Rado and by his close-up exposure to the Soviet system, Foote defected from Communism, first intellectually and then actually by surrendering to British security forces. He died a few years later.

Roessler was brought to trial by the Swiss not just once but twice. The first time he was charged for his wartime activities associated with a foreign power's illegal intelligence service. He was found guilty but then set free because the court decided that he had acted in the best interests of the Swiss state. Hard up for money, he then became an agent for Czech intelligence, was again arrested by the Swiss and was sentenced to a year's imprisonment. He died in Lucerne at the age of sixty-one.

Although the Nazis rid themselves of the scourge of undercover activist dissenters, their deliverance came too late. The informants had done their job: they had told the Soviets what to expect from the Nazis and how to plan their countermeasures so as to turn the war on the eastern front from near defeat to certain victory.

12 Smiting the Axis's Soft Underbelly

ALTHOUGH the Allies did not control the North African coast until mid-May 1943, the decision about where to strike next had been made back in January when Churchill, FDR and their staffs had met at Casablanca. The decrypts of Allied codebreakers had contributed strongly to the decision. Their decrypts had verified that a cross-Channel landing in France that summer, so strongly favored by General Marshall, would face too many German divisions. Nazi power must be reduced before an invasion became feasible. The Allies' choice of a target was what Churchill liked to call "the soft underbelly of the Axis": they would invade Sicily, the triangular island off the toe of Italy's boot. The new front would tie up and decimate German troops who would otherwise be available to fight the Russians or man the defenses on the French coast. Sicily's capture could provide other benefits as well: helping to clear the Mediterranean for Allied shipping, providing a base for invading the mainland and persuading the Italians to drop out of the war.

Axis commanders thought an attack on Sicily the most likely new venture for the Allies, but without codebreakers' coups to back up their theories, they could not be sure: they could only guess.

It was a situation ripe for deception, for convincing the Axis the blow would fall anywhere but Sicily. Among Bletchley Park decrypts was a Luftwaffe Enigma message that disclosed what the Germans considered to be the most threatened areas. While Sicily was first, Crete, Corsica and Sardinia were also viewed as highly possible invasion sites. As Ewen Montagu's book *The Man Who Never Was* told, the decision was made to play to this Axis confusion.

The planning committee gave their scheme the grim code name of Operation Mincemeat. The idea was to float ashore on the coast of Spain the body of a supposed military courier drowned when his plane had crashed in the Mediterranean. He would be carrying a briefcase full of official-looking papers contrived to make the Axis think of targets other than Sicily.

Fantastic fakers, the Brits anticipated every possible question, covered every finicky detail. Where, for instance, should the body come ashore? Answer: the town of Huelva, where there was known to be a very active German agent in cahoots with the supposedly neutral local Spaniards. What could the Spanish authorities be expected to do? They would turn the body over to the British vice-consul at Huelva for burial, but only after the contents of his briefcase had been copied and passed on to the agent. When would be the best time to pull off this stunt? In April, when navy hydrographs confirmed that the winds would be right to push the body ashore at Huelva.

The plotters went to elaborate lengths to make the body itself fit the scheme. It would have to be the corpse of a youngish man who had died of pneumonia, because then he would have fluid in his lungs that would convince a coroner he had died by drowning.

He also should have been taking special precautions against losing his briefcase. Since it was common practice for couriers to chain to themselves the dispatch boxes carrying important papers, the pseudo-officer would have his case chained to his raincoat as though he had been trying to make himself as comfortable as possible on the long flight from London to Tunisia.

It was necessary to give Captain (Acting Major) William Martin a persona. In his pockets would be found a small wealth of documentation: his Marine identification card, a letter from his bank complaining of an overdraft of his account, letters from his fiancée—Pam—and a photo of her, a letter from his father warning that if he did marry Pam he should be sure to make a will, and ticket stubs from a London show he'd seen with Pam.

The ruse would be more convincing if Major Martin were going to North Africa for reasons beyond merely acting as a courier. A fabricated letter from Lord Louis Mountbatten, chief of Combined Operations, to Admiral Andrew Cunningham, the Mediterranean commander in chief, assured that the major was an expert in landing craft and therefore quite able to handle the problem that had come up.

As for the most important letter in the briefcase, the committee cooked up an "old boy" communication from "Archie" to "Alex," Archie being Sir Archibald Nye, vice chief of the Imperial General Staff, and Alex being General Sir Harold Alexander, at the Eighteenth Army Group headquarters in Tunisia. The main thrust of the letter was to sympathize with Alex about the supply problems he was facing, but to inform him that just now he couldn't be given everything he'd asked for. An almost throwaway aside mentioned that the Allied assault would come in the east, falling on Greece. The letter also reported that the idea of using a feint against Sicily as a cover for the Grecian landings had been rejected in favor of using it as the cover for another operation. That alternative went unmentioned—except that a jocular postscript looked forward to the time when these two old friends might sit down over a lunch of sardines.

The committee got permission to use the body of a thirty-four-year-old man who had died of pneumonia. They packed it in dry ice for the submarine trip to the waters off Huelva, dressed it in the proper uniform, chained on the briefcase and had the sub push it off to drift to shore.

Everything went according to plan. A Spanish doctor examined the body and certified that death was due to asphyxiation by seawater. The fictitious Major Martin was given a full military funeral at the cemetery in Huelva. As Montagu noted in his book *Beyond Top Secret Ultra*, written later when he could acknowledge the help of the codebreakers, decrypts showed that the documents had indeed fallen into German hands and that while Axis leaders still believed Sicily was the most likely invasion site, they now felt sure the Allies might try to surprise them by capturing Sardinia first and then come down onto Sicily. Axis commanders also felt compelled to plan against landings in Greece.

Their response was to send troops to both Sardinia and Corsica and to strengthen the islands' defense facilities—at the expense of Sicily. In Sicily they switched forces from the southern beaches to those in the west and the north, better for fending off an approach from Sardinia. As for Hitler, he was so sure the initial landings would be made on Greece that he dispatched Rommel to organize Grecian defenses and shifted a panzer army there as well as some Sicily-based motor torpedo boats. The Germans also laid minefields off the Greek coast. Even after the assault on Sicily had begun, Hitler thought it only a feint covering the real objective, Sardinia.

In the foreword to Montagu's first book, Lord Ismay wrote that Operation Mincemeat "succeeded beyond our wildest dreams." It "spreadeagled the German defensive effort right across Europe, even to the extent of sending German vessels away from Sicily itself."

Sicily: Patton vs. Montgomery vs. the Axis

Partly because of the deception, the Allied landings on the southeast corner of Sicily on July 10, 1943, met with little opposition. They confirmed, however, that a cross-Channel invasion of France that summer would have been premature. The Allies' mastery of amphibious operations was still too weak. The supply of landing craft available was inadequate to meet the needs of so large an undertaking. Command decisions were too rigid: the plan to send American and English glider forces in ahead of the landings was carried out even though high winds were prevailing over that corner of Sicily. The result was that the parachutists were too widely scattered to be effective, and many of the gliders, released against the strong head winds, never reached their landing sites, crashing instead into the sea. Communications were fouled up: navy antiaircraft gunners were not informed that approaching planes were C-47s carrying a reinforcement of paratroops; 22 of the planes were destroyed and 37 badly damaged, with 246 paratroops lost to "friendly fire."

But for the codebreakers the results might have been worse. Harry Hinsley has reported, for example, that the planners of the invasion had assumed that three hundred ships might be lost to air attack off the beaches. But decrypts of Enigma messages revealed that the bomber units based in Sicily were being withdrawn to the mainland. The vastly superior Allied air cover for the landings reduced the losses to just twelve ships.

Once landed in Sicily, Allied commanders benefited from a copious flow of signals intelligence. While the codebreakers were unable to read the Italian high-grade navy and air force codes, they more than made up for this blind spot by their mastery of the German air force Enigma. In addition, they were solving the key used by the Luftwaffe's ground organization in Italy, and that employed in army-air liaison traffic. A new high-level Fish-type German army key for communications between the high command in Berlin and the forces in Italy was soon solved as well.

It was apparent to all the Allied leaders that once the landings were made, the goal was to reach the northeast-corner city of Messina, the closest point to the Italian mainland. It was a maneuver that could, and should, have entrapped Axis troops by the thousands. The push toward Messina, however, degenerated into a petty, publicity-seeking, never-mind-the-casualties race between George Patton and Bernard Montgomery. Under Eisenhower, Britain's Harold Alexander was supposed to be in overall charge of the operation. Both Montgomery and Patton launched major actions without consulting him. Monty, stymied by fierce German resistance in his drive along the eastern seaboard, on his own ordered a portion of his Eighth Army to swing in a westward arc directly across the front of the northward mid-island push by Bradley's II Corps. Monty's idea was that Patton and Bradley should be ordered merely to protect his left flank. Patton, detesting his British colleague, raging against so inferior a role, made his own decision: to spur his Seventh Army in a lightning strike to take the city of Palermo. Although it was on the far western side of the island and its capture no more than a needless diversion, Palermo did win Patton headlines.

He then swung eastward along the northern coast. By a combination of frontal attacks and semisuccessful amphibious end runs around the stubborn Axis defenders, Patton's and Bradley's troops closed in on Messina. Bradley's memoir has divulged how civil dignitaries attempted, on the morning of August 17, to surrender to Lucian Truscott, one of Patton's generals. The general declined. Patton had issued orders that all of that should be left to him. One result, Bradley wrote, "was we had to hold Truscott's men in the hills and watch helplessly as the last of the Germans fled the city. I was so angry at Patton's megalomania that I was half tempted to enter the city myself and greet him on a street corner when he arrived."

Patton arranged a motor cavalcade and a surrender ceremony an hour before the first of Monty's troops entered the city. The victory trappings were tarnished by a major failure of the campaign. The Allies allowed the cornered Axis troops, most particularly the Germans, to escape across the Strait of Messina to Italy virtually unpunished. The failure came about even though the codebreakers warned as early as August 6 that the withdrawals were under way. Headquarters staffs simply seemed unable to accept what the decrypts were telling them. As late as August 10 an HQ summary found "no adequate indication that the enemy intends an immediate evacuation of the Messina bridgehead." Only on August 13 was the Tactical Air Force told that "evacuation is held to have begun," when actually it was nearing completion. Thousands of Axis troops and their armor awaited the Allies on the far shore.

The conquest of Sicily, taking thirty-eight days, was a needlessly costly campaign. Allied casualties ran to 22,811—5,532 killed, 14,410 wounded and 2,869 missing. However, the invasion did succeed in its aims, particularly the goal of driving Italy out of the war and out of the Axis. Allied fliers helped by heavily bombing the railroad marshaling yards in Rome, confirming the belief of many Italians that defeat was inevitable. Magic decrypts of reports from Japan's ambassador to Rome supplied the Allies a day-by-day accounting of Italy's desire for a separate peace, information that told Allied leaders just when to give the Italians ten days to accept an unconditional surrender. On July 25, King Victor Emmanuel III summoned Mussolini to his palace, told him he was dismissed, had him arrested, and appointed Field Marshal Pietro Badoglio to succeed him as head of the Italian government. While pretending, for as long as possible, to remain on Hitler's side, the Italians secretly signed terms of unconditional surrender set by the Allies.

Any elation Allied leaders felt, however, was conditioned by decrypts verifying that Hitler was determined to fight on in Italy and was, in fact, rushing in reinforcements both from the Eastern Front and the Western Wall.

Italy: The Costly Climb up the Boot

Surviving German generals confessed to war historian Liddell Hart after the war that they had expected the Allies, after prevailing in Sicily, to make their next landings well up to the north on the Italian coast. Hindsight suggests that this move would probably have been the right one. Successful invasions near Rome could have saved the Allies from having to fight their way the whole length of the 750-mile-long peninsula—a campaign that became the longest, most grinding, most frustrating struggle of the war in the West. What stopped Allied leaders from such a daring move was that landings so far from their Sicilian bases would have left the invasion forces without fighter aircraft protection. The Allies settled for planning two more cautious landings—one on the toe of the Italian boot, the other 200 miles up on the boot's ankle, at Salerno, south of Naples.

Several factors accounted for the painfully slow progress made by the Allies. Most important was the terrain. It was ideal both for defense and for rearguard delaying actions; it was deadly for the offense. Down the center of the peninsula are the Apennines, a rugged range that presented to the invaders an endless series of soaring mountains. From the central spine steep ridges project east and west toward the seas, and in between are ravinelike valleys through many of which race swift streams. Following the valleys, tortuous ribbons of roads twist through narrow defiles. The German defenders became experts at roadblocks, ambushes, minefields, booby traps.

Their demolition teams grew skillful at blowing up bridges, culverts, viaducts and tunnels. Their surveillance was always from on high, their big guns lying in commanding positions. In such topography tanks were of marginal use; the main task lay with foot-slogging infantry.

A second hindrance was the operation's lack of status. It was always regarded as a secondary show, with the coming invasion of France at center stage. Churchill referred to the Italian campaign as his Third Front, with the Russians first and the cross-Channel attack second. The Allies' main purpose in Italy was not so much to penetrate and conquer the nation itself as to keep German troops occupied south of the Alps and to reduce their numbers. At a key point, seven divisions were pulled out to go to England and prepare for D-Day. Both Eisenhower and Montgomery departed to take up commands for the Normandy invasion. Other divisions were siphoned off for landings on the French Riviera. To make up for these defections, the Allied command pressed into service the resources available to them from around the globe. The Italian battles were fought by what Jesse Jackson would have called a Rainbow Coalition: martial-caste Indians, knife-wielding Algerian *goumiers*, Moroccans, South Africans, Free French, Free Poles, a contingent of Brazilians, Japanese American nisei, newly formed teams of turnabout Italians, U.S. National Guard divisions and, near the end of the conflict, even a division of black infantrymen that the segregated U.S. Army deigned to send into combat. They were, of course, commanded by white officers. While many of these units distinguished themselves by their bravery, their diversity did cause problems in communications and effective coordination. Also, as John Keegan put it, "Recognition of the human fragility of the instrument under their command afflicted all the Allied generals throughout the battle for Italy and deeply affected their conduct of it."

A third factor protracting the campaign was the excellence of German generalship. Hitler told Baron Oshima he was resolved not merely to hold out in Italy but to drive the Allies back into the sea. He assigned some of his best generals to the fight. Divisions in the south were directed by the very able Albert Kesselring, aided by the astute old Prussian infantry commander, Heinrich von Vietinghoff. To head up his last bastion in the north, Hitler called on Erwin Rommel to disarm the Italian soldiery set loose by the Italian capitulation, recapture thousands of Allied prisoners and organize nearly a million captives to prepare the tough fortifications of the Gothic Line, which cut across the peninsula north of Florence.

Against these strong professionals was a mixed bag of Allied commanders. Under Eisenhower as overall commander and Alexander in charge of the Italian campaign, Montgomery was again to lead his Eighth Army. The Americans had a new leader. Patton was out of it because, in two separate incidents at hospitals in Sicily, he had slapped the faces of GIs he'd thought of as malingerers, arousing an outrage that forced Ike to put him temporarily in officerial limbo.

The new face was that of Mark Clark, commanding the Fifth Army. Eric Sevareid, a radio reporter covering the campaign, included in his memoir *Not So Wild a Dream* an insightful assessment of Clark. He had met both Clark and Eisenhower when they had just been made general officers. "I was to see one of them," he wrote, "become the victim of the natural pressures of his position and fame, while the other became their master." Sevareid noted how the jeep carrying Clark was always closely followed by another bearing his photographer, who knew he must not fail to shoot the general's preferred left profile.

Vanity of this sort might be accepted if, as in the case of Patton or MacArthur, it was accompanied by command brilliance. With Clark the evidence suggests otherwise. Worse, his cupidity for acclaim was to lead, late in the campaign, to one of the war's more deplorable decisions.

The Allied plan called for each of Montgomery's and Clark's armies to spread out from its beachhead, jointly cover the two hundred miles separating the forces and, it was hoped, entrap hordes of retreating Germans. It was a plan that called for bold action. But the boldness was all on the German side.

Montgomery had once again shown his cautious nature even before the Eighth's landing on the toe of Italy. He had delayed the invasion until British battleships, American bombers and six hundred field guns had bombarded the coast at Messina for three days—almost enough, it was said, to blow the toe off the boot. When his army did land, they found nothing but some dazed Italians who hurried forward to help unload the assault boats.

He was supposed to launch his attack well before Clark's so that he would be in a position to help Clark if the more vulnerable Salerno landings ran into trouble. But by delaying his start until September 3, Montgomery had too short a period in which to establish his beachhead before Clark made his landing, on schedule, in the early hours of September 9.

Knowing his enemy, Kesselring gambled. He left only one division to block Montgomery while shifting all his other troops, including thousands who had escaped from Sicily, to bottle up Clark's Fifth Army. An Allied decrypt warned of Kesselring's scheme, but Montgomery did not take advantage of the information. When the Germans pinned down both armies, a gap of 140 miles still yawned between them.

Clark's plan for the Salerno landings had one serious flaw. A predominantly British corps was to come ashore in the north while an American corps landed in the south. Between them was a ten-mile gap, which Kesselring quickly seized upon as an opportunity to drive a wedge between the two forces and push them separately back into the sea.

Under a tremendous naval and aerial bombardment, the landings met only moderate opposition. Kesselring had but one division in the immediate area to counter the invasion. But when the Allied attackers did not move aggressively enough to capture the high ground shutting in the Salerno plain, Kesselring's artillery and tanks seized it and used the advantage to ravage the Allied troops. With two German divisions rushed in from the line opposing Montgomery and other thousands of soldiers assembled from elsewhere in Italy, Kesselring thrust his troops into the gap. His plans for the counterattack were minutely detailed in a report to Hitler—the BP decrypt runs five pages long and tells exactly where the German general would strike, what units he would commit and how he hoped to mop up the sundered U.S. and English armies.

He came perilously close to succeeding. Clark in his 1950 memoir, *Calculated Risk*, called Salerno "a near disaster" and wrote of having to consider a lesser Dunkirk.

While Bletchley's decrypt seems not to have had any effect, other factors did. One was pure American grit. Two artillery battalions joined up to place their guns in a deadly row facing the oncoming Germans. While the battalions' officers put rifles into the hands of artillerymen not essential to the firing and rounded up an improvised infantry made up of clerks, cooks and other headquarters troops, the gunners fired eight rounds per minute per gun—an astonishing rate of firepower that, together with the rifle fire of the dug-in GIs, turned back the German thrust not much more than a mile from the beach.

Also helping to stop the Germans was another devastating round of naval gunnery and additional waves of aerial bombers. To secure the beachhead, Clark ordered a landing of paratroop reinforcements. Men of the 82nd Airborne Division were flown in from Sicily and dropped on the beach.

With the German counterattack blunted, Kesselring and Vietinghoff had to settle for a slow, grudging withdrawal northward. On September 16, spearheads from Montgomery's Eighth met with an outward push from Salerno to establish a continuous offensive line across Italy.

The codebreakers kept Allied leaders informed about another important development. A September 9 decrypt detailed orders to the German army to take over Italian warships and merchant vessels—a capture that would have added more than two hundred ships to the German arsenal. The order came too late. On September 8 the Italians fulfilled one of the terms of their withdrawal agreement with the Allies by ordering their navy to surrender. The fleet took off from its ports. Ships on the west coast fled to North Africa; those at Taranto steamed for Malta. The Germans were reduced to trying to destroy the vessels of their late allies. Using new radio-guided glider bombs, they sank an Italian battleship and damaged other vessels. Most of the ships, however, escaped. A longtime worry crease was removed from the Allied brow.

Decrypts also disclosed Hitler's plans to rescue Mussolini, imprisoned in the north. The plans were executed in a daring raid on September 10, and Il Duce was set up as the head of a puppet state, ostensibly commanding the handful of Italian soldiers still loyal to him.

Finally, the codebreakers traced one more development, one that meant bad news for the campaign in Italy. The Germans had adroitly evacuated Sardinia and Corsica, adding nearly forty thousand troops to their defenders on the mainland.

Italy 1943–44: A Winter of Discontent

For a time after the Fifth and Eighth Armies had linked up, decrypts indicated that Hitler might order Kesselring to evacuate southern Italy and make a staged withdrawal to the Rome area. The slow pace of the Allied advance changed the führer's mind. Kesselring and Vietinghoff organized their defenses to check the Allies from reaching a primary goal: the wide Liri Valley, lying beyond the mountain barriers and offering access to Rome. Allied troops made heroic sacrificial efforts to cross the rivers, climb the mountains and dislodge the Germans from their strongholds only to be thrown back. The battle settled into a bitter, bloody stalemate.

Eisenhower and his fellow generals began to consider an amphibious end run that would reach around and beyond the German lines. This landing would take place at Anzio, a coastal town thirty-five miles south of Rome. As with Salerno, Anzio would be preceded by a drive by the armies inland meant to draw the German troops away from the landings. And again, the inland troops were to link up with the invaders. This first Anzio plan came to nought, however, when neither Montgomery's nor Clark's armies could, despite more examples of incredible heroism and tremendous losses, dislodge the Germans from their mountain redoubts. Eisenhower gave up on the idea of an Anzio landing.

Then Churchill weighed in. Obsessed by the calendar that had the invasion of Normandy scheduled for May or June and that of southern France to coincide, the prime minister felt he couldn't allow the Italian campaign to drag on inconclusively. He pressed for what he called a "cat-claw," another reach around the Germans in the west. Coerced from on high, the Allied commanders agreed to organize a new try at Anzio.

Signals intelligence gave a favorable forecast for the mission, set for January 22, 1944. The codebreakers advised, accurately as it turned out, that the only German forces in place to oppose the landings would be at most two divisions, some tanks and a couple of parachute battalions. Decrypts also advised that no strong reinforcements were available within forty-eight hours' journey. Bold and decisive action would catch the Germans unprepared not only at the beach but further inland.

Once again, bold and decisive action was what Clark did not deliver. He seemed to have doubts about the landing's success. He cautioned his general in command of the operation, John P. Lucas, "Don't stick your neck out, Johnny. I did at Salerno and got into trouble." Clark gave Lucas limited objectives: to seize and hold a beachhead, yes, but to risk an inland dash only after getting firmly established ashore. Lucas was sent in without the mechanized troops for a rapid advance, and shortages of landing craft kept him from receiving armor when he most needed it. Kesselring later said of Anzio that it had seemed to him "a half-hearted measure."

The landings began well enough. With their air reconnaissance decimated by Allied fliers, the Germans did not detect the approach of the invasion fleet. The landings met with little opposition, and the first drive inland encountered only two exhausted battalions which had been pulled out of the mountain defenses to rest and refit. They were quickly overrun.

But then the successes stopped. Lucas was only too willing to accede to the warnings of caution. He concentrated on organizing his thumbnail of a beachhead instead of maintaining the momentum of his attack. Kesselring observed "the hesitant advance of those troops which had landed," and wrote, "That morning I already had the feeling that the worst danger had been staved off."

By the time Lucas was ready, on the ninth day, to push toward Rome, his German opponent had put together a formidable defensive cordon around the Anzio beachhead. Hitler helped by rushing in reinforcements from Yugoslavia, Germany, France and northern Italy. Decrypts warned of these transfers and also of the shift of bombers to harass the beachhead.

Lucas's belated offensive was quickly checked, with grim losses. Clark and Alexander ordered him to abandon the attack and dig in. Now it was the Germans' turn. Kesselring planned another of his powerful counterattacks meant to split the beachhead forces and either encircle the fragments or drive them back into the sea. Then occurred what Hinsley termed "one of the most valuable decrypts of the whole war," a revelation that is credited with converting even Mark Clark into a believer in Ultra. It forewarned of the counterattack and predicted precisely where it would hit. When the Germans came, the Allied troops were ready for them. The advance was met by withering fire from Lucas's artillery, tanks, tank destroyers and mortars as well as by some seven hundred sorties by Allied aircraft and shelling by two navy cruisers.

The Germans pressed their first attack for five days, only to be held off by American firepower and GI will. Decrypts pointed up the moment, on February 21, when Kesselring admitted that the offensive had failed. Clark came ashore and relieved Lucas, replacing him with the more aggressive Lucian K. Truscott.

The Germans refused to give up their attempts to smash the Anzio toehold. Further decrypts gave notice that they were organizing another counterattack. Again the Allies knew what to expect and where to mass their power. The German attackers were mauled. On March 1 they sent messages reporting that they were withdrawing to their starting line. A long report from Kesselring advised Berlin that he could not hope to eliminate the beachhead with the forces at his command; the best he could do was to keep it bottled up. For prudence's sake he was rushing the construction of a new defense line to which he could fall back and still prevent the Allies from reaching Rome.

That was the end of German attempts to eradicate Anzio. Kesselring was content to pin in the invaders, keep them separated from the main Allied forces and make life on the beachhead perilous and miserable. His heavy guns and Luftwaffe bombers forced the Allied soldiery to burrow underground and live like beleaguered moles. German radio called Anzio "a prison camp where the inmates feed themselves."

Churchill lamented, "I had hoped that we were hurling a wildcat onto the shore, but all we had got was a stranded whale."

The inland attack ordered by Clark to draw Germans away from the

Anzio landing was an assault across the Rapido River. Clark persisted in carrying out the attack even though he was warned that the strong German defenses and zeroed-in artillery on the far side of the deep, swift-flowing stream doomed it to failure. For the GIs involved, the Rapido crossing quickly turned into a hopeless death trap. So overwhelming was the defeat that it was investigated after the war by a Congressional committee.

With the repulse at the Rapido, with Anzio a stranded whale, a virtual stalemate continued all through March and April and early May. The center and symbol of Allied frustration became the monastery of Monte Cassino. Its great two hundred-yard-long bulk of masonry sat atop the Cassino massif and looked down from a height of seventeen hundred feet on the approaches to it. Below the abbey was Castle Hill, another rugged promontory, and on the banks of the Rapido River the armed town of Cassino itself. By placing heavy guns and artillery spotters on the brow of the massif, by turning the lower reaches into a vast warren of concrete pillboxes, fortified stone houses, minefields and barbed wire entanglements, and by diverting the Rapido to flood the plain below into a quagmire in which armor bogged down, the Germans had made the whole into an impregnable natural fortress.

Allied commanders waged three major battles trying to take the monastery, only to have each of them driven back with severe casualties. Although German gunners placed themselves close to the abbey's walls on either side, their general scrupulously avoided using the structure itself as a fortification, a nicety that Allied commanders refused to accept. Eighth Army commanders called for it to be destroyed—a decision that, to his credit, Clark strongly opposed. The plan went ahead, with heavy artillery combining with a raid by U.S. bombers to reduce the historic structure to rubble.

The bombers were supposed to first drop leaflets on the monastery warning the monks and refugees within its walls to get out at once. That done, the bombers' assault would be followed by having a division of Indian fighters swing around to the abbey's rear and drive out the German defenders. Like so many other actions in the Italian campaign, execution of the plan was botched. The bombers made their terrible run not on February 16 as expected but a day earlier. The bishop and some 250 of the refugees remaining in the shrine were killed. The Indians were not ready and their attack failed. The German troops happily moved into the rubble and used the giant blocks of stone to make their fortress still stronger. Here as at Anzio the stalemate held.

What finally did the Germans in was a plan that depended heavily on their intelligence blindness. Now they were lacking not only cryptanalytic clues; their air reconnaissance had largely been swept from the skies. Astutely employing radio-silent maneuvers at night and camouflage by day, Alexander organized a huge attack force. Kesselring thought he was facing six divisions on the main front when in actuality he was up against more than fifteen. Among them were a division of agile, mountain-climbing Moroccans and a Polish division whose troops had once been captives of the Russians.

As a deceptive move, Alexander had amphibious operations staged near Naples, where German intelligence agents were sure to report them. Kesselring responded as expected: he kept his mobile units in the west to guard against being outflanked by another possible landing.

Alexander's planning was guided by a steady flow of signals intelligence that told him Kesselring's complete order of battle, the sections of the front for which his units were responsible and such other details as the number of his tanks and how many of them were serviceable.

A Bletchley decrypt even informed Alexander when to launch this, the fourth Battle of Cassino. It disclosed that Hitler had summoned several officers to discuss plans with him on May 11 to 12. The news assured Alexander that an attack at that time would be a surprise, and it was.

The offensive was helped by one of Kesselring's rare errors. Thinking the rugged terrain of the Aurunci Mountains would forestall any advance there, he left only a thin line to guard the area. The French mountain troops readily managed the ascent and broke through to a point where they were within reach of the Liri Valley and the road to Rome. The German front crumbled. By May 17 the British had outflanked Cassino. The next day the Poles occupied the monastery ruins and raised their flag over the site, whose capture had claimed nearly four thousand of their colleagues' lives. The Germans were at last in retreat along the entire main battlefront, and their exhaustion and desperation were aptly chronicled by Allied decrypts.

As for the troops at Anzio, Alexander wanted them to break out, drive northward toward the town of Valmontone and block the Highway 6 escape route of the German divisions retreating from the south—a move, he thought, that would bag thousands of prisoners.

He figured without Mark Clark. Along with his own ego driving him to become the liberator of Rome were added the pressures from on high, particularly from Churchill and Marshall, to take the Eternal City before the political significance of its capture was overshadowed by the Normandy landings. Moreover, as Clark recorded in his memoir, "I was determined that the Fifth Army was going to capture Rome." His determination was driven by the belief that "practically everybody else was trying to get into the act."

The Taking of Rome: A Hollow Victory

General Truscott fulfilled his part of Alexander's plan. His troops drove through the German defenses at Anzio and headed north toward Valmontone. Eric Sevareid has left a vivid account of what came next. General Clark, who had earlier endorsed the plan to entrap the Germans, called a press conference at which he now claimed it was "nonsense" to think the Germans could be bottled up by seizing Highway 6, since there were many lesser roads by which they could escape. He ordered Truscott to direct only about a third of his troops toward Valmontone; the main body would head straight for Rome.

The correspondents were dumbfounded. Truscott and other commanders were outraged. But Clark was in charge. Paranoid that the British might take Rome while his troops were busy rounding up Germans, he made sure his Fifth Army got there first.

Even though the Germans were in retreat, they could still manage delaying actions. The most serious holdup came at the Alban Hills, the last breastworks defending Rome. Impatient, Clark sent armor across the flat ground between the hills and the sea. According to Sevareid, "Every vehicle was easily spotted in the enemy's gun sights and within ten minutes we had lost twenty-five tanks."

The Alban Hills impasse was solved by General Fred Walker of the Thirty-sixth Division. He drew two regiments from the main line, circled them stealthily around to the right during the night and sent them climbing the two-thousand-foot height *behind* the German line. His maneuver broke the defense. Most of the Germans, declaring Rome an open city, retreated beyond it. But some maintained a rearguard action.

At one point of delay, Brigadier General Robert Frederick, whom Sevareid described as "the young and capable commander of the special 'commando' regiment of Americans and Canadians," was watching the progress of his men when a jeep drew alongside. Major General Geoffrey Keyes, corps commander, descended. "General Frederick," he asked, "what's holding you up here?"

FREDERICK: The Germans, sir.

KEYES: How long will it take you to get across the city limits?

FREDERICK: The rest of the day. There are a couple of SP [self-propelled] guns up there.

KEYES: That will not do. General Clark must be across the city limits by four o'clock.

FREDERICK: Why?

KEYES: Because he has to have a photograph taken.

FREDERICK [*after a long pause*]: Tell the general to give me an hour.

The guns were silenced, the general and his faithful photographer arrived and the pictures were taken, in Sevareid's words, "of the conqueror and his conquered city."

It was June 5. Clark got his headlines and pictures in the world's press. He had beaten the D-Day deadline imposed on him by his superiors by one day. The next morning he called for a meeting of his corps commanders. Arriving, they found they were to supply a proper martial backdrop for more of Clark's posturing before press photographers. Soon Clark signaled that he wanted to make an announcement. The measure of his myopia was made plain by his opening words: "This is a great day for the Fifth Army." The reporters blanched. His generals reddened with embarrassment, some with anger. What about the much-bloodied Eighth Army? The self-sacrificing Poles? The Free French? The whole of what Clark himself had called a "hodgepodge army" that had united to make this day possible?

For these newsbreaks the chance to encircle Kesselring's entire Tenth Army was lost. The German general took full advantage of the opportunity. His delaying actions at Valmontone fought off Truscott's inadequate force while the bulk of his army safely slipped through to the Gothic Line—to fight, and kill, again.

The rest of the Italian campaign was anticlimactic in terms of its newsmaking value. Churchill envisioned the Allies smashing through the Alps to seize Vienna and possibly even Budapest and Prague before the Russians claimed them, but that remained a dream. The need to transfer combat-hardened divisions to the invasion of southern France drained away strength for tackling the last German redoubts in Italy.

Yet it must be remembered that a main purpose of the war on the peninsula was to tie up and maim German forces that could otherwise have helped throw back the Normandy invasion and/or stop the Soviets in the East. The campaign did that. Hitler's decision to contest every yard of Italian territory played into the Allied hands. For twenty months a score of

German divisions were held there and bloodied. As BP veteran Ralph Bennett has written, "Every man, tank and gun [Hitler] sent to Italy meant one less to defend *Festung Europa*."

Even with depleted forces, Alexander and Clark continued the pressure. Their troops broke the Gothic Line and, as the war in Europe was ending, had the last of Germany's shattered Italian divisions fleeing through the Alps.

Their final drive did have the effect of encouraging Italian partisans to spring up and seize northern Italy. In the process they captured Mussolini and his mistress, then killed them and strung up their bodies by the heels like sides of beef for once-worshiping countrymen now to jeer at and spit upon.

13 The Coming of the Ultra Americans

WHILE the British were happy to see the influx of American fighting men, they were not so sure about the advent of U.S. codebreakers. A serious question arose as to whether the Americans and the British could ever reach an agreement to collaborate in signals intelligence. There were convincing reasons why they should unite their cryptanalytic programs, and a good many lives were lost because of their failures to do so. But there were almost equally powerful reasons why they should not. Chief among these were security concerns. No military unit with a hold on some aspect of Sigint trusts any other unit to protect its secrets. So it was then: security gave teeth to interservice rivalries. The U.S. Navy would not entrust the U.S. Army with its methods of cryptanalysis, much less make them available to the British. The British, for their part, saw American intelligence operatives as gabby, loose-lipped security risks who couldn't even keep the U.S. press from blabbing the Midway triumph. Seen from this perspective, both British and American intelligence seemed riddled with small-minded staffers who used the security issue more to guard their own turf than to question the advisability of cooperation.

Slowly both sides realized, however, that they had significant assets that could be shared. The Americans had their Magic; the British had Ultra. Both sides also had intelligence leaders who saw the need for mutual support. As early as August 1940, the head of the U.S. Army planning staff, Brigadier General George V. Strong, led a contingent to England to propose a "periodic exchange of information" between the British and American governments. Hinsley reported that at this meeting, Strong described U.S. progress against Japanese and Italian ciphers—this before the break-in on Purple was completed!

The British reciprocated by sending some of their most respected and talented representatives, including Alan Turing and Alastair Denniston, to discuss cryptologic matters with the likes of William Friedman. But the response was far from complete openness about the doings at Bletchley Park.

In February 1941 the Americans followed with another act of unprecedented generosity. Four junior American officers, including Friedman's disciples Abraham Sinkov and Leo Rosen, arrived in London bearing the gift of a Purple machine or—the records conflict—possibly two, which the British quickly put to work cracking Japanese diplomatic messages in Europe and the Middle East. In reciprocation the Sinkov team received a whirlwind tour of Bletchley Park that included lectures on the general cryptanalytic methods used by the British.

After these promising overtures, however, advances became a matter of two steps forward and one back. The Sinkov mission actually stoked the fires of U.S. opposition. The Americans' exposure to BP had been so superficial—it did not include even a look at a British bombe—that it was seen as a poor trade for the goodwill shown by the U.S. On the British side, surprisingly, Winston Churchill got his back up about yielding any greater depth of Ultra material to the U.S. and declared himself in favor of a "stiffer attitude" toward sharing secret intelligence. The cause was not furthered by that new indication of American security laxness: Colonel Fellers's unwitting revelations to Rommel of British plans in North Africa.

Nor was it helped by the opinion of the U.S. ambassador to Britain, Joseph P. Kennedy, that the British were doomed to defeat and should not be entrusted with U.S. intelligence secrets.

One event that strengthened cooperative attitudes in both camps was the Lend-Lease Act that Franklin Roosevelt negotiated through Congress in March 1941. The British, with their cash reserves depleted, saw this as an imaginative way to "lend" matériel that no one would be expected to return or make postwar payments for, as had been the case in the Great War. Senator Robert Taft compared it to lending chewing gum: you certainly didn't want it back. To avoid having much-needed U.S. lend-lease cargoes loaded onto ships that would then be sunk by U-boats, both navies became more forthcoming in their exchanges of North Atlantic intelligence. The Admiralty, as noted previously, advised the U.S. on setting up a Submarine Tracking Room similar to that of the Royal Navy. Further, an agreement with the Danish ambassador in Washington allowed the U.S. to establish a base in Greenland and later one in Iceland so that the U.S. took responsibility for protecting convoys over an increasingly broad area of the North Atlantic.

Gradually the collaborationists won out over the die-hard resisters, an evolution that accelerated with American entry into the war. In May 1943, this progress culminated in the BRUSA (Britain and USA) Agreement, calling for a comprehensive exchange of intelligence information. One important decision was what Hinsley called "an effective division of labor." The United Kingdom was to concentrate on the ciphers of the European and Mediterranean theaters while the U.S. took the lead responsibility for securing and disseminating intelligence about the forces of Japan.

An interesting outgrowth of BRUSA was an invitation to have American soldiery join in the British codebreaking effort. In fairly short order during 1943 the U.S. Army Signal Corps organized the 2nd Signal Service Battalion, which was to select and train three outfits to serve in Britain. These were the 6811th, 6812th and 6813th Signal Service Detachments. The original plan called for 485 officers and enlisted men to be assigned, but the number swelled past 500 as more Americans were absorbed into the various detachments. In addition, U.S. Army Intelligence assigned a select group of officers to work at Bletchley Park.

With the integration of these Americans into the Ultra program in late 1943 and early 1944, the promise of effective Anglo-American collaboration could be said, despite a continuance of much bickering and internecine suspicion, to have been, very belatedly, fulfilled.

6811: Interceptors of Axis Radio Traffic

The process of signals intelligence begins with interception. Radio operators must tune in to the rush of Morse *dit-dah* symbols and meticulously copy them down so that the texts cryptanalysts read are as free as possible of skips and garbles. Even for the most dedicated and experienced operators, the copying of Axis radio traffic in World War II posed a demanding test. Enemy transmitters deliberately used only enough power to reach the farthest station in their network. Allied radio ops trying to listen in from well outside the receiving loop had to strain to catch what they weren't meant to hear. Frequently the stream of Morse they were assigned to copy was only the thinnest thread of sound to be picked out amid a welter of booming senders closer in.

"The intercepts had to be fought for, in a battle of skills, wits and wills," British intercept operator Joan Nicholls has reported in her self-published book about her life at Britain's Beaumanor station. "The Germans were adept at placing obstacles in the way of the eavesdroppers."

The obstacles included screening transmissions with "what sounded like military bands, operatic arias, Wagner and speech, all played backwards and at high speed. It sounded like hell let loose in our ears, and underneath it all were the faint sounds of our station." Wavering signals and weather interference could make the job still tougher. A GI operator said it was like going to a noisy cocktail party and trying to listen in on a whispered conversation on the far side of the room.

The Americans had to struggle against the impression of being Johnny-come-latelies. Before the GIs ever arrived, the British network of intercept stations, mostly operated by young women like Joan Nicholls, were doing very well, thank you, without a bunch of Yanks getting into their act. The 7 officers and 195 enlisted men of the 6811th were asked to establish and operate an additional station, which the British labeled Santa Fe. While U.S. help was no doubt useful in covering the widening range of German networks, there was always the feeling among the troops of Santa Fe, of which I was one, that we were added as a courtesy.

To house the station, the Yanks were given an ancient manor, Hall Place, in Bexley, Kent, on the southeastern edge of London. Hall Place was a crumbling relic with some of its walls shored up against collapse. In its cold, drafty interior, whose medieval ceilings seemed to push down on us better-nutritioned Yank residents, the dining hall was converted into a Set Room, with banks of gray-metal Hallicrafters receivers lined up on plank tables. The detachment included one group of radio operators newly trained in the U.S. and a more experienced group transferred from the intercept station they had been manning in Newfoundland.

Santa Fe went into operation on a round-the-clock three-shift basis beginning March 1, 1944. The British assigned it some twenty-five German networks to cover, mostly German air force nets. Many, if not all, of these they were already covering. Redundancy in intercept, we were to learn, is not a waste, since in this game, in which accuracy is needed so acutely, a second operator may correctly copy a signal that the first one partially or wholly missed.

To be assigned a Luftwaffe network meant that the 6811th interceptor had to copy every message sent by all the operators on that net, with the German ops often impatiently waiting their turn. The result was that the Yank was likely to emerge after an eight-hour shift with shaking hands and bloodshot eyes, badly in need of a pint in the nearest pub.

To each shift of radio ops in the Set Room was added a team of eight men rudimentally trained as "cryptographers." Any fantasies the cryptographers harbored of actually breaking significant enemy messages, with generals anxiously awaiting the decrypts, ran up against the reality of our identifying nomenclature: we were the CRR teams, for "Compilation of Reports and Records."

In fact, because of the limitations of the "need to know," the common soldiers at Santa Fe never learned whether the masses of five-letter code transmissions the radio ops received and the cryptographers processed were ever broken. The outfit settled into the routine of handling endless yards of gibberish and making sure that each unit of it was accurately filled in and correctly identified as to time, network and frequency, without ever knowing the content of any of it.

In addition to the radio operators and us cryptographers, each of the shifts also included a small team of Teletype operators who forwarded the intercepts by landline to "Station X"—in actuality, Bletchley Park. On the telephone links to British intercept stations and to X, the fine female British voices oozed condescension toward us late-come Americans.

To do our job, we cryptographers did need to know one important secret. This we summed up in three words: "predicted call signs." In military radio the senders of coded messages try to obstruct interceptors as well as codebreakers. One of the ways they do this is by regularly changing the letters identifying their stations. Unlike commercial radio stations, which want to be recognized as WOR or WLW, military senders try to leave interceptors floundering uselessly in the ether by abruptly switching to a different frequency and employing a whole new set of call signs. What was ABC on 4031 kilocycles suddenly becomes XYZ on 2778 kilocycles.

For their systems the Germans devised fat books of call letters, forty thousand three-letter call signs to a book. At changeover times, usually shortly after midnight, the German ops were armed with a daily numerical shift. The shift told them where to move forward or backward in the call sign books to arrive at their new rows of call letters.

By the time the 6811th set up shop, the British had this whole call sign mechanism completely pinned down. Santa Fe was supplied with the "Elephant" book, which meant that it was the fifth in the series. It hadn't simply been captured somewhere; it had been compiled by infinitely patient analysts. It had blanks in it that were filled in as new call sign lists and placement coordinates came down from X.

The significance of predicted call signs was clear. If a German spy should hear any reference to the prediction, the result could be calamitous. He would know that the German system had been compromised, and if that phase of it was broken, he could arouse suspicions that the whole German encoding superstructure was breached. Many of us had nightmares in which we had one too many glasses of bitters in a pub and blurted out our most closely guarded secret in the presence of a German agent.

The kind of minuscule contributions the Yank cryptographers were able to make is exemplified by one that I recall as probably my singly most important deed of the war. It came on a day in March 1945. At that late date, with the war collapsing around them, the Germans managed to do what they had not done earlier: they made a clean break to a whole new call sign and frequency system. Suddenly everything in the radio spectrum was chaos. The German networks weren't at their usual frequencies, and what was by then the *F* book was dead without anything to replace it. The CRR could no longer provide predicted call signs. Each radio operator went on search, trying to find his network by detecting the sending idiosyncrasies of one or more of his German transmitters. In preparation for this moment, we and our operators had been boning up for days on any distinguishing quirks of the nets assigned to Santa Fe.

I was leaning over the shelf beyond which Jim Hammet, one of our brighter operators, was twiddling his dials trying to latch on to something recognizable. "That's funny," he said.

"What's funny?" I asked.

"This net leaves a space between the first three letters and the last three letters of the indicator. See this: *ARZ* space *DLY*. That's different from my net. They run all six letters together without a pause."

Excitement swelled within me. "We have only one network that does that. Benny Abruzzo's. Give me the frequency and a couple of the call signs and let me have Benny check it out."

I carried my slip of paper to Benny's set. He turned his tuning dial with the delicacy of a safecracker. His face lit up. "That's him! That's one of my guys! I'd know that Heinie meat fist anytime, anywhere!" He grabbed his pad and pencil and began happily copying.

So we three pinned down one frequency and one set of call signs for one day of that one net's operation. It was just such small victories, endlessly accumulated at Station X and fitted like pieces in a giant jigsaw puzzle, that helped the geniuses crack the Germans' systems.

It did seem to me, when I reported our find to Station X, that the British female voice at the other end of the line was, this time, not quite so patronizing.

Other than for moments like this, the work was tedious in the extreme.

Even so, everyone in the 6811th went at his tasks with one thought ever in mind: that this message, or the next one, or the one after that, could, when broken, make the difference for some soldier or sailor or airman, perhaps for a whole contingent of soldiers or sailors or airmen, out there on the fighting front. Any examples of surrender to ennui were few and far between.

The prevailing attitude can best be characterized by an incident in September 1944 when Hitler began sending over his V-2 rockets. One hit so close one day that it broke out windows and brought down a ceiling or two in the manse. A radio operator named Arthur Koester, a T/5 corporal, was at work copying his net when the frame of a window above him was ripped out and hurled on top of him. The wood and glass tore a gash in his head, sending blood coursing down over his face. Koester never stopped copying. Sergeant Vernon Pemberton, the Set Room chief, quickly had another op tune to Koester's net and begin copying the same traffic. Then he yelled at Koester, "You can break off now, Art. We've got your net covered." Koester just waved him away. "Come on now, Art," the sergeant pleaded. "Break if off so we can start taking care of you." Koester simply growled and set himself more firmly. Finally the sergeant grabbed Koester's pad and jerked it from under his hands. Koester shot to his feet, shouting at his NCO, "You stupid son of a bitch. Can't you see I'm copying?"

Art was one of two Purple Heart recipients in the 6811th. Our captain was so craven for recognition of the unit that he refused to distinguish between Koester's deserving wound and that of another GI who was hurt when a V-2 hit near the house in which he was shacked up with his British girlfriend.

6812: Operators of the Bombes

Bletchley Park relied on members of the Wrens to operate the bombes used to determine Enigma key settings. As the number of the Germans' Enigma-based ciphers increased, so did the numbers of bombes needed. At the peak, nearly two thousand Wrens were operating the bombes round the clock. For the women it was heavy going. Petty Officer Diana Payne subsequently recalled work on "the monster deciphering machines" as "soul-destroying but vital." After many months of this merciless routine, the strain began to show. As Payne reported, one Wren collapsed, rendered unconscious by overstrain. Another began to have nightmares from which she woke up desperately clutching a phantom drum of the sort she had been loading onto the bombes day after day. A girl who was due to have an operation became frantic with the thought that under the effects of the anesthetic she might give way and talk.

When in early 1944 fresh cadres of Americans began to move into that corner of Britain to help operate the bombes, their arrival was most welcome. These were the men of the 6812th Signal Service Detachment, 5 officers and 149 enlisted men. Whoever was doing the code-naming of the American outfits must have been a railway buff. The name for this unit was Rock Island. The troops were billeted on the northwest outskirts of London until they could get their own camp built, partly by their own labor, in the Middlesex town of Eastcote. Their three-shift work assignment was to operate an array of bombes in a building they called the Factory. They were close enough to London to be on the receiving end of a few V-weapons that overshot their target, but far enough away from Bletchley Park that they never went there and knew of its existence only via phone lines and teleprinter links. Here, too, the "need to know" limited the GIs from learning definitely that the messages on which they worked were ever broken. "We did what we were told," Paul Best of the detachment remembered later, "and had to take it on faith that our work was being effective in helping to solve the German messages."

Their orders came from Bletchley Park in the form of "menus" instructing them what to do. As Best explained,

Each drum of a bombe was an analogue of a rotor of the Enigma machine, with 26 letter positions on each drum. BP would send us a menu based on a crib of a German phrase that they hoped would be found in the message. The operator would place the drums on the bombe in the order specified by BP, turn them to the menu positions, plug in the cables at the rear, again according to the menu instructions, and switch on the machine. Essentially we were seeking a yes-or-no answer as to whether the crib was actually a part of the message. If the answer was no, we would keep the bombe running through its fifteen-to-twenty minute cycle and nothing would happen. We would call BP and report, "Sorry, that menu was no good." But if there was a "hit," the bombe would hunt for a voltage that indicated a circuit closing and would stop. We would note all the rotor positions and set up our replica of an Enigma machine in those positions to test whether the hit was confirmed. Then we would send the confirmation back to BP and wait for our next menu. With all that array of bombes in the Factory, we could check out hundreds, thousands, of possible cribs in a single day.

As with the men of the 6811th, those of the 6812th were haunted by their secret knowledge. "It was a load to carry," Best recalled. "Here we were, operating replicas of the Germans' encoding machines and, what's more, also operating the still more complex machines that, we felt sure, were being used to conquer the German machines. We dreaded the possibility of one of us going off his rocker and being unable to hold it in any longer. It never happened, but the possibility hung over us like an inescapable cloud."

Here, too, the work was a triumph of determination over boredom. The Americans did something the Wrens hadn't been doing. They kept records of the bombes' performance. Harold Keen, BP's representative at the British Tabulating Machine Company, which produced the bombes, was delighted. He used the GIs' records to make improvements in subsequent bombes.

At BP, Two Groups of American Codebreakers

The first American serviceman to be stationed at Bletchley Park was a young navy lieutenant junior grade. Joe Eachus had been one of the bright lads looking after Alan Turing in his 1942 visit to the U.S. Impressed, Turing had him assigned, in the autumn of that year, to Hut 8. Eachus later recalled those times when denizens of the Hut were struggling with the U-boat codes. "You could tell by people's faces how we were doing," he remembered. "When we were locked out, the faces were grim and discouraged, because we knew what havoc the Germans were creating out there on the seas. But when we were cracking the codes and helping our ships evade the U-boats, there were smiles all around."

Eachus was a special case. Only when the BRUSA Agreement was reached were sizable contingents of Americans invited to join in the codebreaking at Bletchley Park. In the last half of 1943 two separate groups began arriving.

First were the men of the 6813th. Of the three Signal Corps detachments of "Ultra Americans," this one was clearly the elite. To be assigned to it, the men had to have achieved particularly high scores on the Army Classification Tests. They received the more prestigious title of *cryptanalysts* while the members of the other units were identified as *cryptographers*, *traffic analysts* and the like. The 6813th heavily featured Ph.D.s, college academicians, chess masters and accomplished mathematicians. Completing the U.S. railroad cover designations, the unit was labeled Rio Grande.

Second of the U.S. groups at BP was a contingent that reported directly to Military Intelligence at the Pentagon. When it came to staffing U.S. Army Intelligence, Secretary of War Stimson looked to Alfred McCormack, like Stimson a former Wall Street lawyer. As reported in Thomas Parrish's book *The Ultra Americans*, McCormack slipped directly into the uniform of an army colonel and went at his wartime job with great energy and unflagging intelligence. An important task he took on was to organize and oversee the daily summaries of Magic decrypts that did so much in shaping the decisions that U.S. leaders made about the conduct of the war. With the signing of the BRUSA Agreement, Secretary Stimson also asked him to seek out the best available men for duty at Bletchley Park.

When he visited Bletchley he saw it as a "personnel heaven" because the codebreaking program got first pick of the best brains available. It was not that way in the U.S. Official personnel channels confronted McCormack with the rigidities of the civil service and the stifling rules of the military branches. It was maddening, since he was determined to send only first-class minds to BP, men who would fit into that select group without embarrassing the U.S.

McCormack found ways to get around the barriers. One was to comb the ranks of men already in the service. That way he came up with Lewis Powell, an air force intelligence officer who in later life became a justice of the Supreme Court, and Alfred Friendly, subsequently editor of the *Washington Post* and a television personality. McCormack also used his contacts at Ivy League schools to enlist men such as Telford Taylor, a Harvard Law School graduate then serving as general counsel of the Federal Communications Commission.

The two groups reported to different commanders and were billeted separately. Heading the 6813th was Captain William Bundy, of a Boston Brahman family and married to the daughter of Dean Acheson, then the undersecretary of state. In charge of McCormack's group, which became known at Bletchley Park as 3-US because they were assigned to Hut 3, was Taylor.

Three members of the 6813th supplied the vanguard of the U.S. troops dispatched to BP: Paul Whitaker, Selmer Norland and Arthur Levenson. Whitaker and Norland, both fluent in German, were assigned as translators in Hut 3; Levenson worked as a cryptanalyst under Gordon Welchman in Hut 6. He was soon joined there by Bundy.

Varied placements would become the rule for the members of the 6813th. Instead of functioning as a cohesive unit, they were integrated piecemeal into the complex British operation, a few here and a few there. The unit's Walter Sharp has recollected, "We came to BP on the same trucks, dispersed to our assigned offices and under the principle of 'need to know' didn't chatter about what we or the other fellows were up to."

Sharp's assignment was in what was called the Machine Room because each of the operators there sat before an Enigma clone. "The head of the shift," he recalled,

> was responsible for directing those operating the bombes, located at several remote stations, as to what problems they should attack. The rest of us were there to test the "stops" that the bombe crews telegraphed in. Once we had proved that a particular key for a given army or air force unit was broken for the day, the settings were sent to the Decoding Room, where all the messages for that day were deciphered, then to be passed on to translators, intelligence analysts and disseminators. At the same time, the bombe team working on the now-broken key was pulled off that and given another task.

Of his work in Hut 3, Norland remembered, "When a message was broken, the plaintext German was still in five-letter groups. We had to sort that out, try to fill in garbles and omissions and render the message into understandable English. Then we submitted it to the analyst on the watch, who determined its degree of priority and to whom it should be distributed."

A memoir by the late Jim Nielson told of his work in the Quiet Room. Here the operators took on messages that had resisted deciphering and for which there were no verified call signs. The Quiet Room's personnel made a second go against the messages to see whether they could be made to yield.

George Vergine, whom Parrish described as "a brilliant young cryptanalyst," wrote a memoir "for my relatives to tell them what I did during the war." At Bletchley Park, he worked for a time on the Enigma and then transferred to the "Newmanry," where he collaborated with Max Newman on deciphering Fish teleprinter codes. To read his memoir is to marvel at the mathematical complexities young minds could master under the pressure of breaking the codes that revealed "the thinking and planning of the whole German High Command."

As for McCormack's 3-US men, a number of them, after learning the ropes at Bletchley Park, were assigned to Special Liaison Units attached to

American operational units. Don Bussey, for example, transferred over to the continent to become an officer in the intelligence section of the U.S. Seventh Army.

By being spread throughout Bletchley Park the Americans learned virtually every phase of the codebreaking program. "If someone had decided to pull all the Americans together and set them up as an operational unit," according to Sharp, "I think we could have done very well. By the end of the war we would have gained from our experience with the British folks most of the arcane skills needed to identify enemy communications, direct their interception, read and translate messages, and have some idea what to do with the information they contained."

The Americans of the 6813th were also the elite in their off-duty hours. At BP they were part of a diverse group that included many civilians and that ignored the niceties of military rank. They all were known to each other by their first names. The GIs drew neither KP nor guard duty; all that was done by people specifically assigned to those jobs. At their billet the Americans had their own very good cooks; "We probably ate as well as any Americans, at home or abroad," said Sharp. In the mess hall, officers and enlisted men did seat themselves separately. "Someone among the officers," Sharp reported, "had the idea of hanging a curtain between the two sections. The first time it was drawn, the racket from the EM side was such that the officers got the message. The curtain was not drawn again."

For the Ultra Americans, Praise and Honors

By war's end, the U.S. soldiers involved in Ultra had pretty well erased the idea that they were mere tokens of Anglo-American cooperation. They had earned their way. Recognition of their efforts came from the European theater's chief signal officer, Major General William S. Rumbough.

To those of the 6813th he wrote, "The extreme value of your work has been recognized." He commended the 6811th for "operating on a par with British intercept stations which had been in action for a period of three years or more and, in numerous instances, actually surpassing them in performance." He also congratulated the Teletype operators for their accuracy and reliability. The 6812th received a similar commendation from the general. The detachment's work was also praised in David Kahn's writings for "producing two to three times as many solutions as a comparable Wren unit, not because it ran the machines faster but because the men changed setups much more quickly."

British appreciation of the Ultra Americans' contributions at BP is indicated by the postwar awards they approved for individual performance. Bundy received the Order of the British Empire, while Norland was recognized as a Member of the British Empire. Robert Carrol, George Vergine, Cecil Porter and Harold Porter of the 6813th were awarded the British Empire Medal.

While the war continued, and for those thirty secret years afterward, the three Signal Corps detachments were almost entirely unaware of each other's existence. This changed when Fred Winterbotham's *The Ultra Secret* opened the floodgates of information. One member of the 6811th, Robert Fredrickson, gave himself a retirement career of locating the members of the three detachments and bringing them together. Now, more than half a century later, the Ultra Americans have begun to hold the kind of reunions that have become old hat to most World War II servicemen. In addition to posting regular newsletters and organizing the yearly reunions, Fredrickson periodically leads a trip back to the outfits' old haunts. They marvel at Hall Place, handsomely restored and with beautiful gardens replacing what had been GI drill grounds and ball fields, and they enjoy finding their way to Eastcote and the Factory. At Bletchley Park they are pleased to see that the mansion and its huts have been saved from the bulldozers bent on converting the grounds into a housing development during the thirty years when the wartime activities there remained a mystery. They are gratified to see BP made into a cryptology museum and to take part in the tours that have made it an increasingly popular tourist attraction. And in the mansion's library the American visitors take a moment to reread a plaque mounted on the oak-paneled walls that offers these lines of summary from Shakespeare's *Henry V*, act 2, scene 2:

> The King hath note of all that they intend,
> By interception which they dream not of.

14 Up the Island Ladder Toward Tokyo

JAPANESE intelligence about Allied plans never played a serious role in the Pacific war. For the Allies the main intelligence problems came when their codebreakers were blacked out by the system changes the Japanese introduced as security measures. Then Allied commanders were prone to the same fumbling and bungling that characterized many of the Japanese operations.

Perhaps because of that unprincipled press release that broadcast the role of codebreaking in the defeat of the Imperial forces at Midway, the Japanese became rigorous in revising their code systems during the summer and autumn of 1942. The May 28 change from JN-25b to JN-25c plunged Allied crypto teams into almost total eclipse. As the summer progressed, troublesome changes were also made in the Imperial Navy's call sign systems. In August, just as Allied analysts were making some headway with JN-25c, the Japanese made another fundamental switch, from JN-25c to JN-25d. As Nimitz's staff report on August 1 noted dolefully, "We are no longer reading the enemy mail, and today we must depend almost entirely on traffic analysis to deduce enemy deployment."

Allied codebreakers struggled mightily to regain their mastery. A few useful decrypts resulted from an occasional Japanese regression to superseded codes. Otherwise, intelligence was reduced to the less exact arts of direction finding, traffic analysis and photoreconnaissance. Invaluable aid also came from the network of coast watchers, brave men the Australians put in place to transmit observations from within the Japanese perimeter.

This extended period of frustration for the cryptanalysts came at the time when the Japanese made landings in the Solomon Islands in late June and early August, and began constructing an airfield on Guadalcanal. Word of the development came primarily from the coast watchers.

Allied commanders knew they could not allow this venture to succeed. Guadalcanal would give the Japanese a new operational center 560 miles east of their major base at Rabaul in New Britain. From the new field, the emperor's bombers and Zero fighters could provide air support for landings on still more easterly islands. To prevent the Japanese from severing the lifeline between the U.S. and Australia, Guadalcanal must be retaken before the airstrip was completed.

In long, rancorous meetings in Washington, the U.S. high command had already decided on how the war in the Pacific should be conducted. The question was how to divide responsibilities between the two strong leaders Nimitz and MacArthur. Nimitz believed that the best route to Tokyo lay along the small islands in the mid-Pacific. MacArthur, obsessed with his pledge to return to the Philippines, favored a great arc north out of Australia and northwest along the big islands of New Guinea and New Britain, concentrating on seizing Rabaul. The Joint Chiefs of Staff had compromised by endorsing both plans and drawing a line of demarcation with MacArthur in charge to the west and Nimitz commanding operations to the east. Guadalcanal lay just barely within Nimitz's vast area of control.

Being surprised had become almost standard operating procedure for the clueless Japanese military. So it was with Nimitz's August 7 landing on Guadalcanal. The small Japanese contingent on the island, mostly laborers, offered little opposition to the invaders. In just thirty-six hours the Marines had captured the airstrip, which they named Henderson Field in honor of a flight commander who had died leading an attack at Midway. Tulagi, the island adjacent to Guadalcanal, was seized after suicidal resistance by the Japanese troops occupying it.

American commanders, having to proceed without guidance from their codebreakers, were also vulnerable to surprise. That came on the night of August 8, when a Japanese fleet slipped past Savo Island off Guadalcanal and attacked the warships protecting the landing. Four heavy cruisers—three American and one Australian—were lost to the Japanese guns and highly superior Long Lance torpedoes. The ships supplying the Marines ashore backed off after delivering only half their supplies and food. When the engineering equipment needed for work on the airfield was withdrawn, the Marines used abandoned Japanese machines to do the job.

In a tragic twist, Allied intercept operators had delivered into cryptanalysts' hands the message detailing the Imperial Navy's planned course of action off Guadalcanal, but the codebreakers were unable to solve it until two weeks after the battle had been fought.

The Battle of Savo Island was the first of seven naval engagements that battered both antagonists over the next six months. Each side had twenty-five ships sunk—so many that the waters there came to be known as "Iron-bottom Sound." As noted by Guadalcanal veteran Phil Jacobsen on his Web history of the Pacific war, the total of Allied sailors who lost their lives at sea was more than three times that of Marines and GIs killed on land.

Meanwhile, the struggle on Guadalcanal surged back and forth in the island's fetid jungles and malarial swamps. The Japanese, recognizing that the loss of the island would punch a dangerous hole in their defense perimeter, were as determined to retain the island as the Americans were to drive them out.

Japanese movements were being tracked by an unseen foe. Even when Hypo and Melbourne were blacked out, the coast watchers filled in. On September 30, 1942, for example, they warned of a cruiser force heading toward Guadalcanal to bombard the Marines there and put Henderson Field out of commission. So warned, an American fleet met them in the Battle of Cape Esperance. It was a confused struggle, a strategic draw in terms of damage done, but the Japanese ships turned back.

The time of drought for the main Allied cryptographic centers finally ended. In late August they began breaking into the new JN-25 code and by late September were reading it expeditiously enough to supply useful tactical information. When on October 1 the Japanese activated a new substitution table meant to throw off cryptanalysts, the Allies broke it in two days.

With Henderson Field planes controlling the air by day and Allied intelligence units guiding the destruction of large-scale attempts to reinforce and supply Imperial troops on Guadalcanal, the Japanese were reduced to night runs, which became known as the Tokyo Express. Even a number of these runs, however, were anticipated and the transports sunk.

Frustrated, the Japanese high command decided in November to mount one more strong effort to dislodge the Marines. The Tokyo Express landed so many reinforcements that for the first time, the Japanese outnumbered the Americans on the island. Admiral Yamamoto, revered despite the Midway disaster, commanded a task force that sought to add to those gains by bombarding Henderson Field while eleven transports ferried in additional infantrymen and tons of supplies.

The codebreakers told Bull Halsey, now in overall charge of the American and Australian fleet, what to expect. There followed three days of vicious fighting, the two naval battles of Guadalcanal. Poorly commanded American ships suffered severe losses, but the Japanese fared even worse. Most important, eight of the Japanese transports were sunk and thousands of the soldiers drowned.

By the first week of December, the Tokyo Express was limited to runs by submarines bringing in wholly inadequate supplies to the sick and starving troops. Allied decrypts foretold another desperation measure: a run by fast destroyers bearing 1,200 drums of supplies. Halsey saw to it that the destroyers were shot up and turned back. Only 220 of the drums reached land.

The time for the denouement on Guadalcanal had arrived. In late January 1943, decrypts alerted the Allies to a Japanese plan for a new series of warship runs to the island. What the messages failed to disclose was that the ships were not there to bring in reinforcements. Their purpose was evacuation. The Tokyo Express rescued thirteen thousand emaciated soldiers, all that were left of the thirty-six thousand who had come there to fight. By contrast, American losses were just over a thousand dead.

Nimitz sent out a message that read, "Once again radio intelligence has enabled the fighting forces of the Pacific and the Southwest Pacific to know where and when to hit the enemy." He added, "My only regret is that our appreciation, which is unlimited, can be extended only to those who read this system."

Bull Halsey liked to think of the islands of the Pacific as a ladder, with each newly won island a rung in the climb toward Tokyo. Guadalcanal, now finally and irrevocably in Allied hands, was the first rung of the ladder to be ascended.

Hitting the Japanese Where They Weren't

In the division of Pacific war responsibilities dictated by the Joint Chiefs, Nimitz was required to provide MacArthur with naval support. In another of his smart decisions, Nimitz sent Halsey to work with The General. The two of them hit it off swimmingly, forming an ardent mutual admiration duo. In his MacArthur biography, *American Caesar*, William Manchester has told how MacArthur, after his first meeting with Halsey, clapped the admiral on the back and said, "If you come with me, I'll make you a greater man than Nelson ever dreamed of being."

Together they put into practice the strategy of finding out from intelligence where the Japanese were most expecting an attack and then striking their weaker spots somewhere else. For example, Halsey found out that the Japanese, after losing Guadalcanal, anticipated that the next target in the Solomons would be the island of Kolombangara, and they armed the island with ten thousand troops. Instead, Halsey bounded past them and seized Vella Lavella, garrisoned by fewer than a thousand. Outflanked, the Japanese had to evacuate Kolombangara, giving it up with scarcely a shot being fired. Similarly, on the large island of Bougainville, Halsey leapfrogged past the most strongly fortified base, at Buin, and sent his troops ashore at Empress Augusta Bay, farther along the coast. So he and Nimitz began climbing the island ladder.

MacArthur planned similar tactics on New Guinea. His first try, however, did not work out as he had hoped. When the Japanese had been stopped short of Port Moresby and their disease-ridden remaining troops were ordered to withdraw back over the Owen Stanleys, he directed that a pincer attack be made at Buna, on New Guinea's northern coast. His idea was to have a newly arrived American infantry division press from the land while an amphibious force came in from the sea. The General expected a quick victory over a weak garrison. The importance he attached to the Buna offensive is indicated by his final words to his field commander, General Robert L. Eichelberger: "Bob, take Buna or don't come back alive."

His twin attacks did surprise the Japanese, but then MacArthur encountered his own surprise. Instead of facing a few jungle-weakened, battle-weary survivors, his troops faced a large cadre of fresh reinforcements. The battle for Buna turned into a protracted, costly campaign.

Buna taught MacArthur several lessons. One was that he could not afford never going to the battle sites himself. By staying back at his spacious, elegant quarters at Port Moresby and letting his field commanders direct the fighting at Buna, he strengthened his GIs' estimation, and for many their detestation, of him as "Dugout Doug." Second, he learned not to allow his field officers to send their troops in direct frontal assaults if any other course was possible. On Buna these tactics cost almost twice as many men as were lost on Guadalcanal. And he might well have learned not to deepen the common soldiers' antipathy by issuing more of his grandiloquent communiqués, one of which at Buna claimed, in the face of what every GI knew to be false, that "probably no campaign in history against a thoroughly prepared and trained army produced such complete and decisive results with so little an expenditure of life and resources." This last lesson, though, was probably more than his imperial character could absorb.

Although Buna was a low point for him, the ultimate defeat of the

Japanese there did force them finally to abandon any lingering hope of taking Port Moresby. It gave MacArthur a foothold to begin his daring moves up New Guinea's northern coast. And yes, Eichelberger did come back alive.

After Buna, The General corrected his image by becoming almost too visible to his combat troops. When his paratroopers were making their first landing on the New Guinea coast, he insisted on going along in the lead plane. When his troops made beach landings, he arrived while the fighting was still intense, striding forward helmetless, in his pushed-up gold-braided cap and noncamouflaged khakis, smoking his corncob pipe, and persisted in walking so near the front lines that he could poke with his toe at the still-warm bodies of snipers shot out of the trees. When others in his entourage dived for cover, he remained upright, presenting a target that, miraculously, never got hit.

In March 1943, Allied codebreakers set up another victory. A decrypt warned that the Japanese, determined not to give up another inch of the New Guinea coast, were dispatching to their base at Lae an infantry division of seven thousand troops, transferred from Korea and north China. The soldiers were to be conveyed from Rabaul in eight transports, escorted by eight destroyers.

Major General George C. Kenney, MacArthur's air chief, had already been working closely with the codebreakers in planning his air strikes. He read their decodes about the convoy as a fine opportunity to test out new antiship tactics he'd instituted. Bombs dropped from a great height, he had decided, rarely hit their targets. His alternative was to train his medium-range bomber crews to swoop in at a low level and send their fragmentation bombs skipping over the water like flat stones thrown from the beach. The bombs were timed to detonate only after they had penetrated the ships' hulls.

His skip-bombing techniques won the day in the Battle of the Bismarck Sea. Told by the cryptanalysts where to look, Kenney's recon planes spotted the convoy. Its ships were first intercepted by Flying Fortresses employing their precision bombing from on high. They sank only one ship. The next day, when the Japanese Zeros were high up in anticipation of another Fortress raid, Kenney's skip bombers sneaked in just above the wave tops—a neat turnaround on the tactics that had won at Midway. All eight of the transports, as well as four of the destroyers, were sunk, with the loss of thousands of Japanese troops. The battle put an end to Japanese attempts to move anything larger than a small barge by daylight when they were within range of Allied aircraft.

In the months that followed, MacArthur made slow, slogging progress up New Guinea's northern coast. By late January 1944, he had still gone only about a third of the way and faced strengthened Japanese defenses along the island's western two-thirds. However, another important cryptologic change had taken place. Previously MacArthur had been largely dependent on decrypts of Japanese naval codes; the army codes resisted penetration. But as the Allied troops pushed back the Japanese in the battles at a place called Sio, an engineer with a mine detector discovered a bonanza. The retreating infantry had buried a steel trunk that contained the division's entire cipher library. Within days Central Bureau was decoding army messages by the thousands.

The army and navy decrypts combined to tell MacArthur that the Japanese were expecting his next amphibious attack to be launched against Wewak and Hansa Bay, not far from his previous advance. They were so sure of what he would do that they had begun reinforcing their defenders at these sites, including shifting troops from their base much farther along, at Hollandia (now called Jayapura). On the strength of this information, The General decided not to take the small, expected step. He would make the big leap to Hollandia.

Most commanders regard military strategy from within the confines of their own particular service. Army officers, for example, are apt to regard water as a hostile environment. Not MacArthur. He, with Halsey in charge of his naval wing and Kenney the air, became adept at what the admiring Churchill called "triphibious" operations. According to Manchester's biography, during the Pacific war MacArthur made eighty-seven end-around thrusts from the water, and all of them were successful.

None was more so than his triphibious operations at Hollandia. Nimitz contributed by supplying carrier-based air support, but, concerned about exposing his carriers to Japanese bombers, he limited their participation to just three days. MacArthur responded by planning an additional landing at Aitape, 125 miles southeast of Hollandia. Capture of the Japanese airfield there would assure him of continuing air cover. His staff also worked out an elaborate series of deceptions. Kenney's planes played to Japanese preconceptions by bombing and strafing Hansa Bay defenses and by conducting highly conspicuous reconnaissance flights. Torpedo boats made themselves obvious in the area. Submarines left empty rafts ashore to suggest that patrols had been there to investigate landing sites. And when the Allied flotilla sailed toward Hollandia, the ships made feints toward the Wewak and Hansa Bay strongpoints, then at night swerved toward their real target.

MacArthur's quantum leap went off with few hitches. The landings at both Aitape and Hollandia were unopposed. Troops of the small Japanese garrisons faded into the jungle, most of them dying of starvation or succumbing to disease while trying to reach the nearest friendly base. The airfields were captured, and Nimitz's carriers retired without loss. A strong Allied force held the ground separating Japanese strength to the west from that to the east.

Edward Drea's *MacArthur's Ultra* summed up the Hollandia offensive as the codebreakers' "single greatest contribution to The General's Pacific strategy." Drea also saw it as a masterpiece of integrating signals intelligence "into operational planning to deceive, outmaneuver, and isolate an opponent."

By this one daring leapfrog of an attack, MacArthur had extended his control to halfway along New Guinea's fifteen-hundred-mile northern coast—and a lot farther toward his goal of stepping again on Philippine soil.

Perhaps the most telling commentary on MacArthur's tactics was that given after the war by Japanese intelligence officer Colonel Matsuichi Juro. He called The General's envelopment techniques "the type of strategy we hated most." Juro described how, repeatedly, MacArthur, "with minimal losses, attacked a relatively weak area, constructed airfields and then proceeded to cut the supply lines. . . . Our strong points were gradually starved out. . . . The Americans flowed into our weaker points and submerged us, just as water seeks the weakest entry to sink the ship. We respected this type of strategy . . . because it gained the most while losing the least."

While these land and air battles were proceeding satisfactorily, the Allied and Imperial navies were battering each other in a series of engagements. Although in these battles the Japanese generally sank more ships than they lost, the factor of fleet attrition was coming to the fore. The fighting in the South Pacific claimed far more warships, especially destroyers, than Japan's production could replace, while American shipyards were sending veritable armadas of new vessels down the ways. Also, Yamamoto had expended much of the cream of Japan's experienced fliers in ill-advised attacks, many of which were tipped off by Allied codebreakers, against strongly fortified targets. Well-trained airmen were another resource Japan was not replenishing.

It was in these waters that John F. Kennedy, skippering patrol torpedo boat *PT-109*, had his close call with early death. Patrolling off the Solomons on August 2, 1943, Kennedy had his boat rammed, split in half and set afire by a Japanese destroyer. Two of the crew of thirteen were killed outright and a third was badly burned. Towing the injured man by clenching the ties of his life jacket in his teeth, Kennedy led the others on a four-hour swim to Plum Pudding Island, well within the Japanese area of control. Fortunately the destruction of *PT-109* had been sighted by a coast watcher. After six days of hiding out and of desperate recon swims by Kennedy, who had been on the Harvard swim team, the eleven survivors were found by natives who were pro-Allies, and a rendezvous was arranged with another torpedo boat. Kennedy's life was spared probably by the impotence of Japanese cryptanalysts. The codes used by the coast watcher in reporting the loss of his boat and arranging his crew's rescue were ones that even a moderately skilled analyst should have solved. But only Allied receivers read the messages, and the rescue operation went off without interference.

Codebreakers Plot Yamamoto's Fall

One of the most thankless but necessary tasks of intelligence units was the deflation of exaggerated battle reports. Allied codebreakers could set the records straight, but Admiral Yamamoto had no comparable service to correct his fliers' overoptimism. His spirit was buoyed, therefore, by the inflated claims of success by his aviators in their series of raids meant to blunt any planned offensive the Allies might try after Guadalcanal. The admiral came south to Rabaul to begin a tour in which he would review operations and encourage his men. Allied cryptanalysts intercepted messages that offered a tempting possibility: Yamamoto's itinerary would bring him within range of planes lifting off from Henderson Field. Since Yamamoto was known to pride himself on his punctuality, he and his retinue could be expected to follow a precise schedule. Did the Americans dare an aerial ambush?

It was a vexing question. Japanese confidence in their code systems still held. But if American planes suddenly appeared in the correct time and place to intercept Yamamoto's tour—wouldn't that convince the most diehard believer that the Japanese system had been compromised?

When Admiral Nimitz was presented with the decrypts, his answer was to go for it. The removal of so venerated a leader would count for far more than the possible jeopardy to this one phase of Allied codebreaking. Besides, the coast watchers provided a viable cover story: personnel involved in the mission, and thus vulnerable to capture, would be told that the information came from informants at Rabaul. Nimitz secured the approval of the higher-ups in Washington.

On the morning of April 18, 1943, a flight of sixteen fighters took off from Henderson Field and flew at wave-top height to sneak under radar detection and avoid sightings by pro-Japanese coastal watchers. The American timing had to be precise. Even with drop tanks, the four-hundred-mile distance to the point of interception was at the far edge of the P-38s' limits; they couldn't wait around for Yamamoto and his escorts to appear.

There was no need to worry. The two Mitsubishi bombers bearing the admiral and members of his staff, along with protecting Zeros, were right on time. Part of the American flight soared up to take on the Zeros and provide cover. The other planes slipped in, raked the bombers with fire and sent the one bearing Yamamoto flaming into the jungle.

The admiral's death had the desired effect. When it was belatedly reported to the public in May, the Japanese people were profoundly shocked. Many later traced their disheartenment with the war to that moment. Yamamoto, always a dangerous offensive force, was replaced by a conservative, defense-minded strategist.

As David Kahn summed up the episode, "Cryptanalysis had given America the equivalent of a major victory."

Nimitz Goes Island-Hopping

While MacArthur was making end runs up the long coast of New Guinea, Chester Nimitz was intent on forcing the Japanese to contract the perimeter of their Greater East Asia Coprosperity Sphere.

He was having to plan without the services of Joe Rochefort. In the autumn of 1942 the credit war claimed Rochefort as victim. His superiors in Washington, regarding him as a prickly obstacle in the way of their earning plaudits for major intelligence coups, continued to be incensed that he had made fools of them in their off-the-mark predictions. In October he received orders to report for temporary duty at the Office of Naval Operations in Washington. His staff thought this would be good for him. He would gain a respite from the hard work and bad air-conditioning at Pearl Harbor that had given him a persistent bronchial cough and caused him to lose a lot of weight. He might, in transit, get to spend a few days with his family in California. He might even be given a decoration or promotion.

Rochefort knew better. Benefits were not what Washington had in mind. By then Naval Intelligence had been taken over by Admiral Joseph R. Redman, who had eased out Laurance Safford, OP-20-G chief and a good friend of Rochefort. In Safford's place, Redman had installed his younger brother, John. For Admiral Redman, a primary personal objective was to gain control over the intelligence network of the U.S. Navy. As Rochefort said in his reminiscences, Redman wanted "to have somebody on Hypo that would be a creature of his, and this obviously was not going to be Rochefort." Turning over to Jasper Holmes a package of personal papers and the keys to his desk, Rochefort predicted to his doubting colleagues that he would not return to Pearl Harbor.

His assertion was quickly verified when he reached Washington. He was accused of "squabbling" with Nimitz's staff members, opposing a recent reorganization and failing to keep his headquarters informed. After a brief stay in Washington, he was eventually assigned to the Tiburon peninsula in California, where he served as an instructor in the Floating Drydock Training Center. With Rochefort out of the way, the Redman brothers wrote their own history that claimed Midway as an OP-20-G triumph and gave Rochefort only the briefest, most grudging mention.

So mean-spirited were they that when Nimitz recommended Rochefort to receive the Distinguished Service Medal, they saw to it that the award was blocked. In 1958, when Nimitz tried again, he was told that the time had passed for awarding medals in recognition of World War II service. It was not true: Rochefort was granted the medal. The only trouble was that by that time he had been dead for nine years.

The Navy's chief of staff, Admiral Ernest J. King, did salvage some of Rochefort's intelligence skills and knowledge. In late 1944 he recalled Rochefort to join a special group preparing intelligence summaries for him. But Rochefort's time in the Floating Drydock Training Center was a long year lost to Allied intelligence—and what a mockery of an assignment it was for the man responsible, in the words of his associate Holmes, for "the greatest intelligence achievement in the Navy's history."

Meanwhile, late in March 1943, Hypo's codebreakers warned Nimitz that a Japanese convoy was being sent to reinforce the troops holding the Aleutian islands of Attu and Kiska. Nimitz organized a task force to intercept. In an inconclusive sea battle, the Americans succeeded in turning back the reinforcements only because the Japanese vice admiral, at the critical moment when his way was actually clear to make the landings, chickened out and withdrew—and was summarily relieved of his command.

During May, Nimitz assigned an infantry division to retake Attu. The conquest cost the Americans more than five hundred lives, but of the Japanese garrison of twenty-five hundred men only twenty-eight survived after one last banzai sake-soaked suicidal charge. When the U.S. troops moved on to attack Kiska, they found that under the cover of an impenetrable Aleutian fog the Japanese had evacuated their entire force. The northern arc of Japan's defense ring no longer extended to American shores.

In Nimitz's island-hopping campaign across the central Pacific, his targets were much different from MacArthur's. The General most often plotted his course over large land masses—New Guinea is approximately the same in land area as Alaska. The great coastal distances gave him opportunities for his clever triphibious operations. Nimitz, on the contrary, faced clusters of tiny atolls, mere pinpricks of land in the vast reaches of the Pacific. His formula for success had to be quite different: send in ships and planes to bombard the immediate island as near to rubble as possible; then dispatch troops in landing craft headed for the beaches and cover their approach with air bombardment and naval gunnery. MacArthur complained to the chiefs of staff about the enormous losses of lives resulting from Nimitz's tactics, but one wonders whether he could have managed a real alternative or was just undercutting a rival commander. This much is true: when The General did have to take a small island, such as Biak, off the northwestern end of New Guinea, he used a frontal attack, ran into fanatical dug-in Japanese resistance and suffered a considerable number of casualties.

On November 20, 1943, Nimitz launched the first of nine atoll landings he would make in his approach to the Philippines. His objective: atolls in the Gilbert Islands, most particularly Makin and Tarawa. These bits of sand and coral, on the outer edges of Japan's defense perimeter, Nimitz regarded as threats that must be eliminated before he moved on to more important seizures in the Marshall Islands.

The Americans faced unprecedented challenges in conducting this kind of atoll warfare, and their first try was a disaster. Even though signals intelligence identified the Japanese units and determined their numbers almost to a man, the Sigint advantage could not offset the botched execution of the invasions. The opening aerial and naval bombardments, which seemed annihilating to the officers involved, actually did little to weaken the defenders, holed up in caves and tunnels or protected by parapets of concrete and palm logs. The bombardments were not well coordinated, leaving lapses that allowed the Japanese soldiers to recover and reestablish themselves. Confusions and snafus in the landing operations exposed men needlessly to Japanese fire.

Makin, now named Butaritari, was known to be only lightly garrisoned and was expected to fall in hours. Instead, its die-rather-than-surrender Japanese held out so stubbornly that only in the third day could the U.S.

field commander radio, "Makin taken." The delay gave a Japanese submarine time to sneak in and sink, with heavy loss of life, an aircraft escort carrier that would long since have withdrawn if the battle ashore had gone more swiftly.

The horrors of Tarawa shocked the nation. U.S. Marines descended on the main island of Tarawa's ring of atolls expecting to find the enemy dead or dazed by the fierce prelanding bombardment. Instead they encountered Japanese gunners zeroed in to blast many of the landing craft out of the water. Because of bad forecasts, the invasion fleet headed for the beaches at the time of an exceptionally low tide, with the result that the landing craft hung up on hidden reefs. The Marines had to wade in thigh-deep water for more than a hundred yards under devastating fire. The remnants of the main force who made it ashore had to fight for the island inch by inch, using hand grenades and flamethrowers to subdue the defenders. The battle went on for a murderous seventy-six hours. Photos of dead Marines sinking facedown in Tarawa sand brought to the American public a fresh awareness of what victory in the Pacific war would entail.

Tarawa was a hard learning experience. By the time Nimitz was ready to invade the Marshalls, he made sure more accurate data foretold water levels and tide changes. Teams of frogmen went in with demolition charges to clear away barriers. Improved landing craft were designed and rushed to the Pacific. Scores of other improvements included more destructive bombardment patterns, better disembarkation procedures, stronger ground-to-air radio liaison and new methods to subdue Japanese strongholds.

Nimitz, as ever, based his decisions for the Marshalls strike on what his codebreakers were telling him. Decrypts confirmed that the Japanese were expecting the attacks to fall on the outer rim of atolls and in this expectation were shifting troops out of centrally located Kwajalein to these peripheral outposts. Nimitz's decision to land on Kwajalein startled his staff as well as the Japanese.

Decrypts had also shown that the Marshalls' defenders lacked the aircraft to mount a full-scale surveillance of their perimeter and were consequently focusing their searches on the most likely approaches from the south and southeast. Nimitz directed his U.S. Navy task force to drive in from the unguarded northeast. As a result, conquest of Kwajalein and its neighboring atolls in early February 1944 went forward in an orderly fashion, with a third of the casualties suffered at Tarawa. The taking of Eniwetok, farther west in the Marshalls, was more savagely contested by another suicidal Japanese defense, but it, too, fell in five days and was secured by February 21.

Meanwhile, in the southwest Pacific, MacArthur had cleaned the Japanese out of New Guinea except for guerrillas hiding and starving in the hills and had seized the islands of Wakde and Biak, off the big island's northwest coast.

Originally the Nimitz-MacArthur pincer movement was meant to close in on the Japanese stronghold of Rabaul. Now they no longer saw the need to spend lives battling the hundred thousand Japanese troops stationed there. Rabaul could be reduced by bombing and naval firepower and left to wither on the vine. The more northerly fortress at Truk was similarly pounded into a smoking ruin and bypassed.

With all of this favorable news unfolding, MacArthur could look northward with lip-smacking anticipation: his next move would land him on Philippine soil.

Massacre of the Marus

Studying the reports on the war in the Pacific, one can't help but wonder how the Japanese failed to conclude that their codes were being broken. This wonderment pertains especially to the movements of Japanese transport vessels, the marus trying to shift troops or bring supplies to Japanese outposts and meet the import needs of the Japanese nation. Having broken JN-11, the "maru code," the codebreakers time and again foretold when Japanese ships were scheduled to leave port, the planned course of their voyages, their stops for refueling and their expected times of arrival at their destinations. And time after time the marus were intercepted by Allied ships, submarines or planes and destroyed. The decrypts became so numerous that the informants no longer concocted cover stories as to how else the information might have been obtained. They simply sent out a message and let the Allied attackers follow up on it, confident that the Japanese would never lose faith in the inviolability of their codes.

Allied submarines, in particular, showed up wherever Japanese ships went. The accepted explanation seemed to be that the Allies had so many subs they simply blanketed the Pacific with them. A Japanese prisoner reported that in Singapore it was a common saying that one could walk from that port to Japan on American periscopes. The reality was summed up in Jasper Holmes's memoir: "There were nights when nearly every American submarine on patrol in the Central Pacific was working on the basis of instructions derived from cryptanalysis."

Historian John Winton has determined from official sources that while submarines constituted only two percent of the American war effort in the Pacific, they sank two-thirds of the total merchant-ship tonnage and one out of every three Japanese warships sent to the bottom.

American subs achieved these results despite having to rely on torpedoes that, for nearly the first two years after Pearl Harbor, often proved defective. They had two main flaws: their guidance systems frequently caused them to go too deep and pass under their targets, and even when they hit, their faulty detonators failed to make them explode. Submarine captains often heard their torpedoes thump against the sides of the enemy vessels without going off. Ordnance officials continued to claim that the trouble lay with the captains: they were incompetent; they couldn't aim properly. But the contrary evidence mounted, bolstered by codebreakers' receipts of Japanese messages reporting such incidents as ships arriving in harbor with unexploded torpedoes embedded in their flanks. New designs finally corrected the flaws, and the submariners' scores improved.

The Japanese were indefatigable reporters. They not only supplied the Allies with full information about their shipping schedules; they also aired their losses. The codebreakers were, consequently, able to confirm the results of Allied raids.

In the last months of 1943 and throughout 1944 the sinkings reached incredible rates. In November 1943, a total of 120 decrypts were transmitted to the submarines, with another 40 messages adding to or correcting the originals. These guided the subs in sinking 43 ships, of 285,820 tons, and damaging another 22 vessels, of 143,323 tons, making a total of 429,143 tons in one 30-day period. In December a U.S. sub scored the first Allied sinking of an aircraft carrier.

During 1944 the sinkings reached their peak. No less than 548 vessels totaling 2,451,914 tons, went down. So many tankers were sunk that fuel became a desperate problem. The subs sank a converted ferry, gunboats, a cruiser. Trying to reinforce threatened island garrisons by transferring troops from Taiwan and Manchuria, the Japanese had many transports sunk, with heavy losses of soldiers adding to those of the sailors.

While at the outset of the war the submarine strength of the Imperial Navy roughly equaled that of the U.S. Navy in the Pacific, the Japanese made ineffectual use of their subs. One important reason was that their submarine crews disdained attacking merchant vessels; they were at war to take on warships. The result was that they never tried to cut off the supply lines from the U.S. to Australia. As the war proceeded, the Japanese began more and more to use their subs in all sorts of tasks, such as carrying supplies, that might better have been left to other types of vessels. The subs became so ineffective a threat to Allied shipping that the U.S. soon stopped bothering with convoys and began sending out transports unescorted.

As 1945 began, the rate of sinking by Allied submarines declined, for one significant reason: they simply ran out of targets. Their stranglehold on the Imperial war machine and the Japanese economy was all but complete.

The postwar tribute penned by U.S. Vice Admiral Charles Lockwood included a compliment that, though a bit backhanded, says it all: "During periods, which fortunately were brief, when enemy code changes temporarily cut off the supply of Communication Intelligence, its absence was keenly felt. The curve of enemy contacts and of consequent sinkings almost exactly paralleled the curve of Communication Intelligence available."

15 France: Invasions from North and South

At their Quebec conference in August 1943, Eisenhower and his Joint Chiefs had decided that their cross-Channel invasion would fall on the Caen section of the Normandy coast, and had set a target date of May 1, 1944. As they settled into their final planning for the offensive, one of their most reliable information sources was their inadvertent spy on the continent, Baron Hiroshi Oshima. Nazi generals continued to handle "Hitler's Japanese confidant" with kid gloves. As part of his treatment, Lieutenant General Günther Blumentritt, chief of staff under Rundstedt, gave him a thorough briefing on German defenses from the Netherlands to the French Mediterranean coast, a report that included the order of battle for all German armies engaged in coastal defense.

Oshima went to see for himself. He toured the fortifications and learned firsthand how the Germans had aligned themselves along the coast and what divisions they held in reserve. His military attaché, Colonel Seiichi Ito, accompanied the baron to record his own observations.

All this exposure to German plans the Japanese wrote up in lengthy reports that they transmitted to Tokyo, using the Purple machine. The reports were, of course, before Allied eyes as quickly as the baron's superiors in Japan saw them. As one U.S. translator later noted, "In the end we produced a pamphlet, an on-the-ground description of the North French defenses of 'Festung Europa,' composed *dictu mirabile* [*sic*] by a general."

Armed with reliable information from their codebreakers, Allied commanders could plan with confidence. Historical accounts of the Normandy landings written in the years soon after war's end gave them a mythic quality of bloody and heroic but never-in-doubt triumphs. Only decades later has it become clear what a near miss the gamble was and how much its success depended on the massive deception program that was an integral part of the Allies' plans. While the overall code name for this great series of hoaxes was Operation Bodyguard, that main part of it relating to the Normandy invasion went by the code name Fortitude. What has also been made evident is how much the outcome of Fortitude depended on signals intelligence. Without this superstructure of inspired fakery, and the intelligence to know that it was succeeding, the best guess is that the Normandy invasion either would not have been tried at that time or would have been driven back into the sea.

The Germans in their planning were not merely lacking reliable input. The eyes they trusted to inform them about the situation in Britain were those of double agents relaying skillfully slanted misinformation. The conditions were ripe for the most ingenious bit of military artifice since the Trojan horse.

The Allies were aided by German preconceptions. If the situation had been reversed and the invasion left up to the German generals, there would have been no hesitation as to where the blow would have fallen: on that northern jut of French coast called the Pas de Calais. It was, after all, the planned jump-off point for their invasion of Britain in 1940. The Germans could argue, persuasively, that it narrowed the Channel crossing to just twenty miles and was easier to defend from the air. In addition, landings in this easternmost sector offered the most direct route to the Rhine and the German heartland. The high command were so convinced by their reasoning that, as BP decrypts made clear, they positioned the entire highly mechanized, veteran Fifteenth Army in the Pas de Calais as a key element of Army Group B, which Erwin Rommel had been called upon to lead as a subordinate to the commander in charge of West Wall defenses, Field Marshal Gerd von Rundstedt. The commanders also believed that landings anywhere else would be only diversions preceding the main attack.

Hitler himself feared every possible eventuality. As General Blumentritt told Liddell Hart after the war, "Hitler was constantly on the jump—at one moment he expected an invasion in Norway, at another moment in Holland, then near the Somme, or Normandy and Brittany, in Portugal, in Spain, in the Adriatic. His eyes were hopping all around the map."

Lacking reliable information, the German commanders felt obliged to be ready to fend off the full range of possibilities. The navy admirals felt sure the landings would come near Le Havre, since the Allies would need a large port. The Nazi generals could make a case for an attack in all the places Hitler worried about and some others besides. Hitler confided to Oshima, whose report was decrypted by Magic, that while invasion across the Channel was the most effective action the Allies could take, they might judge it too hazardous and decide to land in the less heavily defended areas around Bordeaux or perhaps in Portugal. As D-Day approached, although the Germans' focus narrowed to the north coast of France, and Hitler came to believe that at least the first phase of the attack would come in Normandy, they could never be sure. They continued to hold divisions in place to counter all of these potential landing sites.

This was precisely what the Allied tricksters wanted Fortitude to accomplish: to scatter German divisions in as many places as possible other than Normandy and hold them there even after the landings were made. They also sought to fool the Germans as to the timing of the invasion, to convince them it couldn't possibly come before July.

To carry out the varied deceptions it was necessary to create ersatz armies. At the spy-training camp he had established in Canada, William Stephenson had his "Magic Group," headed by well-known British magician Jasper Maskelyne. The group had become expert in fashioning dummy tanks and guns, trick air bases, false fleets of landing craft and other impedimenta of war. With its aid the British put into place in Scotland their Fourth Army, which the Germans believed to be an expeditionary force of 250,000 men assembling for an attack on Norway. In actuality, the "army" consisted of 28 overage officers and 334 enlisted men. The army's radio operators used a British invention that enabled one operator to simulate the traffic of entire networks. The delusion was strengthened by British special units mounting a series of raids against industrial and military installations in Norway, as though scouting the way for the larger force. Also, Allied planes stepped up reconnaissance over the fjords. Because of all this activity, twenty-seven divisions in Scandinavia stayed put to withstand the Fourth Army's coming assault.

An even more ambitious stroke of Fortitude artifice was the creation of the First U.S. Army Group (FUSAG) in southeastern England opposite the Pas de Calais. FUSAG had several real fighting units and a real commander: George Patton, released from punitive limbo, making himself highly obvious in the area with his pearl-handled pistols, his pampered bulldog mascot and his intemperate spoutings-off to the press. But the group's main forces were nonexistent; the army was fake. Aerial recon by Axis planes found the fields filling with tanks and guns. The pilots spotted tracks off into the woods suggesting that even more armor was hidden there—the tracks had been made at night by real tanks. German scouts looked down on field hospitals, kitchens, troop encampments, oil docks and clusters of landing craft—most of which were concoctions of canvas, plywood, papier mâché and inflated rubber. Postwar, German general Alfred Jodl recalled that fifteen divisions had been held in the Pas de Calais, ready to turn back landings that never came.

In the Middle East another semifictional army was spawned. As with FUSAG, the British Twelfth Army, based in Egypt, included both real and imaginary elements. Its role, so the Germans were led to believe, was to launch a drive through Crete and Greece at the same time that the Russians attacked from the north. Again, augmented reconnaissance flights and air attacks as well as a buildup of bogus landing craft to be seen by German recon planes lent credence to the hoax. The Germans shifted additional troops to the Balkans to hold off that invasion.

John Masterman, the Double Cross Committee and the networks of double agents set about the "grand strategic deception" for which their earlier chicaneries were rehearsals.

Reporting from Scotland, the agents code-named Mutt and Jeff told their controllers about the units making up the Fourth Army; they added the titillating bit that a Soviet military mission had arrived in Edinburgh to discuss plans for a Russian invasion of Scandinavia to coincide with the Fourth's landings in Norway. In his postwar report, *Fortitude*, Roger Hesketh, who has been described as "the quiet genius behind Fortitude," pointed out that the Germans would have needed no more than one hundred thousand troops to garrison Norway and Denmark but, out of fear of invasion by the largely fictitious Fourth Army, they maintained an average of two hundred fifty thousand there.

Under his code name Tricycle, Dusko Popov traveled to Lisbon to deliver to his spymaster the complete order of battle of the FUSAG forces.

The Polish agent known as Brutus told his spymaster that he had had himself assigned to General Patton's headquarters to serve as liaison officer between FUSAG and the Polish high command. He kept his controller informed daily on the changes in FUSAG's order of battle and on its increasing strength.

The agent known as Tate, who had impressed the Germans with his ability to make friends among the British, made a new friend in Kent—a railway clerk. Tate learned from this gabby—and entirely fictitious—clerk, and reported to Germany's secret service, all the rail arrangements for moving the FUSAG forces from their concentration areas to the embarkation ports, thus affirming the Germans' belief that an invasion of the Pas de Calais was imminent.

A woman agent code-named Bronx had been given a code system by her spymaster that she could use to indicate possible invasion sites. She would telegraph her bank in Lisbon the amounts she needed to withdraw to meet dental and medical needs. A request for thirty pounds meant a landing south of Sweden, forty pounds one in Norway, and so on. With that invasion's target date delayed into June, she wired to her bank on May 15 that she needed fifty pounds for the dentist. The interpretation of her message was that she had definite news that a landing would be made in the Bay of Biscay area on the west coast of France on or about June 15. Her purpose was to make sure that the Eleventh Panzer Division, quartered in the Bordeaux region, would stay there rather than hurry northward to help repel the Normandy landings. The German high command ordered the division to remain where it was.

Most of all the committee looked to Garbo to deceive the Germans. He and his invented network of agents transmitted convincing details about the massing of troops in Scotland and the steady growth of FUSAG. To increase his credibility with his Abwehr spymasters, the committee allowed him to be the first to reveal that troops of the First Army had been transferred in from Italy, and the first to announce that FUSAG was under Patton's command. By helping burnish Garbo's reputation within the Abwehr to a high glow, these measures would soon pay rich dividends to the Allies.

Allied schemers' efforts to confuse the Germans about the timing of the attack also bore fruit. German commanders were lulled into thinking that a Channel crossing couldn't possibly come in early June. The Soviets cooperated in the scam by leaking misinformation that their offensive in support of the invasion would be delayed until July. As D-Day approached, even the weather joined in the subterfuge. A Bletchley Park decrypt revealed the belief of Field Marshal Rundstedt that the Allies could not make a cross-Channel assault unless they could anticipate four consecutive days of good weather. Since in those first days of June the weather turned foul, the marshal assured Hitler that the invasion was not imminent. Having lost their weather ships in the North Atlantic, the Germans had no way of knowing, as Eisenhower did, of the temporary letup foreseen for June 6. The decrypt of Rundstedt's message influenced Ike's decision to seize upon the slight clearing. To catch the Germans off guard, he judged, would more than compensate for the less-than-fair weather the invaders would encounter. Since the May target date for the invasion had been missed because of a shortage of landing craft, Ike was also more than a little desperate not to lose out on the best June cycle for the offensive.

One of the ways his decision paid off was that when the invasion came, Rommel was back in Germany conferring with Hitler, and several other generals had left their posts to participate in a war game. Rommel had even suggested to the high command that in view of the impossible weather, the armies on the West Wall be given a time of relaxation from their intense vigilance.

Allied tricksters took advantage of the Germans' belief that Normandy couldn't be the sole objective of the landings because that coast lacked a port large enough to support so massive an operation. The Allies built artificial harbors, code-named Mulberries, and floated them into place soon after the troops had gone ashore. Protected by breakwaters formed of huge sunken concrete blocks and intentionally grounded ships, the Mulberries for a time provided an unloading site whose capacity was greater than any natural harbor in northern France.

With all these guileful preparations working in the invasion's favor, D-Day was a surprise to the Germans and a success for the Allies. Yet the hold on the beaches was slim, the whole enterprise vulnerable to a massive counterattack. It was time for the second phase of Fortitude to begin—to confirm the German leaders' conviction that Normandy was only a sideshow meant to divert attention and resources from the main assault on Calais.

At this point Fortitude hinged on Garbo. To further strengthen his image as the Germans' most reliable source of inside information, Eisenhower had agreed to a further step recommended by the Twenty Committee. On the morning of D-Day, Garbo would give the Germans warning that the invasion ships were on their way across the Channel—too late for the defenders to do much about it but early enough to enhance Garbo's standing with his controllers. Ike specified, however, that the message was not to be sent until three o'clock on the morning of the landings, which were set for six thirty. Since Abwehr operators were off duty from midnight to seven a.m., the timing was a problem for Garbo. Ever inventive, he cooked up a scheme that required the operators to stay on duty throughout the night. Despite the agreement, and much to Garbo's annoyance, on D-Day morning the ops were not at their sets; his message was read only after the beaches had been invaded. How he blasted his controller for their failure! He and his agents had gone to all this trouble and danger to find out when the attack would begin and it had all been in vain!

With the Abwehr now set to believe anything he transmitted, Garbo was ready for the climactic moment of his double-agent career. On D plus one, he told his contact, "It is perfectly clear that the present attack is a large-scale attack but diversionary in character to draw the maximum of our reserves so as to be able to strike a blow somewhere else with assured success. The constant aerial bombardment which the area of the Pas de Calais has suffered and the strange disposition of these forces give reason to suggest an attack in that region of France which at the same time offers the shortest route for the final objective of their delusions—Berlin."

His message went straight to Hitler, and it had a dramatic effect. After mulling over the situation for several days, the führer made his decision. As elements of the Fifteenth Army were moving out of the Pas de Calais to mount a powerful counterattack against the beachhead, he not only ordered the troops not to move; he also called back the ones who had already departed for Normandy.

On June 10, when Churchill and General Marshall joined the Allied chiefs in London's Operation Room, a secretary brought in the Ultra decrypt that revealed what Hitler had ordered. "We knew then that we'd won," Ron Wingate, one of the generals at the meeting, later recalled. "There might be very heavy battles, but we'd won."

The success of the grand deception was enhanced by the Germans' overestimates of the Allied forces arrayed against them. Accepting Garbo's order-of-battle assessments, they believed that in Britain they were opposed by seventy-five divisions; the actual number was less than fifty. In the Mediterranean theater they estimated that to mount a Balkans attack the Allies commanded seventy-one divisions, whereas the true figure was thirty-eight—a difference of 250,000 men. As for their own troops, the Germans were deluded into deploying ninety divisions all over Europe, ready to fight invading armies that didn't exist.

Essential to the whole undertaking was the role of the codebreakers. As Don Bussey, one of Bletchley Park's Ultra Americans, wrote, "Ultra made a tremendous contribution to the success of the deception planning for the Normandy landing because we were able to follow through Ultra not only what the German forces were doing but also that Fortitude was working so well. The Germans still believed well into July that Patton had an army in southeastern England that was going to come across to the Pas de Calais, so they couldn't send reinforcements to Normandy." General Omar Bradley said of the deception that because of it the enemy was "paralyzed into indecision" and made the grave tactical error of "committing his forces piecemeal."

Eisenhower, in his report to the Combined Chiefs of Staff, summed up Fortitude's success: "The German Fifteenth Army, which, if committed to battle in June or July, might possibly have defeated us by sheer weight of numbers, remained inoperative throughout the critical period of the campaign, and only when the breakthrough had been achieved were its infantry divisions brought west across the Seine—too late to have any effect upon the course of victory."

Stalemate in Normandy

Prior to D-Day, the codebreakers had informed Allied chiefs of a deep split in German generals' attitudes as to how best to repulse the invasion. As overall commander in the West, Rundstedt believed that in view of the vast expanse of the coastal area, the sensible course was to depend primarily on mobile reserves held inland, ready to move in strength to wherever the Allies landed. Erwin Rommel, arriving to take up his new duties, came to an opposite conclusion. He felt strongly that the Germans must meet and overwhelm the Allies on the beaches, must hold the coast "absolutely." He was aware, from his experiences in North Africa, how reserves could be made immobile by Allied air supremacy. He also argued that experience in the Mediterranean theater had shown that the Allies did not move quickly and boldly away from their bridgeheads; a continuation of that cautious pattern would provide him the opportunity, with powerful forces close to the coast, to smash the attackers before they could gain a foothold.

The two generals settled on a compromise. Rundstedt agreed to move infantry divisions forward while keeping nine armored divisions in reserve. Rommel was also bound by Hitler's orders not to move his strongest command, the Fifteenth Army, out of the Pas de Calais.

The division of forces worked in the Allies' favor. As Omar Bradley observed, "The result was a defensive crust on the beaches that was too thin to destroy us and reserves too small for von Rundstedt's war of maneuver."

Eisenhower resolved that the Normandy landings would not follow the Mediterranean pattern. The troops were to land and then immediately begin to push inland. After Montgomery's British and Canadian troops, as a lead example, had made their landings on their three assigned Normandy beaches, Monty's Second Army was to drive toward Caen and take this important road and railway hub the first day.

What frustrated this bold plan was partially the result of an odd shortfall in BP's information. Montgomery's landings were only lightly opposed, and the Second Army did begin its push toward Caen. Ultra had warned that a German infantry division at Caen had been replaced by the much more formidable Twenty-first Panzer Division. Further, Ultra disclosed that instead of remaining in place as a cohesive unit, the division had dispersed in the Caen area. Details of this deployment, unfortunately, were not revealed. It remained for Montgomery's army to discover how cleverly the panzer division had disposed its strength. The division's infantry and antitank gun units had been placed at great advantage on the Périers Ridge. Behind them was a battalion of field guns. Still farther back were the tanks, grouped to launch a counterattack. Progress for the Second Army quickly ground to a halt, four miles from Caen.

When the troops and the tanks of the Twenty-first did counterattack they succeeded, for a time, in opening a corridor that linked them with the troops still holding out on the beaches. It was a moment of great peril for the Normandy invasion. If Rommel had been free to rush the mobile forces of the Fifteenth into the battle, he might well have made good on his coastal strategy. Thanks to Fortitude, however, the Fifteenth stayed in place. Monty's troops put up a gritty defense, knocking out 50 of the Twenty-first's 127 tanks. When a large Allied glider fleet sailed over the beaches and behind the battle lines, the Twenty-first withdrew and the beachhead was saved.

The Allied timetable, however, was shredded. Caen was not taken until late July. The Americans to the west became locked in vicious fighting in the difficult French hedgerow country known as the *bocage*. All over Normandy the fighting was stalemated.

As June and then July wore on, though, the Allies were relieved that at least the worst nightmares about the invasion had not come to reality. Rommel had not forced another Dunkirk. With each passing day, more men, armor and supplies flowed into Normandy. There was growing confidence that the Allies' foothold in France could not be dislodged.

When FUSAG made no move and the Pas de Calais attack saw no landings for weeks after D-Day, it might be supposed that the Double Cross agents had exhausted their credibility and brought their usefulness to an end. Not so. Masterman has noted that "no single case was compromised. Those agents who took part were more highly regarded by the Germans than ever."

Garbo and friends, reporting to their German controllers, had an explanation as to why their predictions about FUSAG hadn't materialized. The tough German resistance in Normandy demanded that troops be transferred there from FUSAG to save the beachheads, thus requiring time for FUSAG to be reinforced.

In addition, the idea of a Pas de Calais invasion was so deeply implanted in the Germans' minds that they couldn't shake it. Not until July 27 did the chief of the Wehrmacht's Intelligence Division, noting the withdrawals from FUSAG, concede that it was "improbable now that it will be used at short notice to attack a strongly fortified coastal sector." General Günther von Kluge, who had replaced Rundstedt as commander in chief in the West, persuaded a reluctant Hitler to begin shifting troops, including units of the Fifteenth Army, out of the Pas de Calais. Kluge finally concluded on August 7 that a second major landing was "improbable" and ordered all possible formations to be sent to the Normandy battlefront. By then, however, the Allies had more than a million troops on French soil.

Bradley has recorded one other major Ultra contribution to the early going. The decrypt warned that a panzer grenadier division Rommel had shifted eastward from Brittany was about to attack the lightly armored 101st Airborne Division at Carentan—a move that, as Bradley noted, had the potential of splitting the Allied line and thrusting all the way to the beaches. He ordered tanks and an armored infantry battalion to reinforce the paratroops. "The Germans attacked Carentan exactly as Ultra had forecast and were thrown back with heavy losses."

Hitler Thrusts His Armies into a Noose

On July 20 a cabal of German officers carried out a plot to assassinate Hitler. The attempt failed, and many of the officers were shot, hanged or hung on meat hooks to have their nooses slowly garrote them to death. The effect on Hitler was to make him more suspicious than ever of his generals and to impel him to take command of the war more fully into his own hands. The result was a defeat that came close to breaking the back of the Wehrmacht, that should have broken the back of the Wehrmacht.

On July 31, Hitler was at his "Wolf's Lair" secret headquarters in East Prussia, conferring with General Alfred Jodl, his chief of staff. The situation in the west seemed to the professionals to call urgently for withdrawal to a new defensive line north of the Seine. For weeks the Allies and Germans had been mauling each other along the battle line that stretched across Normandy. Many German units were depleted and exhausted. The Americans had overrun the Cotentin Peninsula and were now squeezing through a narrow corridor at Avranches, the seacoast town on the far western side of the peninsula. The orders for the Yanks' VIII Corps were to turn their backs on the main combat and close in on the ports farther west along the coast of Brittany—ports badly needed for bringing in supplies to the Normandy armies. Patton had finally crossed the Channel to take charge of the real Third Army instead of the notional FUSAG. The Third was pushing through the Avranches defile, poised to press south and east. Two of Omar Bradley's corps had seized Saint-Lô and were also threatening to charge eastward to encircle their German opponents. As Churchill recorded, "The whole German defense west of the Vire was in jeopardy and chaos." The only sensible course, Hitler's generals believed, was to fall back and regroup on the north bank of the Seine.

Hitler had other ideas. He was in the mood not for defense but for attack. In his eyes the Allied bottleneck at Avranches presented a golden opportunity. Both of his main commanders in the West were now gone. Rommel had been injured in the crack-up of his staff car trying to elude a strafing Allied plane, and his support of the plot against Hitler subsequently led to his forced suicide. Rundstedt was temporarily under a cloud. When asked what should be done, after the success of the Normandy landings was evident, he had responded, "Make peace, you idiots. What else can you do?"

Hitler gave his new commander, Günther von Kluge, his order to "prepare a counteroffensive aiming to break through to Avranches with the objective of isolating the enemy forces and ensuring their destruction."

Kluge and his subordinates were dismayed by the order. Already extended too far west, they were in danger of having to extricate themselves from a corridor forming between the Allied forces to the north and those now making a U-turn eastward around Avranches. To push still farther west would only make their exposure worse. But orders were orders, and Kluge prepared his attack.

The obvious launching point was the village of Mortain. The plain before it offered the shortest route to Avranches, and the hilly terrain behind it would provide cover for the assembly of his forces. Kluge planned his offensive to begin the night of August 6.

Ultra's part in warning of the attack is in question. Winterbotham claimed that Bradley's armies were informed well in advance, which Bradley vehemently denied, writing in 1983, "Ultra alerted us to the attack only a few hours before it came, and that was too late to make any major defensive preparations." Hinsley supported Bradley, noting that the timing of the intercepts was either very close to or after the launching of the offensive.

There is no question, however, that Patton was warned. From the time of the formation of the Third Army, he had had a British-manned Special Liaison Unit assigned to his headquarters. In addition, an American major, Melvin Helfers, had been in place as the link between the SLU and Patton. However, the general also had a highly protective intelligence officer, Colonel Oscar Koch, who stood between Helfers and Patton. The most Helfers had been able to do thus far was supply summaries of Ultra decrypts to Koch, who then decided what, if anything, would be passed on to the general.

When Helfers saw the decrypts about the Mortain attack, he immediately recognized their importance. This time he was not to be denied. He went to Koch's tent and showed him the Ultra materials as well as a map he had hastily prepared. Koch agreed that Patton should get the news without delay. According to Koch's own memoir, he and Helfers picked up Patton's chief of staff, Brigadier General Hobart "Hap" Gay, en route to Patton's trailer. It was the first time Helfers had been admitted to the general's presence.

The officers spread Helfers's map on the floor and squatted over it as Helfers explained the decrypts. Patton was not one to ignore advantageous information. As he wrote in his diary the next day, "We got a rumor last night from a secret source that Panzer divisions will attack west from . . . Mortain . . . on Avranches. Personally, I think it is a German bluff to cover a withdrawal, but I stopped the 80th, French 2nd Armored, and 35th [Divisions] in the vicinity of St. Hilaire just in case something might happen."

Bradley's Thirtieth Infantry Division was already in place. Its men, with help from Patton's divisions and from intense aerial forays once the weather cleared, checked the German panzers in three days of bloody, desperate fighting.

When it became clear that the Mortain counteroffensive was failing, Bradley told the visiting Secretary of the Treasury Henry Morgenthau, "This is an opportunity that comes to a commander not more than once in a century. We are about to destroy an entire hostile army. If the other fellow will only press his attack here at Mortain for another 48 hours, he'll give us time to close at Argentan and there completely destroy him."

Kluge and his fellow generals would not have given the Americans those additional forty-eight hours, but Hitler did. He ordered a new offensive: "I command that the attack be presented daringly and recklessly to the sea." By then decrypts of Kluge's orders were flowing to Allied commanders almost as swiftly as they were to his own generals. In the end the attack never really came off. The most that Hitler's order did was slow the with-drawal and allow the Allies to tighten the noose around the battered Ger-man armies.

Patton, now starting each day with a report by Helfers, swung around to the south and raced eastward ahead of the retreating Germans. Colonel Koch had become an Ultra convert as well. His assistant reported, "An army never moved as fast and as far as the Third Army in its drive across France and Ultra was invaluable every mile of the way."

The Germans were closed into a narrow corridor on three sides and had to run a gauntlet of fierce artillery fire and air attacks. The only way out was via a gap at the town of Falaise. With Patton pressing up from the south and Montgomery's Canadians pushing down from the north, it ap-peared that the gap would be closed and most of Kluge's Fifth and Seventh Panzer Armies trapped inside.

Kluge himself was no longer in charge. When he set off on a tour of the pocket in which his armies were confined, his staff car was strafed by fighter planes just as Rommel's had been earlier, and he was unable to reach his headquarters until midnight. By then Hitler had become con-vinced that Kluge was planning "to lead the whole of the Western Army into capitulation." He had replaced Kluge with Walther Model. Ordered to return to Germany, Kluge, surmising correctly that he would be met by the Gestapo, took poison instead.

Sadly for the Allies, the Falaise gap was not closed in time to capture the whole of the German armies. With two major Allied forces now head-ing directly toward each other, it was Montgomery's duty to define the lim-its of advance to avoid a collision. He set the town of Argentan as the point beyond which neither of the approaching armies was to go. Units of Pat-ton's army reached Argentan while Monty's Canadian troops were still miles away and making painfully slow progress. Patton pleaded with Bradley to be allowed to advance farther; in fact he ordered his field com-mander there to push on slowly until meeting up with the Canadians. Bradley, knowing that Patton had exposed himself to a flank attack, was adamant that Patton stay at Argentan. Stay he did, while German troops poured through the gap to fight again. There are conflicting accounts of why the Allied armies failed to close the Falaise gap. Bradley blamed it in part on faulty intelligence that told him the main German divisions had al-ready escaped when, in actuality, they were still in the trap. Many place the blame on Montgomery, claiming that because the rapid American advances were grabbing the headlines while his own troops were stalled, he was determined not to allow the Americans to gain still more credit and so delayed giving the orders that would have allowed Patton to move northward. Whatever the cause, Montgomery's own intelligence officer later admitted, "Monty missed closing the sack."

Even so, Falaise was a German disaster. Ten thousand men were killed and fifty thousand captured, and huge quantities of tanks, artillery and other equipment were lost. The Germans were deprived of the strength to stop Patton from making his slashing drives to the east and south. The Battle of Normandy had, at last, ended in triumph.

Up from the South: The Riviera Invasion

When most of Italy was in Allied hands and Rome captured, the question became, where next? Churchill, ever weighing the political aspects, looked past the war at hand and contemplated the potential war to come. He wanted the Allies to push northeastward, up through Trieste, then into Austria, Czechoslovakia and southern Germany, so as to deny these areas to Russian Communism. Eisenhower, though, had a one-track mind: the first order of business was to whip the Germans, and the best way to do that was to concentrate Allied strength in the west. He stood steadfast, with FDR behind him, to follow the plan agreed on earlier: to carry out Operation Dragoon, the invasion of the south of France. Dragoon's goal was to drive out the Germans there and link up with the Allies breaking free in Normandy. Muttering in discontent, Churchill eventually gave in.

On August 15 another great collation of ships, this one nine hundred strong, converged on the Riviera and began unloading warriors onto the beaches and the playgrounds once reserved for the wealthy. The invasion was an enormous feat of planning and organization that came off with few fumbles. This was no narrow Channel crossing. The ships that arrived together on the fifteenth had come, on varying schedules, from Italian ports such as Naples and Taranto, from Oran on the north coast of Africa, from the islands of Malta, Sardinia, Corsica and Sicily. Plans for the landings were based on an intelligence file that, according to William Breuer in his book *Operation Dragoon*, exceeded that for the Normandy invasion. This "mountainous pile of information" on every detail of the German defenses had been obtained from photoreconnaissance, the French underground and Ultra decrypts. Despite an early morning fog that caused some units to be landed well away from their drop zones, the parachute and glider operations were unusually successful. The beach landings met with little opposition, bringing ashore ninety-four thousand men and eleven thousand vehicles in a single day. The drive inland held to its schedule.

Ultra codebreakers began quickly to decrypt messages with an astonishing import: Hitler was ordering a withdrawal to a defense line well back from the coast. He did want troops left at the fortresses such as Toulon and Marseilles, and these defenders were of course to hold out to the last man. Otherwise, concerned that the breakout in Normandy was threatening to cut off his Nineteenth Army in southern France, he ordered his commanders to move quickly to the north.

Aided by decrypts that covered the Germans' every move, General Lucian Truscott, commanding the invading Seventh Army, foresaw that most of the retreating enemy would follow the Rhône River northward. At Montélimar, eighty miles north, was a gorge that could be turned into a deadly bottleneck. Truscott sent a task force racing ahead to close off the gorge and trap the Germans trying to pass through it. Too cautious action by the task force's commander allowed two German divisions to escape, but other retreating units were encircled. Ultra warned when two German divisions were to combine their forces in a desperate breakout effort. Some German units did fight their way through but with heavy losses.

The codebreakers enabled the Allied generals to direct their forces with certainty and efficiency. In just two weeks' time they had driven the Germans out of southern France. The Riviera invasion ended up not unlike the Battle of the Falaise Gap. Many Nazi troops succeeded in making it through to help firm up the home defenses. Thousands of others, however, were killed, thousands more captured and tons of matériel were left behind in the rout.

With both the northern and southern invasions now rapidly contracting the Germans' defenses and in the process destroying legions of soldiers and masses of equipment, the situation in Europe bred relief for the Allies. But it also fed a spirit of inflated hope and cocksure confidence that presaged trouble ahead.

16 CBI: Winning the "Forgotten War"

IN the broad sweep of World War II history, the battles of the China-Burma-India theater can seem in retrospect to be an aside, a series of viciously lethal struggles that were only a back eddy to the main conflict. Those who fought there ruefully regarded it as "the forgotten war," the front with the lowest priorities, the arena whose demands of men and matériel were most begrudged.

Yet it seemed inarguable at the time that the Japanese had to be stopped there. The Allies could not assume, early on in the Pacific war, that either Nimitz's island-hopping or MacArthur's climb from New Guinea would succeed. The CBI theater offered an alternative: it could serve as a launching base for the aerial bombardment and ultimate invasion of the Japanese homeland. It was even more essential to deny the Japanese their continuing exploitation of Southeast Asia's boundless natural resources and endless ranks of manpower that could have built them into an unbeatable foe. The farther reaches of the Indian subcontinent must not be opened to them. The glimmering vision of an Asia–Middle East linkup that would put the Axis powers on their way to ruling the world could not be allowed to come to pass. Allied leaders would have seemed irresponsible if they had not believed the CBI war had to be fought—and won.

Nor can the role of CBI's codebreakers, vital in turning defeat into victory, be overlooked. Their contributions, though, were late in coming. Before the war and during its early stages, the British had established an extensive network of intercept stations, direction-finding units and cryptanalytic teams to keep tabs on Japan. But the onslaught of Japanese advances kept the Sigint forces on the run. Some hopped from Hong Kong to

Singapore to Ceylon and even to eastern Africa. Others fled to Australia. The British, Australian and Indian intercept and cryptographic teams tried valiantly to regroup in their new locations and did reestablish linkages with Bletchley Park, Cast, Hypo and Op-20-G. However, months passed before Sigint could begin to have much of an impact.

In the meantime, the entire Southeast Asia theater had been a sequence of disasters for the Allies. Before the war, the Japanese had begun their expansion by conquest with the annexing of Manchuria in 1931, the capture of eastern China's major cities and the occupation of the Chinese coast. When the war came, and the Allies wished to support Generalissimo Chiang Kai-shek's Nationalist army, the only supply line was through China's western back door. Chiang's needs were met by landing supplies at Rangoon, Burma's capital and major seaport, transporting them by rail through Burma and completing the journey to his Kunming wartime capital by truck on the Burma Road, built in 1936–37.

Chiang looked primarily to the U.S. for aid. In 1937 he enlisted Clare Chennault, a flamboyant Great War pilot, to develop an effective Chinese air force. Chennault did so by retraining Chinese fliers, hiring mercenaries wherever he could find them and welding his polyglot band into what was officially called the American Volunteer Group (AVG). The group became far better known as the Flying Tigers from the fact that its U.S.-built planes had winged tigers painted on their tails. Toothy shark faces on the aircrafts' noses also contributed to their lethal appearance. For the first seven months in 1942, at a time when the American public hungered for success stories, Chennault's Tigers racked up impressive headline-grabbing scores against Japan's planes. Because the AVG was a private air force functioning outside official channels, the U.S. reorganized it in July 1942 as the Chinese Air Task Force, still under General Chennault. With an influx of regular U.S. Air Force fliers who volunteered for duty and the arrival of a U.S. bomber squadron, Chennault's Tigers continued to harass the Japanese throughout the war. Eric Sevareid, transferring to China for his CBS reports, wrote that Chennault became "the great American hero to the Chinese" and that his "very face in its grim, scarred belligerence had come to be a symbol of China's resistance."

To help Chiang develop a more professional army, the U.S. sent him an able field commander and trainer who had spent fifteen years in China and spoke the language fluently, General Joseph W. Stilwell. His nickname was "Vinegar Joe," an appropriate label for his no-nonsense, to-hell-with-tact personality. General William Slim, Stilwell's British counterpart in the Burmese command, said of him that "he could be as obstinate as a whole team of mules," but Slim added that when Stilwell "said he would do a thing, he did it," and while others found him impossibly abrasive, "I liked him."

Stilwell faced a tough task in trying to shape an effective Chinese army. Chiang's understrength divisions were ridden with corruption and incompetent leadership. The soldiers were low paid, malnourished and ill equipped. American supplies meant for them often ended up on the black market and were likely to be traded to the Japanese. In addition, Chiang himself was never sure which war took precedence, the one against Japan or that against the Chinese Communist armies under Mao Tse-tung, which Chiang's forces had driven into a corner in China's northern mountains. Despite signing an agreement with Mao to fight together against the Japanese, Chiang kept a quarter of his army standing guard against a possible move by the Communists. Stilwell quickly came to have a low regard for the devious Chiang, referring to him privately, and too often publicly, as "Peanut."

In the triumphant takeover of Southeast Asia, the Japanese viewed the capture of Burma as the means to shut off aid to China. Neighboring Siam put up only a five-hour fight before allowing passage to Japanese troops and becoming Japan's ally. The invasion of Burma began on January 31, 1942. Thousands of British, Australian, Dutch and Asian prisoners the Japanese had captured in their conquest of Southeast Asia were condemned to slave labor building the Siam-to-Burma railroad, which was to be Japan's invasion route into India. When the Japanese attacked Rangoon, the British, knowing the port's importance, fought them off for the first two and a half months of 1942. Then the sheer numbers of the Japanese and their dominance in the air forced the British-led troops to retreat northward.

At this point Slim was called in from his previous post in Iraq to take charge of the defense of Burma. Commanding the British, Burmese and Indian divisions of the Fourteenth Army, he joined with Stilwell and his Chinese troops to form a defensive line in central Burma 150 miles north of Rangoon. The Allies' numbers were too few, the Japanese attackers were too well versed in jungle fighting, and their air superiority was too overpowering for the line to hold. In what CBI veteran Louis Allen, in his comprehensive history *Burma: The Longest War*, has called "the longest retreat in the history of the British Army," Slim's forces withdrew for 900 miles, all the way back into India. The whole of Burma fell under Japanese control. Stilwell, too, escaped to India, arriving with the remains of his command only after a harrowing 140-mile jungle trek. The Burma Road was no longer usable. Supplies to China had to be transported from India by indomitable American fliers ferrying cargo planes over the southern spurs of the Himalayas, which they called "the Hump." So many of their planes went down that the pilots claimed they could plot their course to China by the line of smoking wrecks on the mountainsides.

Before leaving their post at Colombo on the island of Ceylon, the code-breaking crew had tried to avert a naval disaster. On March 28, 1942, they had broken a Japanese naval code foretelling a carrier-based air raid on the harbor at Colombo. Accordingly, Admiral James Somerville, commanding the Royal Navy's Eastern Fleet, heeded the warning and withdrew his ships to their Indian Ocean hideaway in the Maldive Islands. Merchant ships left for a port in India. When two days passed and the raid had not come, however, the admiral decided the codebreakers were wrong and returned his fleet to Colombo. What no one on the Allied side knew was that the Japanese admiral had merely delayed his attack until Easter Sunday, believing he would find the British less alert then. Subsequently Colombo intercepts of plain-language air-to-ground messages warned that enemy aircraft were less than five hundred miles away. Somerville tried to scatter his ships, but there was not time. In this and a further raid the next day, the Japanese sank three cruisers, an aircraft carrier and two destroyers.

At this lowest point in the CBI war, a self-appointed messiah stirred hope. Orde C. Wingate had led irregular forces in North Africa, once bluffing fifteen thousand Italians into surrendering to his own force of less than two thousand. Now he arrived to apply the same audacious tactics in Burma. Wingate was a deliberate eccentric who gloried in wearing grimy uniforms, an ever-present pith helmet and a great bushy beard. He was given to such bizarre behavior as straining his tea, and that of his guests, through his dirty socks. He proposed beating the Japanese by what he called "long-range penetration." He would lead a specially trained infantry brigade far behind enemy lines, where, supplied by air and communicating via radio, his troops would wreak guerrilla-type havoc on the Japanese. The world press fastened onto a new word: *Chindits*, the name Wingate's outfit acquired. Wingate coined it when he misheard the Burmese word *chinthe*—the name of the mythical beast that guarded Burmese temples.

During the outfit's first weeks in the jungles the Chindits fulfilled Wingate's expectations and gave newspaper readers throughout the Allied nations a small feast of excitement amid otherwise dreary gruel. They destroyed bridges, sabotaged the Japanese army's supply railroad, attacked outposts and set up ambushes. The raid proved that penetration forces could be supplied by airborne drops. But the toll on the men was too great: the Japanese were too powerful. Wracked by disease more than by bullets, only remnants of Wingate's guerrillas made it out of the jungles and back to safety.

Summing up this first try by the Chindits, Slim wrote in his memoir, "As a military operation the raid had been an expensive failure." Yet he added, "There was a dramatic quality about this raid, which, with the undoubted fact that it had penetrated far behind the Japanese lines and returned, lent itself to presentation as a triumph of British jungle fighting over the Japanese." It gave a lift to the people of Britain and to all the Allies. For the troops in the CBI "it seemed the first ripple in the turning of the tide." Slim judged Wingate's adventure "worth all the hardship and sacrifice his men endured."

It remained for Vinegar Joe, however, to render the final verdict on the first Burma campaign. "I claim we got a hell of a beating," he told a press conference. "We got run out of Burma and it is humiliating as hell. I think we ought to find out what caused it, go back and retake it."

Stilwell's Drive to "Mitch"

Winston Churchill was not convinced that the tremendous costs of retaking Burma were worth the effort. He foresaw that the replacement for the Burma Road that Stilwell pressed the Allies to undertake was "unlikely to be finished until the need for it had passed." Strategically, Burma was too remote to be of use in the conquest of Japan. As for conducting war there, "one could not choose a worse place for fighting the Japanese."

The Americans, nevertheless, persisted. The Pacific campaigns were proving slow and costly. U.S. leaders thought they still might have to strike at Japan through China. Besides, Chiang's clever, Wellesley-educated wife, Madame Soong Mei-ling, traveled to Washington and charmed FDR into maintaining full support for Chiang and Chennault, and even for Stilwell.

After sixteen months of reorganizing and strategizing by the Allies, the second Burma campaign was ready to begin in October 1943. It would be under the overall command of a new leader, Lord Louis Mountbatten.

By now the cryptologic resources of the Allies were in full interplay. The East African contingent had returned to Colombo for closer surveillance of Japanese naval traffic. Outside New Delhi the British had established "Bletchley Park East," another operation officially identified by a misleadlingly low-key name: the Wireless Experimental Centre. WEC had two Indian intercept and cryptologic outposts, one in Bangalore, in southern India, and the other in Barrackpore, near Calcutta. The latter was specifically assigned to meet the signals intelligence needs of Slim's Fourteenth Army and to operate mobile stations that stayed close to the fighting fronts. Special Liaison Units served Mountbatten, Slim, Stilwell and the U.S. bomber command in China.

In addition, a Tactical Air Intelligence Section at Slim's headquarters intercepted and broke the signals of Japanese aircraft flying into and out of airfields in Burma. The section directed a squadron of U.S. long-range fighters in successes that decimated Japanese planes and gave the Allies air superiority for the coming offensives. The voices of Japan's militarists were, all unbeknownst to them, being overheard and understood by an untiring legion of eavesdroppers.

Forced back to India's eastern border by their earlier defeats, the Allies planned for three main forces to carry out their offensive to retake Burma. One would be Stilwell's American-trained Chinese divisions. The second: Wingate's Chindits, expanded to twenty thousand troops. Third would be Slim's British and Indian armies.

Stilwell's assigned task was to clear the Japanese out of northern Burma, an offensive essential to breaking the blockade of China. That Burma Road alternative that Churchill disparaged had been under construction since the autumn of 1942. American engineers were directing the building of a two-way all-weather road leading from Ledo, in India, southeastward into Burma to join up with the Burma Road's upper reaches. If Chiang's armies were to receive the help they needed, a new overland truck route must replace dependence on planes flying the Hump. Also, alongside the Ledo Road the engineers built a pipeline to carry fuel to the B-29 bombers expected to attack the Japanese in eastern Asia and in Japan itself.

To reach his north Burma objectives, Stilwell would have to push for 150 miles through jungles, over mountains and across rivers to capture the rail, air and road hub that the maps named Myitkyina and the Americans called "Mitch."

Trained in India by Americans, the Chinese soldiers had rounded into formidable fighters. As Sevareid described them in his reports from India, "Now husky, well fed, imbued with fighting spirit by the Americans and their own young and able officers . . . they were at least the equal of the Japanese." They offered "a startling contrast with the rest of Chiang's starved and spiritless army."

The Thirty-eighth Chinese Division had not penetrated far into Burma before they encountered stiff opposition. At the same time the Allies in India had been planning their campaign, the Japanese commanders, as decrypts began to verify, had developed their own offensive plans, whose objective was nothing less than to smash the Allied armies in their path and take India. As the ever useful Baron Oshima had radioed to Tokyo—and to Magic codebreakers—Foreign Minister Ribbentrop had told him, "Germany would eagerly welcome a Japanese invasion into the Indian Ocean whereby contact between Europe and Asia might be achieved." Bent on fulfilling their part, the Japanese had been moving troops into north Burma in preparation for their Indian campaign. They met and slowed the advance of Stilwell's Chinese fighters.

Vinegar Joe, however, now had a new source of strength. This was an American combat unit that was to gain fame as "Merrill's Marauders" because it was under the command of Brigadier General Frank D. Merrill. The outfit, trained in India with the Chindits, was only three thousand men strong, but it included veterans of combat duty in the Pacific plus a number of toughs volunteering to avoid guardhouse time.

Stilwell expected more of the Marauders than guerrilla-type missions. In what he called a "left hook," he sent them around the Japanese facing the Chinese attackers and had them take up a position blocking a Japanese retreat. The commander of the Japanese Eighteenth Division threw his full strength against the Marauders, ordering charge after charge. The Americans held firm, piling up Japanese bodies on the approaches to their lines. In the end the Eighteenth had to give up the attack and slip away through the jungles to escape. It was Stilwell's first major victory in Burma—and a tonic for Allied spirits everywhere.

Stilwell's second try at having the Marauders swing around the tenacious Eighteenth was less successful. He planned a two-way hook meant, this time, to bottle up the division and destroy it. The trouble was the terrain the Marauders had to cross. The combination of jungle and mountains made their treks long and exhausting. Short of supplies and water, they fell ill to dysentery and jungle diseases. They did establish a roadblock, but when a Chinese brigade came to their relief, the Chinese let the Eighteenth again escape annihilation.

Even though the Marauders were weary and ill, and had lost their leader to an incapacitating heart attack, Stilwell called on them for yet another desperate mission, this one in response to a captured Japanese document. From this bit of intelligence, Stilwell knew he had to block the attempt by a Japanese battalion to mount their own left hook and outflank the Chinese. The Marauders stationed themselves to stand off the attack, dug in and held on for a week. They were aided by a different kind of intelligence. A Japanese American sergeant, Roy H. Matsumoto, nightly crawled close to the enemy's perimeter and, listening in on their conversations, learned of their plans for the following day. He also learned Japanese intentions by clipping into their telephone lines. In one critical attack, when the first wave of the Japanese had been shot to pieces, Matsumoto yelled "Charge" in Japanese to a follow-up wave, who also rushed into wholesale slaughter. The sergeant's information helped the Marauders turn back the try at encirclement.

But Stilwell was still ninety miles from Mitch. He faced the necessity of stirring the Chinese into exerting more aggressive pressure on the main front. He also had to motivate the Marauders to take on one last grueling mission, despite their being down to half their original numbers and looking for relief rather than further action. The assignment was to make a long eastward swing, code-named End Run, and close in on Myitkyina from a direction the Japanese would least suspect.

To meet the first demand, Stilwell used all his powers of persuasion, flattery and bullying to make the Chinese generals step up their attacks. He walked into the front lines and made himself a visible target, knowing that the Chinese commanders would fear their superiors' wrath if Vinegar Joe was killed. To lessen this chance, they ordered their men forward. "It pays to go up and push," Stilwell wrote in his diary. "At least, it's a coincidence that every time I do, they spurt a bit."

As for the Marauders, he convinced them that there was no one else who could do the job. Also, he increased their numbers by adding two Chinese regiments as well as a band of Burmese guerrillas who were experienced in operating behind Japanese lines.

The drive became a terrible ordeal. Stilwell was forced to send in more Chinese troops and to strip engineers off the Ledo Road project and convert them into infantry. In addition, the monsoon rains arrived early. By late June 1944, however, End Run had succeeded. The airstrip at Mitch had been seized, and after more bitter fighting, so had the town itself. Just as important, the enemy's Eighteenth Division had at last been broken and its remnants sent fleeing to the south. Having the Myitkyina airstrip in Allied hands meant that air transport could avoid the Hump and double the tonnage lifted to China. This development made Churchill's prediction of the needlessness of the Ledo Road almost come true. By the time the road was completed, Stilwell's capture of the Mitch airstrip had brought a far larger flow of supplies to Chiang—forty thousand tons of them in fourteen thousand transport flights—than was moved over the new truck route.

Not that the Generalissimo was inclined to show any gratitude. Instead, still incensed by Stilwell's too freely expressed estimation of him, Chiang pressed for, and in October 1944 succeeded in achieving, Vinegar Joe's recall.

Stilwell had worn so many hats, it took three generals to replace him. The North Central Area Command passed to his subordinate Daniel Sultan. In China, Albert Wedemeyer was chosen to be Chiang's adviser. And Raymond Wheeler became Mountbatten's deputy supreme commander for the Southeast Asia Command.

Stopping the Japanese at Imphal

To the small tales of success that Orde Wingate and his Chindits had achieved in the first Burma campaign, he hoped to add big news in the second. He had more than three times as many troops assigned to him. He also had his own air force, including U.S. planes to supply his behind-the-lines incursions, as well as gliders to carry in his troops. Above all, he had the strong backing of Winston Churchill and even of Franklin Roosevelt. Churchill had invited him to the Quebec Conference, where he had made so strong an impression that the Allied leaders instructed him to appeal to them directly if his immediate superiors were thwarting his plans.

General Slim, in his memoir, *Defeat into Victory*, told of an incident in which, when he denied Wingate's demand that an Indian division be added to his Chindits, the brigadier let him know that he had a loyalty above that to his immediate commander. To whom? Slim asked. "To the Prime Minister of England and the President of the United States," Wingate replied, and added that this was an occasion when he must so appeal. "I pushed a signal pad across my desk to him," Slim wrote, "and told him to go and write his message. He did not take the pad but he left the room. Whether he ever sent the message I do not know, nor did I inquire. Anyhow, that was the last I heard of his demand for the 26th division."

For their part in the campaign, the Chindits were assigned to give extraordinary support to Stilwell's offensive. To do this, they had their gliders towed far to the south, beyond Myitkyina. Landed there, the glider troops established three airstrips while a larger group marched overland to join them. The Chindits eased the pressure on Stilwell's Chinese divisions by cutting the Japanese supply routes and creating other behind-the-lines mayhem. Their planes protected both the Chindits and Stilwell's troops from Japanese air attacks. In a reminiscence, Delhi-stationed code man Alan

Stripp told of the "punched-in-solar-plexus anguish" of the Japanese, as revealed in decrypts of their reports of the Chindits' exploits.

In the midst of the operation, Wingate himself was killed in a plane crash. Churchill recorded his distress: "With him a bright flame was extinguished."

Both the Chindits and the Marauders were, in Slim's words, "asked to do more than was possible." By August 1944 "they had shot their bolt." Their remnants were withdrawn.

Meanwhile, Slim himself was attempting to carry out his part of the campaign. His own word for his objectives was "modest": to lead his divisions out of India and drive down the India-Burma border to Burma's west coast. For a while the operations of his Fourteenth Army went well. Michael Smith's recently published book *The Emperor's Codes* has recorded how India-based codebreakers combined with mobile intelligence units to provide Slim's army with the signals intelligence it needed for its invasion of Burma.

Then, at the beginning of February 1944, Slim's divisions began to encounter the same force that had slowed Stilwell's advance: the reinforced Japanese effort to mount their own powerful offensive, their "March to Delhi." While the troops carrying out the Allies' coastal thrust inflicted some setbacks to the Japanese and proved, once again, that the British could defeat the enemy in jungle warfare, Slim soon had to reorganize his divisions to meet the more serious threat of a major Japanese drive into India by pressing up through central Burma.

As Allied decrypts revealed, the Japanese no longer regarded Burma as an aside in their war. Success in Burma could completely isolate China and, it was hoped, drive the Chinese to sue for a separate peace. The Japanese organized Indian and Burmese anti-British armies. Magic decrypts of Oshima's messages revealed how the Burmese rebel Subhas Chandra Bose, who had opposed Gandhi's nonviolent rebellion in favor of an armed one against the British and had fled to exile in Germany, was transported in a German U-boat to Japan as preparation for his leadership of pro-Japanese forces in the CBI theater. The Japanese were encouraged to believe both Burma and India were ripe for revolution and would fall into their hands. As Japanese commanders proclaimed in exhortations to their troops, victory in Burma could change the whole course of the war.

Properly handled, the Burma offensive could ease the supply situation by seizing Allied supplies. The Japanese were so confident in this hope that they sent units of gunners without guns so they could take over captured British artillery.

Faced with this grave new threat, Slim and his commanders drew together a defense line south of the Indian town of Imphal. Slim planned to begin resistance on this new line and then, at the strategic moment, withdraw to the Imphal Plain and there "fight the decisive battle on grounds of our own choosing."

He later admitted that he made not just one "cardinal error," but two. With timing all-important, he allowed the withdrawal decision to be left to his field general. This was wrong, he acknowledged, because he himself was much better informed and in receipt of much more comprehensive intelligence reports. As it was, the withdrawal was delayed too long. The Japanese were able to send roadblocks around the retreating British troops and force them to fight their way through, with serious losses of men and equipment.

Slim's second error was in badly underestimating the capacity of the Japanese. Driven by their desire to capture British supplies, they showed themselves capable of accomplishing the sort of large-scale, long-range infiltration at which the Allies had become adept.

Slim had thought the Japanese would send only a regiment against the town of Kohima, north of Imphal. Copies of the Japanese maps and plans, recovered from a fallen officer's dispatch case, informed him otherwise. The entire Thirty-first Division of the Imperial Fifteenth Army was pressing the attack. Both Kohima and Imphal were quickly surrounded.

The British commanders were acutely aware that if the Japanese overran these strongpoints, their way was clear to strike virtually unopposed into the Indian subcontinent.

In two of the war's more admirable examples of courage, the garrisons held out. At Kohima, wounded men left their hospital beds, took up rifles and joined defenders. The Japanese kept pushing in the perimeter until, at one point, Kohima's no-man's-land consisted of a former swell's tennis court. Air teams dropped food, water and ammunition. The garrisons fought on, from April through May and into June.

In addition, as Slim's postmortem affirmed, he was saved from his mistakes by the "bullet head" and "unenterprising" nature of Kotoku Sato, the Japanese general directing the siege of Kohima. Sato could have left a small detachment to keep the garrison penned in while he dispatched the bulk of his division to take the vital but lightly protected center of Dimapur and open India to his advance. Instead, he spent his force by senselessly ordering wave after wave of bloody frontal attacks against the defenders. Allen has contested Slim's opinion of the Japanese general, claiming that Sato was "neither stupid nor unenterprising" but was the victim of orders he received from his superiors.

However it was, the staunch defense at Kohima and Imphal by Slim's Fourteenth Army allowed him to implement a new strategy. He had troops at his Arakan command on Burma's west coast that he could transfer to the Imphal-Kohima battles. He thought at first of moving the reinforcements by road and rail. When, however, he learned from his intelligence officers the full extent of the Japanese commitment to that area, he knew the shift must be done by air. He had U.S. and British aircraft at his disposal, most of them C-47 Dakotas. He needed C-46 Commandos from the Hump route— planes each of which could carry a load equivalent to that of thirty Dakotas.

Mountbatten took the initiative and secured the loan of the Hump aircraft. The airborne transfer of the coastal divisions to Imphal, according to Slim, brought the turning point. They arrived just in time, lifted the two sieges in vicious fighting and checked the Japanese short of replenishing themselves from Allied supplies. The Allies' defeat of the Fifteenth Army was aided as much by hunger and disease as by ammunition and bayonets.

The codebreakers' emphatic role in the turnaround was spelled out by Slim in talks with Winterbotham when the Ultra official traveled from Bletchley Park to check up on the CBI situation. "General Slim told me," Winterbotham wrote in *The Ultra Secret*, "that the intelligence from Ultra about the Japanese forces had been invaluable throughout the campaign, but the real triumph had been the information which led up to the final attack by the Japanese at Imphal and Kohima. It had become very evident from Ultra that the Japanese supply position was desperate and that their attack was being planned to capture the Fourteenth Army supply depots, so as to keep the Japanese army 'in business.'"

Winterbotham also learned that the codebreakers had shown "that the Japanese air force in the area had dwindled so as to be practically useless." The information was put to practical use in two ways. Allied air crews were able to supply the Fourteenth Army from the air without being menaced by Japanese fighters, and the decision to use the Hump cargo planes to fly in a whole division was made with the knowledge that it could be done without enemy interruption.

This time, the BP emissary concluded, "the Japanese retreat was for good."

The Recapture of Rangoon

To keep pressing the attack, Slim drew up new plans. The battles at Imphal-Kohima had crushed Japan's Fifteenth Army. Now he was faced by the Thirty-third Army, which he resolved to smash as well. He sent his troops south toward the cities of Mandalay and Meiktila. However, "it was not Mandalay or Meiktila that we were after," Slim wrote in his memoir, "but the Japanese army."

He devised a grand deception, relying on his Sigint teams to tell him if it was succeeding and whether or not it had been detected.

His scheme was to engineer his own Chindit-style end run penetration to block the Japanese retreat. Alan Stripp's memoir, *Codebreaker in the Far East*, has detailed the elaborate precautions Slim took in order to keep his encirclement a surprise.

Since the operation was to take place in Burma's dry season, the hundred-mile swing to the west had to avoid revealing itself by plumes of dust kicked up by the advancing men and armor. The construction crews laid a track of asphalt-impregnated dust-gathering hempen cloth at the rate of a mile a day. In the mountains they cantilevered tracks out from the cliff faces. To cross streams they installed seven prefabricated bridges. Teams of elephants were brought in to fell trees, help with the bridge building and collect timber for five hundred river barges used to transport troops and equipment. Drums filled with gasoline were floated on rafts of empty drums lashed together. The RAF prowled the skies to prevent any wandering Japanese plane from spying the end run.

Beaten in the Imphal-Kohima battle, the Japanese had retreated to the east side of the Chindwin River and stood ready to repel the Fourteenth Army's attempt to cross it. While they waited, Slim pulled off the second phase of his deception plan. He left a single division of his army there, along with a dummy headquarters and a radio communications unit that whipped up a storm of fake transmissions to suggest the busy traffic of forces readying for the crossing. The other divisions took to the concealed roadway, crossed the Chindwin one hundred miles south of the key town of Mandalay and took positions across the Japanese escape route.

Due to his secret encircling maneuver, the Thirty-third Army disintegrated. Small units tried to escape through the jungle and down the streams, but most of them were hunted down and wiped out.

Combining overland drives with airborne and amphibious assaults, the Allied armies converged on Rangoon. On May 2, 1945, an RAF pilot flying over the city saw a message written by Allied prisoners of war on top of their jail. It read JAPS GONE. The flier landed his plane at a nearby air base and walked into the city center, where he was greeted by the POWs. His cheeky report on the incident claimed that Rangoon had been taken by the RAF.

The Japanese had left the port sabotaged and smashed. Slim marshaled engineers and laborers to repair and reopen it. "They succeeded beyond my hopes," he wrote. "In six weeks we had 3,000 tons a day coming over the patched-up wharves; the maintenance crisis was passed."

One More Army to Destroy

Although the war in Europe was now over and the Allies' climb up the Pacific island ladder far advanced, generals who did not know about the atomic bomb had no choice but to anticipate months, possibly even years, of further warfare in Asia. For the generals of the CBI theater, this meant they still had to defeat another Japanese army, the largely intact Twenty-eighth, cornered in eastern Burma by the Allied victories. The aim of Japanese commanders was to save the army and withdraw it so it could fight again in Malaya, Singapore or even in the homeland. The result was the Battle of the Breakout.

Again, codebreakers and intelligence teams gave the Allies an enormous advantage. Allen has written of Lieutenant General Francis Tuker, who was directing the Allied attack, "Naturally enough, his Intelligence had given him the entire picture on a plate."

The richest intelligence source was, once more, a captured document that gave the Allied leaders the clues they needed to thwart the Japanese and destroy the Twenty-eighth with a minimal expenditure of their own troops. In the foothills northeast of Rangoon, a patrol of Gurkhas ran into a Japanese contingent, killed a number of them and drove off the rest. Among the debris the Japanese left in their retreat was a leather dispatch bag. By the time the Gurkhas found it, it was soaked by the monsoon rains. A British intelligence officer, Lieutenant L. Levy, and a U.S. nisei sergeant, Katsu Tabata, carefully dried the papers from the bag, pieced them together and translated them. They disclosed the Twenty-eighth's breakout plans, including the routes they meant to follow. From that point on it was, as military historian S. W. Kelly noted, "largely a gunners' battle." The Allies massed artillery at main points in the Japanese passage and used metal rather than men to massacre the retreating forces.

Unknowing, disbelieving pockets of Japanese troops were still resisting well after the atomic bombs were dropped and the war ended.

In winning the China-Burma-India war, the Allies did more than stop the march to Delhi. They tied up the more than 300,000 troops Japan sent there and killed three-fifths of them, allowing only 185,000 to return home. They routed the subservient armies whose victories would have turned Burma and India into Japanese puppet states. They kept China in the war. In so doing, they achieved at least one of the U.S. goals: in the weeks before Hiroshima, U.S. China-based planes did join in the bombing of the Japanese home islands.

As for the codebreakers' contribution to the hard-fought turn toward victory in the CBI, Hugh Denham, a BP-trained analyst who served in India, has told of Louis Mountbatten visiting his unit at war's end and saying of the CBI cryptographic teams that they were "worth ten divisions." Hyperbole, of course, but nonetheless a gratifying commendation for the men and women who spent countless hours, often in unspeakable conditions, to wrest the contents out of the multiple codes used by the Japanese and to read for Allied commanders the minds of their opposing brass.

17 Europe: The Bitter Fruits of Complacency

ROBERT A. Miller's book *August 1944* claimed this was the climactic month of the war in Western Europe. At the month's beginning, the Allies' hold on their beachhead in Normandy was still tenuous. The pivotal town of Caen had not been taken. The Americans were bogged down in the *bocage*. Everywhere the Allies were well behind their planned schedules of advance.

By the month's end, all had changed. Caen had fallen; the Americans had held off the mad offensive Hitler had ordered at Mortain and Patton was making ground-eating drives toward the German frontier. Paris had been liberated. The entrapment at Falaise had seriously weakened the Wehrmacht.

Euphoria set in among Allied leaders and lower ranks alike. Official summaries included statements such as "The August battles have done it; have brought the end of the war in Europe in sight." December 31 was marked as the ultimate date for victory. GIs sang, "I'll be home for Christmas."

Unfortunately, along with the euphoria came complacency, overconfidence, carelessness. Signals intelligence was never more complete or timely, but it was in crucial instances disregarded. Ambitious plans would not be altered because of a few misgivings conveyed by Special Liaison Units.

Churchill, for one, was by no means convinced that the scene on the continent was as rosy as it appeared. He read the Ultra reports of how masterfully the Germans were pulling their forces together to form a new defense line from the North Sea littoral to the Swiss border. Freshly formed fighting divisions were being scraped together by combing able-bodied men out of rear echelon troops. Underused Luftwaffe and navy personnel were being reassigned. Men not previously thought to be soldier material were being sworn in and hustled forward to fill in the gaps while battered panzer divisions were withdrawn to be reorganized and reequipped. Decrypts told him of divisions being transferred from the stalemated front in Italy. German war production, adroitly dispersed by Albert Speer, was turning out more matériel than at any previous time of the war. Most significantly, the prime minister noted that the Allies, in their eastward sweep, had still not captured a major usable port. Although Montgomery's armies had taken the port of Antwerp, finding it surprisingly intact, the harbor could not be used until the winding Schelde River estuary that connected it with the sea, as well as the islands offshore from the estuary, could be wrested from German control. Churchill saw these worrisome details, and no doubt growled into his sherry, but by then he was trying to leave the direction of the war to the generals.

Another disturbing element, as Anthony Cave Brown has noted in his book *Bodyguard of Lies*, was that having pulled off their enormous ruses to fool the Germans about the landings in Normandy, the Allies had no grand deceptions left. Now it was frontal assault against dug-in defenses, conventional arms rather than skillful artifice, and the war would, as Brown expressed it, "deteriorate into dull carnage." The progress was slow and the casualties were heavy, far heavier during the plotless march to Germany's borders than in those heady times when subterfuge dominated.

The Allied leaders could not claim, though, that they lacked for knowledge of German intentions. For example, a flood of decrypts should have made clear to Montgomery the importance the Germans placed in holding the approaches to Antwerp. Those coastlands north of the city denied the port to the Allies. They also provided an escape route for the Germans' Fifteenth Army, strung out along the Normandy coast. But Monty, with the concurrence of Eisenhower, regarded the Schelde as an annoying diversion from his main objective: to push on eastward toward the Ruhr and the Reich heartland. The First Canadian Army, which he assigned to clear the estuary, was not strong enough to do the job. Not until eighty-five days later did the first Allied transports finally enter Antwerp, and in the interim Allied operations were greatly handicapped by problems of supply. In a moment of refreshing candor, Montgomery was later to admit that in underestimating the difficulty of opening up the Schelde he had made "a bad mistake," adding, "I reckoned that the Canadian Army could do it *while* we were going for the Ruhr. I was wrong."

A serious setback for the Allies, in blood and in spirit, came in September when Montgomery decided he could speed his penetration into the

Reich and bring the war to an end in 1944 by dropping paratroops and glider crews behind the German lines in Holland. He code-named his plan Market Garden and won Eisenhower's approval of it. The plan called for a British airborne division to land near the town of Arnhem, capture the bridge there over the Rhine River and hold it until an armored relief column could arrive. Two American airborne divisions were to seize key bridges leading up to Arnhem while the armored British XXX Corps broke out of its beachhead on the Meuse-Escaut Canal, more than fifty miles to the rear, and drove to Arnhem. If the operation succeeded, it would forge a corridor through the German defenses and across the Rhine.

As Peter Harclerode has detailed in his book *Arnhem*, the plan was flawed from the beginning and became "a tragedy of errors." In the first place, it began too late. Launched sooner, it would have caught the Germans reeling back, disorganized by their defeats in Normandy. By the time Eisenhower had stopped vacillating in his support and Montgomery had pressured for every ounce of scarce supplies he could obtain, the opportunity was gone. The Germans had firmed up their defenses.

Then the operation was undertaken too hurriedly; commanders were given only six days to prepare, not enough time for them to reconnoiter what they would be up against. The British commander sensibly sought to have the paratroops land near Arnhem, but the RAF, believing that antiaircraft fire there would be too intense—an unfounded fear, as it turned out— would agree only to drop zones eight miles away. The number of planes was inadequate to carry out so large an operation, with a result that the paratroop and glider landings were spread out over three days, losing much of the advantage of surprise. Among other errors, the field radio equipment was too low powered to overcome the distances involved and enable the various outfits to communicate with each other.

Most damaging of all, Montgomery persisted in carrying out Market Garden despite copious intelligence warnings of the grave hazards it would encounter. BP decrypts and air reconnaissance showed that the failure to seize control of the Schelde had allowed some seventy thousand German soldiers, with much of their equipment, to be ferried out of Normandy and to begin to regroup in Holland. Admonitions from Ultra were supplemented by those of Prince Bernhard of the Netherlands, who brought to Montgomery's headquarters a briefcase full of Dutch Resistance reports on the buildup of German forces in the lowlands. Montgomery rejected the prince's advice. He belittled the Ultra decrypts. Not once but twice he brushed aside the cautions of his own intelligence officer. And he waved away the objections to his plan brought to him by Eisenhower's chief of staff, Walter Bedell Smith, and the British intelligence chief of SHAEF (Supreme Headquarters of the Allied Expeditionary Force), Kenneth Strong.

The hazards pointed out to Montgomery included not only the troops of the Fifteenth Army who had escaped across the Schelde estuary, but also two panzer divisions that were in the Arnhem sector to be reequipped with new tanks. Moreover, two companies of parachute troops were there, plus ten battalions armed with heavy antitank guns. To round out this murderers' row, another BP decrypt revealed, Field Marshal Walther Model had established a headquarters just four miles from Arnhem; he would be on the spot to mobilize and direct the annihilation of the invaders.

As Hinsley has noted, Ultra decrypts even revealed that the Germans anticipated an Allied thrust toward Arnhem and believed that it might involve airborne landings.

Montgomery was not to be deterred. His only response was, when the operation was obviously faltering, to send in a reserve brigade of Polish paratroops to be added to the awful stew in what became known as the "caldron."

Even with all these adversities going against it, Market Garden came close to succeeding. Courageous British paratroops did reach Arnhem, seize the bridge and hold out, not for the two days specified in the plan but for three days and three nights. The American paratroops captured their assigned bridges and held open the corridor despite having their ranks thinned by repeated German counterattacks. What caused Market Garden ultimately to fail was that the armored ground forces could not make the connection. The only road for the linkup was one tank wide and six feet higher than the surrounding marshy terrain, making the deployment of tanks impossible, assuring German defenses easy targets. The Rhine crossing at Arnhem became, in the phrase Cornelius Ryan made famous, "a bridge too far."

After nine days of slaughter, the airborne units were ordered to save themselves if they could. Of the original force of ten thousand men, only about two thousand escaped, some by swimming the wide expanse of the Rhine. The rest were killed or taken prisoners.

The setback of Market Garden proved that the German armies, instead of deteriorating after their hard knocks in Normandy and in southern France, were still capable of mounting a surprisingly strong resistance to Allied advances. Still, the Allied generals were obsessed by their desire to bring the war to a quick end, to finish off the Wehrmacht and be in Berlin by Christmas. Their overconfidence that Allied troops could bring this about led to another horrific bloodletting.

This was the Battle of the Hürtgen Forest. A dense tangle of woods, ridges and ravines south of the German city of Aachen, it lay in the way of the plans being developed by Eisenhower, Bradley, Courtney Hodges and their staffs. They had decided that the quickest way for a breakthrough into the Ruhr industrial sector lay in the relatively flat terrain of the Aachen valley, where armor could roll in full force. They saw the forest as a double obstacle. German troops hidden there could spring a flank attack on the Ruhr-ward push. Also, they could open dam gates on the forest's streams to flood the valley and any Allied armor in it. Hürtgen Forest, the Allied commanders decided, must be taken.

Believing in the power of their troops to overcome weakened Nazi garrisons, the generals were sure the Hürtgen threat could be overcome in a matter of days. The taking required more than a month—a month in which division after division was fed into the German meat chopper. U.S. general James Gavin reported later that American casualties amounted to thirty-three thousand men—twenty-four thousand battle casualties and nine thousand cases of trench foot and respiratory diseases resulting from the miserable weather. Hardly mentioned, barely remembered, the battle nonetheless chewed up more men by far than Market Garden, with little more to show for their sacrifice.

The failure to open the port of Antwerp, the defeat at Arnhem and the grim details of the Hürtgen Forest offense were major contributors to the deceleration of the Allied drive toward Germany. Stung by Arnhem, Monty reverted to his usual caution and stopped to recuperate. The U.S. First Army captured the German city of Aachen but then came up against what Ultra decrypts recognized as two reinforced panzer divisions and settled into a stalemate. In the south, Patton's gasoline-starved armor was frustrated by its inability to subdue the stubborn fortress at Metz. Any hope of ending the war that winter evaporated.

And after being duped time and again by Allied deceptions, Hitler was about to have his turn.

The Bulge: When Ultra Missed the Main Point

On a bitterly cold night in late December 1944, my group of "cryptographers" sat over the dregs of our coffee at Hall Place in Bexley, Kent. We had finished our evening shift and our midnight snack. Our mood was one of despair, for we had just learned the news of what was to become known as the Battle of the Bulge. The German counteroffensive through the Ardennes forest had come as a stunning surprise. The lines of raw, newly arrived, half-trained GIs, and of battle-weary troops sent there for R and R, spread out over too wide a front, were being overrun by giant panzer tanks and waves of German infantry.

Our question was, how could this be happening? How had the Allies been caught so completely off guard? How, if Station X was breaking these endless streams of code we were so diligently processing, could some message have failed to warn of this vicious counterstrike by the Germans? Was our whole war effort an empty charade? Were those masses of message forms we'd intercepted and processed just piling up in some Limey warehouse hopefully awaiting the day when *some*one *some*how would find the key to them?

Never had the limitations of the "need to know" been so galling to us, so frustrating. We longed to hear that the work we were doing, this activity in lieu of bleeding and dying, did make some worthwhile contribution, did have some meaning. Reassurance seemed essential if we were to pick ourselves up on the morrow and continue to do our job.

But we were common soldiers, below that broad dividing line of the military caste system separating enlisted men from officers, the system that ruled that we were there merely to do and not to know. There was nothing for it but to overcome our doubts, crawl into our frigid bunks and get the sleep that would let us, out of deference to those poor guys across there on the continent, keep plugging away with the same care as before.

Most of us didn't learn the truth until years later, until the walls of secrecy came tumbling down.

It may have been, we learned, that the Germans had become aware that their Enigma systems had been compromised. As a result, Hitler directed that none of his orders, or those of his generals, relating to his surprise attack were to be sent by wireless. A counterintelligence report prepared by SHAEF in November 1944 stated that a Dutchman, Christiann Antonius Lindemans, recruited as an agent by the German secret service, had wormed his way into the confidence of Dutch authorities and betrayed both the Allied plans for the Arnhem landings and the secrets of Ultra. Lindemans's disclosures, the report asserted, convinced the Germans to limit their use of the Enigma, even though the task of completely replacing its far-flung dispersion could only partially be met by the end of the war.

Whatever the truth of the Lindemans story, the Germans achieved a definite drop-off in the volume of Enigma traffic. BP decrypted messages ordering units to avoid the use of radio. Selmer Norland has recalled seeing a message that read, "*Fuer Alle SS Einheiten funkstille*," or "For all SS units, radio silence." Winterbotham has told of orders being delivered to the front "by hand by motor-cyclists."

This decline in traffic was in itself viewed by BP analysts as a warning of something big brewing. Norland recognized the importance of the SS message: "It was what we called a five-Zed message, five Zs for 'top priority.' It was a clear indicator of what was going to happen."

Hinsley's history has detailed scores of messages portending a major action by the Germans. As early as August, Baron Oshima was reporting on a "very thorough" mobilization by which Hitler was expecting to form 110 to 125 new divisions and to rebuild the German air force so that it would be able to stand up to the Allies. In September, Oshima used his Magic machine to tell of his latest interview with Hitler, in which the führer confided that a million new troops were ready, together with units withdrawn from other fronts, to undertake a great offensive in the West.

Enigma decrypts showed panzer divisions being withdrawn east of the Rhine for rest and refitting. Their places in the defensive line were taken by new "Volksgrenadier" divisions made up of reassigned air force and navy troops, overage men and Hitler Youth teenagers. Other decrypts revealed the formation of a new Sixth Army and of the reorganization of the Fifth Panzer Army. Decoded railway Enigma messages reported train after train of men and supplies being conveyed to the western front. Luftwaffe decrypts told of Göring energetically gathering together aircraft to replace the close-support operations that had been all but eliminated during the fighting in Normandy, and of preparing the new formations for a "lightning blow."

BP analysts noted the skillful resistance against the Allies being conducted by Rundstedt and wondered, in view of this sensible use of the army, whether Hitler might be "unwell," allowing Rundstedt to function "without higher intuition."

Available at Britain's Public Record Office is Bletchley Park's own twenty-seven-page analysis of what went wrong, written as the crisis was ending. Having by then substantiated "Source" rather than Boniface as the supplier of its information, BP said in its summary, "Source gave clear warning that a counteroffensive was coming. He also gave warning, though at short notice, of *when* it was coming." The trouble was that "he did *not* give by any means unmistakable indications of *where* it was coming, nor . . . of its full scale."

There was the catch. Because of "new and elaborate deceptions staged by German security," the word *Ardennes* never appeared in the decrypts. Although the Ardennes was where Hitler had achieved his great success in 1940, it was now in 1944 regarded as the least likely point of a German attack.

As Hinsley observed, the generals of both the Allied and German armies agreed what the Germans *should* do in the waning months of 1944. They should husband their depleted forces to wage a stubborn withdrawal west of the Rhine and then use that great natural barrier for a last-ditch stand to protect the Reich. They lacked the troops, ammunition and fuel for a counteroffensive other than a minor "spoiling" action to blunt the coming Allied advances.

All of this sensible military prognosis figured without Hitler. Living more and more in his fantasy world, he refused to accept the reports of inadequate resources. As the Allies thinned out their Ardennes defense lines to strengthen their offensives north and south, he saw the opportunity for another grand coup. He would confuse any spies of Allied intelligence by giving his armies new names: the Fifth would become the "Gruppe von Manteuffel," after a young and able general whom Hitler trusted, while the Sixth would be designated, in English translation, the "Rest and Refitting Staff 16." He would further befuddle observers by shifting his troops back and forth across the entry to the Ardennes, moving three divisions one way and two back while holding the extra one for the offensive's buildup. Then, with his Volksgrenadier divisions holding the line, his Fifth and Sixth Panzer Armies would file through to launch the attack.

His delusional idea was that his panzers would smash through the weak American lines, turn north into Belgium, drive to Antwerp, split off the British divisions in the north, force them into another Dunkirk and so dishearten the British people—who were already suffering the demoralizing effects of the V-2 rockets being rained on England—that they would drop out of the war.

Hitler's generals, knowing they were far short of the men and matériel to carry out so grandiose a scheme, tried to persuade him to accept a lesser plan such as a drive toward Liège that stood a chance of encircling large numbers of British troops. He remained adamant. They must carry out the counteroffensive exactly as he had envisioned it.

Despite the partial wireless blackout, the codebreakers at Bletchley Park knew a great deal about these developments. Decrypts told of Luftwaffe pilot aircraft being brought up to guide fighters and fighter-bombers to their targets, as well as the pulling together of a paratroop division. The formation of Volksgrenadier divisions and their dispatch to the front were also amply reported. BP read Hitler's orders for a special operation to be made up of volunteers fluent in English and American idioms and for "captured U.S. clothing, equipment, weapons and vehicles" to be collected for these troops.

All that was missing was where these forces would head once the offensive began.

Partly, Hitler succeeded because he kept his secret even from his own generals for so long. Not until November did Rundstedt and the other top officers learn of the plan. The lower-echelon generals were given only a few days' notice, so short a time that they could not do adequate planning.

Tragically, the earlier tip-offs by Ultra and Magic had bred among Allied commanders a dependence on their output. Without having German plans and intentions verified by the codebreakers, Allied leaders discounted warnings from other sources. From the Ardennes sector came GI reports of hearing the muffled roar of powerful engines, POWs' confessions that a great attack was in the offing and local residents' accounts of seeing armor and men massed behind the front. All was ignored. As the BP analysis put it, "There is a risk of relying too much on Source. His very successes in the past constituted a danger."

Allied commanders were so convinced the war was in its midwinter doldrums that when the blow fell Montgomery was playing golf in Belgium and had received Eisenhower's permission to go back to England to celebrate Christmas with his family. Eisenhower was attending his valet's wedding, and other officers were on R and R in Paris. While some Allied intelligence officers expressed concern about the buildup, none felt sure enough to counter their generals' prevailing expectations.

Before dawn on December 16, the area that German messages had referred to as "the quiet sector" erupted. Artillery blasted the green or tired GIs crouched in their frozen foxholes. Searchlights bouncing their beams off low-lying clouds provided light for the "storm battalions," made up of the most battle-experienced officers and men, to infiltrate the American lines. A special operation of English-speaking Germans, dressed in U.S. uniforms and driving jeeps, slipped through to create confusion and near panic among the rear echelons. The big tanks of the Sixth Panzer Army, followed by those of the Fifth, rolled over the defenders. SS troops once again followed the fighting legions to perpetrate such atrocities as the massacre of American prisoners at Malmédy.

Hitler's new version of an Ardennes surprise had its moment of success. But in the end the counteroffensive went as his generals had predicted. The Germans simply lacked the strength to push through to Antwerp. Even though the American troops' shock was great, they put up a defense stubborn enough to throw the offensive off schedule on its very first day. The Germans' drive to capture Allied fuel dumps to replenish their fast-waning supplies came within a quarter mile of the huge reserve at Stavelot in Belgium but could advance no closer. Similarly, the push to gain control of the road and communications hub of Bastogne and make the Americans there surrender was frustrated. The Germans sent to negotiate the capitulation received General Anthony McAuliffe's famous single-word reply, "Nuts," which had to be translated for the Germans as "Go to hell." When the bad weather ended, the GAF's efforts to support the army were overwhelmed by masses of Allied planes swarming over the German columns. As soon as the drive started and full use of wireless was resumed, BP was decoding every phase of the attack. According to Hinsley, "Thanks to the exceptionally prompt decryption of copious high-grade Sigint, the Allies encountered no surprises once they had overcome the initial shock." Eisenhower and his generals, reading the German commands' operational and reconnaissance orders for each day, knew when the Sixth Panzer Army changed its course from trying to reach Antwerp to trying to take Liège, when the Luftwaffe reached its peak and began its precipitous decline and when the attack finally stalled.

Hitler's dream soon became a nightmare. Pummeled by Allied aircraft, pounded from the south by Patton's divisions and from the north by Americans temporarily assigned to Montgomery, hamstrung by Hitler's refusal to countenance withdrawals, the German armies suffered losses far greater than those of the Allies.

Bradley later wrote in his memoir that he and other U.S. generals foresaw, as GIs grimly slowed down the German drive, the opportunity to turn from defensive to offensive operations and cut the German salient at the waist, entrapping the fuel-starved German armies. But as at Falaise, Montgomery foiled the plan by having to "tidy up" his lines before launching his attack, a full five days after Patton had begun his assault. Monty's caution, combined with foul weather that held up both offensives, permitted the bulk of German forces and equipment to escape.

Nevertheless, the battle left the Wehrmacht badly wounded. As Churchill summed up, "This was the final German offensive of the war. It cost us no little anxiety and postponed our own advance, but we benefited

18 Closing In on the Empire

As the Japanese were forced to surrender island after island, further rich treasures in captured documents fell into Allied hands. They included codebooks, copies of strategic plans, and manuals relating to such equipment as radar and underwater sonar gear. On Makin the captures amounted to basketfuls; on Kwajalein they rose to more than a ton; on Saipan they soared to more than fifty tons. This tremendous inflow pressed new cadres of translators back at Pearl Harbor and in Australia to the limit.

One especially useful trove of information came in a single recovered briefcase. On the night of March 31, 1943, Admirals Mineichi Koga and Shigeru Fukudome were inspecting defenses in the Palau islands. When a patrol plane reported, mistakenly as it turned out, that a U.S. fleet was approaching, the two admirals decided to leave for a safe haven at Davao, in the Philippines. They took off in planes that became separated from each other in a storm. The plane bearing Koga, commander in chief of Japan's Combined Fleet, was never seen again. When strong head winds made Fukudome's plane run short of fuel it made a crash landing off the Philippine island of Cebu. The admiral survived by clinging to a seat cushion for eight and a half hours. He was rescued, but not by Japanese troops. His captors were native fishermen loyal to Allied guerrillas on the island. All this time Fukudome had held on to his briefcase, which the fishermen recovered and turned over to the guerrillas. Soon an American submarine was carrying it to the Allied Translation and Interpretation Section in Melbourne. The contents included Koga's Decisive Battle plan for the approaching phase of the war as well as a highly informative study of carrier fleet operations.

Although the Japanese should have expected that their code materials had, by captures such as these, fallen to the Allies, they continued to make only routine obligatory changes in their code systems. It was as though, cryptologically, they had already surrendered. The changes did more to complicate the tasks of Japanese code clerks than to frustrate Allied cryptanalysts. After the June-to-August blackout in 1942, Allied codebreakers were never again shut out for more than short periods.

The new information strengthened the arsenal of intelligence the Allies brought to the next big battles. Although the Japanese warlords knew that a major new Allied fleet operation was forming up to strike them, they could only guess where the blow would fall. They were ripe for another grand deception. Air raids against their bases in the Palau islands convinced them that these would be the objective of the Allied offensive. Instead, Nimitz ordered a giant leap past the Palaus and into Guam, Saipan and Tinian, three of the main islands in the Marianas chain. While Guam was the primary objective, Nimitz directed the first attack against the more northerly island of Saipan, since possession of it would cut off Japanese air support of the garrison on Guam.

One morning the inhabitants of Saipan looked out on serene waters. The next morning they saw the front edge of an invasion fleet that totaled more than six hundred ships. The contrast with the skimpy three-carrier force the U.S. was able to scrape together for the Battle of Midway was a tribute to American productivity. The task force bearing down on Saipan included seven battleships, twenty-one cruisers, scores of destroyers and fifteen aircraft carriers. Transports carried more than 125,000 troops. The landings came on June 15, 1944, at the same time that the Allies in Europe were trying to hold on to their Normandy beachheads.

Control of the Marianas was another of those crisis points vital to both sides. Allied leaders thirsted for the strategic advantages that bases there would provide. They would bisect the supply lines connecting Japan and the Asian mainland with their strongholds in the south. An airfield on Saipan could put Japan itself within reach of America's new B-29 Superfortresses. Also, recapture of Guam would have spirit-lifting significance: it had been a U.S. possession for forty-three years before the small Marine garrison had been overwhelmed two days after the raid on Pearl Harbor.

For the Japanese, their Marianas bases were bastions of the inner defense ring to which they had withdrawn after the first wave of Allied island-hopping successes. They, too, knew that from Saipan U.S. planes would come within striking distance of their homeland, the Imperial Palace, the emperor himself. The Marianas must be held at all costs.

Even though the invasion of Saipan surprised the Japanese by its boldness, their military chiefs had been anticipating that they would have to fight battles such as this closer to home. Characteristically, their planners were not content with a purely defensive posture. They continued to ready their depleted forces for the Decisive Battle. This could come, they believed, in the next big clash between the Allied and Imperial fleets. The Japanese plan called for smashing the Allied ships in a three-phase attack. First, submarines would waylay the Allied fleet and reduce its numbers. Second, the newly organized First Air Fleet would use the islands still under Japanese control as "stationary aircraft carriers" to send land-based bombers and fighters against the Allied ships. And third, the Mobile Fleet would then sally forth to administer the coup de grâce. The plan was, of course, another variation on the strategy that had yielded the legendary success of 1904.

Once again, though, the Japanese were at the enormous disadvantage of having their plans revealed by signals intelligence. Decodes precisely spotted the locations assigned to the submarines, which were dispatched one after another by a trio of Allied destroyer escorts. One of these vessels, the USS *England*, made six kills in just twelve days. Further, once the Japanese plan for using the islands as stationary carriers was known, the airfields were subjected by Allied forces to incessant air and naval bombardments that destroyed many of the planes before they could go into action. Thus, two phases of the plan were neutralized before the real battle began.

Nevertheless, the Mobile Fleet, under Admiral Jisaburo Ozawa, sailed on into the Marianas, observing radio silence in order to avoid detection. The mighty new battleships *Yamato* and *Misashi*, which had been steaming south to blast the ships protecting MacArthur's invasion at Biak, were called back to join Ozawa.

Allied submarine sightings and direction-finding combined with decoded messages to keep Allied commanders informed as to when and where *Yamato* and *Misashi* and their escorts would link up with Ozawa's force, where they would refuel, and what course they would follow. The powerful additions to the Mobile Fleet were worrisome; each battleship was a behemoth the length of three football fields, protected by fourteen inches of armor plate and carrying giant 18.1-inch guns capable of hurling a 3,200-pound shell nearly thirty miles.

But the combat would feature aircraft and submarines, not battleships. On June 18, the eve of the battle, when his scout planes sighted the U.S. fleet, Ozawa felt obliged to break his radio silence and send a message to coordinate the next day's carrier- and land-based air attacks. He had no way of knowing that the Allies' preemptive air and naval bombardments had put the stationary carriers almost out of commission. Allied signal teams pounced on his broadcast and used it to gain an exact fix on his fleet's location. Admiral Spruance, in charge of the Allied task force, surmised that Ozawa, to keep his ships beyond the range of U.S. carrier aircraft, would launch his planes from well out, expecting them to land on Marianas airfields rather than return to their carriers.

There followed, on June 19 and 20, what U.S. fliers dubbed the "great Marianas turkey shoot." Inexperienced pilots flew most of Ozawa's planes, for the veterans had been shot down in earlier battles. Intelligence units aboard the U.S. warships awoke to the fact that the Japanese were using flight coordinators who, by radio, assigned targets and lectured the green pilots on how to attack. Translations of these instructions were quickly radioed to combat-hardened Hellcat pilots who gleefully agreed on their countermeasures. Of the sixty-nine planes that lifted off from Ozawa's carriers in his first wave, forty-two were lost. In addition, about fifty of the land-based planes from Guam went down. In this one day Japan's naval arm lost three-quarters of its waning stock of aircraft while doing only negligible damage to the Allied fleet.

Making matters worse for Ozawa, U.S. submarines stole in among his ships and sank two of his carriers, including Japan's newest, which he was using as his flagship.

Operating with minimal information, Ozawa presumed that many of his planes had made it to Guam rather than been shot down and would return to his carriers the next day. What came instead were hordes of Hellcats. They sank a third carrier, seriously damaged other ships and destroyed additional planes. Of four hundred aircraft with which Ozawa had entered the battle, he retreated with only thirty-five able to fly. The troops in the Marianas were left to fend for themselves.

American flyboys had enjoyed a rousing couple of days. For the marines and infantry GIs invading Saipan the story was much less buoyant. In a scenario that was becoming all too familiar, the prelanding bombardments did far less damage than the Americans had hoped, the invaders faced enemy soldiers holed up in caves carved into the island's foundation rock, progress had to come redoubt after burned-out redoubt, and the Yanks had to hold against a final sacrificial charge by soldiers emboldened by sake and beer. In planning this last attack, the Japanese commanders ordered all wounded men unable to walk and bear arms to be shot; the others hobbled into battle carrying sticks and stones because there were not enough rifles to go around. Two American divisions were all but wiped out before the hysterical charge could be stopped. Many of Saipan's civilians joined the troops and their commanders in committing suicide. Admiral Nagumo, hero of Pearl Harbor, now demoted to the command of a land-based sailor contingent, was one who died there by his own hand.

Spruance subsequently drew some criticism for not being more aggressive in seeking out the Japanese fleet and sinking more of Ozawa's capital ships. He preferred to protect the invaders of Saipan and let Ozawa come to him.

The island of Tinian fell within a week. Guam was another matter. Even though the navy tried to do a better job than on Saipan, bombarding the island mercilessly for thirteen days before the troops went ashore, the battle was long and lethal. Partly this was due to geography. The largest of the islands, Guam has a mountainous core into which the defenders had burrowed with molelike energy. Also partly responsible was one of the two Japanese generals in command. Takashima Takeshi had seen the folly of suicidal charges, and he instructed his men to conduct cool, calculated forays. One of these efforts infiltrated the combat line and finally had to be stopped by an impromptu assembly of truck drivers, Seabee construction crews, headquarters troops and wounded men firing from their hospital beds. U.S. casualties in the Marianas campaign ran into the thousands, and those for the Japanese into the multithousands. The U.S. Navy added to the mayhem by sinking three more Japanese aircraft carriers and destroying seventeen submarines—losses that were confirmed by decrypts.

The mass of documents captured on the islands soon enabled Allied commanders to know almost as much about the enemy's fleet organization and order of battle as their own admirals did.

While the fighting was still going on, work was started on airfields from which the Superforts could fly. They made their first raid against Japan on November 24.

Japan's defeat in the Marianas and the initial U.S. attacks on the homeland had another important consequence. Prime Minister Hideki Tojo, architect of the empire's war effort, resigned and was replaced by the more moderate Kuniaki Koiso. It was the beginning of a rift in war attitudes that would divide Japan's leaders until the end of hostilities.

With Nimitz closing in from the east and MacArthur driving up from the south and west, the Philippines were now gripped in a giant pincers. At this point in the war the Americans under Nimitz had evolved a resourceful approach to command. For a couple of months, as in the Marianas, Admiral Spruance would head the huge Task Force 58. During this period Admiral Halsey would be preparing for the next phase, when the Allied fleet would become Task Force 38. Invasion of the island of Leyte, in the Philippines, came on Halsey's watch.

The original plan was for him to first take the islands of Peleliu and Angaur, in the Palaus, while MacArthur invaded the Philippines' southernmost island of Mindanao. When Halsey's carrier-based planes struck at the midarchipelago island of Leyte, however, they found the defenses there surprisingly weak. He advocated leapfrogging the Palaus and Mindanao and landing directly on Leyte. The change, he argued, would advance the timetable by at least two months.

The new plan was approved—except for one detail. Nimitz was concerned about having the untamed Palaus on his flank. Over Halsey's objections he held out for subduing Peleliu and Angaur. For once Halsey was right and Nimitz was wrong. In hindsight it can be seen that the Palaus could have been left to wither as Rabaul and Truk were now withering. The cost of nearly two thousand Americans killed and more than eight thousand wounded for these conquests was too high a price to pay for the islands' limited strategic value.

Eugene B. Sledge in his memoir, *With the Old Breed*, has left an indelible impression of what it was like to be a raw young marine fighting for thirty days on Peleliu's chunk of coral rock so hard the soldiers couldn't protect themselves by digging holes. To have come through without being killed or wounded made him feel he "hadn't been just lucky but was a survivor of a major tragedy."

When the Palaus were overcome, even Nimitz was ready to reclaim the Philippines.

A Close Call on Leyte

By October 1944, Douglas MacArthur had taken Morotai, the northernmost island of the Molucca chain, only three hundred miles from the Philippines, without losing a man. His bypass strategy had left two hundred thousand Japanese uselessly guarding islands not chosen for assault. It was time for The General to redeem his pledge.

He had first to win out over Admiral King, who argued that the next step in the Pacific war should be against not the Philippines but the island of Taiwan. MacArthur presented his case in masterly fashion before FDR, the Joint Chiefs and operational commanders and won their authorization to capture Leyte as the opening wedge in his Philippines campaign.

Here the Japanese desperation to make a stand was redoubled. To surrender the Philippines would completely block access to their pockets of troops farther south. Defeat there would also be a stunning blow to civilian morale in the homeland. Most important, losing the Philippines would sever the Japanese pipeline to Indonesian oil and immobilize their war machine. To prevent the Americans from taking over, the military leaders were ready to commit much of their remaining ships, their aircraft and their veteran troops.

On the Allied side there was a great deal more to the plan than to stroke the ego of a vainglorious general. The Philippines were seen as an essential stepping-stone to the conquest of Japan itself. Air and naval bases there would supplement those under Nimitz's control. In the war of attrition the land and naval battles would give the vastly superior Allied forces the opportunity to eliminate more Japanese ships, planes and soldiers that would otherwise be available to defend the home islands.

Aboard his flagship, the cruiser *Nashville*, MacArthur headed a seven-hundred-ship, hundred-mile-long flotilla bearing two hundred thousand troops ready to carry out his carefully devised battle plan. At daybreak on October 20, the U.S. warships began their bombardment of the Leyte beaches. Heedless of the Japanese planes buzzing overhead, The General stood on the bridge observing the Higgins boats ferrying the assault troops to the landing site. In his memoir MacArthur says he went in with the third wave, but in truth the invasion was four hours old before he, his staff, the soon-to-be-restored Filipino leaders and the necessary gaggle of war correspondents and photographers descended into a barge and made for the shore. MacArthur was dressed immaculately, expecting a dry landing. Instead, a harried beachmaster was too busy directing vitally needed traffic to honor Mac's small boat's request for pier space. "Let 'em walk," he said, not knowing who " 'em" was. Trying to reach the beach, the overloaded barge grounded fifty yards from shore. Waiting only for the cameramen to precede him, MacArthur leaped into the knee-deep surf and waded in, setting up one of the war's most renowned photographs.

On the beach, with combat guns blazing in the background, he spoke into microphones and recording devices, delivering the speech he had been preparing for years: "People of the Philippines, I have returned," he said. "Rally to me."

Meanwhile the intelligence blindness of the Japanese was leading them to two calamitous blunders. The first involved Japan's diminishing supply of aircraft. Not knowing when the invasion would come, the admiral directing the defense of the Philippines ordered hundreds of land-based and naval aircraft to the islands prematurely. The planes of Halsey's fleet enjoyed another turkey shoot, destroying some five hundred aircraft before the battle for Leyte began.

Second was a grave mistake at sea. The miscalculation was triggered when Japanese land-based planes broke through the protective screens of Halsey's Third Fleet and hurled torpedoes at the U.S. ships. The returning Japanese pilots exultantly claimed great successes: the sinking of two battleships and no less than eleven carriers, with other ships severely damaged. The triumph was trumpeted on Tokyo radio, which inflated the number of carrier sinkings to nineteen. Unlike the Americans, whose Hawaii-based Estimate Section used decrypts to reduce overoptimistic reports to hard facts, the Japanese had no way to verify the actual results of the raid. Consequently, Japanese navy chiefs were convinced that the American fleet had been seriously weakened and could be defeated by an all-out attack. Assessing the Philippine seas as perhaps their last chance to win the Decisive Battle, they committed still more of their warships.

In actuality, the Japanese fliers had grossly overestimated their results. Halsey's fleet had suffered damage only to two cruisers, hardly a dent in so huge a force.

The American plan was for Halsey's Third Fleet to coordinate with Admiral Thomas Kinkaid's Seventh Fleet to protect the Leyte landings and perhaps to engage in a showdown if the Japanese contested them at sea. Decrypted messages assured the U.S. admirals that a showdown was exactly what their opponents had in mind.

Although the Japanese were, as ever, surprised by the Allies' choice of an island to invade, they responded quickly in two ways. One was to shift reinforcements from other islands to Leyte. The other, deriving from their belief in a severely damaged Allied naval task force, was to mount a complex series of offensive sea maneuvers meant to hammer the remaining U.S. ships from all sides.

Two straits in the Philippines gave ready access to Leyte Gulf: San Bernardino in the north and Surigao to the south. The Japanese plan was to have four different fleets converge on Leyte. Two would link up as the Southern Force and attack through Surigao. The main formation, the Center Force, under Vice Admiral Takeo Kurita, was to descend on Leyte through San Bernardino. The fourth unit, the Northern Force, made up largely of the aircraft carriers and the handful of planes Admiral Ozawa had been able to salvage from the Marianas defeat, was to sail down from Japan and offer itself as a sacrifice to lure Allied ships away from Leyte.

Except for Ozawa's decoy operation, the plan was poorly carried out. Half the Southern Force never did meet with the other half, which alone tried to run through the Surigao Strait. It was ambushed there by Kinkaid's lurking ships and was all but wiped out. Informed by decrypts, U.S. subs shadowed the approach of Kurita's Center Force and sank two of his heavy cruisers, including his flagship, and damaged a third. The next day Halsey's carrier-based planes sank the superbattleship *Musashi* and damaged other vessels. Kurita turned back to regroup his battered fleet.

Then Halsey made a mistake—one that brought the Leyte landings to the brink of disaster. Thinking that Kurita had been defeated and was withdrawing, and not wanting to chance the kind of criticism directed at Spruance, the impetuous admiral resolved to attack Ozawa's carriers. In doing so, he overlooked an earlier captured document outlining Ozawa's plan to use his ships as a diversionary force to draw the American carriers away from their coverage of the landings. He also ignored the warnings of his own radio intelligence unit that he was proceeding into a trap. Saddest of all, he failed to heed instructions from Nimitz that, in effect, no matter what else he did, a part of his fleet, Task Force 34, must guard San Bernardino Strait against a possible Japanese assault on the Leyte landings. In his obsession with the carriers, Halsey swept all the main ships of Task Force 34 along with him. The consequence was that the only warships left to guard the San Bernardino Strait were a handful of small, light, slow escort carriers, a few destroyers and some PT boats from Kinkaid's Seventh Fleet.

While Halsey chased Ozawa's dangled bait, Kurita reorganized his formation, turned about, entered San Bernardino and made for Leyte. All that stood in the way of his wreaking havoc was that thin screen of hopelessly overmatched American "jeep" carriers and their escorts.

They proved to be a game lot. For two and a half hours, while their radio crews filled the airwaves with appeals for aid, these lesser craft managed a kind of naval fan dance, using smoke instead of Sally Rand's plumes to fool the eyes of Kurita's gunners.

The Japanese, never good at ship identification, persisted in thinking that the gray ships darting in and out of their smoke screens were not destroyers and light carriers but cruisers and big fleet carriers. The U.S. ships survived longer than they should have because they were so thinly armored that many of the Japanese shells passed through them without detonating. Still, the plucky Americans lost two of their carriers, three destroyers and more than one hundred planes. In exchange, however, they sank three of Kurita's cruisers and damaged other ships in his fleet.

On the morning of October 25, just at the point when Kurita's gunners had pounded the U.S. minifleet into near helplessness and when Halsey's fleet and Kinkaid's main warships were still too far away to be of help, just when the Japanese might have won if not the Decisive Battle then at least a devastating victory, Kurita checked his advance: he ordered his ships to withdraw. Why? One explanation is that he lost his nerve, but the more probable answer is cryptologic. He had no reliable intelligence to call on, so he didn't realize his true advantage. He had to guess. His guess, conditioned by the earlier ravaging of his ships, was that every minute he waited, he courted increasing danger. He ordered a retreat, and the last serious Imperial Navy threat of World War II retreated with him.

As Churchill wrote, Kurita "had been under constant attack for three days, he had suffered heavy losses, and his flagship had been sunk soon after starting out from Borneo. Those who have endured a similar ordeal may judge him."

The Battle of Leyte Gulf produced a celebrated bit of cryptologic mischief. While the light American ships were making their gallant stand against Kurita, Nimitz fired off a message to Halsey: "Where is Task Force 34?" The U.S. cryptographic system specified, as a security measure, that to the beginning and ending of a message meaningless padding must be added and set off from the real contents by double letters. Nimitz's message, as transmitted, read, "Turkey trots to water—FF—Where is, repeat, where is, Task Force 34—JJ—the world wonders." Responding too quickly, the decoders on Halsey's flagship tore off the front part of the padding but failed to remove the end part, so that the message Halsey received read, "Where is, repeat where is, Task Force 34 the world wonders."

In his rage at what he saw as a misplaced piece of irony, Halsey later admitted, "I snatched off my cap, threw it on the deck and shouted something that I am ashamed to remember."

On land, meanwhile, the Leyte landings quickly developed into a protracted, vicious struggle. The GIs had to battle monsoon rains and knee-deep mud in addition to reinforced hordes of Japanese infantrymen. As Allied decrypts revealed, the Japanese high command had resolved to make Leyte the climactic battle of the Philippines, possibly the turning point in the Pacific war. They poured in reserves of manpower and resources prodigally, drawing troops from as far away as Manchuria and planes from homeland defenses.

But for Allied decodes, the fighting would have gone worse for the GIs. Allied codebreakers supplied precise information about the routes of reinforcement convoys, and U.S. planes and submarines sank nearly three hundred marus and transports during the battle. One reinforcement flotilla was so thoroughly mauled that the only soldiers to reach the island were the ones who swam in from their sinking transports. Another convoy, bearing troops from Manchuria, was smashed by wolf packs of U.S. subs even before it could leave the China Sea.

Although MacArthur drove his commanders impatiently, he maneuvered to avoid costly frontal attacks. He kept the defenders off balance with strikes where they least expected them and with another triphibious end run that cut the enemy forces in two. The ground battles on Leyte destroyed more than five Japanese divisions.

The General would have fought against admitting it, but Leyte was, as Edward Drea has documented, a codebreakers' victory, one in which signals intelligence had "a starring role." As Drea summed up, "The Japanese high command, operating on woefully bad intelligence, gambled all at Leyte and lost. The American high command, acting on very good intelligence, took a well-calculated risk and won." The island was finally secured at Christmastime in 1944.

Aided by Filipino guerrillas, the Americans had already invaded Mindoro Island. MacArthur needed it as a stepping-stone toward his main objective, the large island of Luzon and its capital city of Manila. The assault on Luzon began January 9, 1945. This was MacArthur's old stomping ground. Everywhere he saw symbols that stirred his vanity and fed his craving for speedy successes. He drove his field commander, the patient and dependable Walter Krueger, unmercifully, setting the date for the liberation of Manila on January 26 to coincide with his own birthday. He also began to plan a victory parade down the city's boulevards. When his subordinate generals became convinced that the numbers of Japanese defenders on the island were much larger than MacArthur's sycophantic intelligence chief had estimated, he rejected their claims—which in the end turned out to be correct.

In a crude effort to speed up Krueger's timetable, MacArthur dangled the reward of a promotion and a fourth star if his field general would move more quickly to take Manila. He was impervious to Krueger's protest that to extend his lines so recklessly would open him to Japanese flank attacks.

The General was also sure that the Japanese would abandon the city after token resistance. His final step to goad Krueger was to establish his own headquarters twenty-five miles nearer the front lines than Krueger's command post.

Krueger refused to launch his attack on Manila until he was reasonably ready. As he expected, the city was fanatically defended by the Japanese troops there. It could be taken only by furious, costly street fighting, building-by-building combat. The battle went on for three bloody weeks. Reluctantly, MacArthur authorized heavy artillery support of the infantry but refused the aerial bombardments asked for. The struggle for Corregidor, that other symbol held dear by MacArthur, claimed an additional thousand-plus U.S. casualties.

The General was not granted his birthday present. The Japanese in Manila held out until February 25. Outside the city, the Japanese troops retreated into the Luzon hills and were still fighting as guerrillas when the war ended.

In the midst of the Philippines struggle came an ominous development for the Allies. The Japanese high command had thought of a new weapon. On October 21, Vice Admiral Takijiro Ohnishi traveled to Mabalacat, one of the main airfields on Luzon, and met with pilots of the Twenty-first Air Group. He proposed that the fliers arm their Zeros with 550-pound bombs and crash-dive onto Allied warships. A total of twenty-three petty officer pilots immediately volunteered. While improvised suicidal flights had been made against the Allies at Saipan, the meeting on Luzon was the first systematic organizing of sacrificial squadrons. It was the full-bore beginning of *kamikaze*, the "Divine Wind," a reference to a time in the thirteenth century when violent storms had destroyed the Mongol fleets bent on invading Japan. The Divine Wind's first victory came on the last day of the Leyte Gulf battles. One of the two escort carriers opposing Kurita's fleet was sunk by a kamikaze.

The decision to ask young pilots to immolate themselves to save the empire was a symbol of the desperate straits to which Japan's leaders had come. By then the Nimitz-MacArthur pincer strategy was all but fulfilled. MacArthur's conquest of the Philippines deprived the Japanese war machine of the Southeast Asian oil it needed to keep on operating. Nimitz's island-hopping had drawn the ring around the homeland tight enough that American bombers were routinely devastating Japanese cities. Not knowing of the deus ex machina relief to be delivered by the atomic bombs, the Allied leaders began planning their final steps toward the defeat of Japan through the waging of conventional warfare.

19 Europe: High-grade Decrypts Abet Allied Victory

FOR those GIs who lost friends in the Battle of the Bulge, it is difficult to look past that terrible bloodletting of American soldiers and see it the way military experts regard it: as ultimately a boon to the Allied cause. In the cold statistics of attrition the Germans lost heavily. The slaughter of their forces in the Ardennes, joined with the unrelenting drain of German strength by the Soviets, left the armies of the Reich unable to put up more than crumbling resistance, temporary holding actions and doomed counterattacks. GI sacrifices in the Bulge sped the Allied war machine toward triumph.

As the war in Europe entered its final stages, Allied commanders benefited from what Hinsley has described as "a large volume" of "high-grade decrypts." Merely to list all the main Enigma and Fish keys Bletchley Park was breaking took up a long paragraph in his intelligence history.

Information from these secret sources pointed up the inadequacies of German resources to meet the demands of the three frontiers in which the Nazi armies were engaged. In the west they tried to make the Rhine an impenetrable barrier. On the Russian front their defensive East Wall extended for two thousand miles from the Baltic in the north to the Black Sea in the south. And in Italy they sought to hold at bay the Allied armies under Alexander and Clark.

The decrypts also chronicled the frenetic shifts that Hitler and his generals ordered in their attempts to prevent a breakthrough. Now troops rushed eastward to check a Russian advance, now south to shore up Italy's Gustav Line, now west to try to fend off an Allied encirclement in the Ruhr. The German army no longer had reserves; all the fighting manpower was thrust into the front lines.

Germany's plight contrasted with the gathering might of the Allies. Both in manpower and matériel the Allied advantage was mounting to overwhelming proportions. Victory in the Battle of the Atlantic was allowing the unhampered flow of U.S. troops and supplies into Europe and enabling the Americans to fight their kind of war, which was to hurl vast barrages of steel against the enemy in order to limit the hazarding of men.

While Soviet losses were forcing the call-up of men outside the normal ages for military service, the Russians were still able to build their offensive capabilities to awesome levels. They were equipping their troops as never before: to the productive cornucopia from the factories they had moved behind the Urals was added the great influx of lend-lease supplies from the U.S. The Red Army was made mobile by Detroit-built trucks; the soldiers walked in thirteen million pairs of frostbite-defying felt boots manufactured by Americans to Soviet specifications; supplies were hauled by two thousand American-made locomotives and eleven thousand freight cars.

Hitler deepened the German troubles by further refusals to admit when his armies were overextended and facing insuperable odds. Still dreaming of tapping into southeast Russian oil, he issued stand-fast orders to his generals in the Crimea only to have more legions of German troops surrounded, captured and doomed to the rigors of Soviet prison camps.

To all these rising barometers for the Allies was added an unexpected bit of luck. In the West the Allies faced the necessity of crossing the Rhine, whose eastern banks were defended by troops fanatically determined to protect the homeland. On the morning of March 7, 1945, a Ninth Division recon pilot was aloft in a Piper Cub along the Rhine when he saw an incredible sight: the railroad bridge at the town of Remagen stretched across the river still intact, undestroyed by the Nazis. He radioed the news back to his general, William Hoge, who immediately ordered the nearest unit of the Ninth Armored Division to take the bridge before a German demolition team could bring it down. GIs under twenty-two-year-old Lieutenant Karl Timmerman found the bridge, dashed across it even as some charges were detonated and routed the Germans on the far side. This first American contingent was soon followed by four divisions of Omar Bradley's First Army, establishing a bridgehead several miles deep. The bridge was damaged and collapsed in a few days, but by then army engineers had six pontoon bridges spanning the river. As historian Martin Gilbert has pointed out, this was the first time an enemy invader had crossed the Rhine into Germany since Napoléon's crossing in 1805.

Sigint's Edge in the Air War

As the war in Europe wound down, Allied dominance owed much to the growing superiority of Allied air power. The Luftwaffe, having expended much of what was left of its strength in support of the Ardennes offensive, was all but wiped from the skies. Allied fighters and bombers roamed almost at will over a prostrate enemy. The planes of Britain's Bomber Command and the U.S. Air Force put the finishing touches on their devastation of the German economy.

This ascendancy came only after a long and perilous journey. And only when Allied intelligence combined with British and American science to win the struggle against German technological advances, the battle of measures versus countermeasures. German scientists proved to be a formidable source of lethal innovations that the Allies had to neutralize in order to keep their bomber losses and aircrew casualty rates from becoming "insupportable." But because of Enigma and Fish decrypts, Magic disclosures of what Japanese military attachés were learning and reports from secret agents and resistance fighters, the work of German scientists was no more secret than the plans of the military.

After British scientists and technicians had, early on, won "the battle of the beams" and had helped to foil Hitler's plans for invasion, their attention turned to advancing the technology of Britain's only offensive weapon: the planes of Bomber Command. Their goal was twofold: to reduce bomber losses by mastering German air defense systems; and to strengthen the accuracy, effectiveness and self-protection of British bombers.

Dr. R. V. Jones, Churchill's young science adviser, developed a close relationship with Bletchley Park and depended on BP decodes to keep him abreast of German technical developments. In his memoir he told how he and others of Britain's scientific team worked to understand the radar-based defenses the Germans were putting in place.

The scheme was ingenious. Along the northern coast of Europe the Germans installed a belt of radar detectors that gave early warning of the nighttime approach of streams of British bombers. This radar front line was tied in with an inland belt of more powerful units that were used for three purposes: to turn on a barrage of searchlights that picked the bombers out of the night sky, to alert the crews of antiaircraft gun batteries along the bombers' path, and to guide hordes of night fighters in intercepting the incoming raiders.

Percentages of bombers lost on each of the raids gave a measure of

British technology's successes in thwarting the German systems. A "reasonable" loss was in the three-to-four-percent range, meaning that perhaps only a dozen bombers failed to return and fewer than one hundred men died that night. "Unacceptable" losses came when percentages soared above ten percent, as they did on the night of March 30, 1943. Then 96 of the 795 planes sent against Nuremberg, or more than twelve percent, went down. During 1943, the odds of a bomber crewman's surviving a tour of twenty operations were roughly one in six.

Against this grim backdrop, Britain's technical teams devised new ways to cut bomber losses. When one method of jamming enemy radar was countered, they introduced another, and then another. They put into use long strips of aluminum foil, called "window" by the British and "chaff" by the Americans, which on being dropped by diversionary planes caused German radar to see dense flights of bombers where there were none. Bomber Command's Air Marshal Arthur "Bomber" Harris has described the success of this development in his memoir, *Bomber Offensive*:

> The use of window had an immediate effect. On the first night of the attack the night of July 24th–25th, the radar controlled searchlights waved aimlessly in all directions, the gunfire was inaccurate, and in England the stations which intercepted the enemy's wireless traffic were immediately aware of hopeless confusion in the German ground control stations. In fact, the ground controllers gave the whole situation up, their instruments behaved as though the sky was filled with thousands of hostile aircraft, and they could do nothing to help them. A ground controller was overheard saying, "I cannot follow any of the hostiles—they are very cunning."

RAF bomber losses, for a time, nose-dived. The tech advisers instructed Bomber Command in launching "spoof" or mock raids that, combined with screens of window, misled the night fighters into attacking the decoys rather than the main force.

When the Germans began using a radioed "running commentary" to direct their night fighters, the British counterfeited the controller's voice over a powerful transmitter and ordered the fighters to land because of the danger of fog. When the Germans substituted a woman as controller, the British were ready with a German-speaking Waaf to override *her* voice. Nearly always in the air war the advantage lay with the Allies because signals intelligence not only forecast what new measures the Germans were planning to introduce but also revealed when Allied technologies were fading in effectiveness and needed to be replaced.

An important turn in the technological struggle came when Bletchley decrypts began to suggest that the Germans were using the various types of electronic transmissions from Allied bombers to home in on them. Bomber crews left on their IFF (Identification Friend or Foe) equipment in flights over Germany, used airborne radar to detect attacking planes and made profligate use of radio in their communications—all of which provided beams the new German equipment utilized in seeking out the senders.

It took Marshal Harris a long time, and many needless deaths, to agree that his planes should avoid using transmission devices. Here, once more, Enigma decrypts supplied the clincher. A German message boasted of their new technology, claiming that in December 1943, 9 out of the 41 aircraft downed in a raid against Berlin and 6 of 26 in a later raid were hit due to exploitation of the IFF beams.

The change in the "missing rate" was dramatic. After banning transmissions, Bomber Command began achieving complete surprise in some of its raids. In an attack on Kiel, for example, it lost only 4 of 629 aircraft.

Ultra decrypts had another salutary effect on the air war. They brought reality to the delusion ardently championed by Marshal Harris that "area bombing"—the unloading of huge amounts of bombs onto broad targets such as major German cities—could by itself bring Germany to its knees. Harris held to this belief so resolutely he forbade the transfer to Coastal Command of the long-range bombers that could have narrowed the "Air Gap" that left Allied convoys vulnerable to the U-boats. BP decrypts, Baron Oshima's Magic reports from Berlin and photorecon all verified that the effectiveness of area bombing was far below the exaggerated claims endemic among aircrews. Of 1,729 sorties in a series of raids against Berlin, for example, only 27 delivered their bombs within three miles of the aiming point. As historian Keegan put it, British fliers "were dying largely in order to crater the German countryside."

Similarly, Bomber Command's claims that area bombing was destroying aircraft production facilities were shown to be far wide of the mark. But for these corrections, Allied commands would have believed they were facing a much weakened GAF at a time when, under Albert Speer's energetic direction of Nazi production, the numbers of German fighters were actually increasing.

Reluctantly, Harris gave up his indiscriminate "area bombing" and, aided by new guidance equipment, began to concentrate more on specific targets.

Slowly, the informational and technological advantage, together with burgeoning numbers of aircraft, swung the balance. The U.S. Eighth Air Force, which for a time in the final months of 1942 had been forced by severe losses to abandon its raids, came storming back when new long-range Mustang fighters arrived to escort the bombers on their precision bombing daylight flights. The U.S. Fifteenth Air Force took off from bases in Italy against such targets as Romania's Ploesti oil refineries. Bomber Command finally joined in attacks on aircraft factories and oil facilities. BP decrypts tallied the results: the decreases in aircraft production, the desperate efforts to commandeer and train new fighter pilots, the mounting problems in rail transport and, most seriously, the immobilizing shortages of fuel.

The end of the air war could be summed up by the decrypt of one plaintive order from the Luftwaffe. Asking its pilots to avoid wasting gasoline in taxiing to and from their airstrips, it suggested that the pilots have their planes towed into place by oxen.

Across the Rhine and on to Victory

The U.S. First Army's capture of the Remagen bridge did more than provide the Allies a passage over the Rhine. It changed the minds of George Marshall and Dwight Eisenhower on the future course of the war. Previously they had agreed to have Montgomery's northern armies cut through the low countries, cross the Rhine and lead the way toward Berlin. Churchill greatly favored this plan, but Ike himself was not entirely comfortable with it. Monty's tendency to dot every i and cross every t before making a move tore at Eisenhower's patience. Now, suddenly, a new door was open. Remagen was in Omar Bradley's sector. "Bradley," Ike has been quoted as saying, "has never held back and has never 'paused to regroup' when he saw an opportunity to advance." He told Bradley to push ahead.

However, having the Western Allies' main advance made this far to the south aimed their direction not toward Berlin but across Germany's midsection. Its success would cut Germany in two. Marshall and Eisenhower at that point put military, not political, objectives first. As they saw it, to send Bradley's troops slashing across Germany and linking up with the Russians would end the war in Europe more swiftly than to have Montgomery force his cautious way across the north.

Besides, the Soviets were thirty-five miles from Berlin; Ike's troops were two hundred miles away. He knew that the Allied leaders had agreed at their February meeting in Yalta that after the war, Berlin was to be in the Soviet occupation zone. Why should he rack up casualties to take a "prestige objective" that must subsequently be shared with the Russians? He was also aware that a more southerly drive could crush whatever the Germans were rumored to be planning for a "National Redoubt" in the Harz Mountains, a center from which to carry on guerrilla operations.

Eisenhower asked Bradley to estimate how many casualties it would cost to take Berlin. Bradley's answer: one hundred thousand. And in fact that was close to the Russian losses in taking the city.

On March 28, Ike sent a telegram directly to Stalin announcing the decision to join hands with the Soviet forces on the river Elbe, leaving the Russians to take Berlin. The decision outraged Churchill, Montgomery and the British generally. Churchill addressed a message to Roosevelt emphasizing the political aspects, the symbolic importance, that he thought Eisenhower had overlooked. FDR, nearing his death on April 12, was too enfeebled to respond. The reply fell to Marshall, who of course sided with Ike. Churchill, already foreseeing Stalin's plans to extend an Iron Curtain across Europe, could do no more than push Montgomery to seize the North Sea ports facing Britain in order to keep them out of Soviet hands. On his bidding, Monty also drove his troops to take the city of Lübeck, whose capture would keep Denmark and its portal to Scandinavia from falling into the Soviet orbit.

With Montgomery spurred to attack in the north, Bradley moved quickly to exploit his Remagen bridge advantage. Patton's armies in the south pushed across the Rhine and into Germany. The deterioration of the German armies accelerated. The Allies encircled the Ruhr and took more than three hundred thousand prisoners. General Walther Model dissolved his army group, and he himself committed suicide. Allied advances sliced almost at will through the pockets of German resistance.

Signals intelligence continued its strong support. Although the volume of decrypts diminished as German-controlled territories shrank, the quality remained high. Sigint tracked virtually all of Hitler's frantic orders and mindless shifts of commanders as well as his armies' final desperate maneuvers.

Notably, the Allied codebreakers were able to warn Soviet leaders of a last-gasp Hitler-ordered counteroffensive in the southeast. Magic decrypts of Baron Oshima's Tokyo reports told of Hitler's decision to accept the temporary loss of eastern territory and resources in order to group his armies for a surprise attack against the advancing Russians. BP knew when he transferred the Sixth Panzer Army to the eastern front and shifted Luftwaffe squadrons there. Bletchley decrypts also disclosed that the ultimate objective of the offensive was to reenter Hungary and recapture Budapest in the hopes of securing Hungarian oil—information that the British Military Mission in Moscow passed on to Soviet leaders. Of course, the Russians may also have been tipped off by the Cambridge clique and other sources, but unknowing, the British fulfilled their obligations as allies. In any case, when the offensive began on March 5, 1945, it made only minimal advances before being overwhelmed by the Red Army.

Hitler's empire began to come apart. Countries thankfully shook off their German oppressors only to fall under Stalin's control. The Romanians changed sides, as did the Bulgarians and the Hungarians. Vienna fell to the Russians. The Soviets signed a treaty of friendship with Yugoslavia's Tito.

The Russian armies opened their offensive against Berlin on April 16, and on April 30 they raised the Red flag on the roof of the Reichstag, in the city's center. The Americans linked up with Russian troops at the Elbe on April 25. Bletchley Park decrypted Hitler's final flurry of futile orders, including his demand that Göring be arrested for daring to suggest that if Hitler had lost his freedom of action in Berlin, he, Göring, in southern Germany, should assume control of the Reich. Hitler also ordered the arrest of Himmler for trying to open peace negotiations with the Allies. Then on April 30, as Russian shells shook the ground above his bunker, Hitler married his mistress, Eva Braun, and retired with her to his quarters, where they both committed suicide.

From then until Victory-in-Europe Day, May 8, the war became merely a mopping-up operation—a matter of reducing the last bits of organized resistance, seizing prisoners by the tens of thousands, signing surrender papers and making a start toward dealing with the great miseries that came in the battles' wake.

Hitler's V-weapons: The War Ends None Too Soon

One of the factors in Eisenhower's decision to seek the fastest possible end to the war was his fear of what Hitler still might spring in the way of his secret V-weapons—*V* for *Vergeltungswaffe*, translated either as "Vengeance" or "Retaliation weapons."

Hitler had begun boasting of them as early as September 1939. All through the war they continued to buoy his fantasies, and toward the end they became his last hope that he could still wrest victory from the closing jaws of defeat. He kept promising his beleaguered generals, as he did Manstein in the fight against the Russians, that "weapons unique and hitherto unknown are on the way to your front."

For the Allies, the fear persisted that, given a greater time span, German science might bring still other V technologies to fruition and seriously alter the course of the war.

Foremost was the specter of a German nuclear bomb. Hitler regarded it as one of his *Wunderwaffen*, his "wonder weapons" that could reverse the course of the war.

The Reich's nuclear experts had met to consider the possibilities of an atom bomb in September 1939—two weeks before Albert Einstein had sent his letter to Franklin Roosevelt warning of the German potential and suggesting that the U.S. counter with a development program. Acting on this advice from one of Germany's Jewish émigrés, FDR set up a "Uranium Committee" ten days later. It was the start of the technological race in which Anglo-American cooperation in the Manhattan Project was to be victorious.

At the time, however, Allied success could not be presumed. Uneasiness grew in late 1942 when it became known that at Germany's direction, activity at the heavy-water Vermork plant in Norway had increased. Heavy water was the medium in which plutonium for nuclear weapons could best be processed. Concern was also expressed that Niels Bohr, the Nobel Prize–winning Danish scientist respected as an international authority in atomic research, might be pressed into helping the Germans. That his mother was a Jew made the prospect more ominous.

The leader of the German nuclear program was the brilliant Werner Heisenberg, a prewar Bohr protégé. Heisenberg's role in the project remains equivocal. Did he vigorously pursue the development of a German bomb? Or did he, as he claimed after the war, deliberately work from within to keep an atomic weapon from being delivered into Adolf Hitler's hands? Bohr himself had no doubt that Heisenberg did his utmost to produce the bomb. In an unsent letter Bohr wrote to Heisenberg after the latter's visit to Copenhagen in 1941—a meeting dramatized in the play *Copenhagen*, by Michael Frayn—he said that "under your leadership, everything was being done in Germany to develop atomic weapons." His heirs made Bohr's letter public only in February 2002. Whatever the truth of it was, the German efforts were never so clearly directed as those of the Allies.

The British, in planning countermeasures against the Vermork plant, were helped by the widespread hatred of the Nazis. In October 1942 they gained the cooperation of Jomar Brun, Vermork's chief engineer, who supplied them with detailed drawings and photographs. Brun himself was spirited out to England, where he briefed the British team that was assigned to go in and destroy the plant. The plan, however, went disastrously awry. The British saboteurs were to land near the plant in gliders. But in heavy weather over Norway the gliders crashed and the survivors were quickly rounded up by German ski troops. The injured men were killed immediately; the others, after being interrogated, were shot—even though they were in British army uniforms. Defenses around the plant were strengthened.

Even so, the British felt they had to put the plant out of business. This time they organized much more carefully. With Brun's aid they built a model of the plant and the surrounding terrain. They formed a team of Norwegian volunteers and gave them rigorous training so that they could parachute into Norway and concentrate on destroying the eighteen stainless steel cells used to concentrate the heavy water. The team landed safely and, on a Sunday morning in February 1943, entered the plant through a cable duct that Brun had described. Securing the cooperation of the only workman on duty, a Norwegian, they placed their charges and set their fuses. The workman was told to find a safe place away from the area to be bombed. As the team scrambled away over the tough mountainous terrain, they heard the satisfying booms when their explosives went off, destroying all eighteen cells and more than a ton of heavy water.

Britain's next step was to remove Niels Bohr from German control. In September 1943, he was aided in escaping from Norway and flown to London. Instead of assisting the Nazis, he became an adviser to the Anglo-American nuclear program.

German atomic scientists still refused to give up. First, they put the Vermork plant back in operation. Then, after it had produced a considerable amount of heavy water, came the word that the whole installation was to be evacuated to Germany. Transfer of the machinery itself did not greatly worry the British experts—they knew that Germany lacked the tremendous amounts of hydroelectric power needed to operate the plant. But the Germans could make good use of the plant's existing stores of heavy water.

Again, Nazi-hating Norwegians aided the British response. Brun's replacement at the plant told the plotters that the heavy-water consignment was to be shipped in railcars to a ferry that would cross a Norwegian lake and then be carried by rail to a waiting German ship. The weak point, the Norwegians figured, was the lake crossing. If they could sink the ferryboat in the deep lake, the heavy water would be irretrievably lost. The saboteurs were aware they would have to contend with special teams of Germans and a squadron of reconnaissance aircraft along the entire route.

Stupidly, the Germans did not guard the ferry beforehand. The Norwegian agents boarded her the night before the shipment was to arrive. In the hold they secured plastique bombs, detonators and a timer. The plan worked perfectly. When the ferry reached the deepest waters of the lake, the charges went off and tore a hole in the bow that sank the boat.

With it sank any German hopes of developing an atomic bomb before war's end.

It was in aerial warfare that Hitler's programs stirred the strongest anxiety among the Allies and came nearest to succeeding. Of concern were the three main areas of development: jet- and rocket-propelled aircraft, V-1 pilotless bombing craft and V-2 rocket-powered missiles.

Ironically, it was a British inventor, Frank Whittle, who in 1937 ran the first jet engine and patented its principles. No one in Britain had the foresight to make his discoveries classified information, and engineers around the world seized upon his advance and began independent development of jets. In Britain, Whittle met with the hidebound opposition of aviation authorities. In Germany his ideas found fertile ground.

If the Nazis had concentrated their development on a few promising designs, they might well have made their jet aircraft a devastating reprisal weapon. However, too many competitors—Dornier, Focke-Wulf, Heinkel, Junkers and Messerschmitt, among others—vied for the favor of Göring and Hitler. German science and German resources were burdened by demands both to improve conventional aircraft and to develop too many varieties of jets. Great effort was also expended on an aircraft propelled by rocket fuels that was supposed to render all existing aircraft obsolete. Most telling of all was the fact that the Luftwaffe, having to compete for scarce resources with the V-1 and V-2 programs, was left virtually leaderless as Göring slipped more and more into self-indulgence and drug addiction.

Ultra decrypts were of little help in the formative stages of these new planes, but Nazi haters filled the intelligence gap. As the pressures on German aircraft development and production increased, skilled men from occupied countries were recruited for service in factories and research centers. Many of them were only too willing to supply information that kept Britain's Air Ministry abreast of virtually every line of development.

Later, BP decrypts began to weigh in, as messages disclosed the transfer of specialists to jet production, the training of jet mechanics and pilots and the schedules for the entry of new planes into service. A Magic decode of a Japanese attaché's Berlin report back to Tokyo in 1943 revealed that the Germans expected to have at least one line of jets in service by 1944, and other reports disclosed that Hitler intended to hurl his new jets against any invasion attempt by the Allies.

Fortunately, the combination of observers' reports from the continent, photoreconnaissance and Ultra decrypts pinpointed the production sites. Allied bombers knew exactly where to go to smash the factories. On just five good-flying-weather days during the operation code-named Big Week, beginning February 20, 1944, U.S. Air Force bombers, protected by their long-range fighters, conducted massive daytime raids on aircraft manufacturing plants. Together with RAF nighttime sorties, the raids destroyed more than seventy-five percent of the targeted buildings and over seven hundred jet aircraft. German plans and schedules were torn apart, the danger of the rocket plane was eased, and on D-Day the German jets proved to be no threat.

The Germans, nevertheless, persisted. Demands on Allied bomber commands occasioned by the invasion and the Normandy battles gave the Nazis' aircraft planners the rest that they needed to disperse production and locate much of it underground. Again a Japanese military attaché betrayed the Germans' expectations of producing a thousand jets a month by January 1945. And again the Allied bombers, able to break off from their ground war support, knew where to strike to delay work on the jets.

As the war approached its end, Hitler hoped to organize a corps of five hundred jets and reserves of fuel for them to be used as a "trump card." There were too many obstacles. The card was never played.

More serious threats were posed by the V-1s and V-2s. Once more a Nazi hater first tipped off the British about these and other German technical developments. Shortly after the war began, a never-identified source in Oslo left with the British embassy there an analysis of Germany's progress in weapons research. This "Oslo Report," passed on to the Air Ministry in London, accurately forecast what the Germans were planning in both pilotless aircraft and rocket missiles. It also disclosed to the British for the first time that the German center for technological experiments was on Peenemünde, an island off the Baltic coast.

The reported plans were so far ahead of British weapons development that at first they were dismissed as airy imaginings. But in early 1943 an

Ultra decrypt reported the transfer of a Knickebein team to Peenemünde. Anti-Nazis' reports quickly confirmed that this was the center of German work on advanced aerial weapons. Ultra removed any confusion about what these weapons were. At one end of the island, development was going forward on what became known as the V-1 pilotless aircraft; at the other end a team of rocket scientists under the direction of Wernher von Braun was developing the V-2 rocket. French Resistance observers began reporting on launch sites in northern France that were plainly positioned to aim the V-1s toward London.

When these secret reports identified the work going on at Peenemünde, Churchill personally ordered Bomber Command to attack the island. Carried out on the night of August 16, the raid pulverized Peenemünde and set back this phase of German weapons development by months. Braun's team moved to a new underground center in Bavaria, and a new test site was built in Poland. Allied bombers slowed up the first firings of the new weapons by destroying many of their launch sites in France.

Because of the delays and design problems with the weapons, the Allies had landed in Normandy before the V-1 buzz bombs began their guttural flights to Britain. They would pulse-jet ahead until their inner "air logs" had clicked off the requisite number of miles, shut down their fuel supplies and sent them into their deadly dives. For those of us stationed at Hall Place, the odds of survival were suddenly diminished. On the first long June night when V-1s began to arrive in full force, our captain ordered one of our guards to station himself in a cupola atop our roof and try to sound an alarm if the bomb came directly toward the manse. That poor sweating GI counted sixty-seven V-1s buzzing past and over him before dawn.

What we didn't know was that because of Ultra decodes and other intelligence, the British had had six months to get ready for the buzzers. In May 1944, as an example, Tricycle's spymaster sent a warning that this most valued of German agents should move out of London as soon as he could so as to escape Hitler's secret weapons targeted on the city.

We at Hall Place gained a firsthand view of one of the defensive steps taken by the British. On the second morning of the V-1s' arrival we were amazed to look southward and find that, overnight, a whole line of barrage balloons had been raised across the largely unpopulated heathlands, with cables forming a steel fence between them. Even as we watched, a buzz bomb tangled itself on one of the wires and came down in a harmless flash.

When the V-1s first started coming over, the antiaircraft batteries near us fired their shots ridiculously far behind the small, scudding craft. We didn't know that the British and American scientists were cooperating to correct that problem. Masses of antiaircraft guns equipped with American-developed proximity fuses were lined up on the south coasts to shoot down the V-1s before they could reach land.

On another day my shift was doing calisthenics outside Hall Place when a V-1 came toward us. We hurried to flatten ourselves against the wall as we realized that on the buzz bomb's tail was a Spitfire whose guns were chattering away as it sought to bring the V-1 down short of London. Fortunately, both planes went over the hill beyond our digs before the bomb exploded. Again, we learned later that the speeds of RAF fighters had been increased and Britain's own small fleet of jet planes pressed into use to run down the buzz bombs, mostly out at sea. As the summer went on, fewer and fewer of the bombs came our way and we began to breathe easier.

Although the V-1s destroyed more than a million homes and killed some ten thousand people, their reign was far shorter and less corrosive in terms of morale than the Germans had hoped. The launch sites originally chosen for them, in the Pas de Calais, were soon overrun by the Allies, forcing the Germans to fire the bombs from greater distances in Holland. Given this advantage, the RAF shot down more of them over the sea, and the coastal AA batteries were better able to track the ones that got through. In August the kill rate rose to seventy-four percent, and it climbed to eighty-three percent in the last days before the offensive ended in September. Hitler himself admitted, "The V-1 unfortunately cannot decide the war."

The V-2s were another matter. They required little in the way of launch sites, and there was no defense against them. The giant rockets, prototypes of ballistic missiles, simply soared into the stratosphere, arced over Britain and smashed down with an impact that sent powerful shock waves radiating outward to remind war-weary Britons of the men, women and children who lay dead or dying at their epicenters. Braun and his colleagues managed a successful firing in October 1942. Seeing a film of the launch, Hitler called the V-2 "the decisive weapon of the war" and envisioned thousands of the missiles pouring down on England to pummel the cities into rubble and force the people, even at this late date, to sue for peace.

How near the Germans came to turning this last great fantasy of Adolf Hitler into reality is hard to assess. War historians seem to take it for granted that the plucky Brits, who had weathered so much, would also have endured this one without folding. As one who lived through that time, I am convinced that the threat of the V-2 rockets has been underestimated. Certainly, given more time, the Germans could have pounded much of England into dust, killed or maimed civilians by the thousands and hundreds of thousands and wiped out the masses of the Allied troops assembled there. And although it now seems inconceivable that British morale could have collapsed, I can testify that the V-2s' psychological impact was more powerful than their physical blows. There was no warning of them, no sirens wailing, no drone of approaching motors. There was just this brilliant flash and you and everything yards around you were gone, ionized, blown to bits. English people told me that the V-2s drove fear into the psyche as no earlier experience had done.

Add to this the fact that Braun's team was already working on a two-stage rocket that could have hurtled over the Atlantic to reach the U.S. Work was also under way on a rocket that could be launched from a platform towed by a U-boat.

The V-2 was a near thing. Its defeat in World War II was a matter of timing. The delays caused by the bombing of Peenemünde and other sites pushed back the beginning of the missiles' attack until September 8, 1944. On March 29, 1945, Allied troops overran their last launch sites. The countermeasures engineered by the British and their anti-Nazi colleagues on the continent limited the V-2 onslaught on Britain to 1,115 rockets, as calculated by Dr. Jones and his staff. In all they killed "only" about twenty-five hundred people in Britain. Their deaths were tokens of what might have been.

The Germans rained even more of the rockets on the Belgian cities of Antwerp and Liège after they were in Allied hands.

A footnote. For those of us Americans billeted in Kent's "Bomb Alley," the V-weapon attacks held an irony that we learned about only decades later. Lacking adequate air reconnaissance, the Germans decided to use their spies in Britain as forward observers for their unique artillery. The agents were instructed to report where the V-weapons hit and at what time, enabling the German specialists to correct their trajectories so as to deliver more of them on London rather than too far north or too far south. But of course the spies were under British control. Churchill's scientific guru, the ubiquitous Dr. Jones, devised a scheme whereby these pseudo observers reported the actual point of strike of bombs that had hit the central part of London coupled with the time of strike of those that had fallen short. This stratagem caused the Germans to believe the shorter-range setting was correct. Obligingly they set the timing mechanism so that more of them fell—where? On the approaches to London, on Bomb Alley. We at our intercept station were, unknowingly, helping to bring Hitler's vengeance weapons down on our own heads. That they landed all around us, without doing us in, was a matter of chance.

The "Final Solution" Delivers an Ultimate Message

As Allied armies smashed across Germany and its occupied territories in April 1945, the troops encountered phenomena that pierced even their war-hardened mind-sets. These were the Nazi death camps, where what Nazi Walter Schellenberg had called the "Final Solution" to the problem of the *Untermenschen*, the so-called inferior peoples, was being administered. GIs and Tommies alike were horrified by the scenes the open gates disclosed: the pathetic masses of gaunt, hollow-eyed survivors clad in fragments of filthy, lice-ridden striped cotton, the thousands of unburied emaciated corpses left to rot like great piles of garbage. A man as tough as George Patton vomited when he witnessed the barbarism of the camp at Ohrdruf.

In early 1941, Bletchley Park began receiving messages relating to the massacres of those the Nazis classed as undesirables. BP was breaking the non-Enigma codes of German police units assigned to the elimination of "inferior races" and was also breaking one of the codes used by Himmler's killing squads.

By August 1941, Churchill was sufficiently enraged by the information he received through Bletchley decrypts that he decided to speak out against the German atrocities, even though his so doing might jeopardize Britain's codebreaking operation. In a public broadcast he expressed his horror that "scores of thousands—literally scores of thousands—of executions in cold blood are being perpetrated by the German police troops." He added that not since the Mongol invasions of Europe had there been such methodical, merciless butchery on such a scale. "We are," he said, "in the presence of a crime without a name."

When Churchill issued his public denunciation, the BP decrypts had not yet made clear that the main thrust of the SS and the police was to eradicate the Jews of Europe. So his speech made no reference to Jews. As Richard Breitman acerbically noted in his book *Official Secrets*—an in-depth review of "what the Nazis planned, what the British and Americans knew"—Churchill's " 'crime without a name' was not the Holocaust."

The Nazi massacres should not have been a surprise. In *Mein Kampf*

Hitler dwelled on his hatred of Jews, his theories of "inferior races" and his assertion of the German people as the apotheosis of Aryan supremacy. He claimed that World War I would have turned out differently if a large segment of "Hebrew corrupters" had been eliminated by poison gas.

As Breitman has carefully documented, however, despite the steady infusion of BP's incriminating decrypts, official recognition of the Jews' plight was painfully slow in coming. Left over from the Great War was a hearty skepticism toward purported atrocities. No one could believe that men this side of Attila could do such heinous things as line up people along the edge of the ditch they had just dug and then shoot them so that they conveniently fell into their own graves. Added to this was the harsh fact that many high-placed Allied officials themselves harbored anti-Semitic prejudice.

Evidence of the Final Solution's reality nevertheless mounted, and it affected Allied leaders, particularly Churchill and Roosevelt. On December 17, 1942, with the concurrence of Stalin, came the joint Allied Declaration denouncing the Nazis' killings of the Jews. In Parliament it was read on the floor of the House of Commons, and a moment of silent prayer was observed.

Still, words and prayers fell far short of action to carry out rescue operations and save Jewish lives. It seemed that strong objections could be found to reject every rescue proposal. To evacuate refugees into the Middle East would upset Muslim allies and might also arouse unrealistic hopes for a Jewish homeland. To have neutral countries take in thousands of Jews raised the necessity of providing massive amounts of food, medicine, housing and other forms of support—in those times of dire shortages, who was willing to assume these extra demands? Attempts to supply aid to Jews in German-occupied Europe would, it was argued, only weaken the Allies' blockade and forestall Germany's collapse.

What became the prevailing view was expressed by Adolf Berle, U.S. assistant secretary of state: "Nothing can be done to save these helpless unfortunates except through the invasion of Europe, the defeat of the German armies and the breaking of German power."

Of all this, most people were only dimly aware. Concerned with their own wartime responsibilities, having to conduct their lives under difficult conditions, they failed to let recognition of the Holocaust penetrate. They saw the photos of men and women having to wear the yellow Star of David sewn on their outerwear and of the shop windows of Jewish-owned stores shattered by hoodlums and the like, but to accept that these signs of depravity extended to state-ordered mass shootings and gas oven executions and baskets of gold teeth knocked out of the jaws of Jewish corpses and of lamp shades crafted of human skin—these were beyond human understanding.

That is, until the Allies liberated the death camps, until the press photographers sent back their horrifying pictures of Nazi evil. Only then did the public at large awake to the proofs of a nation gone rabid.

For those whose beliefs in that European phase of the war had been buffeted by what often seemed senseless slaughter, the waste of young lives under posturing generals, the loss of family members and good friends, the sheer cruelty and horror of it all, suddenly all doubts were wiped away. World War II was, after all, a necessary war; it had to be fought and won; the tremendous sacrifices were justified. We of what Tom Brokaw has labeled "the greatest generation," who are now of an age that he, not to miss a sentimental beat, has called "the twilight of their lives," we who are now disappearing at the rate of more than a thousand a day, look back with satisfaction on a job that needed doing and was, with the inestimable help of the codebreakers, well done.

20 In the Pacific: Last Battles, Final Decisions

ONCE MacArthur had retaken the Philippines, the time had come to close in on the Japanese homeland. Even though the outcome of the war was now clear, the Nipponese were ruled not by a sense of reality so much as by the Bushido code of the samurai, one of whose tenets was to prefer suicide to defeat or dishonor. Still in the grip of the military, the people prepared to apply the code to the nation as a whole rather than just to individual warriors.

Allied planners fixed on the outlying islands whose possession was deemed essential as the last stepping-stones to Japan. The first was the small island of Iwo Jima, 625 miles north of Saipan and 660 miles south of Tokyo. Second was Okinawa, the large island the Japanese had occupied since 1879 and had made a prefecture of greater Tokyo. Peopled by farmers and fishermen loyal to the empire, it was only about 350 miles from Japan's southernmost island of Kyushu and less than a thousand miles from Tokyo.

The taking of Iwo Jima was dictated in large part by the needs of U.S. Superfortresses. Flying from Saipan, the big bombers had made devastating raids on Japan, but since the long distances precluded the protection of fighter escorts, the costs were high. Japanese fighters stormed up to meet them. By January 1945 the crew of a B-29 setting out for Japan could expect to be subjected to an average of eight fighter attacks. Between December and March, thirty-seven B-29s were shot down.

Air bases at Iwo Jima would mean greater security for the Forts and their crews. The island could provide navigational beacons for flights from Saipan as well as emergency landing sites for crippled planes. Most important, long-range fighters could launch from Iwo Jima's airfields to accompany the Superforts.

Responsibility for the attack on Iwo Jima shifted to Spruance and his Fifth Fleet. Spruance showed his continuing belief in the efficacy of signals intelligence by assigning a codebreaking team to his flagship as well as placing teams on four of his other ships. The main cryptanalytic crews in Oahu, Washington and Melbourne backed them.

One incident illustrates the Allied mastery of Japanese codes at this late stage of the war. On April 1, 1945, the Japanese navy changed to a new codebook, a real attempt to make their communications more secure. Yet the code was broken the next day, and within two days Japanese messages were again being read routinely. The Japanese high command could make scarcely a move without having word of it passed on to Allied commanders.

By contrast, the Americans put into use at Iwo Jima an additional type of code communications that proved impenetrable to the Japanese. This was the language of the Navajo code talkers. The Navajo tongue has such a complex, irregular syntax that few people outside the tribe can understand it. Consequently, use of the Navajo code talkers speeded up battlefield communications by eliminating the need for encoding and decoding. A few Choctaw code talkers had served in World War I. In the Pacific, it was the Navajos who were enlisted: four hundred of their code talkers literally "fought with their tongues." Lacking Navajo words for modern military equipment, they developed equivalents: *tas-chizzie,* or "swallow," meant a torpedo plane; *jay-sho,* or "buzzard," stood for a bomber; *da-he-tih-hi,* "hummingbird," was a fighter plane. At Iwo Jima, in the first forty-eight hours of battle, the code talkers sent and received some eight hundred messages without an error—and without the Japanese ever gaining the first understanding of the guttural chatter that came over their intercept receivers.

Spruance's battle fleet tried hard to ensure that the Iwo Jima invasion would be less deadly for the Marines than previous invasions. The island was subjected to almost constant air and naval bombardment before the February landings. Once again the intended softening up had little effect. The Marines faced an enemy dug into Iwo Jima's core rock, especially into its one volcanic peak, Mount Surabachi. Interconnected tunnels led to stoutly protected artillery, mortar and machine-gun emplacements. The prudent commander of Iwo Jima's garrison kept his troops underground during the pre-landing pyrotechnics, allowed the Marines to reach the beaches virtually unopposed, but then had his men emerge to contest every yard of the Americans' advance. Whereas the U.S. commanders had hoped to take the island in a matter of days, the killing went on for over a month.

Here also the Allies were beset by dense flights of kamikazes. To combat them, radio intelligence units teamed up with radar to warn of the approaching waves. Most of the suicide planes were shot down, but enough of them got through the screen to sink an escort carrier and damage five other ships.

Iwo Jima gained a legendary status in the war's history at least in part because of Joe Rosenthal's photograph of Marines triumphantly raising the American flag atop Mount Surabachi. Meatgrinder Hill might have made a more fitting symbol: it was taken and lost by the Marines five times before it was finally held. Of the twenty-two thousand in the Japanese garrison, only a few hundred gave themselves up as prisoners.

The objective was finally gained. Superfortress raids on Japan were stepped up. Iwo Jima did become a haven for damaged bombers. By the end of the war some twenty-four hundred B-29 landings were made there. As one B-29 pilot said after an emergency landing on Iwo Jima: "Whenever I land on this island, I thank God and the men who fought for it."

Okinawa: The Pacific War's Final Battle

The struggle for Okinawa, the southernmost of Japan's four main home islands, followed the same script as that for earlier islands, only writ much larger. On an island that stretched more than sixty miles in length, the Japanese garrison was a large one, and the soldiery were dug in on a scale surpassing that of anything previous. The underground warren of defenses even included a rail line to carry ammunition to the firing emplacements. The general in charge was another who rejected beach resistance and banzai charges in favor of conserving his men to kill methodically from behind their buttresses of concrete, steel and carved rock.

Japanese plans for this last-ditch stand included a much greater use of suicide weapons. The high command, which no doubt included men steeped in the tradition of haiku, kept coming up with poetic names for their awful devices. To "Divine Wind" kamikazes, they added *kaiten*, or "turned toward heaven," for human-guided torpedoes launched from submarines. *Ohka*, or "cherry blossom," stood for small rocket-powered sacrificial wooden aircraft. *Fukuryu*, or "crouching dragons," were suicidal divers who swam out to sea to fasten themselves, along with powerful mines, to invasion craft. As for the kamikazes, the Japanese invented a new term: *kikusui*, "floating chrysanthemums," for massed attacks of the immolating aircraft.

To these death-dealing smaller weapons they added a suicidal naval fleet. Desperately short of fuel, they filled their superbattleship *Yamato* with just enough gasoline for a one-way voyage and sent off with her the cruiser *Yahagi* and eight destroyers. The warships were either to go down fighting or to beach themselves on the island and add their crews to the ranks of the defenders.

The Allied decision that the island must be taken was based on securing a staging area essential to the invasion of Japan. From airfields on the island, preassault bombardments could be intensified, and planes could provide air cover for the landings. Its great expanse could also serve as a huge supply base supporting the attack.

The Allied fleet for the invasion, now including a task force of 22 British ships, was more enormous than ever: 3,025 vessels that included 18 carriers. No less than six Radio Intelligence units were aboard the command ships. After a weeklong bombardment and the taking of small ancillary islands providing logistic bases and a useful anchorage, the initial landings were made on April 1, Easter Sunday, 1945. The first reports were euphoric: virtually no opposition on the beaches and very little as the troops swept inland. In the first hour the Americans put ashore sixteen thousand men and on the first day fifty thousand, with the eventual buildup running into hundreds of thousands.

Then came the crunch. Lieutenant General Mitsuru Ushijima, knowing he lacked the strength to defend the entire island, had concentrated his defenders on the craggy terrain of the southern sector. From their elaborate subsurface quarters, the Japanese soldiers trundled out huge mortars, uncovered powerful antitank guns and emerged for sudden counterattacks. They made the Marines and GIs pay dearly for every advance and stretched the campaign out for weeks, delaying plans for the invasion of the mainland.

Japanese resistance forced much of the protecting Allied fleet to remain in place, making it vulnerable to the suicide weapons. The Americans had precluded one use of sacrificial offense when, in taking the outlying islands, they had found and destroyed some two hundred and fifty explosives-laden plywood boats cached there to smash their loads against Allied ships. Still the Allies had to defend against the *ohkas* and kamikazes. The *ohkas* were ferried in by regular planes and, over their targets, released to dive to the destruction of their pilots and, so it was hoped, the warships below. As for the kamikazes, an appeal went over all Japan to assemble nonmilitary and obsolete aircraft to provide wings for self-sacrificing pilots.

On April 6, Japanese commanders sent aloft the first of ten *kikusui* raids. Regular pilots led the waves of kamikazes off fields on Taiwan and the homeland island of Kyushu and guided them to the Allied ships.

To counter these attacks, American intelligence units figured out when the mass kamikaze flights were launched and how long they would take to reach the Allied fleet. Marine Colonel Bankston Holcomb would then relay the information to Admiral Spruance. "He always listened," Holcomb later recalled, admiring how coolly Spruance issued his orders for meeting the incoming suicide planes. Once forewarned, navy gunners shot down an estimated sixty to ninety percent of the kamikazes and *ohkas* short of their targets.

Even so, the carnage was great. A total of 34 warships were sunk and 368 damaged, including 8 carriers, 4 escort carriers, 10 battleships, 5 cruisers and, because of their exposure in forward picket lines, 63 destroyers. Casualties among shipboard crews were the heaviest in the war.

British ships in the fleet fared better because of their armor-plated decks. None of their ships were sunk, although all four of their carriers as well as other vessels were damaged.

Meanwhile, on April 7 the suicide sortie of Japanese surface ships formed around the *Yamato* and arrived to do battle against Spruance's fleet. It goes almost without saying that Allied codebreakers knew the makeup of the fleet and the exact route and schedule of its approach to Okinawa. Sightings by a submarine and a B-29 confirmed the decrypts. Admiral Marc Mitscher, in charge of the Allied fleet's Task Force 58, had his riposte all worked out. One of his groups of strike aircraft was to concentrate on the *Yamato*, a second on the *Yahagi*, and after sinking these prime targets, all units would go after the eight destroyers. The Americans launched 386 aircraft against the suicide force, including 98 torpedo bombers.

It was no contest. Torpedo after torpedo slashed into the *Yamato*, causing her to roll over and go down, taking the fleet's admiral with her. The U.S. planes quickly dispatched the *Yahagi* and sank four of the destroyers. The other four limped back to Japan, three of them badly damaged. The Japanese navy had virtually ceased to exist.

The land battle of Okinawa continued until the beginning of July. Seeing their resistance crumble, Ushijima and his fellow general Isamu Cho killed themselves on June 22, leaving only ten days of American mopping-up operations to follow. This final battle of the Pacific war was also the bloodiest. Allied losses included over 12,000 army and navy men killed. More than 100,000 Japanese troops died. Because they callously used natives of the island as little more than cannon fodder to buy time for the buildup of defenses, an estimated 150,000 civilians were killed or joined in mass suicides.

Japan: The Greatest Battle Never Fought

In the early months of 1945 there seemed to be no alternative to preparing for the staged invasions of Japan. The Joint Chiefs of Staff settled on a plan for two major landings. The first, code-named Olympic, would invade the southern island of Kyushu on November 1. If Japan had still not surrendered by March 16, 1946, the follow-up would come. Code-named Coronet, it would target the main island of Honshu, whose broad Kanto Plain led to Tokyo. Douglas MacArthur was designated as commander in chief of the United States Army forces in the Pacific, including its air force units. Admiral Nimitz was designated the commander of all U.S. Navy units, while General Carl Spaatz was placed in charge of the Strategic Air Force.

An important question troubling Allied leaders, especially Harry Truman after he became president, was the number of Allied casualties likely to result from these invasions. During the final week of July, at the Big Three conference in Potsdam, Germany, Marshall gave his answer, based on estimates received from his subordinate commanders. Truman later wrote that Marshall told him that the invasions would cost "at a minimum one-quarter of a million casualties and might cost as much as a million." Even the lesser total would outnumber by far all losses in the Pacific campaign, including those at Iwo Jima and Okinawa, and would exceed Western Allied casualties in Europe from D-Day through the Battle of the Bulge.

Certainly the million figure seized the attention of Winston Churchill. He wrote, "To quell the Japanese resistance man by man and conquer the country yard by yard might well require the loss of a million American lives and half that number of British—or more if we could get them there; for we were resolved to share the agony."

MacArthur's judgment concerning the numbers was conditioned by his obsession with commanding the greatest amphibious invasion in history, one that would surpass Eisenhower's forces on D-Day by a wide margin. Since the question of unacceptable casualties might jeopardize this glory-seeking prospect, he seized every opportunity to play down both the estimate of Japanese strengths on the islands and the expectations of Allied losses. He let it be known that he did not anticipate a "high rate of loss" in the attacks on Japan and assured military planners, "The invasion of the Tokyo plain should be relatively inexpensive." He was opposed to "the slightest thought of changing the Olympic operation."

To take this stand, he had to fly in the face of his own codebreakers. As decrypts from those times have been declassified, they have accentuated the horrors that lay in wait for Allied invaders. The Japanese high command had come to the same conclusion reached by Allied leaders: that on Kyushu only three beaches were suitable for large-scale landings. Japanese planners made those beaches the most formidable death traps their fervid imaginations could devise.

Broken message after broken message detailed the enormous buildup of troops on the islands. To the two general armies, numbering two and a half million men, the Japanese added reinforcements from the Asian mainland—four divisions from Manchuria, others from Korea and north China. Additional troops came from the northern Kuril Islands and Hokkaido. Levies of remaining manpower called for raising new divisions totaling more than a half million men. In addition, there was the National Volunteer Corps—twenty-five million untrained children, old men, and women serving as a labor force but ready to convert to warriors armed with sharpened bamboo spears, pitchforks, rusty bayonets and even dynamite charges strapped to their bodies.

If the underground fortresses built by the Japanese on Pacific islands had presented deadly barriers to American GIs, these were nothing compared with the networks of subterranean tunnels, corridors and firing points constructed for defense of the homeland. Heavy guns mounted on rails could roll out from behind steel doors, fire their shots and retreat behind the closing doors before an answering shot could be made. Decrypts warned of the construction of underground hangars and concealed bases for aircraft. Acres of mines were sown in harbors and coastal areas. The National Volunteer Corps labored throughout the torrid summer to build bunkers, field fortifications and connecting tunnels along the shoreline.

Most of all, the high command relied on its newest weapon—the willingness of the young to die in suicide missions. As revealed by a steady stream of decrypts, plans called for a massive employment of this horrible strategy. Thousands of planes, largely obsolete, were rounded up to serve in kamikaze operations. A Japanese aircraft firm began designing a craft specifically for carrying a one-thousand-pound bomb on suicide missions. Hundreds of *kaitens* and *ohkas* awaited their sacrificial moment. At naval bases, midget submarines were stashed in sardinelike rows, most of them scheduled to be used as suicide craft. *Fukuryu* frogmen waited to turn themselves into human mines. Along the coasts riflemen dug themselves into fortified pits, expecting to die in the preinvasion bombardments but hoping to survive long enough to take a few Americans with them. Perhaps saddest of all were the new aircraft specially built with reusable landing gears: since the planes were destined to go only one way, why waste scarce rubber when the planes on takeoff could drop their wheels?

Despite the overwhelming proofs of the grim ordeals faced by Allied invaders, MacArthur continued to assert that the invasions would not involve serious losses. As Drea has pointed out, MacArthur consistently dismissed codebreakers' evidence "that failed to accord with his preconceived strategic vision."

Encouraged by the colossal defensive preparations being carried out by their people, Japanese planners clung to an unrealistic but persuasive goal: that their trained military forces and their multitudes of sacrificial volunteers could inflict such mayhem on the invaders that the Allies would agree to a negotiated peace.

To compel Japan to surrender, the Allies assembled a force of five million men. These were largely American but also included three British Commonwealth infantry divisions, a contingent of supporting RAF fliers and the British Pacific Fleet. Troops idled by the end of the war in Europe were being shipped to the Pacific theater as quickly as the transport system allowed. Seeking all possible help, the Joint Chiefs urged FDR, at his Yalta meeting with Churchill and Stalin, to exact Russia's promise to come into the war and join in the attack on Japan. The U.S. chiefs told the president and the prime minister to make whatever concessions were necessary to ensure USSR participation.

Meanwhile, Allied warships and aircraft were doing their utmost to reduce Japan to a wasteland. Almost with impunity navy ships cruised along the coasts and shelled inland targets. Carrier-based aircraft heaped destruction on airfields, naval bases, shipping, rail lines and communications. Superfortresses added another form of attack to their high-level daytime bombing. At night they swept in at low altitudes to drop thousands of incendiaries on Japanese cities. In one raid the Superforts burned out sixteen square miles of Tokyo. Five other cities were similarly devastated, which left thousands dead and hundreds of thousands homeless.

Magic decrypts now seized center stage. They revealed that Japanese diplomats, blind to the fact that Stalin had already pledged to come into the war on the Allies' side, had traveled to Moscow to persuade the Russians to act as intermediaries for peace negotiations. The decrypts also made clear that although a peace faction had been formed at the upper levels of power, its leaders could not prevail against the military hierarchy.

The sticking point for the Japanese, as it had been for the Germans, was the idea of "unconditional surrender." Early in the war, on the final day of the summit meeting in Casablanca, Roosevelt had used the term when ad-libbing in a press conference. The extreme term greatly distressed Winston Churchill, who recognized how it would block any hope of a negotiated surrender. Once an Allied leader pronounced it, though, the term stuck. Anyone questioning it ran the risk of being judged guilty of "appeasement." For the Japanese it had the inadmissible meaning of dethroning the emperor.

The concept of unconditional surrender was discussed when Truman arrived in Potsdam, Germany, for his first Big Three conference, as recounted by David McCullough in his *Truman* biography. Churchill and Stalin were in favor of easing it to allow the monarchy to be preserved. Along with his chief advisers, Truman was not so sure. The president had his reason for thinking the Japanese would agree to an outright unconditional surrender. He had delayed the start of the conference to July 17 because he knew that, on the day preceding, the first atomic bomb was scheduled to be tested at Alamogordo, New Mexico. The test was successful, meaning that the Allies now had the power to end the war on their own terms. Churchill was told explicitly that the "babies" had been "satisfactorily born." Truman told Stalin, almost as an aside, only that the Allies now possessed "an entirely novel form of bomb, something quite out of the ordinary, which we think will have decisive effects upon the Japanese will to continue the war."

Truman, Churchill and the representatives of China issued the Potsdam Declaration, offering Japan "an opportunity to end the war" before Allied military power completely destroyed the Japanese forces and reduced the homeland to utter devastation. The declaration took into account what decrypts had been disclosing about the divided states of mind among Japanese leaders, demanding that the nation decide "whether she will continue to be controlled" by those who had brought her "to the threshold of annihilation" or whether she would follow "the path of reason." It set down hard terms for the disarmament of the military and the elimination of those who had "deceived and misled" the people. It did limit the call for an unconditional surrender to "all of the Japanese armed forces."

With the militarists still in control, however, the offer was rejected out of hand.

The moment had come for Harry Truman to make up his mind about dropping the A-bomb. Churchill later wrote that "the decision whether or not to use the atomic bomb to compel the surrender of Japan was never even an issue." It was also clear that President Roosevelt had had every intention of using it. General Marshall, Admiral King and several other top Allied commanders were in no doubt. Still, as the hour approached, the prospect aroused controversy.

The idea of exploding a bomb in a "non-military demonstration" in order to awe Japanese leaders into surrender was suggested—and rejected. "We could not afford the chance that it might be a dud," explained atomic scientist and Manhattan Project member Arthur H. Compton.

Another idea was to give the Japanese a warning in advance of dropping the bomb on a predesignated area. That, too, was turned down because, as Secretary of State James F. Byrnes put it, "if the Japanese were told that the bomb would be used on a given locality, they might bring our boys who were prisoners of war to that area." Fear of the bomb's failure to explode was also a factor.

Truman had formed an Interim Committee of top government officials and bomb-building scientists to advise him on the use of the bomb. Committee member Harvey H. Bundy expressed a belief held by scientists such as J. Robert Oppenheimer: that it was necessary to employ the bomb in order to assure world peace. "Unless the bomb were used," Bundy said, "it would be impossible to persuade the world that the saving of civilization in the future would depend on a proper international control of atomic energy."

Not all the commanders acquiesced in using the bomb. Eisenhower, judging from afar that the Japanese were on the point of collapse, expressed "grave misgivings" and pled with Truman not to rely on "that awful thing." Chief of Staff Admiral William D. Leahy thought neither the bomb nor an invasion would be necessary: the navy alone could finish off the Japanese will to fight. MacArthur was not consulted in advance, but if he had been, he would no doubt have given the opinion he expressed later that the A-bombing was "completely unnecessary from a military point of view."

As a counter, McCullough has offered one other cogent reason to release the bomb: "How could a President, or the others charged with responsibility for the decision, answer to the American people if when the war was over, after the bloodbath of an invasion of Japan, it became known that a weapon sufficient to end the war had been available by midsummer and was not used?"

All of these ideas revolved in the head of the studious, hardworking American president, but in the end the main determinant for Truman seems to have been his concern for the lives of American fighting men. That concern grew stronger as decrypts revealed more and more divisions being mobilized on Kyushu. From the original estimates of six combat divisions and two supporting "depot" divisions, the verified number had, by early August, grown to fourteen combat divisions plus below-division-sized units such as mixed brigades, tank regiments and artillery units. Truman faced the fact that the Japanese military had changed Kyushu into a bristling fortress of death for the invaders and, true to the Bushido spirit, were prepared to sacrifice seventy million civilians rather than surrender.

Not having received any response to the Potsdam Declaration, he ordered the bombing to proceed.

To enable the U.S. to assess accurately the effects of the bomb, the decision was to drop the first bomb on a city that had not been previously damaged by air raids. It was also deemed desirable to choose a city reported to be free of Allied prisoners of war. Hiroshima filled the bill. The *Enola Gay* crew dropped "Little Boy" on the city's center on August 6, 1945.

In one blinding moment, some eighty thousand people died, including a small number of American POWs. Thousands more would die from the effects of radiation. More than two-thirds of Hiroshima's buildings were destroyed.

When news of the Hiroshima bomb reached MacArthur's headquarters, according to members of his staff, "General MacArthur was livid" and later seemed to be "in a daze." His reaction was understandable: gone were all those visions of leading the greatest amphibious et cetera.

The second bombing was not scheduled until August 11, but the air force command was given leeway for the timing, depending on the weather. When the forecasters predicted bad weather for that day, the mission was moved forward two days. Also, it was supposed to be dropped on the city of Kokura. Finding that city obscured by industrial haze and following orders to bomb only a visual target, the captain of *Bock's Car* dropped the plutonium "Fat Boy" on his alternate choice, the *Madame Butterfly* city of Nagasaki, on August 9. Nearly fifty thousand more people were added to the atomic death toll.

Although none of the other Allied leaders now wanted it to happen, the Soviet Union declared war against Japan on September 8. Russian troops immediately crossed the border into Manchuria to begin pushing back the depleted Japanese defenders.

As to what happened in Japan following the nuclear bombing, the best analysis has been given by Robert J. C. Butow. After the war he went to Japan, interviewed the surviving leaders, read voluminously in the documents and presented his findings in his book *Japan's Decision to Surrender*.

The shortened interval between the two bombings, he made clear, was unfortunate. The devastation at Hiroshima was so complete, and reports out of the city were so fragmentary, that the leaders in Tokyo lacked the time to learn what had hit them. The peace faction and the militarists remained deadlocked. The minister of war declared, "It is far too early to say that the war is lost," adding that upon the Allies' invasion, "it is by no means impossible that we may be able to reverse the situation in our favor, pulling victory out of defeat."

As Butow reported, the two factions finally did the unprecedented: on the night of August 10 they stated their cases before the emperor, who was traditionally limited to having only to endorse unanimous decisions. His response was emphatic: "I cannot bear to see my innocent people suffer any longer. Ending the war is the only way to restore world peace and to relieve the nation from the terrible distress with which it is burdened."

A reply was quickly drafted and dispatched, accepting the Potsdam ultimatum "with the understanding that the said declaration does not comprise any demand which prejudices the prerogatives of his Majesty as a Sovereign Ruler."

To accept this condition outright went against the Allied grain. U.S. Secretary of State Byrnes wrote a reply that stated, "From the moment of surrender the authority of the Emperor and the Japanese government to rule the state shall be subject to the Supreme Commander of the Allied powers who will take such steps as he deems proper to effectuate the surrender terms." The reply also demanded that the emperor issue orders to the military to cease active operations and stated, "The ultimate form of government of Japan shall, in accordance with the Potsdam Declaration, be established by the freely expressed will of the Japanese people."

In Tokyo, Byrnes's reply rekindled the bitter debate between the hawks and the doves. In researching his book *Downfall: The End of the Imperial Japanese Empire*, Richard Frank found that Japanese militarists had argued the war should be continued because the U.S. had no additional atomic weapons. The fierce clash continued until August 14 when, again, the two factions presented their arguments to the emperor. He was no less decisive. Having studied the terms set by the Allies, he said, "I consider the reply acceptable." He also ordered that machinery be set in motion so that he could broadcast the decision to the people. For the first time in history the Japanese nation heard the voice of the emperor himself, proclaiming in a shaking voice that because "the enemy has begun to employ a new and most cruel bomb," Japan would accept the Allies' peace terms and cease all hostilities.

Despite some violent reactions by a few military extremists, the Japanese war machine was closed down. The transfer of thousands of GIs from the European theater to the Pacific ended. For the codebreakers, Japanese traffic declined to just a few plaintext messages. Nevertheless the Allies stayed on the alert, scarcely daring to believe that the words of one man could bring the Japanese war effort to a complete halt. Bull Halsey warned his ships to maintain a close watch. "Any ex-enemy aircraft attacking the fleet," he signaled, "is to be shot down in a friendly manner."

The stage was set for Douglas MacArthur to make another dramatic landing, this one by plane to an uncertain reception in Japan on August 30. To the great relief of his party, he found the people compliant and their officers polite. Aboard the battleship *Missouri* in Tokyo Bay on September 2, he conducted the peace-signing ceremonies. His brief speech, to which he had given most careful thought, forecast the magnanimity toward the defeated that he would exercise in his control of Japan's postwar recovery. Toshikazu Kase, the American-educated diplomat chosen to give the official report to Emperor Hirohito, described The General as "a man of light." It was, he went on, "a piece of rare good fortune" that "a man of such caliber and character should have been designated as the Supreme Commander" to "shape the destiny of Japan."

Of this glowing report, William Manchester has commented, "MacArthur himself could hardly have improved upon it."

For the Allies, these were the happiest, most celebratory days of the twentieth century. All too soon that relief and joy would end in anger and fear. As early as 1943 the virus of a new conflict had been detected by U.S. codebreakers. Cryptanalysts of the Signal Intelligence Service had begun breaking Soviet codes whose messages revealed the extensive Russian intelligence network operating in Britain, among de Gaulle's Free French, in the Scandinavian countries, in Australia and, most critical of all, in the U.S. The U.S. net was made up of outright agents and Americans enamored of Communism. All through the McCarthy flimflam the genuine news about

Russia's secret allies had to remain hidden within what became code-named as the Venona project. The import of the decrypts was chilling. They told of Soviet spies penetrating the Manhattan Project, the Los Alamos test site, the War Department staff, the Office of Strategic Services and the British embassy in Washington. They penetrated past the cover names to identify many of the spies, including Britain's Cambridge moles and such U.S. deniers as Alger Hiss. They traced the flow of vital techno-logical data to Moscow. The Venona secrets remained classified until 1995, after the USSR had crumbled and the Cold War been brought to an end.

In World War II's long aftermath, the predictions of Harvey Bundy, Robert Oppenheimer and other scientists of the Interim Committee have been borne out. Those who died in Hiroshima and Nagasaki are our mod-ern martyrs; the horror of their vanquishing seared into the minds of the world a fear of nuclear war that maintained a fragile, trigger-happy peace all through the militaristic temptations of the Cold War and that has contin-ued its hold down to the present day.

Conclusion

To review World War II from the perspective of the codebreakers is to wonder at the fragility of the thread that bound their story together. How easily that thread could have broken at any of many places. If the Poles hadn't had the foresight to concentrate the minds of brilliant young mathematicians on the problem . . . if French signals intelligence had been in the hands of a less determined man . . . if a German code worker hadn't picked this moment to sell out his country . . . if the Poles had lacked the initiative at the last hour to pass on their secrets to their allies . . . if the Japanese had been able to change over to new naval codes on schedule . . . if one of these or any of the other potential threats had materialized, the thread would have snapped, the story ended.

Because the thread held, Allied commanders at the critical turning points of the war gained the upper hand by securing advance knowledge of their opponents' next moves. The contention here is that this advantage was decisive in producing Allied victory.

Agreement on this point is hardly to be expected.

Harry Hinsley gave a guarded answer: "In attempting that assessment we may at once dismiss the claim that Ultra by itself won the war."

His assertion is, of course, made inarguable by his inclusion of "by itself." Obviously an Alan Turing sitting in a Bletchley Park hut couldn't shoot down Luftwaffe planes or brew up Tiger tanks. Nor could a Joe Rochefort holed up in an Oahu cellar sink the battlewagons of Yamamoto. For the Allies to win demanded that many factors work together, from the Rosie riveters on the home front to the G.I. Joe infantrymen on the firing line. Victory, in Charles Ameringer's words, "would have been impossible without troops and guns and leadership and resolve," but it was Ultra, he added, that determined "the conduct of the war."

That is the point. The codebreakers supplied the information that shaped the strategies. They influenced the decisions of what would be done, and then the men and guns and leadership and resolve *carried out* what these revelations had shown to be the most promising courses of action. Or, as Edward Drea wrote about a U.S. campaign, "American GIs paid in sweat, pain and blood to reap the harvest that intelligence had sown."

D-Day offers a prime example. If Eisenhower had not known that Hitler had been fooled into ordering Rommel to hold his main strength in the Pas de Calais, and if Rommel had been allowed to shift his Fifteenth Army into Normandy, would Ike have tried his tremendously vulnerable five-pronged landings?

From his disclaimer that Ultra did not alone win the war, Hinsley swung to the other pole by asserting that the Normandy invasion "would have been impracticable—or would have failed—without the precise and reliable intelligence provided by Ultra about German strengths and order of battle."

So it was at all the pivotal points of the war: the Allies' superiority in secret intelligence turned the tide of combat.

In the early stages, remember, Allied codebreaking *kept the war from being lost*. Even though British cryptology was in what one commentator called "its dark ages," Bletchley Park did help get the British army out of France, it did aid in warding off the German air force in the Battle of Britain and it was a main factor in keeping Britain from being strangled by the U-boats.

Similarly, secret intelligence provided the edge that turned back the Germans at Moscow, prevented Rommel from taking Egypt and saved the U.S. Navy from a more definitive Pearl Harbor at Midway Island.

Diana Payne, a bombe operator at Bletchley, expressed it well: "Without the priceless foreknowledge of German plans the war could well have been lost before the Allied forces were sufficiently armed and trained to achieve complete victory."

After staving off defeat, the codebreakers assumed a more critical role: *They took much of the guesswork out of Allied command decisions.*

German leaders accepted the belief of military theorist Hans von Seekt that "uncertainty and chance are inescapable characteristics of war." The Nazi commanders had no other choice. After early successes, German codebreakers were progressively shut out and reduced to relying on the lesser non-codebreaking elements of direction-finding and traffic analysis.

Allied leaders, on the other hand, came gradually to the realization that they could, to a large degree, refuse to accept uncertainty and chance as inescapable. Confident that their codebreakers would tell them what their opponents were planning, they could issue their orders on solid information. In war's shifting seas, the codebreakers supplied an anchor of truth.

Further, *codebreaking made victory possible by being "the mother of deceptions."* Recall that in Normandy and elsewhere, the codebreakers gave the Allies the advantage of being able to undertake enormous feats of what Churchill liked to call "legerdemain" and to know whether their duperies were succeeding.

Likewise, deception together with codebreaking set up the Eighth Army victories in North Africa, eased the landings in Sicily, thwarted the Germans at Monte Cassino and, as in the capture of Hollandia, fooled the Japanese repeatedly.

The true value of Allied codebreaking is underscored *by those times when it failed*, when Axis security measures temporarily blacked it out.

Pearl Harbor, it will be recalled, happened because, while U.S. codebreakers were reading Japanese diplomatic messages, they had made only an insufficient dent in Japan's naval codes that would have forewarned them of the Japanese attack.

Other instances include the Battle of the Atlantic, where the U-boats' scores against Allied shipping soared when the Germans were reading British Admiralty codes while Bletchley Park was shut out of decoding German traffic. Blackouts of U.S. codebreakers led to such tragic defeats as that of the navy at Savo Island. Most telling of all was Hitler's surprise 1944 replay of his Ardennes offensive. Thousands of Allied soldiers died unnecessarily because, for once, Ultra was not positive enough in determining where the Nazi buildup was aimed. Nothing says more about the powerful hold that the codebreakers gained on Allied decision making than this: when Allied generals were deprived of warnings relayed to them by their Ultra liaison units, they refused to heed other indicators of looming enemy action. Shorn of Ultra, Allied commanders became suddenly less godlike, more humanly fallible, more bumbling, as they would most likely have been throughout the war without the codebreakers' skills in backing them up.

The codebreakers' vital role is also underscored by the serious Allied setbacks that occurred *when generals ignored their advice*, as Mark Clark did in the disastrous effort to cross Italy's Rapido River, Bernard Montgomery did in the ill-fated airborne landings at Arnhem and Jack Fletcher did in one of the preliminary battles in the Coral Sea.

Conversely, most Allied leaders became adroit *in using the advantage given them by their codebreakers*. Montgomery's victory at El Alamein, Patton's and Bradley's at Mortain and Falaise, Clark's in stopping the counterattacks at Salerno and Anzio, Zhukov's at Stalingrad and Kursk, Spruance's at Midway and MacArthur's at Hollandia and elsewhere were all based on effective use of superior intelligence.

Lastly, Allied cryptanalysis provided the opportunities *to frustrate Axis technological developments*, delay their progress and keep them from becoming the scourges they might well have been. Nuclear bombs, fearsome new U-boats, jet aircraft, V-1s, particularly V-2s, were prevented from realizing their potential before they could hamstring the Allies' march to triumph.

For such reasons as these, it is not excessive to claim that in World War II the main determinant of Allied ascendancy was not warriors and armor, essential as they were, not U.S. industrial might, overpowering as it became, but codebreaking by brilliant Polish codebreakers in Warsaw, geniuses at Bletchley Park, self-sacrificing informants in the Red Orchestra and superlative cryptanalysts among the Americans.

David Kahn cited U.S. Navy Vice Admiral Walter Anderson as saying of wartime codebreaking, "It won the war!" Kahn added, "Hyperbole, to be sure, but indicative nevertheless." He went on to remark that a summation written by George Marshall, "who was certainly in a position to know, tends to support the hyperbole."

Dwight Eisenhower wrote that "Ultra was decisive." Winston Churchill declared, "We owe to the arm of General Menzies that we won the war."

The premise of this book, then, is not without support from the war's leaders. As intelligence documents that have been locked in secrecy since the war years continue to be declassified, they make the case ever stronger. The more we learn about those times, the more evident it becomes: of the many factors that contributed to the winning of the war, none had so powerful an effect as the advantage that came from the breaking of enemy messages and the guidance those decrypts gave Allied commanders. The evidence that has been assembled here points to one conclusion, whose validity the reader is asked to judge: to reassess World War II fairly is to grant that it was a codebreakers' victory.

Acknowledgments

WORK on this book has been a race against time. The idea for it came to me only six years ago—in a reaction, as I've noted, against the previous reading I'd been doing since Fred Winterbotham opened my eyes fully to what, in my wartime duty, I had been a part of, an element in. I could see that the project would be hugely demanding: to assess the effects of secret intelligence in all the major theaters of the war and render defensible judgments in readable prose would be a daunting undertaking for a much younger writer. I was then in my late seventies. In the time I had left, could I possibly conduct the intensive research and manage the vast reading that the writing would entail?

Fortunately, my genes have been kind to me, allowing me these six years, plus the requisite wits and energy, to get the job done. Yes, I would have liked months rather than just days at the Public Record Office, where Britain so efficiently stores its immense detritus of once-secret intelligence from the war. Yes, my stay with John Gallehawk, archivist at Bletchley Park, was all too short. Yes, I would have welcomed more time in the U.S. National Archives and Records Administration files in College Park, Maryland—more time to allow NARA's World War II guru, John Taylor, and his associates to guide me through that labyrinth of information. Yes, I would have appreciated more opportunity to explore what I know are rich resources at the U.S. Army Military History Institute in Carlisle, Pennsylvania, the Washington National Records Center and the United States Naval Institute in Maryland, and other such troves as the MacArthur Memorial Bureau of Archives in Norfolk, Virginia. And yes, there are scores of other books, articles and Web sites I would gladly have scanned as well as further interviews with the waning ranks of survivors from the war I could have pursued.

No complaints. I've had the six years to make the most of what I could accomplish. I'm fortunate in having Patricia, my wife of fifty-five years, hang in with me, not as a "golf widow" but certainly as a "writer's widow," and in addition give me great help in getting the manuscript ready for review. I'm grateful that my fellow Ultra Americans and my friends in Britain have rallied round to lend their support. And I'm most fortunate in having Richard Curtis as my ever-encouraging literary agent and Dan Slater as my ever-resourceful editor at Penguin Putnam. I thank all of you for giving me the great adventure of having my first book published as an octogenarian.

Now to notes on sources I *have* been able to call upon.

For general coverage of the war I've relied, of course, on Winston Churchill's magisterial six-volume history. I've made a run-through of Samuel Eliot Morison's equally massive *History of United States Naval Operations in World War II*. Primarily, though, I've concentrated on histories written after the walls of secrecy about World War II intelligence came down, histories that could begin to take into account the contributions of the codebreakers. My copy of John Keegan's *The Second World War* has fallen apart from overuse. Martin Gilbert's history with the same name has provided a diurnal record of the conflict—and supplied the most compendious and useful index imaginable. Otherwise, I've drawn snippets about the war from dozens of other writers—Accoce to Ziegler.

To my knowledge, there are no books aside from this one that regard the entire war from the perspective of the codebreakers. The five-volume *British Intelligence in the Second World War*, compiled by Harry Hinsley and three other historians, and nicely condensed by Hinsley into a one-volume abridged edition, focuses almost entirely on the war in Europe. Donald Lewin's *Ultra Goes to War* also deals with Europe, while his *American Magic* tries, less successfully, to cover codebreaking in the Pacific theater. The revised edition of David Kahn's great tome *The Codebreakers* includes an account of Allied successes against the "scrutable orientals" as well as rather cursorily added-on reports on the attacks against Enigma. Otherwise, writers have dealt with specific aspects of the story rather than overall assessments.

Introduction

Churchill's quote about the golden eggs: Oliver Hoare's booklet *Enigma*. Churchill's lines about "the secret war" are from his own *Their Finest Hour*.

The first, virtually unnoticed break in the secrecy about conquest of the Enigma came in Wladyslaw Kozaczuk's 1967 book, *Struggle for Secrets*, followed by Gustave Bertrand's equally unnoticed *Enigma* in 1973. It was Winterbotham's *The Ultra Secret*, published in 1974, that first drew world attention to the Ultra program.

Chapter 1. Belligerents: Choose Your Code Machines

The brief history of cryptology borrows from David Kahn's *The Code-breakers*, Stephen Budiansky's *Battle of Wits*, James Gannon's *Stealing Secrets, Telling Lies* and Simon Singh's *The Code Book*.

The account here of the Battle of Tannenberg is condensed from Barbara Tuchman's *The Guns of August*, while the story of the Zimmermann telegram is from her book of that title.

Painvin's success: Simon Singh, *The Code Book*.

Herbert Yardley's Great War experience: his *The American Black Chamber*.

William Friedman's breaking Pletts's machine: Ronald Clark's *The Man Who Broke Purple*.

As for Scherbius's Enigma, a number of cryptographic specialists, including Kozaczuk, Kahn and Budiansky, have described its inner workings in enthusiastic detail. The account here is a synthesis, drawing particularly from Bletchley Park veteran Peter Calvocoressi's *Top Secret Ultra*.

Several writers, including Robert Leckie in *Delivered from Evil*, have mentioned the connection between Elgar's composition and the naming of Scherbius's machine.

Disclosure by Churchill of Britain's breaking of the German naval code in the Great War: Kahn's *The Codebreakers*.

The inventions by Hebern, Damm and Hagelin, as well as developments by the Russians and the Italians, are described by Kahn in his *The Code-breakers*. Clark's book tells of the work of Friedman and Rowlett on an American machine. Ralph Erskine is the source of material on Britain's Typex.

Michael Smith in *The Emperor's Codes* reports Japan's work on code machines.

Chapter 2. Breaking the Enigma: Poles Show the Way

Of the many tellings of the Poles' cracking of the Enigma, I've relied primarily on Rejewski's account in the appendixes of Kozaczuk's *Enigma*, on Kozaczuk's own version and on Kahn's explanation, the clearest and most readable, in *Seizing the Enigma*.

The incident of the 1929 arrival of an Enigma-holding crate at the Warsaw customs office is from Kozaczuk.

For a fuller review of the stories of Hans-Thilo Schmidt and Bertrand, Kahn is also a good source.

Details of the Poles' course at Poznan and of their initial breaking of the Enigma are in Kozaczuk's *Enigma*, which includes Rejewski's description in the appendixes.

Rejewski's reminiscences of his final victory over the Enigma are from a typewritten copy collected by Jozef Garlinski, author of *The Enigma War*.

Bertrand's quote about "*un moment de stupeur*" is from his *Enigma*.

Peter Twinn tells of Dilly Knox happily chanting "*Nous avons le QWERTZU*" in his contribution to *Codebreakers*, edited by Harry Hinsley and Alan Stripp.

Chapter 3. *Britain Takes Over the Cryptologic War*

British Intelligence in the Second World War, by Hinsley et al, is the essential source of information on the Ultra work at Bletchley Park.

Andrew Hodges has written the fine biography *Alan Turing: The Enigma*, while Gordon Welchman has told of his own days at BP in *The Hut Six Story*. More on Welchman is reported in Nigel West's *The Sigint Secrets*.

Details of Alastair Denniston's contributions are from numerous sources, especially Kahn's *Seizing the Enigma*.

The report on Herivel's tip relies mostly on Michael Smith's *Station X*, while that on "cillis" is drawn from Welchman.

The Wrens' problems with the bombes: Diana Payne's essay "The Bombes," in Hinsley and Stripp's *Codebreakers*.

In *Ultra Goes to War*, Ronald Lewin tells of Welchman's organization plan for BP.

An entire section of Hinsley and Stripp's *Codebreakers* is devoted to various slants on Fish. Other useful texts: Michael Smith's *Station X*, Lewin's *Ultra Goes to War* and Singh's *The Code Book*.

These sources have been supplemented by personal research in the historical files of Bletchley Park, at Britain's Public Record Office (PRO) and at Hall Place, Bexley, Kent, where the Santa Fe intercept station was operated. Also by interviews with Pat Bing and Molly Brewster of the BP staff, with Anthony Sale, who rebuilt the Colossus as a BP exhibit, and with the late George Vergine, an Ultra American who worked on Fish and who left with me a copy of his own reminiscences of those days.

Chapter 4. *BP Begins Exploiting Its "Gold Mine"*

To the usual sources of Churchill, Winterbotham, Hinsley, Calvocoressi, Kahn, Lewin, Keegan and Gilbert, I've added Len Deighton and Max Hastings's *Battle of Britain*, Peter Wescombe's *Bletchley Park and the Luftwaffe*, R. V. Jones's *Most Secret War* and Correlli Barnett's *The Desert Generals*.

The Welchman quote about the gold mine is not from his *Hut Six Story* but from his later essay "From Polish Bomba to British Bombe: The Birth of Ultra," in *Codebreaking and Signals Intelligence*, edited by Christopher Andrew.

The commander's quote about the Germans' knowledge of British shipping is from Hinsley et al.

Hinsley tells of his post-*Glorious* improvement in status with the Admiralty in his essay "Bletchley Park, the Admiralty and Naval Enigma," in *Codebreakers*.

Frederick Pile's quote about Dowding: Deighton and Hastings.

Hitler's furious response to the bombing of Berlin: Lewin. His quote about the losses from a Channel crossing: Gilbert.

The doggerel about the local scorn BP males had to endure: Irene Young's *Enigma Variations*.

The Brauchitsch quote is from Liddell Hart's *The German Generals Talk*, and that of Kesselring from his *A Soldier's Record*.

Churchill's words about the German leaders' passing the buck to Göring is from his *Their Finest Hour*.

The debate over Churchill's competence as a wartime leader is covered at length by Christopher Hitchens in his article "The Medals of His Defeats," in *The Atlantic Monthly*, April 2002.

Much of the section on O'Connor's victory in North Africa follows Barnett, with Ultra details from Hinsley. The section on Matapan is told well by Sebag-Montefiore.

Chapter 5. Battle of the Atlantic: Cryptologic Seesaw

Since Harry Hinsley not only wrote the official history of British intelligence in World War II but also played a major role in winning the fight against the U-boats, his writings were a main source for this chapter.

David Kahn's far more readable account in *Seizing the Enigma* was especially useful concerning the efforts of Hinsley along with Turing and his associates in Hut 8 to engineer the capture of materials that broke open the tough German naval codes.

As a general history of the U-boat war, Barrie Pitt's Time-Life book, *The Battle of the Atlantic*, proved a good source.

My report on B-Dienst's successes in breaking British Admiralty codes borrows from *The Battle of the Atlantic* by Terry Hughes and John Costello, and from Patrick Beesly's *Very Special Intelligence*.

If my accounts of the methods used by B-Dienst and, conversely, by Turing are understandable, thank Budiansky's *Battle of Wits* and Sebag-Montefiore's *Enigma: The Battle for the Code* for their skillful explanations.

Rolf Noskwith's own memoir of breaking the Offizier code is included in Hinsley and Stripp's *Codebreakers*.

The section on the war against Germany's surface raiders synthesizes material from Hinsley, Kahn, Calvocoressi and Hughes and Costello, as does the section on Shark.

Martin Gilbert recounts the story of the German sailors trapped within the *Tirpitz*.

Hinsley is the source for the Admiralty's fears of defeat in early 1943.

The report on the *Petard*'s capture of *U-559*, and on the sacrifice of Fasson and Grazier, condenses Kahn's account in *Seizing the Enigma*.

The climax of the Atlantic battle reflects the very full treatment in Michael Gannon's *Black May*.

Again, research at the PRO strengthened my accumulated knowledge of this long and sanguinary struggle.

Chapter 6. *When Superior Intelligence Was Not Enough*

Among its offerings, the Internet presents a translation in English of the whole of *Mein Kampf*. My reading left me wondrous of how opposing leaders during the war could have so ignored its import.

The facts about Paul Thummel and other British agents on the continent are from Hinsley et al.

Churchill's quote doubting that Germany would attack the Soviets is from his volume *Their Finest Hour*, as is his "lightning flash" conversion to believing it would happen. His riposte about Hitler invading hell is cited in Nicholas Bethel's *Russia Besieged*.

Hinsley details Britain's intelligence heads' resistance to the idea of a German attack on the Soviets and their turnaround to accepting the idea that Hitler might be anticipating "a lightning victory."

Churchill's lines about Hitler's tantrum over the coup in Yugoslavia are from *Their Finest Hour*.

As noted, the section on William Stephenson and William Donovan draws, rather gingerly, on William Stevenson's overblown biography of Stephenson, *A Man Called Intrepid*, and, more confidently, on H. Montgomery Hyde's *The Quiet Canadian*. Nigel West's *Counterfeit Spies* documents the incredible fictionalizing by Stevenson of his near namesake's story.

The section on Crete owes much to John Keegan's *The Second World War* for its historical coverage and to Hinsley for the codebreakers' role. Churchill's *Their Finest Hour* is again the source for his quotes about Crete and about Moscow being saved by the delayed start of Barbarossa.

Chapter 7. The Spies Who Never Were

Any account of the double agents who served Britain while convincing the Nazis they were serving *them* must begin with J. C. Masterman's *The Double-Cross System*. Since it was drafted soon after the war's end but not authorized for publication until 1972, it can only hint at the Ultra secret. That aspect is well covered by Hinsley. Other books that proved to be useful sources: Kahn's *Hitler's Spies*, Cave Brown's *Bodyguard of Lies*, Jeffrey Richelson's *A Century of Spies*, Ewen Montagu's *Beyond Top Secret Ultra* and Ernest Volkman's *Spies: The Secret Agents Who Changed the Course of History*.

I'm indebted to Nigel West's *Operation Garbo* for additional information about Garbo-Pujol and the belated recognition given his incredible wartime services.

Tricycle—Dusko Popov—also could not get his memoir, *Spy/Counterspy*, approved for publication until well after the war. The pro-FBI counterattack against his version of his failed attempt to alert the U.S. to the approach of the Pearl Harbor raid is detailed in Thomas Troy's "The British Assault on J. Edgar Hoover: The Tricycle Case" and in B. Bruce-Briggs's "Another Ride on Tricycle."

Chapter 8. The U.S. Tackles Japan's Codes

This chapter in particular benefits from personal research at the U.S. National Archives and Records Administration facility.

Sources for the story of William and Elizebeth Friedman, include Ronald Clark's *The Man Who Broke Purple*, Kahn's *The Codebreakers* and Frank Rowlett's *The Story of Magic*.

My account of Joseph Rochefort and his Hypo operation is also compiled from many sources, led by his own oral history recorded by navy scribes. Others: Edwin Layton's *And I Was There*, Jasper Holmes's *Double-edged Secrets*, Lewin's *The American Magic*, Winton's *Ultra in the Pacific* and Kahn's *The Codebreakers*.

The reference to Admiral Stark's memorandum to FDR is from Joseph Persico's *Roosevelt's Secret War*.

Among the scurrilous publications claiming that FDR conspired in the

Japanese raid on Pearl Harbor in order to bring the U.S. into the war, my favorite dart target is Mark Emerson Willey's *Pearl Harbor: The Mother of All Conspiracies*. Refutations abound, as noted in the text, including books by Prange, Wohlstetter, Keegan and Persico, among others.

Source for the near misses in sounding the alert: Kahn's *The Codebreakers*. The account of Ralph Briggs's reception of the East Wind message is by Ellsworth Boyd in the November 2000 issue of Primedia's *World War II* magazine.

John Prados's *Combined Fleet Decoded* supplies a clear analysis of Japanese thinking behind the raid.

Layton's memoir expresses his indignation at the treatment of Kimmel and Short.

The admiral who in Prange's interview scanted the Japanese destruction at Pearl Harbor was Claude C. Bloch.

Admiral Morison's quote about Pearl Harbor being a "strategic imbecility" is from his *The Rising Sun in the Pacific*.

Layton and Prados expressed sharp criticism of MacArthur for the follow-up losses on Luzon.

In the use of Japanese names, I've followed the Western practice of putting the surname *after* the given name. In Japanese style, it's the reverse.

The section on Baron Oshima relies mostly, as mentioned, on Carl Boyd's *Hitler's Japanese Confidant*. Also, Bruce Lee documents in his book *Marching Orders* the incredibly diverse flow of information provided by the Magic summaries placed daily on the desks of General Marshall and Secretary of War Stimson.

Chapter 9. North Africa: A Pendulum Swung by Codebreakers

The terrible story of Bonner Frank Fellers was not to be overlooked by writers. Kahn tells it in a couple of his books. Welchman dwells on it. So does Cave Brown. They all gave me aid in forming my own account.

Both Welchman and Kahn tell of Seeböhm's field intercept unit and its fate.

A prime source for coverage of the North African battles is Barnett's *The Desert Generals*, despite his obvious animus toward Bernard Montgomery.

Rommel quotes are from *The Rommel Papers*, edited by Hart with the aid of Rommel's family. Kesselring's quote is from his *A Soldier's Record*.

The Edgar Williams and William Mather quotes are from Nigel Hamilton's *Monty: The Making of a General*.

Hinsley is, as ever, indispensable in pinning down specific decrypts that were of great benefit to British generals. His quote about the number of submarines and recon aircraft based on Malta is from his answer to a question following his 1993 lecture at a Security Group Seminar.

The section on Operation Torch is compiled from Keegan, Gilbert and Lewin, with Ultra information from Hinsley and from Omar Bradley's autobiography.

Chapter 10. Turnaround in the Pacific War

Details of the Japanese double delay in changing JN-25 come from Lewin's *The American Magic* and Edward Van Der Rhoer's *Deadly Magic*.

Layton's memoir sets forth clearly the effects of Doolittle's raid, as does Frederick Parker's *A Priceless Advantage*, from the United States Cryptologic History available on the Web. Yamamoto's quote about the "disgrace" of the raid is from Layton.

As cited, Prados's *Combined Fleet Decoded* proved a valuable resource for understanding all the Decisive Battles of the Pacific war.

Sources for the treatment of the Battle of Midway include Rochefort's own *Reminiscences*, Layton, Holmes, Kahn and particularly Prange's *Miracle at Midway*.

The David Kennedy quote is from his essay "Victory at Sea," in the March 1999 issue of *The Atlantic Monthly*.

Admiral Nimitz's postbattle praise of Rochefort is from Winton's *Ultra in the Pacific*.

In addition to the sources cited, the section on MacArthur's Port Moresby operations includes details from Edward Drea's *MacArthur's Ultra* and William Manchester's *American Caesar*.

Chapter 11. USSR: Intelligence Guides the Major Victories

Most of the sources here are cited in the text. Otherwise, Jozef Garlinski's *The Enigma War* supplied information on the Red Three as well as the Red Orchestra.

Alexander Foote's quote is from his *Handbook for Spies*.

Material on the Cambridge ring came from Phillip Knightley's *The Master Spy*, among other sources.

My main source on Richard Sorge is Robert Whymant's *Stalin's Spy*.

The David Glantz quote is from his *The Role of Intelligence in Soviet Military Strategy in World War II*.

Keegan supplied Hitler's quote about kicking down the Russian door, while Gilbert contributed the Hitler lines about flouting the Hague Convention rules and the führer's plans for Operation Typhoon.

Rundstedt's quote is from Hart's *The German Generals Talk*, as is that of Kleist.

Churchill's exchanges with Menzies are from Gilbert.

Hitler's Directive 41 is drawn from V. E. Tarrant's *The Red Orchestra*.

For my brief summary of the battle for Stalingrad I've relied mostly on Glantz.

The Cairncross quote about Moscow's acceptance of his information is from Michael Smith's *Station X*.

Zhukov's counsel to Stalin is from Keegan.

Tarrant is the source for the account of the breakup of the Red Orchestra, seconded by Shareen Brysac's *Resisting Hitler*. The postwar treatment of Rado, Foote and Roessler is also from Tarrant.

John Taylor at NARA helped me dig far enough into the files on Martin Bormann to discount Louis Kilzer's claim that Bormann was the main source of anti-Nazi information.

Chapter 12. *Smiting the Axis's Soft Underbelly*

Again, most references are identified in the text. In addition to the works by Keegan, Gilbert and Hinsley, Robert Wallace's Time-Life book, *The Italian Campaign* was a useful source.

At the Public Record Office, copies of the most significant decrypts, such as those warning of Kesselring's planned attacks at Anzio, were efficiently delivered for review.

Kesselring quotes are, once more, from his memoir.

Churchill's quip about Anzio turning into a stranded whale is from his *Triumph and Tragedy*.

As noted, details about Mark Clark's megalomaniacal decisions in Italy are from Eric Sevareid's *Not So Wild a Dream*.

Chapter 13. *The Coming of the Ultra Americans*

Supplementing my own memories, I've interviewed or corresponded with a number of other Americans who participated in the Ultra program. The unpublished memoirs of Walter Sharp, Jim Nielson and George Vergine were especially helpful.

Joan Nicholls's book is *England Needs You: The Story of Beaumanor Station*. Diana Payne's comments are from her chapter in Hinsley and Stripp's *Codebreakers*.

Thomas Parrish's *The Ultra Americans* was a useful, if disjointed, source.

Chapter 14. Up the Island Ladder Toward Tokyo

The historical narrative here follows Keegan, while coverage of the cryptologic developments synthesizes Layton, Drea, Holmes, Prados and Winton, plus personal research at the National Archives.

The quote about Nimitz's staff being unable to read the enemy mail is from Edwin Hoyt's *How They Won the War in the Pacific*.

Firsthand observations of cryptologic work on Guadalcanal have been supplied by Philip Jacobsen's Web history, *The Codebreakers*. An associate of Joe Rochefort at Hypo, Jacobsen was transferred to Guadalcanal and helped operate a field intelligence station there.

The main sources on MacArthur are Manchester and Drea. The Juro quote, as an example, is cited by Manchester, as is The General's order to Eichelberger.

To John Kennedy's own account of *PT-109*, Kahn, in *The Codebreakers*, adds details about coast watcher codes and the Japanese failure to break them.

The story of Yamamoto's fall has been written up repeatedly. Kahn's version in *The Codebreakers* is a good one.

Rochefort's downfall is taken from his own oral history as well as from the memoirs of Holmes and Layton.

Vice Admiral Lockwood's quote is from Winton.

Chapter 15. France: Invasions from North and South

The account here of the Allies' Normandy landings and of the deceptions accompanying them has been compiled from many sources, including my own readings of relevant decrypts at the PRO. For additional coverage of the Sigint side I'm indebted, of course, to Hinsley, but also to Cave Brown, Kahn, Welchman and Lewin.

Oshima's involuntary spy role is from Boyd.

General Blumentritt's quote is from Hart. Jodl's estimate of divisions held in the Pas de Calais is from Masterman.

William Stephenson's Magic Group is described by Stevenson, while Jones's *Most Secret War* tells of the air traffic simulator. The Ronald Wingate quote is also from Jones.

The Don Bussey quote: Smith's *Station X*. That of Omar Bradley is from his *A General's Life*.

The part played by Britain's double agents is, again, mainly from Masterman.

Churchill's proposals for Russia-countering alternatives to the Riviera landings are in his *Triumph and Tragedy*.

Rundstedt's brash words about making peace are quoted from Winter-botham's *The Ultra Secret*.

The incident involving Melvin Helfers's meeting with George Patton is related in Robert Miller's *August 1944*. So is Bradley's meeting with Mor-genthau. Miller is the source for Hitler's order for a new offensive and for Kluge's end.

Principal source for the section on the Riviera invasion: William Breuer's *Operation Dragoon*.

Chapter 16. CBI: Winning the "Forgotten War"

In his massive book *Burma: The Longest War*, Louis Allen, a British veteran of that war, tells more than anyone other than a specialist or a fel-low vet would be interested in absorbing. But Allen, fluent in Japanese, does give a rounded history by recording both sides of the conflict.

General William Slim's memoir, *Defeat into Victory*, presents a much more readable account from his perspective. Philip Ziegler's *Mountbatten* devotes chapters to Lord Louis's part in the campaign. Joseph Stilwell's *The Stilwell Papers* offers a vinegary account from *his* vantage point.

The *China-Burma-India* volume from Time-Life Books' World War II history is a useful source. The editor is Don Moser.

Eric Sevareid's *Not So Wild a Dream* gives penetrating glimpses of the war from his visits to India and China.

Sigint information has been culled from Michael Smith's *The Em-peror's Codes*, Alan Stripp's *Codebreaker in the Far East*, Hugh Den-ham's essay "Bedford-Bletchley-Kilindini-Colombo," in *Codebreakers*, and Winterbotham's *The Ultra Secret*.

Churchill quotes are from his *Triumph and Tragedy*.

Chapter 17. Europe: The Bitter Fruits of Complacency

Hinsley's chapter "The Check in the West" is a compendium of the troubles Allied generals brought upon themselves, often by not heeding their intelligence providers. Montgomery's rueful quote about not clearing the Schelde estuary is from his *Memoirs* and is also cited by Hinsley.

Other sources are noted: Cave Brown, Miller, and Peter Harclerode's *Arnhem*. The brief account of the Hürtgen Forest struggle borrows from Miller and from General James Gavin's 1979 article in *American Heritage* magazine. Oshima references are from Boyd.

Some details such as Eisenhower's attendance at his valet's wedding on the day of the Ardennes attack come from Charles Whiting's *Ardennes: The Secret War*.

The Churchill quote is, once again, from *Triumph and Tragedy*, and that of Rundstedt is from Hart's *The German Generals Talk*.

Chapter 18. Closing In on the Empire

For sources here, a familiar cast reassembles. Holmes tells of the captures of intelligence materials, Layton of Fukudome's briefcase, Van Der Rhoer of the ships for Saipan, Prados of Japanese hopes for the Decisive Battle, Winton of the Marianas turkey shoot and Drea of Koiso's replacement of Tojo. To these add Thomas Cutler's *The Battle of Leyte Gulf*. A navy career officer, Cutler capably dramatizes the battle but shows a fighting man's disdain for secret intelligence by never acknowledging the contributions of the codebreakers.

Cutler, however, can't pass up the story of Halsey's wrath aroused by the Task Force 34 query and tells it well.

The references to MacArthur's leaving two hundred thousand Japanese soldiers useless and details of his Leyte landing are from Manchester's *American Caesar*.

The Churchill quote about Kurita is from *Triumph and Tragedy*.

As noted, Drea's description of The General's Luzon maneuverings was most helpful.

Of the several tellings of the story of Ohnishi and the formalization of the kamikaze tactics, Cutler's is best.

Chapter 19. Europe: High-grade Decrypts Abet Allied Victory

In addition to a final surfeit of decrypt information from Hinsley, this chapter gains from Keegan's lend-lease facts and from Stephen Ambrose's account in his *Citizen Soldiers* of the seizure of the Remagen bridge.

The section on the air war technologies obviously owes much to R. V. Jones, with the final bit about oxen-towed Luftwaffe aircraft contributed by Hyland and Gill's *Last Talons of the Eagle*.

Ambrose's *Eisenhower and Berlin* is the chosen source for Ike's Churchill-annoying decision. The Allies' warning to the Soviets about Hitler's southwest offensive is from Hinsley.

The report on Hitler's V-weapons is, mostly, a briefer retelling of the relevant passages in R. V. Jones's memoir. The summary of Bohr's letter refuting Heisenberg is the *New York Times* article by James Glanz. Cave Brown is the source for the narrative on Norway's heavy-water production. Montagu's *Beyond Top Secret Ultra* contributes the detail of the warning from Tricycle's spymaster.

For information about the Nazis' jet plane developments I have relied on Hyland and Gill as well as Jones and Hinsley. The latter pair are also the chief sources for the account of the struggle against the V-weapons.

For the finale on the "Final Solution," the key source is, as noted, Richard Breitman's *Official Secrets*.

Chapter 20. In the Pacific: Last Battles, Final Decisions

I looked to Prados for facts about the Superfort benefits from the taking of Iwo Jima and to Winton for codebreaking details.

The code talkers' story: Singh's *The Code Book*.

The Superfort pilot's expression of gratitude: Winton.

Japanese plans for the defense of Okinawa: Van Der Rhoer.

Prados contributes the information on Colonel Holcomb and Admiral Spruance as well as the sacrificial mission of Japanese warships.

Drea is one source for the debate over potential casualties from a Kyushu landing, for MacArthur's opposition to changes in plans for the Olympic operation and for details of what awaited the invaders.

Douglas MacEachan's *The Final Months of the War with Japan*, available on the Internet, also details the awesome Japanese preparations to withstand the invasion.

Churchill's quotes about the costs of an invasion and the decision to drop the atomic bomb: *Triumph and Tragedy*.

As cited, McCullough's *Truman* provides a thorough treatment of the president's decision to drop the bomb.

The MacArthur reaction to news of the Hiroshima bombing is recalled in Horace A. Thompson Jr.'s interview with MacArthur's pilot, W. E. Rhoades. The interview transcript is in the MacArthur Memorial Archives.

Magic decrypts revealing the divide in Japanese attitudes toward peace: Van Der Rhoer, among others. As mentioned in the text, Robert Butow's *Japan's Decision to Surrender* is a key source.

Effects of the "Fat Boy" bomb on Nagasaki: Gilbert.

Bull Halsey's line about handling an ex-enemy aircraft attack: Winton.

My brief section on the Venona project summarizes the fuller account in Budiansky's *Battle of Wits*.

Conclusion

Hinsley's quote is from his introduction to *Codebreakers*.

The Ameringer quote is from his *U.S. Foreign Intelligence: The Secret Side of American History*.

Kahn on Admiral Anderson is from *The Codebreakers*.

Eisenhower's opinion that "Ultra was decisive" is cited by Winterbotham, while Churchill's assessment is from Harold Deutsch's essay "The Historical Impact of Revealing the Ultra Secret," in the journal *Parameters*.

Diana Payne's comment is from her essay "The Bombes," in Hinsley and Stripp's *Codebreakers*.

Bibliography

Books

Accoce, Pierre, and Pierre Quet. *A Man Called Lucy*. Translated by A. M. Sheridan Smith. New York: Coward-McCann, 1967.

Allen, Louis. *Burma: The Longest War, 1941–45*. London: Phoenix Press, 1984.

Ambrose, Stephen A. *Citizen Soldiers: The U.S. Army from the Normandy Beaches to the Bulge to the Surrender of Germany*. New York: Simon & Schuster, 1997.

———. *Eisenhower and Berlin, 1945: The Decision to Halt at the Elbe*. New York: Simon & Schuster, 1967.

———. *The Victors: Eisenhower and His Boys: The Men of World War II*. New York: Simon & Schuster, 1999.

Ameringer, Charles D. *U.S. Foreign Intelligence: The Secret Side of American History*. Lexington, VA: D. C. Heath, 1990.

Andrew, Christopher, ed. *Codebreaking and Signals Intelligence*. London: Frank Cass, 1986.

Barnett, Correlli. *The Desert Generals*. Rev. ed. Bloomington, IN: Indiana University Press, 1982.

Beesly, Patrick. *Very Special Intelligence: The Story of the Admiralty's Operational Intelligence Centre 1939–1945*. New York: Doubleday, 1978.

Bennett, Ralph. *Behind the Battle: Intelligence in the War with Germany, 1939–1945*. Rev. ed. London: Pimlico, 1999.

———. *Intelligence Investigations: How Ultra Changed History*. London: Frank Cass, 1996.

Bertrand, Gustave. *Enigma, ou la plus grande énigme de la guerre 1939–1945*. Paris: Plon, 1973.

Bethel, Nicholas, and the Editors of Time-Life Books. *Russia Besieged*. Alexandria, VA: Time-Life Books, 1977.

Boyd, Carl. *Hitler's Japanese Confidant: General Oshima Hiroshi and Magic Intelligence, 1941–1945*. Lawrence, KS: University Press of Kansas, 1993.

Bradley, Omar N., and Clay Blair. *A General's Life*. New York: Simon & Schuster, 1983.

Breitman, Richard. *Official Secrets: What the Nazis Planned, What the British and Americans Knew*. New York: Hill and Wang, 1998.

Breuer, William B. *Operation Dragoon: The Allied Invasion of the South of France*. Novato, CA: Presidio Press, 1987.

Brysac, Shareen Blair. *Resisting Hitler: Mildred Harnack and the Red Orchestra*. Oxford: Oxford University Press, 2000.

Budiansky, Stephen. *Battle of Wits: The Complete Story of Codebreaking in World War II*. New York: The Free Press, 2000.

Butow, Robert J.C. *Japan's Decision to Surrender*. Stanford: Stanford University Press, 1954.

Calvocoressi, Peter. *Top Secret Ultra*. New York: Pantheon, 1980.

Cave Brown, Anthony. *Bodyguard of Lies*. New York: Harper & Row, 1975.

Churchill, Winston S. *The Second World War*. 6 vols.: *The Gathering Storm, Their Finest Hour, The Grand Alliance, The Hinge of Fate, Closing the Ring, Triumph and Tragedy*. New York: Houghton Mifflin, 1948–53.

Clark, Mark. *Calculated Risk*. New York: Harper, 1950.

Clark, Ronald. *The Man Who Broke Purple: The Life of Colonel William F. Friedman, Who Deciphered the Japanese Code in World War II*. Boston: Little, Brown, 1977.

Cutler, Thomas F. *The Battle of Leyte Gulf: 23–26 October 1944*. New York: HarperCollins, 1994.

Deighton, Len, and Max Hastings. *Battle of Britain*. London: Jonathan Cape, 1980.

Drea, Edward J. *MacArthur's Ultra: Codebreaking and the War Against Japan, 1942–1945*. Lawrence, KS: University Press of Kansas, 1992.

Foote, Alexander. *Handbook for Spies*. London: Museum Press, 1964.

Frank, Richard B. *Downfall: The End of the Imperial Japanese Empire*. New York: Random House, 1999.

Gannon, James. *Stealing Secrets, Telling Lies: How Spies and Codebreakers Helped Shape the Twentieth Century*. Washington, D.C.: Brassey's, 2001.

Gannon, Michael. *Black May: The Epic Story of the Allies' Defeat of the German U-boats in May 1943*. New York: HarperCollins, 1998.

Garlinski, Jozef. *The Enigma War: The Inside Story of the German Enigma Codes and How the Allies Broke Them*. New York: Charles Scribner's Sons, 1979.

Gilbert, Martin. *The Second World War: A Complete History*. New York: Henry Holt, 1989.

Glantz, David M. *The Role of Intelligence in Soviet Military Strategy in World War II*. Novato, CA: Presidio Press, 1990.

Hamilton, Nigel. *Monty: The Making of a General*. New York: McGraw-Hill, 1981.

Harclerode, Peter. *Arnhem: A Tragedy of Errors*. London: Caxton, 2000.

Harris, Arthur. *Bomber Offensive*. London: Collins, 1947.

Hart, B. H. Liddell. *The German Generals Talk*. New York: William Morrow, 1948.

———, ed., with assistance of Lucie-Marie Rommel, Manfred Rommel and General Fritz Bayerlein, and translation by Paul Findlay. *The Rommel Papers*. New York: Harcourt, Brace, 1953.

Hesketh, Roger. *Fortitude: The D-Day Deception Campaign*. New York: The Overlook Press, 2000.

Hinsley, F. H. *British Intelligence in the Second World War*. Abridged ed. Cambridge: Cambridge University Press, 1993.

Hinsley, F. H., and Alan Stripp, eds. *Codebreakers: The Inside Story of Bletchley Park*. Oxford: Oxford University Press, 1993.

Hinsley, F. H., E. E. Thomas, C. F. G. Ransom and R. C. Knight. *British Intelligence in the Second World War*. London: Her Majesty's Stationery Office. 1979–1990.

Hodges, Andrew. *Alan Turing: The Enigma*. New York: Simon & Schuster, 1983.

Holmes, W. J. *Double-edged Secrets: U.S. Naval Operations in the Pacific During World War II*. Annapolis: Naval Institute Press, 1979.

Hoyt, Edwin P. *How They Won the War in the Pacific: Nimitz and His Admirals*. New York: Weybridge & Talley, 1970.

Hughes, Terry, and John Costello. *The Battle of the Atlantic*. New York: Dial, 1977.

Hyde, H. Montgomery. *The Quiet Canadian: The Secret Service of Sir William Stephenson*. London: Hamish Hamilton, 1962.

Hyland, Gary, and Anton Gill. *Last Talons of the Eagle: Secret Nazi Technology Which Could Have Changed the Course of World War II.* London: Headline Book Publishing, 1998.

Jones, R. V. *Most Secret War: British Scientific Intelligence 1939–1945.* London: Hamish Hamilton, 1978.

Kahn, David. *The Codebreakers: The Story of Secret Writing.* Rev. ed. New York: Scribner, 1996.

———. *Seizing the Enigma: The Race to Break the German U-boat Codes, 1939–1943.* Boston: Houghton Mifflin, 1991.

———. *Hitler's Spies: German Military Intelligence in World War II.* New York: Macmillan, 1978.

Keegan, John. *The Second World War.* New York: Viking, 1990.

Kesselring, Albert. *A Soldier's Record.* Westport, CT: Greenwood Press, 1981.

Kilzer, Louis. *Hitler's Traitor: Martin Bormann and the Defeat of the Reich.* Navato, CA: Presidio Press, 2000.

Knightley, Phillip. *The Master Spy: The Story of Kim Philby.* New York: Random House, 1989.

Kozaczuk, Wladyslaw. *Enigma: How the German Cipher Was Broken and How It Was Read by the Allies in World War II.* Translated and edited by Christopher Kasparek. Frederick, MD: University Publications of America, 1984.

———. *Struggle for Secrets: Intelligence Services of Poland and the Third Reich, 1932–1939.* Warsaw: Ksiazka i wiedza, 1967.

Layton, Edwin T., with Roger Pineau and John Costello. *And I Was There: Pearl Harbor and Midway—Breaking the Secrets.* New York: William Morrow, 1985.

Leckie, Robert. *Delivered from Evil: The Saga of World War II.* New York: Harper & Row, 1987.

Lee, Bruce. *Marching Orders: The Untold Story of World War II.* New York: Da Capo Press, 1995.

Lewin, Ronald. *The American Magic.* New York: Farrar Straus & Giroux, 1982.

———. *Ultra Goes to War: The First Account of World War II's Greatest Secret Based on Official Documents.* New York: McGraw-Hill, 1978.

Long, Gavin. *MacArthur as Military Commander.* New York: Batsford, 1976.

Manchester, William. *American Caesar: Douglas MacArthur, 1880–1964.* New York: Little, Brown, 1979.

Masterman, J. C. *The Double-Cross System in the War of 1939 to 1945*. New Haven: Yale University Press, 1972.

McCullough, David. *Truman*. New York: Simon & Schuster, 1992.

Miller, Robert A. *August 1944: The Campaign for France*. Novato, CA: Presidio Press, 1996.

Montagu, Ewen. *Beyond Top Secret Ultra*. New York: Coward, McCann & Geoghagen, 1978.

———. *The Man Who Never Was*. New York: J. B. Lippincott, 1954.

Montgomery, Bernard Law. *Memoirs*. New York: Collins, 1958.

Morison, Samuel Eliot. *History of United States Naval Operations in World War II*. 15 vols. Boston: Little, Brown, 1947–62. Specific citations: vol. 3, *The Rising Sun in the Pacific*, and vol. 5, *Coral Sea, Midway and Submarine Actions*.

Moser, Don, ed. *China-Burma-India*. Alexandria, VA: Time-Life Books, 1978.

Nicholls, Joan. *England Needs You: The Story of Beaumanor Station*. London: self-published, 2000.

Overy, Richard. *Russia's War*. New York: Penguin, 1997.

Parrish, Thomas. *The Ultra Americans: The U.S. Role in Breaking the Nazi Codes*. New York: Stein and Day, 1986.

Persico, Joseph E. *Roosevelt's Secret War: FDR and World War II Espionage*. New York: Random House, 2001.

Pitt, Barrie, and the Editors of Time-Life Books. *The Battle of the Atlantic*. Alexandria, VA: Time-Life Books, 1977.

Popov, Dusko. *Spy/Counterspy: The Autobiography of Dusko Popov*. New York: Grosset & Dunlop, 1974.

Prados, John. *Combined Fleet Decoded: The Secret History of American Intelligence and the Japanese Navy*. New York: Random House, 1995.

Prange, Gordon W., with Ronald M. Goldstein and Katherine V. Dillon. *At Dawn We Slept: The Untold Story of Pearl Harbor*. New York: McGraw-Hill, 1982.

———. *Miracle at Midway*. New York: McGraw-Hill, 1982.

Richelson, Jeffrey T. A. *Century of Spies: Intelligence in the Twentieth Century*. New York: Oxford University Press, 1995.

Rochefort, Joseph J. *The Reminiscences of Captain Joseph J. Rochefort—U.S. Navy (Retired)*. Rev. ed. Annapolis: U.S. Naval Institute, 1983.

Rowlett, Frank. *The Story of Magic: Memoirs of an American Cryptologic Pioneer*. Laguna Hills, CA: Aegean Park Press, 1998.

Sale, Anthony. *The Colossus Computer and How It Helped to Break the German Lorenz Cipher in WWII*. Cleobury Mortimer, Shropshire: M&M Baldwin, 1998.

Sebag-Montefiore, Hugh. *Enigma: The Battle for the Code*. New York: John Wiley & Sons, 2000.

Sevareid, Eric. *Not So Wild a Dream*. New York: Alfred Knopf, 1946.

Singh, Simon. *The Code Book: The Evolution of Secrecy from Mary Queen of Scots to Quantum Cryptography*. New York: Doubleday, 1999.

Sledge, E. B. *With the Old Breed at Peleliu and Okinawa*. Novato, CA: Presidio Press, 1981.

Slim, William. *Defeat into Victory*. New York: David McKay, 1961.

Smith, Bradley F. *Sharing Secrets with Stalin: How the Allies Traded Intelligence, 1941–1945*. Lawrence, KS: University Press of Kansas, 1996.

———. *The Ultra-Magic Deals and the Most Secret Special Relationship, 1940–1948*. Novato, CA: Presidio Press, 1992.

Smith, Michael. *The Emperor's Codes: Bletchley Park and the Breaking of Japan's Secret Ciphers*. London: Bantam Press, 2000.

———. *Station X: The Codebreakers of Bletchley Park*. London: MacMillan, 1999.

Stevenson, William. *A Man Called Intrepid*. New York: Harcourt Brace Jovanovich, 1976.

Stilwell, Joseph. *The Stilwell Papers*. New York: William Sloane Associates, 1948.

Stripp, Alan. *Codebreaker in the Far East*. New York: Frank Cass, 1984.

Tarrant, V. E. *The Red Orchestra: The Soviet Spy Network Inside Nazi Europe*. London: Cassell, 1995.

Tuchman, Barbara. *The Guns of August*. New York: Dell, 1962.

———. *The Zimmermann Telegram*. New York: Ballantine, 1994.

Van Der Rhoer, Edward. *Deadly Magic: A Personal Account of Communications Intelligence in World War II in the Pacific*. Lincoln, NE: Authors Guild, 2000.

Volkman, Ernest. *Spies: The Secret Agents Who Changed the Course of History*. New York: John Wiley & Sons, 1997.

Wallace, Robert, and the Editors of Time-Life Books. *The Italian Campaign*. Alexandria, VA: Time-Life Books, 1978.

Welchman, Gordon. *The Hut Six Story*. New York: McGraw-Hill, 1982.

West, Nigel. *Counterfeit Spies: An Astonishing Investigation into Secret Agents of the Second World War*. London: St. Ermin's Press, 1998.

————. *The Sigint Secrets: The Signals Intelligence War, 1900 to Today, Including the Persecution of Gordon Welchman*. New York: William Morrow, 1986.

West, Nigel, with Juan Pujol. *Operation Garbo: The Personal Story of the Most Successful Double Agent of World War II*. New York: Random House, 1985.

West, Nigel, with Oleg Tsarev. *The Crown Jewels: The British Secrets at the Heart of the KGB Archives*. New Haven: Yale University Press, 1999.

Whiting, Charles. *Ardennes: The Secret War*. New York: Dorset Press, 1987.

Whymant, Robert. *Stalin's Spy: Richard Sorge and the Tokyo Espionage Ring*. New York: St. Martin's, 1996.

Willey, Mark Emerson. *Pearl Harbor: The Mother of All Conspiracies*. Philadelphia, XLibris, 2000.

Winterbotham, F. W. *The Ultra Secret*. New York: Harper & Row, 1974.

Winton, John. *Ultra in the Pacific: How Breaking Japanese Codes and Ciphers Affected Naval Operations Against Japan*. Annapolis: Naval Institute Press, 1993.

Wohlstetter, Roberta. *Pearl Harbor: Warning and Decision*. Stanford: Stanford University Press, 1962.

Yardley, Herbert O. *The American Black Chamber*. Indianapolis: Bobbs Merrill, 1931.

Young, Irene. *Enigma Variations: A Memoir of Love and War*. London: Trafalgar Square Press, 2000.

Ziegler, Philip. *Mountbatten*. New York: Alfred A. Knopf, 1985.

Pamphlets

From the Bletchley Park Trust:
Carter, Frank. *The First Breaking of Enigma: Some of the Pioneering Techniques Developed by the Polish Cipher Bureau*.
Gallehawk, John. *Convoys and the U-boats*.
————. *Some Polish Contributions in the Second World War*.
Wescombe, Peter. *Bletchley Park and the Luftwaffe*.
From the Center for Cryptologic History, National Security Agency:
Miller, Ray. *The Cryptographic Mathematics of Enigma*.
Wilcox, Jennifer. *Sharing the Burden: Women in Cryptology During World War II*.
From Britain's Public Record Office:
Hoare, Oliver. *ENIGMA: Codebreaking and the Second World War*.

Articles

Ballard, Geoffrey. "1944—and Ultra sets the agenda for the Pacific War." *Reprint of Papers from the 1995 Enigma Symposium*, ed. Hugh Skillen. Pinner, Middlesex, England: 1995.

Boyd, Ellsworth. "Briggs believes a lost warning could have saved Pearl Harbor from destruction." *World War II*, November 2002, pp. 18–21.

Bruce-Briggs, B. "Another Ride on Tricycle." *Intelligence and National Security* 7, no. 2 (1996), pp. 79–100.

Erskine, Ralph. "The Development of Typex." *The Enigma Bulletin* no. 2 (1997), pp. 69–81.

Gavin, James. "Bloody Hürtgen." *American Heritage*, December 1979, pp. 32–44.

Glanz, James. "New Light on Physicist's Role in Nazi Bomb." *The New York Times*, March 7, 2002, p. 1, continued on p. 8.

Hitchens, Christopher. "The Medals of His Defeats." *The Atlantic Monthly*, April 2002, pp. 118–137.

Kennedy, David M. "Victory at Sea." *The Atlantic Monthly*, March 1999, pp. 54–74.

Troy, Thomas F. "The British Assault on J. Edgar Hoover: The Tricycle Case." *International Journal of Intelligence and Counterintelligence* 3, no. 2 (1989), pp. 169–209.

Unpublished sources

Nielson, James. "Military Time." Section of a memoir recalling his experiences at Bletchley Park.

Sharp, Walter. "The 6813th Signal Security Detachment." Memoir telling of his duties in the "Machine Room" at BP.

Vergine, George. "Technical Sergeant at Bletchley Park." Memoir including a precise technical explanation of how "Fish" was broken.

Internet

Hinsley, F. H. "The Influence of ULTRA in the Second World War." Cambridge Security Group Seminar, 1993. www.cl.cam.ac.uk

Jacobsen, Philip H. "The Codebreakers: Intelligence Contributions to U.S. Naval Operations in the Pacific." www.microworks.net/pacific/intelligence

MacEachin, Douglas J. "The Final Months of the War with Japan: Signals Intelligence, U.S. Invasion Planning, and the A-Bomb Decision."

Monograph posted by the Center for the Study of Intelligence. www.
cia.gov/csi/monograph/4253605299/csi9810001

Parker, Frederick D. "A Priceless Advantage: U.S. Navy Communications
Intelligence and the Battles of the Coral Sea, Midway and the Aleutians." National Security Agency—United States Cryptologic History,
1993. www.ibiblio.org/hyperwar/PTO/Magic/COMINT-CoralSea

Interviews and correspondence

Best, Paul, on operations of 6812th Signal Security Detachment.

Bing, Patricia, on life as a young assistant to Alan Turing.

Brewster, Molly, on the role of young women at BP.

Eachus, Joseph, on being the first "Ultra American."

Fredrickson, Robert, a devoted provider of useful information on all three
Signal Service Detachments in Britain.

Manuel, Richard, a 6811th officer knowledgeable about the drastic March
1, 1945, change in the Germans' radio transmission procedures.

Norland, Selmer, a faithful consultant on all phases of the Americans' contributions to Ultra.

Sale, Tony, who rebuilt a Colossus at BP and helped me reach an understanding of it as well as other technical functions at the Park.

Sharp, Walter, another reliable adviser on the Ultra Americans at Bletchley.

Titus, William M., Jr., a 6811th officer with an acute memory of Set Room
operations at Hall Place.

Vergine, George, very possibly the smartest American at BP, the man to
whom the British gave some of the toughest work to be done on
"Fish."

Index

338 • *Index*